A Right to Flee

C000152672

Why do states protect refugees? In the past twenty years, states have sought to limit access to asylum by increasing their border controls and introducing extraterritorial controls. Yet no state has sought to exit the 1951 Refugee Convention or the broader international refugee regime. This book argues that such international policy shifts represent an ongoing process whereby refugee protection is shaped and redefined by states and other actors. Since the seventeenth century, a mix of collective interests and basic normative understandings held by states created a space for refugees to be separate from other migrants. However, ongoing crisis events undermine these understandings and provide opportunities to reshape how refugees are understood, how they should be protected, and whether protection is a state or multilateral responsibility. Drawing on extensive archival and secondary materials, Phil Orchard examines the interplay among governments, individuals, and international organizations that has shaped how refugees are understood today.

Phil Orchard is a lecturer in International Relations and Peace and Conflict Studies at the University of Queensland and a senior researcher with the Asia-Pacific Centre for the Responsibility to Protect. He holds a PhD from the University of British Columbia and previously worked as the assistant to the representative of the UN Secretary-General for Internally Displaced Persons. His research focuses on international efforts to provide institutional and legal forms of protection to civilians and forced migrants, and his work has been published in *Global Governance*, *International Affairs*, and the *Review of International Studies*.

A Right to Flee

Refugees, States, and the Construction of International Cooperation

Phil Orchard

University of Queensland

CAMBRIDGE
UNIVERSITY PRESS

CAMBRIDGE
UNIVERSITY PRESS

University Printing House, Cambridge CB2 8BS, United Kingdom

Cambridge University Press is part of the University of Cambridge.

It furthers the University's mission by disseminating knowledge in the pursuit of education, learning and research at the highest international levels of excellence.

www.cambridge.org
Information on this title: www.cambridge.org/9781107431690

First published 2014
First paperback edition 2015

A catalogue record for this publication is available from the British Library

Library of Congress Cataloguing in Publication data
Orchard, Phil, 1976–
A Right to flee : Refugees, States, and the Construction of International
Cooperation / Dr. Phil Orchard, Lecturer in International Relations
and Peace and Conflict Studies, University of Queensland.
    pages   cm
ISBN 978-1-107-07625-9 (hardback)
1. Internally displaced persons – Protection – International cooperation.
2. Refugees – Protection – International cooperation.   I. Title.
HV640.O74   2014
325′.21–dc23

                                    2014010864

ISBN 978-1-107-07625-9 Hardback
ISBN 978-1-107-43169-0 Paperback

To my mother, Carole Anne Orchard, and my father, Donald Bryce Orchard (in memoriam)

Contents

Figures

Tables

Acknowledgments

This book began more than a decade ago, in 2001, when I began working on the issue of internal displacement at the United Nations. I was surprised at the time by international relations scholars' neglect of internally displaced persons (IDPs) as an international issue. As I began my PhD, I realized that deeper questions existed around the basic state practices that underpin policies toward both IDPs and refugees. Even as the events of 9-11 and its aftermath saw the rights of asylum seekers and refugees challenged dramatically, no state sought to leave the 1951 Refugee Convention or abandon the wider international refugee regime. Why, then, were some norms around refugee and IDP protection so fragile, whereas others had proved to be incredibly robust? This book is my attempt to explain that puzzle. The answer is a complex one, one that requires a trip back as far as the seventeenth century to understand how these basic practices were first created, then shaped, replaced, and created anew through four successive refugee regimes.

I am indebted to many people. At the University of British Columbia (UBC), where this project began as a doctoral dissertation, Brian Job's guidance and advice was critical to the shape the project eventually took, and he worked hard (sometimes successfully, sometimes not) to rein in my broader impulses. Thanks also to my other committee members, Richard Price and Katharina Coleman, who ably helped to guide and shape the project, while Mark Zacher first suggested to me the idea of refugees as a relief valve for the state system. I also owe a range of friends from UBC my thanks for their help, in particular Lesley Burns, Miriam Anderson, Miki Fabry, Jennifer Gagnon, Jamie Gillies, Tania Keefe, Mike Schroeder, Scott Watson, and Karen Winzoski.

The School of Political Science and International Studies at the University of Queensland has since provided an equally collegial and stimulating environment. I would like to thank particularly Stephen Bell, Melissa Curley, Kath Gelber, Seb Kaempf, Matt McDonald, Andrew Phillips, Alastair Stark, Ryan Walter, Heloise Weber, and Martin Weber.

One of my PhD students, Rebecca Shaw, also deserves special mention for making me think differently about norm entrepreneurs.

I would also like to thank a number of other people for their helpful comments on the project at various stages, including Michael Barnett, Alexander Betts, Jeffrey Checkel, Jean-Francois Durieux, George Egerton, Kimberly Hutchings, Charles Keely, Susan Kneebone, Gil Loescher, James Milner, Sarah Percy, and Lisa Sundstrom. I would also like to thank Francis Deng for inspiring the initial project while I was his assistant when he was the Representative of UN Secretary-General for Internally Displaced Persons, and Roberta Cohen and Erin Mooney for their advice. At Cambridge University Press, I would like to thank John Haslam for supporting this book, even as it went through extensive revisions, and Carrie Parkinson for editorial guidance. I would also like to thank two anonymous reviewers for their comments and suggestions.

This book also would not have been possible without the help of a number of knowledgeable archivists. I would like to thank in particular Lee MacDonald and Patricia Fluckiger-Livingstone at the United Nations High Commissioner for Refugees (UNHCR) Archives, and Bernhardine E. Pejovic and Sebastian Vernay at the League of Nations Archives. I would also like to thank the staff at the University of Oxford Refugee Studies Centre Library; Churchill Archives Centre, Churchill College, University of Cambridge; the British National Archives; and the United States National Archives and Records Administration. It also would not have been possible without financial support from the Social Sciences and Humanities Research Council of Canada, the Canadian Consortium on Human Security (CCHS), the Canadian Department of National Defence's Security and Defence Forum, and the University of Queensland.

Finally, it would not have been possible without the help of my family. My greatest thanks go to my wife, Victoria Colvin. Her support, encouragement, editorial skills, and understanding have made this book possible, even as we have been joined by our two daughters, Charlotte and Kate. It was my mother, Carole Orchard, who first introduced me to the reality of flight, whether traveling in Cyprus or Pakistan, or meeting refugees from Sarajevo who became good friends. She continues to support me in all I do. It is to her that this book is dedicated and, in memoriam, my father, Donald Bryce Orchard.

Abbreviations

AU	African Union
DHS	United States Department of Homeland Security
DP	Displaced Person
ECOSOC	United Nations Economic and Social Council
ELV	Exceptional Leave to Remain
EU	European Union
FRUS	*Foreign Relations of the United States*
GAOR	*UN General Assembly Official Records*
ICEM	Intergovernmental Committee for European Migration
ICRC	International Committee of the Red Cross
IDP	Internally Displaced Person
IFRC	International Federation of the Red Cross and Red Crescent Societies
IGCR	Inter-governmental Committee on Refugees
ILO	International Labor Organization
INS	United States Immigration and Naturalization Service
IO	International Organization
IOM	International Organization for Migration
IRO	International Refugee Organization
LNA	League of Nations Archives
LNHCR	League of Nations High Commissioner for Refugees
LPC	United States "Likely to Be a Public Charge" Clause
NATO	North Atlantic Treaty Organization
NBKR	Philip Noel-Baker Archives, Churchill College, University of Cambridge
NGO	Non-governmental Organization
OAU	Organization for African Unity
OCHA	United Nations Office for the Coordination of Humanitarian Assistance
POW	Prisoner of War
PRO FO	Public Record Office (United Kingdom) Foreign Office Records

PWA	Paul Weis Archives, Refugee Studies Center, University of Oxford
ROC	Republic of China (Taiwan)
SHAEF	Supreme Headquarters, Allied Expeditionary Force
STC	Safe Third Country
UN	United Nations
UNHCR	United Nations High Commissioner for Refugees
UNRRA	United Nations Relief and Rehabilitation Administration
UNRWA	United Nations Relief Works Agency
USEP	United States Escapee Program
USNARA	United States National Archives and Records Administration

1 Introduction: a right to flee

When 200,000 Huguenots fled religious persecution in France in 1685, they had little idea that their plight would mark a major change in state practice. Because of this policy shift, the Huguenot flight remained synonymous with the term used to define these individuals into the nineteenth century: *refugees*.[1] Before this event, the flight and expulsion of religious minorities had been commonplace, whether they were Jews expelled from England in the twelfth century or Moors from Spain in the fifteenth century. The Huguenots – primarily merchants and artisans – would bring to their receiving states wealth and knowledge. But they represented an international problem: unlike the situation of earlier groups, Louis XIV forbade the Huguenots to leave France. This prohibition violated a normative understanding, reached in the Peace of Westphalia some forty years earlier, that allowed subjects whose religion differed from that of their prince to leave that territory with their property. The states to which the Huguenots fled faced a dilemma: how could they accommodate the Huguenots in a way that would express their concerns over Louis XIV's actions, but still avoid conflict with France?

The decision by their receiving states to accommodate and protect them under domestic law caused the Huguenots to be recognized as a distinct category of migrants, ones who, because they could no longer count on the protection of their own state, should be allowed to leave that state and receive protection elsewhere. It is this basic understanding that was codified in the 1951 *Convention Relating to the Status of Refugees*, which defines a refugee as:

Any person who owing to well-founded fear of being persecuted for reasons of race, religion, nationality, membership of a particular social group or political

---

[1] As late as 1796, the third edition of the *Encyclopaedia Britannica* noted that the term "refugee" had been applied to the expelled French Protestants and that only in recent times had the term "been extended to all such as leave their country in times of distress, and hence, since the revolt of the British colonies in America, we have frequently heard of American refugees" (Marrus 2002: 8–9).

opinion, is outside the country of his nationality and is unable, or owing to such fear, unwilling to avail himself of the protection of that country.[2]

This understanding remains the basis for how we understand who a refugee is, even if it appears to be at odds with current state practice. Rhetorically, governments across the developed world acknowledge their commitment to refugee protection, asylum, and the refugee regime, yet they prioritize national interests such as immigration and border control over broader humanitarian interests, including refugee protection and acceptance. President George W. Bush could reaffirm the U.S. "commitment to protect and assist refugees, promote their right to seek asylum, and provide opportunities for their resettlement, as needed" (Bush 2002) while arguing that the United States will "turn back any [Haitian] refugee that attempts to reach our shore" (Bush 2004).

A simple interest-based explanation exists for this. Refugee admissions during the Cold War were in the interests of most developed states. As Teitelbaum (1984: 439) argued, "refugee admissions policies have been guided ... by the belief that refugee outflows serve to embarrass and discredit adversary nations." A generous U.S. refugee policy during this period could be viewed as nothing more than the result "of interest calculations in which international norms played no role" (Hartigan 1992: 711). Since the end of the Cold War, states have faced increased numbers of refugees requesting entrance and have therefore prioritized intake restrictions in order to maintain control over their borders.

The restrictionist practices that have developed over the past quarter-century led a number of commentators to conclude that the international refugee regime is today in crisis, unraveling, or split between the interests of the developed and developing worlds (see, among others, Keely 2001; Crisp 2003; Gibney 2004: 229; Betts 2009). Yet even while states challenge aspects of the regime, few challenge the refugee regime itself. No government has adopted the strategy advocated by former British Conservative Leader Michael Howard in 2004. Howard said that, if elected, "we will pull out of the 1951 Refugee Convention, as is our right... Its authors could not have imagined that it would come to be exploited by tens of thousands of people every year" (Howard 2004). Indeed, Gibney suggests that current responses to asylum seekers and refugees are schizophrenic: "great importance is attached to the principle of asylum but enormous efforts are made to ensure that refugees (and others with less pressing claims) never reach the territory of the state where they could receive its protection" (Gibney 2004: 2). Simply

---

[2] Article 1 A.(2), *Convention Relating to the Status of Refugees*.

concluding that changes in state interest have led to changes in refugee policy cannot explain the continued relevance of the regime.

The shift to restrictionism that began in the early 1990s is not the first such crisis to affect refugee protection. When the modern refugee regime was created in the five years following the Second World War, states faced a far larger displaced population than today. The war had created more than 40 million refugees and displaced persons. New flows in the millions were generated by the partition of India, the creation of Israel, and the Korean War. By 1950, when thirteen governments met to negotiate the 1951 Refugee Convention, refugees were fleeing across the Iron Curtain into West Germany at a rate of 15,000 per month, a continuous refugee flow with little prospect of ending. Yet, rather than restricting refugee protection, that Convention strengthened what had been an ad hoc system of legal protections by introducing the first comprehensive definition of refugee status and establishing a new legal obligation for states to not "expel or return ('refouler') a refugee in any manner whatsoever to the frontiers of territories where his life or freedom would be threatened."[3]

There is a puzzle here. Why did states in this earlier period agree to a regime now unacceptable to them? And why do these states seek to restrict asylum even while otherwise abiding by the Refugee Convention and acknowledging the importance of the refugee regime? An interest-based explanation may answer the first question, but not the second. One alternative explanation focuses on the possibility that refugees may pose an international problem – that they "may fall outside the state system and become a source of instability or a threat to state security" (Betts 2009: 7). The notion of the refugee regime providing stability and thus serving common interests and goals offers an explanation for ongoing international cooperation, but it fails to explain both the forms cooperation has taken and its durability.

I propose a third explanation, one reflected in the fact that the Refugee Convention, along with the associated creation of the United Nations High Commissioner for Refugees (UNHCR), reinforced a norm-governed view of refugees first established by the French Huguenots. Because refugees were outside their own state and could no longer count on its protection, they became a problem for the international community, one that could only be solved through international cooperation. And although creating the Convention was a watershed event, it was neither the beginnings of state cooperation nor a substantial break with past practice, a view contrary to "most conventional accounts [that]

---

[3] Article 33.1, Ibid.

identify the refugee 'problem' as a particularly twentieth century phenomenon" (Nyers 1999: 11; see also Haddad 2008: 65; Long 2009: 135). This is also at variance with an alternative explanation for the durability of refugee protection in the post-Cold War period that suggests it is associated with the wider growth in human rights norms since 1945 (Rosenblum and Salehyan 2004).

Instead, refugee protection marks a critical example of continuity and change in state practices. Some practices have been continuous. Since the Peace of Westphalia was signed in 1648, states have held intersubjective social understandings of refugees as different from other migrants; upheld that they should be allowed to leave their own state; and, crucially, recognized that they require some form of protection because they can no longer count on the protection of their state and are outside of its territory.

The basis for this entrenched normative understanding has been and remains law: as Helton has argued, when we speak of refugee protection, "we mean legal protection. The concept must be associated with entitlements under law and, for effective redress of grievances, mechanisms to vindicate claims in respect of those entitlements" (Helton 2003: 20). This core understanding of refugee protection is readily apparent in the 1951 Convention but also in earlier international conventions, such as the 1933 Refugee Convention.

This consistent basic understanding of who refugees are exists because refugees are part of a small set of actors in international society who do not conveniently fit into the Westphalian system based around the primacy of territorially based states. They are, in one sense, a transterritorial problem (see Ruggie 1998a: 191); the international system, Cronin has argued "is not equipped to deal with individuals or groups who are not under the authority or protection of a state" (2003: 152). This problem, however, does not arise as a consequence of a breakdown in international society. Rather, as Haddad suggests, refugees are an inevitable if unanticipated result of the Westphalian system: "as long as there are political borders constructing separate states and creating clear definitions of insiders and outsiders, there will be refugees" (Haddad 2008: 7; see also Keely 1996: 1046). In fact, refugees help solve a larger issue for international society. As Bull argued, in such a society:

in which rights and duties applied directly to states and nations, the notion of human rights and duties has survived but it has gone underground... The basic compact of coexistence between states, expressed in the exchange of recognition of sovereign jurisdictions, implies a conspiracy of silence entered into by governments about the rights and duties of their respective citizens. This conspiracy is mitigated by the practice of granting rights of asylum to foreign political refugees. (2002: 80)

Refugees, in other words, are a relief valve for the state system. European history, as Hirschman suggests, would have either "been far more turbulent or far more repressive and the trend toward representative government much more halting, had it not been possible for millions of people to emigrate toward the United States and elsewhere" (1981: 226–27; see also Dowty 1987: 50).

Although there are continuous understandings around refugees' basic identities, there are also sweeping changes that have occurred in how states practice refugee protection. Although refugee protection may be anchored in law, this protection was initially provided at the domestic level, in documents such as the 1832 French law that defined refugees as "unprotected persons."[4] It was only over time that refugee protection shifted from the domestic level, to the bilateral level, and finally to the international level.

Equally critical, although the basic understanding of a "refugee" as a person fleeing state persecution has been commonly understood for centuries, what state acts qualify as "persecution" and even who falls within the refugee category have been significantly redefined over this period. In the seventeenth and eighteenth centuries, states accepted that people fleeing religious persecution (and only religious persecution) in Europe qualified as refugees, whereas in the nineteenth century individual political exiles were added to this list. Since the 1951 Convention, states have accepted that refugees are those who flee individualized state-based persecution, although broader interpretations are included in regional international law (such as the Organization for African Unity [OAU] 1969 Refugee Convention) and in domestic policy. Other changes have seen the locus of primary responsibility for refugees shift from individual states to international organizations and refugee assistance move from being an ad hoc and voluntary activity to being enshrined as a critical norm in the current regime.

Explaining the origins and evolution of refugee protection

I have suggested that how states approach refugee protection reveals a mixture of continuity and change in their practice. This behavior exists not only because of collectively held interests on the part of states to ensure international order, but also because of deeply entrenched normative understandings. As such, my goal is to use the issue of refugee

---

[4] *Loi Relative aux Etrangers Réfugiés Qui Résideront en France* (IX, Bull. LXXV, no. 165) passed on April 21, 1832.

protection as a way to understand how state cooperation can be created and sustained by the interaction of structures and agents over a long historical period.

Although I lay out this argument in detail in Chapter 2, here I briefly summarize the interplay between those structures and agents that help to form international cooperation around refugee protection. First, I offer a framework of analysis that focuses on the mediating effects of three levels of international structure: fundamental institutions, regimes, and norms. Four fundamental institutions, elementary rules of practice within international society (Reus-Smit 1997: 557), play a key role in framing how states have responded to refugees. Initially, the institutions of territoriality and international law, and subsequently, popular sovereignty and multilateralism, provided commonly held understandings that created a political space offering incentives for states to cooperate to provide refugee protection.

Regimes reflect the basic understandings embodied within these fundamental institutions (Reus-Smit 1999: 14–15; Buzan 2004) but also create webs of meaning by linking together individual norms (Neufeld 1993: 43; Hasenclever et al. 1997: 165). Norms are shared understandings of appropriate behavior for actors with a given identity that isolate a single strand of behavior (Jepperson et al. 1996: 52; Finnemore and Sikkink 1998: 891). Because a regime bundles together what might otherwise be disparate norms, it provides a clear sense of the scope of the international behavior and of how states within international society should deal with the problem. Thus, regimes provide a mechanism through which the appropriate standards of behavior suggested by the individual norms are linked together to create a response within the complexity of the issue area. In so doing, the regime brings increased regularity to state practices than would otherwise be the case.

State practices have not been static. Regimes contributed to the generation of state identities and the creation of notions of legitimate state behavior within international society that led to a level of stability. Yet these shared understandings between states have also changed dramatically over time, following a punctuated equilibrium framework. As such, I bring together constructivist and historical institutionalist approaches to make my argument.

I argue that a critical source of variance comes from crisis events caused by dramatic and sustained changes in either the number of refugees in the international system or the nature of refugees (such as the emergence of political refugees following the French Revolution). Crisis events disrupt policy stability by exposing new or preexisting contradictions within a refugee protection regime. This forces states to engage in an information search in order to reconcile their normative beliefs to the changed reality of the situation (Berger 1996: 33; Checkel 1997: 125; Price 1998: 622). International and domestic norm entrepreneurs are therefore presented with an opportunity to introduce new norms that favor refugee protection and broader humanitarian interests or, alternatively, that favor restrictionist policies designed to protect state sovereignty.

The sets of norms that end up being internalized by states depend on the norms' congruence with domestic interests and culture, as well as with the ability of norm entrepreneurs to reframe their arguments within a context acceptable to domestic veto-playing or gatekeeping institutions (Finnemore and Sikkink 1998: 893; Checkel 1999; Risse and Sikkink 1999). This is successful when the new norm either reflects existing domestic understandings or is in an area in which there are no preexisting understandings. Thus, in 1920, states were "convinced" by the League of Nations and the International Committee of the Red Cross that a formal international organization was the best way to provide protection to refugees fleeing the Russian Revolution, whereas in the 1950s and 1960s the UNHCR successfully convinced states to expand the legal basis of refugee protection away from a Eurocentric to a global focus.

By contrast, when discordance exists between the new international norm and prior normative understandings at the domestic level, norm internalization will be more difficult. Either the international norm will not be internalized at the domestic level, or it may be only rhetorically supported and weakly internalized. Thus, although states may rhetorically support norms at the international level, until they are internalized domestically by veto-playing institutions they may be subject to violation or avoidance even when supported by elite decision makers (Müller 2004; Krebs and Jackson 2007). Thus, in the 1930s, the League of Nations, the United States, and the United Kingdom all argued in favor of some mechanisms to protect the Jews fleeing Nazi Germany. However, the domestic immigration policies of both the United States and the United Kingdom created substantial barriers to entry for these same refugees. Rhetorical commitments led to inaction not accompanied by domestic policy change.

Even in this pattern, however, successful internalization can occur through active persuasion on the part of domestic norm entrepreneurs who can reframe the new norm within the domestic context. For example, following the Second World War, American President Harry S. Truman successfully convinced the U.S. Congress that providing a broad-based refugee resettlement program was not only in the interests of the United States, but also served as an important weapon in the Cold War.

This is not a progressive history; not all emergent norms are positive in their impacts on refugees. New norms introduced since the end of the Cold War have focused on the regionalization and restriction of refugee movement and rights. During other periods, most notably the 1930s, international cooperation unraveled entirely. As domestic-level factors change, in particular as states mediate between their humanitarian impulse to protect refugees and the need to protect national interests and sovereignty, even established international norms can quickly be challenged and replaced.

Norm content, state interests, and practices

Norm breakdowns do not point to an inability by international actors to bring about normative change (Moravcsik 1999), nor do they indicate either domestic interests or a logic of consequences trumping international norms (Krasner 1999). Both of these patterns of action do represent norm-governed behavior. The issue, then, lies in the content of those norms. Many norms proscribe behaviors that states should not undertake (Price 1997; Percy 2007), such as not blocking people from fleeing the state or not returning (refouling) refugees to their state of origin. By contrast, within the area of refugee protection, there are relatively few prescriptive norms – those that require a positive duty or action on part of states (Glanville 2006: 154–56). Positive duties in the refugee regime would include offering asylum to refugees who are not within a state's territory and providing assistance and protection to refugees who remain beyond the state's borders. Equivalently, we could frame this within the conception of responsibilities. A direct responsibility exists to refugees who have reached the state's territory. By contrast, a broader, diffuse responsibility exists toward refugees as a whole, created (and interpreted in different ways) by successive international refugee regimes.[5]

Because of this issue of positive action, there exists a gulf between bare observance of the international norms that constitute the international refugee regime at any one time and the states accepting that they have an active obligation to provide protection to all refugees globally and acting on that obligation. This gulf, as Weiner (1996: 171) has noted, is brought about by a moral contradiction "between the notion that emigration is

---

[5] By responsibility, I follow Erskine (2003: 7) that "to be responsible for some act, event or set of circumstances is to be answerable for it." Diffuse responsibilities, as Welsh and Banda (2010: 219) note, "can make it easier for states and international organizations to shirk their obligations."

widely regarded as a matter of human rights ... while immigration is regarded as a matter of national sovereignty." Developed states today argue that they support refugees and fulfill their international legal obligations by providing support to the UNHCR, even while providing only token resettlement opportunities and minimizing their own obligations to accept refugees as much as possible. Thus, the main costs of refugee admissions are borne by countries of first asylum, which are almost exclusively in the developing world (Loescher and Milner 2005; Betts 2009).

This mix of proscriptive and prescriptive international norms leads to two distinct forms of state practice. Within the state, refugee admittance falls within the realm of domestic policy and hence interacts with other domestic interests and the myriad numbers of pressures that governments face from their own citizens. Outside the state, seeking to ensure that refugees in general receive protection at the international level falls within the goals of foreign policy and hence not only reflects the state's role in the world, but is also affected by a range of collective and humanitarian interests within international society. For norm entrepreneurs who favor increased refugee protection, these variant forms of state practice mean they can find themselves playing a modified two-level game (Putnam 1988), trying both to diffuse new norms at the international level while simultaneously convincing domestic actors of the importance of those norms and situating them within domestic interests.

With refugees, and with broader immigration policy, these two forms of practice overlap. Immigration policy can be a "symbol that can be used to pursue a state's interests" (Fitzgerald 1996: 9; see also Greenhill 2010). But immigration admissions go beyond mere interest and sovereignty to echo, as Walzer argues, "the shape of the community that acts in the world" (1983: 61–62). As Shacknove notes, "refugee policy has always been at least one part State interest and at most one part compassion... When interests of State are fundamentally at odds with other values, as is increasingly the case with asylum, then it is unlikely that compassion, solidarity, or human rights will prevail" (Shacknove 1993: 517–18). Interests are at play, however, in different ways and at different times.

Traditional rationalist explanations see cooperation through the lens of state interests. States cooperate when it is in their interests to do so. Realists would go further, arguing that when it is not in the state's interests, cooperative regimes will be allowed to wither away (for the extreme variant of this, see Mearsheimer 1994). But if one of the justifications for the regime is stability, with the primary issue being a problem of collective action and the provision of public goods, then defecting states will result in an iterative suboptimal outcome: the regime will erode over time due to trust issues.

An alternative to the realist explanation is provided in the notion that states can be motivated by common political interests to ensure the preservation of the values and institutions of international society (Wolfers 1962; Cox 1969: 207; Cronin 2003: 12). Thus, within a neoliberal perspective, Cronin (2003) argues in favor of international protection regimes designed to protect clearly defined classes of people. But the neoliberal perspective creates two weaknesses here. First, for Cronin (2003: 154), formal cooperation alone is important; tacit or informal understandings are not examined. Second, although Cronin can explain why international protection regimes emerge, it is unclear how they change once established. As he notes, states' individual preferences will gradually aggregate "in ways that produce a consensus around a common good... Over time, international order can become durable and self-sustaining through both domestic and international processes" (Cronin 2003: 40–41). Thus, whereas in Cronin's view collectively held interests may lead to the creation of protection regimes and arguably to the creation of normatively held beliefs, analytically, his model does not explain how these regimes change or are replaced.

Within my constructivist justification of regime formation, change, and replacement within state provision of refugee protection, interests remain important but are subject to two important limitations. The first, as Müller (2004: 416) notes, is that in negotiations (and, by analogy, in other forms of behavior), "it is appropriate for actors to pursue their self-interest unless it collides with a valid norm that prescribes different behaviour." The simple presence of self-interest by itself does not presume that states are acting against existing norms or the broader logics of appropriateness.

The second is that interests are not fixed but are instead fluid and depend in part on the state's identity within a given context. Weldes argues that national interests "are social constructions created as meaningful objects out of the intersubjective and culturally established meanings within which the world, particularly the international system and the place of the state within it, is understood" (1999: 10; see also Finnemore 1996; Adler 1997: 337; Wendt 1999: 96–97). Classical realism advanced a similar contextual understanding of interests – as Morgenthau noted – whereas the "idea of interest is indeed of the essence of politics and is unaffected by circumstances of time and place . . . the kind of interest determining political action in a particular period of history depends upon the political and cultural context within which foreign policy is formulated" (1978: 8–9). Fluid interests introduce an element of contestation and perception into any claim made around the state's interests. Furthermore, this suggests that how states respond to refugees, how refugees are perceived as a problem, and even how refugees are perceived at all are affected by international society and are subject to change (Haddad 2008).

Methods, cases, and process tracing

Although a number of states and international organizations have been important in shaping norms of refugee protection, this book focuses on two critical states: the United States and the United Kingdom. Both states were crucial in shaping the initial international response to refugees in the nineteenth and twentieth centuries, and both have contributed substantially to the formal architecture of international cooperation that exists today, including international law and organizations. Examining the formation of policies in both these states provides us with a window to understand why even strong rhetorical support for international norms can be blocked or undermined. Conversely, once these states accepted at the domestic level new norms that also had international implications – such as the United States committing to a strong norm against the refoulement of refugees in the late 1940s or the United Kingdom committing to not return political refugees to their countries of origin in the nineteenth century – the state itself began to serve as a norm entrepreneur, arguing in favor of a normative position already accepted as correct behavior by its domestic institutions and public. Success here can be measured by whether other states also adopt the norm.

To uncover how a state initially adopts the norm, I focus on the domestic level. This requires that I do not treat the state as a single entity but instead focus on key institutions within it, generally the foreign ministries (the State Department in the United States, the Foreign Office in the United Kingdom) and the executive branches.

Beyond states, international organizations have also played critical independent roles in creating shared understandings of how cooperation should proceed toward refugees. The League of Nations High Commissioner for Refugees (LNHCR) successfully introduced a norm that favored anchoring refugee protection in international law in the 1920s, whereas the UNHCR successfully ended a Eurocentric focus on cooperation and shifted efforts to the global level. Therefore, to adequately explain change within the refugee issue area, I focus on both the interplay between states and international organizations at the international level and the policy formation process within the United States and the United Kingdom.

In the period following the Peace of Westphalia in 1648, I identify four separate international regimes governing refugee protection. I treat these four regimes as cases, with the caveat that because they are chronologically successive within the same issue area, they cannot be considered independent. I engage in both synchronic and diachronic investigations of each case (Gerring 2004) by exploring the role of different actors at the international and domestic levels and the roles played by both the United Kingdom and the United States.

I am interested in both causal and constitutive explanation here and thus base myself within a scientific realist epistemology (Wight 2006; Jackson 2011).[6] I do not seek to bracket the role of structures and agents (as an example, see Finnemore 1996) – not because I disagree with the intent behind this approach but because, as Checkel (2008: 125) notes in a trenchant critique, "bracketing means, first, to hold structure constant and explore agency's causal role, and, then, to reverse the order, holding agency constant while examining structure's role. These are very linear processes." The complexity and dynamism of the international system defeats this, just as it defeats efforts to fully differentiate causal and constitutive processes at the margins (Betts and Orchard 2014). At what point, for example, does a causal feedback loop transition into constituting the identities of actors?[7] Within this study, therefore, I provide one level of constitutive theorizing, focusing on the role played by the deeper structures of the international system, in particular fundamental institutions.

Within the political space created by these institutions, I trace out the causal and constitutive processes by which normative change affects state practices. Therefore, within the individual regimes, I use process tracing to explore the causal chains through which these changes occur (George and Bennett 2005; Checkel 2008). This, by necessity, is contingent due to the historical scope of the project and the number of actors involved at any one time, although this is balanced with a focus directed at the norm entrepreneurs working in any one period.

To inform this work, I draw on three main sources of data. The first is a range of archival records, including documents from the successive League of Nations and United Nations (UN) agencies with a core mandate of refugee protection (based on materials gathered at the League of Nations Archives and the UNHCR Archives, both in Geneva), the British government (particularly the records of the British Foreign Office), the United States government (particularly the records of the United States Department of State), and the personal records of a number of individuals. To supplement the archival record, I draw on a range of other primary sources, including official government, League, and UN publications;

---

[6] By scientific realism, I accept a view that "the objects of scientific theories are objects that exist independently of investigators' minds and that the theoretical terms of their theories indeed refer to real objects in the world" (Chernoff 2005: 41).

[7] Wendt's (2001) critique of institutional rational design raises this issue.

other government sources; and the memoirs of participants. Finally, secondary historical accounts and other sources are used to balance against biases within these sources and to fill in gaps in particular areas and periods.

Plan of the book

Crisis events trigger changes in state policies toward refugees, which can bring about regime transformation or replacement. Since 1648, therefore, we can point to four different regimes within the refugee issue area, each providing a basis for international cooperation. Although the individual norms of each regime have varied significantly, each regime possesses three elements that are critical to the functioning of the regime. The first element identifies who has *responsibility* for refugees; whether this responsibility rests on individual states, allowing them to set varying policies, or rests instead within a formal international institutional structure.[8] The second element identifies how *legal protection* is formulated; whether protections are offered at the domestic, bilateral, or international level, and whether refugee status is clearly defined in law. An important corollary is whether refugees are protected against refoulement. The third element identifies how *assistance* is provided; whether states provide assistance directly on an ad hoc or reciprocal basis, whether states rely on voluntary organizations to provide it, or whether states choose to act through an international organization to provide it. As understandings between states and at the domestic level have been redefined over time, different norms have provided different answers to these elements. These three elements and the different norms associated with them in each regime are detailed in Figure 1.1.

Regimes do not emerge instantaneously. As Chapter 3 details, beginning with the Peace of Westphalia in 1648, states began to recognize the right of individuals to leave their own territory if their religion differed from that of their prince. But this right to leave existed primarily on paper until the Huguenots fled France. The Huguenots were recognized for the first time as a distinct group who, because they could no longer count on the protection of their own state, needed an alternative form of protection through the domestic law of the state of asylum. Although the Huguenots triggered an important shift, I argue that this represented a unique

---

[8] Increasingly, there are also suggestions of a growing collective responsibility to prevent widespread displacement, particularly in cases of genocide or ethnic cleansing, as framed by the Responsibility to Protect doctrine (see Evans and Sahnoun 2001; Loescher 2003; Orchard 2010c).

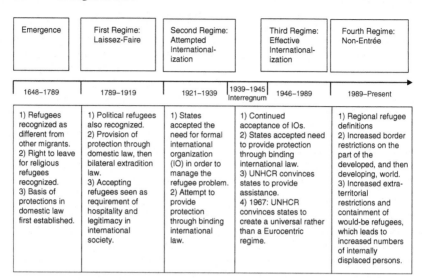

Figure 1.1 The four regimes and their key norms

practice at the time, with no similar status accorded to other religious refugees for the next century. There was no regime because there was no international cooperation or clear understanding of the scope of the problem.

Chapter 4 traces out how state responses to a new form of refugee – political refugees fleeing the French Revolution and other abortive uprisings across the European continent – triggered the creation of a tacit regime in the nineteenth century. In this regime, which existed from 1789 until 1914, states began to apply preexisting practices systematically, recognized political as well as religious refugees, and began to associate the protection of refugees with legitimate practices in international society. I refer to this as a tacit or "laissez-faire" regime (Barnett 2002) because states had no formal constraints on their behavior and states' responsibility toward refugees ended at their own borders. Even so, the idea that refugees needed legal protections – first at the domestic and then bilateral level – was accepted by a core set of states including the United Kingdom, France, and the United States, which then transmitted these understandings across international society through the mechanism of extradition law.

A significant increase in the number of refugees, triggered by the Russian Revolution and territorial changes following the First World War, caused this tacit regime to breakdown. Chapter 5 explores how a new multilateral regime was created through the actions of a handful of norm entrepreneurs – including Gustave Ador, the head of the International Committee of the Red Cross and Fridthof Nansen, who became the first High Commissioner for Refugees. This led to the first international organization created for the express purpose of protecting refugees, the League of Nations High Commissioner for Refugees, and the first international legal protections for refugees. However, international cooperation was challenged by both the start of the Great Depression and the rise of fascism, which cemented restrictionist immigration practices. Even as the United States became engaged with refugee protection in the late 1930s, this meant that for new refugees – the German Jews in particular – there was no easy path to asylum.

Chapter 6 focuses on refugee protection during the Second World War and the postwar period. It argues that the United States took the lead in creating a new, consistent refugee regime based in its own domestically held norms and in the moral beliefs of President Harry S. Truman. As the Cold War deepened, however, and the United States drew away from UN-based multilateral solutions, it initially opposed the creation of the UNHCR while favoring international organizations it could control.

The UNHCR survived this inauspicious beginning, demonstrating its effectiveness as an assistance organization and becoming an important norm entrepreneur in its own right, a change highlighted in Chapter 7. The UNHCR convinced states that comprehensive multilateral assistance was the best way to help refugees. Most notably, it helped to redefine a Eurocentric and geographically restricted regime into one that was universal in scope, arguing that it held a responsibility to refugees everywhere.

Even so, as Chapter 8 documents, growing refugee numbers in the late 1980s and early 1990s produced a new crisis. Developed states responded to this by increasing measures to deter would-be refugees and introducing new extraterritorial measures to circumvent the Refugee Convention. Furthermore, a parallel regime has expanded to offer protections to internally displaced persons (IDPs), people who have been forced to flee their homes but have not left their state. As a result, the vast majority of the world's forced migrants today are under the care of states in the developing world, which have limited resources and are increasingly unwilling to accept this burden (Figure 1.2).

Thus, although the post-Second World War regime was initially strong and effective, state policies directed at preventing the entry of refugees and other asylum seekers fatally undermined the regime's normative basis. It has been replaced with a bifurcated *non-entrée* regime (Chimni 1998) based primarily on containing refugees in the developing world and would-be refugees within their own states as IDPs.

Regime Elements and Norms	Emergence		First Regime (Tacit)	Second Regime (Weak)	Third Regime (Strong)	Fourth Regime (Weak)
	1648	1685	1789–1914	1921–1939	1951–1989	1989–present
Refugees are recognized						
Responsibility is domestic						
Responsibility is international						
Legal protection is primarily domestic						
Legal protection is bilateral						
Legal protection is primarily multilateral						
Legal protection is regionalized						
Non-refoulement						
Extraterritorial restrictions on asylum seekers						
Assistance is a private responsibility						
Assistance provided through multilateral IOs						

Figure 1.2 The different regimes and their normative components (shading represents norms that were in contention)

These regimes each had their own characters. I argue that the laissez-faire regime, given its lack of formal multilateral cooperation, was a tacit regime. The interwar regime, although formally established through a multilateral organization, was weak because of contradictions inherent in its normative understandings. The post-Second World War regime was strong but was undermined by key actors in response to growing refugee numbers. The modern regime, which reinterprets key norms of the post-war regime, is weak because it has no adequate way to reconcile the differing interests of the developed and developing world.

Protection efforts today are hobbled once again by restrictionism and by discordance. As the United States, the United Kingdom, and other developed states have sought to define their role in a globalized world, a humanitarian basis for their refugee policies has been allowed to drift. Although these states continue to follow the key norms of the regime – support for multilateral cooperation, refugee protection in international law, and non-refoulement – they compromise these norms on a day-to-day basis through policies of refugee deterrence, detention, and extraterritorial processes such as interdiction at sea. Although these states provide rhetorical support for refugee protection, it is the UNHCR and the developing world that bear a disproportionate share of the regime's costs. These changes undermine the regime's collective basis and normative coherence. Even if it is in no one's interests, even if it is no one's goal, these changes are causing the modern refugee regime to unravel.

2   Structures, agency, and refugee protection

Explaining refugee protection since the seventeenth century requires an exploration of long patterns of continuous state practice and of important moments of change within that practice. To do so, I anchor my work within a constructivist approach. I present a framework that treats structures and agents in a mutually constitutive manner.

In making this argument, I have two goals. The first is to differentiate the unique properties of nested levels of structures. I explore how three structural components – fundamental institutions, regimes, and norms – work together within international society. These structures interrelate in a hierarchical fashion to provide a basis for the production of shared understandings between states and with other actors. Fundamental institutions – including territoriality, international law, popular sovereignty, and multilateralism – have played a critical role by constituting refugees as an international problem and by creating a political space in which cooperative solutions to this problem are possible. Regimes link together the understandings embodied within these fundamental institutions and in individual norms. Norms within the regime provide shared understandings of appropriate behavior to actors which isolate a single strand of behavior. These norms can provide either behavioral prescriptions or proscriptions (Tannenwald 2007: 10). Regimes mediate the understandings embodied in fundamental institutions in terms of their specific issue of significance, thus framing the scope of the problem. And, by linking together a diverse set of norms, regimes provide states with guidance toward normatively appropriate solutions.

My second goal is to present an agentic view in which actors operate within an environment constituted by structures that they in turn create and change over time. This account is not static. I explore how change occurs by focusing on refugee crises as events that punctuate the status quo and cause states to question preexisting normative understandings. These shocks provide a window of opportunity for norm entrepreneurs at both the international and domestic levels to argue in favor of alternative normative understandings. I am also interested in revisiting the traditional account of norm entrepreneurship – in which an individual or organization with an idea convinces a state to pursue it at the international level – which I argue is overly simplified. Instead, I suggest that a range of actors and institutions at the domestic level matter in the early stages, before the state (as a corporate whole) accepts a new norm. Even once that threshold is passed and the state becomes a "norm leader" (Finnemore and Sikkink 1998: 901–02; Coleman 2013: 166), domestic institutions and actors, as well as international-level actors, remain critical to the ongoing norm institutionalization and implementation process.

Structures forming continuity in state practice

One of the main disagreements between rationalists and constructivists concerns the role played by structures (Fearon and Wendt 2002). Rationalists adopt agent-centered frameworks in which agents (principally states) create structures to further their own interests. For constructivists, this account is problematic. Because the rationalist approach presumes that structure is "an epiphenomenon of the preferences and powers of the constituent states" (Finnemore 1996: 14), interests are exogenously derived and therefore are not affected by structures or identity shifts (Wendt 1992: 393). Interests, in other words, cannot change.

Constructivists, by contrast, treat structures and agents as mutually constitutive. For Wendt (1987: 337–38), although individuals are purposeful actors "whose actions help reproduce or transform the society in which they live," society is also composed of social relationships "which structure the interactions between these purposeful actors." This is, he argues, the heart of the agent–structure problem – whether effects can or cannot be reduced down to independently existing individuals (Wendt 1999; see also Dessler 1989). Structures matter because they not only regulate behavior but also help to construct identities and interests. As Checkel suggests, such a position opens up "the black box of interest and identity formation; state interests emerge from and are endogenous to interaction with structures" (1998: 326). Hence, examining both agents and structures provides constructivists with a way to also examine interest changes.

The constructivist focus on mutual constitution introduces a different reductionist problem: constructivists examine norms as the critical structural element. Early definitions of norms had a clear scope limitation – that norms are shared understandings of appropriate behavior for actors with a given identity, one that isolates a single strand of behavior (Jepperson et al. 1996: 52; Finnemore and Sikkink 1998: 891). An alternative perspective is to equate norms to *any* rules. This is present in definitions such as Woods's, who sees norms as "constitut[ing] the international game by determining who the actors are, what rules they must follow if they wish to ensure that particular consequences follow from specific acts ... [that] can be established and transferred" (1996: 26–27). Finnemore and Sikkink deliberately define norms to avoid this perspective. They note that "institutions emphasize the way in which behavioral rules are structured together and interrelate" and, furthermore, that there is a danger in using norm language because "it can obscure distinct and interrelated elements of social institutions if not used carefully" (Finnemore and Sikkink 1998: 891).

Keohane similarly sees the need to disaggregate norms (and rules) from institutions. He defines institutions as encompassing any "persistent and connected sets of rules, formal and informal, that prescribe behavioural roles, constrain activity and shape expectations" (1990: 732; see also Keohane 1988). Institutions are based in rules but are "related complexes of rules and norms, identifiable in space and time" (Keohane 1988: 383; see also Donnelly 2012: 625).

This form of disaggregation is important in two ways. First, it makes clear that institutions have structural properties beyond their component norms. Norms, in isolation, would not have the same level of suasion as norms anchored within an institution. Second, constructivists focus on change in the international system. Yet, conflating norms, rules, and structures together defeats our ability to explain change in two ways. Relatively prosaically, constructivists can explain some forms of norm change that result in changes to state practices quite easily, such as the evolution of a norm against the use of land mines (Price 1998). Other state practices, such as those based around sovereignty, are not so easily altered.

More problematic is the question of how actors can resolve contradictions between different norms or rules. Constructivism, by and large, presumes that once a norm becomes institutionalized at the international level, that norm's identity is fixed. But this claim is untenable. As Krook and True (2012:104) have recently argued, norms are processes that "tend to be vague, enabling their content to be filled in many ways and thereby to be appropriated for a variety of different purposes." Norms cannot cover every contingency; it is only through practice that they are clarified (Victor et al. 1998: xi; Sandholtz 2008b: 101). Only once domestic implementation has occurred can we presume that an individual state's understanding of a norm is fixed, and even that may be at odds with other understandings that may reopen the process of international contestation (Betts and Orchard 2014). But if a norm's identity is not yet fixed, it can provide little guidance to states and other actors concerning how they should behave. Furthermore, even if a norm is broadly accepted, it provides a binary set of actions for individual actors: to comply or not to comply. Actors need something beyond the norm itself to understand how the norm relates to the issue at hand and its relative suasion in comparison with other norms, which may provide alternative ways of understanding the issue and thus different forms of action or behavior.

One way in which actors may determine normative suasion might be to presume that an international legal convention trumps more informal norms. Legalization, Simmons (2009: 5) notes, signals "a seriousness of intent that is difficult to replicate in other ways." But Finnemore argues that legal norms have power simply because they have legitimacy (Finnemore 2000: 702–03), a property that any settled norm should possess (Betts and Orchard 2014).[1] Furthermore, it presumes that "international law" itself as a structure has some property separate from other rules.

Norms are thus neither necessarily fixed nor interpretable in isolation. Hence, as detailed later, normative contestation is an ongoing process. Furthermore, structures must be more than just isolated rules or norms (Donnelly 2012: 625). Instead, we can think of structure as Wight (2006: 122) does: as "that aspect of social life that ties the various elements together and is probably, in principle, something that can never be brought into the realm of the observable." This suggests that structures have three properties: they are rules, they provide processes to interpret those rules, and they demark who should have a role in interpreting the rules.

It is this broader structural framework that constitutes actors and ensures that those actors accept basic rules as valid (Ruggie 1998a: 20–21, 34). As Searle (1995: 23–28) notes, such institutional facts are rooted in collective intentionality – they make sense only within systems of constitutive rules that create the possibility of such facts, facts that are both iterative (Rust 2006: 12) and self-perpetuating because "each use of the institution is a renewed expression of the commitment of the users to the institution" (Searle 1995: 57). These practices are reproduced "through habitual use and compliance" (Reus-Smit 1999: 17) and therefore some practices may be so "deeply sedimented or reified that actors no longer think of them as rules at all" (Ruggie 1998b: 873).

But Searle (1995: 35) also notes that "social facts in general, and institutional facts especially, are hierarchically structured." Institutional facts require collective agreement or acceptance; they depend, Guzzini (2000: 160) notes, "in their very existence, and not only in their observation, on an intersubjectively shared set of meanings" that presupposes a

---

[1] Frost has argued that a norm is settled "where it is generally recognized that any argument denying the norm (or which appears to override the norm) requires special justification." Violating a settled norm therefore either should trigger a process of justification or will be undertaken clandestinely (Frost 1996: 105–06).

set of actors who can make that agreement. Thus, within international relations, some basic institutions – enduring fundamental practices in Keohane's (1988: 162) view, primary institutions in Buzan's (2004), fundamental institutions in Reus-Smit's (1999) – must exist to provide the basic rules of the game and identify who the players are.

It is these fundamental institutions that, Reus-Smit suggests, provide the "basic institutional framework for interstate cooperation... Without these basic institutional practices the plethora of international regimes that structure international relations in diverse issue-areas would simply not exist, and modern international society would function very differently" (1999: 3).

These institutions are therefore critical in two senses: they enable actors to cooperate, and they help to constitute those actors. Without the basic rules and understandings these fundamental institutions provide, stable cooperation would be impossible. They allow states, Morgenthau (1940: 279) argued, "to put their normal relations upon a stable basis by providing for predictable and enforceable conduct with respect to these relations." Thus, for Bull (2002: 66), the primary goal of states within an international society is to ensure order, which requires a rule-based system. Bull's definition of "international society" is a situation in which states conceive of themselves as bound by common rules and share in the working of common institutions (2002: 9–13). Once in such a society, states will adhere "to the rules and norms ... even when these conflict with their non-vital interests" (Dunne 1998: 144).[2] Thus, fundamental institutions provide states with a means "to judge each other's policies and actions and communicate that normative assessment" (Jackson 2000: 10–11), and they allow for cooperation in the absence of either a central authority or some form of common world culture (Cronin 2003: 17). Authors within the English School tradition, focused primarily on the need for order, argue in favor of a few core fundamental institutions based around law, diplomacy, and conflict.[3]

---

[2] Although any state system may have social dynamics, including mutual recognition (Reus-Smit 2011: 209), I deliberately use society here to highlight its intersubjective and social nature.

[3] Bull points to the balance of power, international law, the diplomatic mechanism, the managerial system of the great powers, and war as serving the role of fundamental institutions (Bull 2002: 71; see also Bull 1966: 48). Wight suggests that diplomacy and trade are vital. Butterfield points to international law, diplomacy, and the system of balance of power as key institutions (Butterfield and Wight 1966). Watson (1984: 24–25) points to the balance of power, international law, diplomatic dialogue, and the Congressional system (akin to Bull's management by the great powers). Mayall (2000: 11–12) accords an important role to diplomacy, international law, and nationalism.

The second way in which fundamental institutions are critical is that they "constitute state actors as subjects of international life in the sense that they make meaningful interaction by the latter possible" (Wendt and Duvall 1989: 53). In this sense, fundamental institutions define the cognitive horizons of institutional architects. They shape the universe of possible institutional choice by "licensing some institutional solutions over others," which results in the reproduction of basic institutional practices. States that wish to engage in stable interactions "encounter strong incentives to employ existing practices" (Reus-Smit 1999: 34, 36; Phillips 2011). Over time, these institutions acquire legitimacy "through their perceived concordance with a shared vision of the good" (Phillips 2011: 17).

This constructivist focus on a constitutive role leads to a more expansive set of fundamental institutions than those highlighted by the English School. Multilateralism qualifies because, without it, basic institutional arrangements such as international property rights would not be defined or stabilized (Ruggie 1992: 567; Reus-Smit 1999: 3). Territoriality also is critical because it is the "most generic attribute of any system of rule," comprising as it does "legitimate dominion over a spatial extension" (Ruggie 1993b: 151; Holsti 2004: 25). Other institutions, such as international law, help to create an underlying "intersubjective expectation that normative prescriptions will be followed because it is good to do so" (Crawford 2002: 92; see also Kratochwil 1989: 71).

Fundamental institutions also contribute to whether a state is perceived as acting legitimately in international society. State-members of international society "debate how legitimate states should, or should not, act" (Reus-Smit 1999: 27). Although some states can survive such negative feedback and reputational effects, most will seek to conform (Finnemore and Sikkink 1998: 903). Furthermore, by establishing how states ought to behave in international society, and by ensuring that territorially based states are the primary actors in that society, these institutions problematize refugees as an international issue and provide a basic framework of rules for state cooperation.

Refugees and fundamental institutions

Four fundamental institutions frame basic state cooperative practices toward refugees: territoriality, international law, popular sovereignty, and multilateralism. These fundamental institutions are not immutable. Reproduction of these constitutive practices at the international level also depends on the reproduction of these practices by domestic actors (Koslowski and Kratochwil 1994: 216). Change in these institutions, however, is limited and occurs over long periods of time. When change does occur, institutions are more likely to gain in complexity than to be replaced wholesale (Holsti 2004: 12–16, 300; see also Reus-Smit 2007; Phillips 2011).

The initial European-based international society that emerged in the seventeenth century was far narrower than today's international society, which is based on mutual territorial recognition. Different principles, Keene notes, were applied within and outside of this system:

> The fundamental normative principle of the colonial and imperial systems beyond Europe, by contrast, was that sovereignty should be divided across national and territorial borders as required to develop commerce and what Europeans and Americans saw as good government... This arrangement was inevitably more centralized and more hierarchical than the Westphalian system... Beyond Europe, however, international order was dedicated to ... the promotion of *civilization*. (2002: 98, emphasis in original; see also Gong 1984; Raustiala 2006: 222)

The importance of territoriality to the state cannot be underestimated – in Weber's (Weber, Gerth, and Mills 1958: 78) classic definition of the state as "a human community that (successfully) claims the monopoly of the legitimate use of physical force within a given territory" – it is directly linked to the basic concept of the state itself, even though there is no requirement for territory as the basis for human organization (Ruggie 1993b: 149; Herbst 2000: 52). The state becomes a geographically contained structure, one created through territoriality and sovereignty (Biersteker and Weber 1996: 2–4). In this sense, territoriality is critical because it provides a basis for both noninterference and state integrity (Herz 1957: 474; Nettl 1968: 562–64).

Within the Westphalian system, territory provides the indelible link between the state and its citizens. Westphalia, Philpott (1999: 570) argues, ensured the "collection of people over whom the holder of sovereignty rules is defined by virtue of its location within borders." These people, he adds, "may not necessarily conceive of themselves as a 'people' with a common identity ... [but] their location within boundaries requires their allegiance to their sovereign" (Philpott 1999: 570).

In an ideal system, Keely suggests, "of formally equal states, with mutually exclusive territories, everyone belongs somewhere ... but this does not accurately describe the real world" (1996: 1052). Instead, we are faced with a fundamental disconnect between the rights of the individual within the state and the status of those who do not have a state or cannot rely on their state's protection. As Hannah Arendt wrote, refugees and the stateless are a unique class:

To be a slave was after all to have a distinctive character, a place in society – more than the abstract nakedness of being human and nothing but human. Not the loss of specific rights, then, but the loss of a community willing and able to guarantee any rights whatsoever, has been the calamity which has befallen ever-increasing numbers of people. Man, it turns out, can lose all so-called Rights of Man without losing his essential quality as man, his human dignity. Only the loss of a polity itself expels him from humanity. (1966: 297)

Given this partitioning of people within territorial spaces, Hindess argues that the system of territorial states requires "regulation of movement from one national territory to another" (Hindess 2000: 1494; see also Joppke 1998: 5–9). But such a system, Liu suggests, creates an exclusionary space without which refugees would not exist (2002; see also Skran 1995: 3). "Functioning alongside sovereignty," she argues, "territory is deployed to problematise inter-state movement in a way that intra-state movement is not." Similarly, Haddad (2008: 43) notes that refugees exist because of the nature of the territorial state system: they are "a political construction posited outside the state-citizen-territory trinity."

Furthermore, aspects of territoriality as an institution have been subject to ongoing change. Borders, for example, are "crucial to basic goals of system perpetuation, state independence, limits on violence, sanctity of agreement, and stability of possession" (Williams 2002: 739–40). Yet borders were readily violated historically (Krasner 1999: 55), and it is only recently that a norm against altering them through the use of force has evolved (Zacher 2001: 216; Holsti 2004: 101; Atzili 2007).

Extraterritorial practices, another aspect of territoriality, have also evolved significantly (Hudson 1998: 89; see also Taylor 2003). The origins of extraterritorial practices reflected the fact that absolute territoriality provided no answers to issues that could not be reduced down to a territorial solution (Agnew and Corbridge 1995). As Ruggie (1993b: 164) notes, it left no space to anchor even "so basic a task as the conduct of diplomatic representation without fear of relentless disturbance." The solution to this issue was the creation of the embassy, "little islands of alien sovereignty" that allowed states to communicate with one another (Mattingly 1988: 244).

Extraterritorial practices directly affect refugee protection in two senses. For Raustiala (2009: 5), extraterritoriality represents a process through which "domestic law extends beyond sovereign borders" in order to "manage, minimize, or sometimes capitalize on legal differences [created as a] direct result of the territorial basis of sovereign rule." Embassies fit this mold. This understanding also underlies a range of international human rights treaties that focus on the protection of individuals under the jurisdiction of the state signatory rather than just within its territory (Meron 1995; Hawkins 2004: 782–83). And it is this understanding of extraterritoriality that underpins the basic notion of refugee protection. As Noll (2000: 18) has argued, "the word 'extraterritorial' expresses the exceptional character of such protection in that it takes place outside the country of origin."

More recently, a new sense of "extraterritoriality" has developed, one linked explicitly to how the developed world approaches its response to asylum seekers and refugees. Although this idea is developed in Chapter 8, this new version represents a deliberate attempt on the part of states to deterritorialize the provision of protection and thereby limit their commitments under international law (Betts 2004; Goodwin-Gill 2007: 28). Rather than extending domestic law beyond the state, extra-territoriality is used to limit the application of international law either at the border or, in the case of programs such as Australia's Pacific Solution, within the territory of the state itself (Kneebone 2006).

Thus, we can see notions of territoriality defining the state as a geographic entity and creating clear rights for citizens within this space. But this provides no answer to how those outside of this space – those who have either fled or who have been expelled – should receive basic rights and protection. International law has been critical in framing the individual's (and thus the refugee's) role toward both the state and international society. Although its development alongside the conception of refugees is explored further in the next chapter, international law is a critical fundamental institution because it provides the basic rules for coexistence between states. Through international law, Kratochwil argues, we gain norms "against lying (protecting the veracity of factual information), norms against the resort to violence (bounding of conflict), and norms against the breaking of promises (*pacta sunt servanda*), as well as norms settling the orderly acquisition and transfer of 'property'" (1989: 71; see also Ruggie 1998b: 872–73).

Multilateralism is a generic institutional form of international life that coordinates relations among three or more states in accordance with generalized principles of conduct (Ruggie 1993a: 7–8). Although Ruggie (1993a: 23) points to a history of multilateral arrangements within international society, only with the formation of the League of Nations was a multipurpose, universal membership organization created "with broad agendas in which large and small had a constitutionally mandated voice." With this shift, multilateralism not only embodied "a procedural norm in its own right," but it also gained "an international legitimacy" (Ruggie 1993a: 23).

The shift toward multilateralism in the period after the First World War not only led to a novel approach by which states could provide refugee protection – through multilateral organizations – but it also provided an important basis for these organizations to develop their own independent authority. At a deeper level, it also reconstituted how states approached the refugee problem. Prior to this shift, although states did accept a normative obligation to protect refugees, governments had no sense that this was a collective responsibility: rather, individual states sought to protect refugees *within their territory*. With the creation of multilateral organizations, states accepted that they bore a collective if limited responsibility to protect all refugees.

Finally, the fundamental institution of popular sovereignty redefined the state–citizen relationship within the guise of a bargain in which citizens perceived their governments as legitimate in exchange for a bundle of rights that increased over time. Popular sovereignty undermined the "ideological and material foundations of dynastic rule." Instead, with it, legitimate state action became tied to the "augmentation of individuals' purposes and potentialities" (Reus-Smit 1999: 122). The state system, in turn, began to be "built around the popular principle, deriving both its domestic and international legitimacy from the claims and consent of the governed" (Haddad 2003: 304; see also Zolberg et al. 1989: 9). As Mayall has argued, the people "are the final source of state legitimacy" (1990: 2; Buzan 2004: 243–47).

Popular sovereignty helped to structure how states and their populations responded to refugees. It provided an important underpinning to an international legal discourse that argued in favor of refugees being allowed to leave their state and of the state's prerogative to allow them entry. As popular sovereignty developed in the nineteenth century, states that acted in bad faith toward their citizens by persecuting them and forcing them to flee were increasingly perceived as illegitimate in international society. This provided an impetus for "legitimate" states, often driven by their domestic publics, to accept the "wayward souls" who had been driven out. Popular sovereignty thus played a key role at both the international and domestic levels in legitimating refugee protection practices.

Historically, the idea of popular sovereignty was a Eurocentric concept not applied to peoples across the globe (Keene 2002; Buzan 2004: 215). In the postwar period, popular sovereignty changed to become an inclusive concept and shifted toward a "non-racial and non-ethnic concept of self-determination as a right of 'peoples' rather than 'nations'" (Rae 2002: 232; see also Crawford 2002). Thus, decolonization triggered a substantial reinterpretation of state sovereignty and ushered in dramatic growth in the number of states.

To summarize, fundamental institutions are historical artifacts created and replicated by states through negotiations and practices. As time passed, these understandings were legitimated in international society because they formed a set of rules that enabled cooperation to occur and allowed for order and stability within that society to be preserved.

Regimes guiding state behavior

These four fundamental institutions created a political space in which states could conceive of refugees as an international problem. However, this provides no direct input into state practices, no direct forms of response to the problem. Another level of structures – regimes – helps to enact "basic institutional practices" embodied within fundamental institutions for a given issue (Reus-Smit 1999: 14; see also Hasenclever et al. 1997; Müller 2004: 420).

I argue that regimes play two roles within a broader structural account. First, by applying the basic ideas of fundamental institutions, they frame the nature and scope of a given problem and provide potential response scripts. Second, regimes also serve as a "web of meaning" in which individual issue-specific norms can interact and become linked together. Regimes therefore function as a behavior guide for states; they provide a basis for cooperation and coherent responses to common problems (Neufeld 1993: 43; Hasenclever et al. 1997: 165).

This conception of regimes is a departure from traditional neoliberal institutionalism. In that school of thought, regimes are arrangements created by states to improve their welfare by solving cooperation dilemmas through reducing uncertainty. They do this through information provision, monitoring activities, and linkages to or nesting with other issues to ease side payments (Keohane 1984: 6, 80; Axelrod and Keohane 1985: 232–34; Müller 1993: 383; Hasenclever et al. 1997: 33–37).

This materialist account of regime creation framed a key disagreement over the basic nature of regimes: were they only formal in nature, or could informal or tacit regimes also qualify? Informal regimes were seen as problematic because they begged "the question of the extent to which state behaviour is, in fact, rule-governed" (Haggard and Simmons 1987: 494; see also Keohane 1993: 27). But this had the advantage of including regimes that emerge spontaneously, rather than only through formal negotiations. This suggested that regimes might exist in the absence of conscious coordination among their participants (Young 1980: 348–52; see also Young 1982: 282–83, 249; Lipson 1991: 498). Most importantly, such a conception opened up the possibility that regimes were "social institutions," as Levy, Young, and Zurn suggest (1995: 274; see also

Ruggie 1982: 380). As social institutions, both formal and tacit regimes can have suasion not only through their benefits to participants, but also through the shared understandings and international norms they embody.

The "consensus" view of regimes had included norms among a regime's four discrete components: "implicit or explicit principles, norms, rules, and decision-making procedures around which actors' expectations converge in a given area of international relations" (Krasner 1982b: 186; for critiques of this definition, see Young 1986: 106; Levy et al. 1995: 270). By conceiving regimes as social institutions, I instead follow Goertz's minimalist concept that regimes are structures of norms and rules, with norms and rules being counterparts for most purposes (2003: 15). Such a position redefines a regime as effectively equivalent to a norm complex, which provides ways "in which behavioural rules are structured together and interrelate" (Finnemore and Sikkink 1998: 891; Bernstein 2000; Phillips 2011). This shift allows for a clearer explanation of why regimes persist even after their original functions have ended and why they fall apart.

On the first point, the question of regime persistence has long been a point of contention. For neorealism, regimes decline as hegemons decline (Keohane 1980: 132; Gilpin 1981). Neoliberalism suggests that regimes can persevere long after their creators decline because they are not affected directly by changes in power or short-term calculations of interest (Krasner 1982b: 186–87; Keohane 1984). This perseverance occurs for three reasons. First, regimes persevere because they are costly to build and because, as they persist and prove themselves effective, "the value of the functions they perform increases" (Keohane 1984: 102; see also Hasenclever et al. 1997: 38–39; Stein 1993). Nesting individual agreements within regimes facilitates their linkage and also lowers costs of future transactions (Keohane 1984: 91–92). Finally, over time, regimes can generate reputational effects by "providing standards of behaviour against which performance can be measured, by linking these standards to specific issues, and by providing forums, often through international organizations, in which these evaluations can be made" (Keohane 1984: 94).

Reputational concerns suggest that, as time passes, governments may, per Keohane and Nye (1989: 259), begin to "define their own self-interest in directions that conform to the rules of the regimes" and "the principles and norms of the regime may be internalized by important groups and thus become part of the belief systems which filter information." This is not a mere changing of "assessments of interest" (Krasner 1982a: 500); instead, through participation in regimes, "iterated acts of cooperation can lead to an internalized commitment to the social practice of cooperation itself" (Sterling-Folker 2000: 112). In effect, the social character of regimes helps to ensure their perseverance: states become used to

cooperating through them. But this also allows for a process of endogenous interest change among states driven by the regime, a feedback
process that further entrenches the regime.

As states conform to the regime, not only do their interests change over
time, but so too do their normative expectations with regard to other
states. In effect, the regime begins to represent a pattern of behavior
that legitimate states ought to follow. In this sense, regimes "represent a
concrete manifestation of the internationalization of political authority"
where authority combines a degree of power with legitimate social purpose (Ruggie 1982: 380–82; Cronin and Hurd 2008: 6).

Institutions, Reus-Smit (2007: 159) notes, can command legitimacy
when "there is a generalized perception that its normative precepts are
rightful, that they warrant respect and compliance for more than self-
interested reasons, for reasons of their normative standing." By contrast,
once a regime's legitimacy is undermined, once it suffers from a crisis of
legitimacy, this can be overcome only through adaptation or disempowerment (Reus-Smit 2007: 167; Phillips 2011). Consequently, the normative
content of the regime is critical – a clear and consistent normative structure helps ensure that a regime is perceived by actors as legitimate.

Outside factors also matter for a regime. For neoliberalism, regimes
have robustness, or staying power, when they are able to survive
"disturbances or to adapt to changing circumstances without losing
their essential or constitutive characteristics" (Young 1999: 133; see
also Powell 1994: 340–41; Hasenclever et al. 1997: 2). A constructivist
alternative to this suggests that challenges posed by alternative norms can
undermine the regime's collective purpose, either by the redefinition of its
individual component norms or by the introduction of new norms
(see Donnelly 1986: 605; Bernstein 2000). This can lead to the
coherence, internal consistency, and thus the compliance pull of the
regime's norms being undermined (Franck 1990: 163–80; see also
Legro 1997: 34; Thomas 2001: 15). Thus, regimes that are embedded
or nested within the deeper structures of international society
(Hasenclever et al. 1997: 16; Ruggie 1982; Alter and Meunier 2009) or
that complement social institutions at the domestic level are more robust
due to their greater acceptance by states (Young 1999: 15).

In an increasingly complex international system, regimes and institutions fill new and overlapping roles. Complexity has benefits – not only
can the positive feedback of individual regimes continue, but weaker
actors also can use the overlap of regimes and rules to their advantage
(Alter and Meunier 2009: 13). It also has drawbacks: notably "unhelpful
competition across actors, inefficiencies, and transaction costs that end up
compromising the objectives" of the regime (Alter and Meunier 2009: 14;

see also Raustiala and Victor 2004). States may use regimes in a very instrumental fashion, including by shifting issues from one regime to another through forum shopping and by picking venues "based on where they are best able to promote specific policy preferences." In the worst cases, states may deliberately create contradictory rules in order to undermine a parallel regime that covers a similar issue (Betts 2010: 14).

State actions may not be deliberate. As new norms that conflict with prior understandings gain salience, they, too, can limit or undermine the strength of a norm (Percy 2008: 30). More broadly, regimes "might not be the product of conscious design but rather emerge out of patterned interactions that become routinized and institutionalized" (Barnett 1996: 159). In other words, they may have path-dependent properties. Early choices, rather than current conditions, may drive institutional change (Sterling-Folker 2000: 98), and "accumulated random variations can lead an institution into a state that could not have been predicted in advance" (Keohane 1988: 389; see also March and Olsen 1998: 958). Sequencing and entrenchment of certain arrangements can therefore "obstruct an easy reversal of the initial choice" (Levi 1997: 28), with the result that "social systems can get 'locked in' to certain patterns by the logic of shared knowledge, adding a source of social inertia or glue that would not exist in a system without culture" (Wendt 1999: 188). As Crawford notes, this may mean that there are no good ethical or practical reasons for a practice, and yet: "for some accidental reason, the practice is accepted and expected. In this situation, no one seems to have what might be recognized as an ethical or logical argument to justify the practice, though post-hoc rationalizations for the practice might spring to mind if practitioners are pressed" (2002:88).

Reconceiving regimes as structures that bundle together individual normative understandings helps to accentuate their social, as opposed to material, properties and to link them more concretely with deeper fundamental institutions. This shift moves regimes away from being solely created by states to fulfil their interests. Instead, routinized practices may also slowly create regimes. Regime legitimacy depends on its normative content, particularly whether the norms bundled in the regime are coherent and consistent. When they are, the regime creates shared interests and understandings between its members and can link those understandings to other structures at the international and domestic levels. Regime legitimacy is also affected by the external environment. Regimes are challenged by events beyond themselves, including dramatic changes such as crisis events or by the development of new alternative norms and practices. It is to how crisis events drive change that I now turn.

Refugee protection crises

Crisis events drive changes in the norms that underpin refugee protection. Refugee protection has elements of a punctuated equilibrium model, one that anticipates "short bursts of rapid institutional change followed by long period of stasis" (Krasner 1984: 242; see also Goertz 2003: 51). "Complex interactive political systems," as Jones, Baumgartner, and True note, "do not react slowly and automatically to changing perceptions or conditions; rather, it takes increasing pressure and sometime a crisis atmosphere to dislodge established ways of thinking about policies" (Jones et al. 1998: 2; see also Hall 1993). I utilize a historical institutionalist approach to analyze the dynamics at play in changes to the refugee protection regime.

The concept of crises as driving change has been criticized. It has been argued that, too often, crises are simply used as default explanations for change (Legro 2005: 15, 28; see also Price and Reus-Smit 1998: 282).[4] Rather than assuming crisis events as a default, per Legro (2000: 420), I identify a two-stage mechanism through which a crisis event generates change. In the first stage, "societal actors must somehow concur, explicitly or tacitly, that the old ideational structure is inadequate thus causing its collapse." Beyond a simple failure, for a crisis to occur, the failure must be "identified and widely perceived" and both become public (Hall 1993: 287; Hay 1999: 324) and see actors question their own self-interests (Blyth 2002); hence, reversion to the status quo will not be feasible. In so doing, the crisis event disrupts policy stasis within governments (Milner and Keohane 1996: 16; see also Goldstein 1989: 32; Hall 1993). By questioning the ideational basis of a regime, a crisis event can also break down the regime's legitimacy (or cause a legitimacy crisis).

This triggers a second-stage process in which new international norms, and even new regimes, may be created to replace failed ones (Florini 1996: 378; Price 1998: 616; Reus-Smit 2004: 288). For constructivists, it is this perception of a crisis that creates a window of opportunity for change during which societal attributes become more malleable (Berger 1996: 331; Price 1998: 622). In short, as Checkel (1997: 7) notes, "under conditions of high international uncertainty or foreign policy crisis, decision makers engage in an information search and are thus more receptive to new ideas." During this window of opportunity, outsiders with knowledge, such as norm entrepreneurs, can influence the decision-making apparatus by promoting new norms (Hass 1992; Simmons et al. 2006: 789).

---

[4] For similar concerns, see Steinmo and Thelen (1992: 16) and Bell (2011: 884).

Rarely, however, does only one idea appear. Instead, the state of uncertainty will trigger a process of contestation among differing ideas. As Hay (2008: 67) notes, "crises thus unleash short bouts of intense ideational contestation in which agents struggle to provide compelling and convincing diagnoses of the pathologies afflicting the old regime/policy paradigm and the reforms appropriate to the resolution of the crisis." Thus, this process may closely follow a garbage can model, with some new ideas being introduced whereas other ideas may simply be "solutions looking for problems" to be grafted on to this new issue (Cohen et al. 1972: 16; Kingdon 2002). Idea proponents, consequently, are working within a contested institutional environment that can both enable and constrain their efforts, with agents seeking institutional enablement, space, and discretion within this setting (Scharpf 1997; Bell 2011: 894–95). As Bell (2011: 900) notes, agents "operate within fields of bounded discretion utilizing institutional resources to help enable or empower action." This extraordinary period ends with the adoption of new norms and a new period of stasis. Institutionalization will cause the new norm to fade "into the background and relative obscurity until something provokes a re-evaluation of that process" (Goertz 2003: 51).

Therefore, I wish to make two additional moves. The first is to elaborate how the concept of crisis events applies to the area of refugee protection. The second, elaborated in the next section, is to develop an expanded account of constructivist norm entrepreneurship that allows these crisis events to trigger the process of normative change.

What constitutes a crisis event within the area of refugee protection? A crisis event, here, is a failure of existing policies triggered by a dramatic and sustained change in the nature and/or numbers of refugees seeking protection. This change must be significant enough that state refugee policies will be unsustainable in the long run without alteration or replacement. Furthermore, it causes states to question preexisting normative understandings and the purpose of the regime. Reversion to the status quo will no longer be feasible. For example, following the First World War, the dramatic growth in refugee numbers meant that the ad hoc response by individual states was no longer sustainable; even so, this response continued until critical states such as France and Britain acknowledged failure in 1921.

Under this definition, the crisis event can have either a material basis (physical refugee numbers) or an ideational basis (new groups claiming protection). Initially, the refugee category was exclusively for those fleeing religious persecution; the French Revolution added political persecution to that category. More recently, people fleeing situations of generalized violence have started to be incorporated within the term, although not yet fully within international law. The material and ideational bases are not mutually exclusive criteria; rather, both often occur in tandem.

This definition of crisis allows for the identification of six major crisis events within the history of refugee protection since the seventeenth century:

1. The *Huguenot flight from France*, precipitated by the Revocation of the Edict of Nantes (1685, detailed in Chapter 3), was a shock caused by a change in the nature and numbers of refugees. Although religious refugees had been common prior to this period, the Revocation challenged key norms reflecting the right of refugees to leave their own state and created more than 200,000 refugees.

2. The *flight of the émigrés from France* during the Revolution (1789–1815, detailed in Chapter 4) was a shock caused by a change in the nature of refugees. For the first time, states were faced with significant numbers of persons fleeing political, rather than religious, persecution.

3. The *flight of Russians* from the Russian Revolution (1917–21, detailed in Chapter 5) was a shock caused by both a change in the nature and numbers of refugees. For the first time, refugees who fled a state also had their citizenship stripped, rendering them nonpersons under existing international law.

4. *German Jews fleeing the Nazis* (1933–39, detailed in Chapter 5) was a shock because of their numbers and the inability of states to successfully coordinate policies.

5. *Displaced persons following the Second World War* (1946, detailed in Chapter 6) were a shock because of their numbers, their inability and/or unwillingness to return to their countries of origin, and the threat they posed to the stability of postwar Europe.

6. *Post-Cold War flight* (1987–94, detailed in Chapter 8) was a shock because of the nature and numbers of refugees. Refugees in this period often constituted a new type – those fleeing situations of generalized violence and persecution by non-state actors.

Crises are crucial to regime creation, transformation, and replacement because they cause states to question the norms and principles associated with the existing regime as it goes through a crisis of legitimacy. An acknowledged crisis opens the "policy window" to norm entrepreneurs to argue in favor of new norm-governed understandings toward refugee protection, which may bring about normative change as well as regime transformation or replacement.

Norm emergence, norm entrepreneurs, and domestic structures

How do norms change? New norms emerge into a contested environment, one in which they must compete with other existing and perhaps countervailing norms (Jepperson et al. 1996: 56). Norm entrepreneurs may help to introduce these norms to states and other actors. Their role, however, is more than this. They may also help to actively build norms. Ideally, they will frame the norms in such a way that they become widely accepted. Thus, norm entrepreneurs are critical to this process because "they call attention to issues or even 'create' issues by using language that names, interprets and dramatizes them" (Finnemore and Sikkink 1998: 896–97).

The content of new normative alternatives is not predetermined and, contrary to many typically constructivist accounts, may result in outcomes that are problematic to refugee protection. I frame new proposals by norm entrepreneurs within two sets of heuristic alternatives. First, norm entrepreneurs advocate *humanitarian-based* solutions by expanding or deepening refugee protection, changes that can occur either by the state changing its policies at the domestic level, by supporting norms at the international level, or both. This is most clearly demonstrated by state practice in the early nineteenth century and following the Second World War. Second, norm entrepreneurs advocate *sovereignty-based or restrictionist* solutions, designed to deliberately or inadvertently narrow refugee protection. This can occur by the state changing domestic policies, such as introducing policies to restrict immigration or asylum, by supporting norms reflecting this at the international level, or both. This is most clearly demonstrated by state practice in the late 1920s and 1930s, and since the end of the Cold War. Such restrictionist arguments tend to emerge at the domestic level but can also play important roles at the international level.

Putting forward new humanitarian-based alternatives is a process fraught with difficulty and danger. Such claims almost invariably entail either greater obligations, resource commitments, or both on the part of the state. Such new obligations therefore tend to bear higher direct costs and can prove a "harder sell" to individuals and institutions within the state (Kaufmann and Pape 1999; Busby 2010). Crucially, because the crisis event has elevated the issue out of the realm of ordinary politics, the status quo is no longer an option. Therefore, if norm entrepreneurs fail in their efforts to introduce new humanitarian-based norms to protect refugees, the historical record demonstrates that, in past instances, the end result was to introduce restrictionist-based policies. Thus, crisis events trigger a high-stakes gamble on the part of refugee protection proponents.

This is not to say that crisis events are the only way that change occurs. In fact, norm entrepreneurs can play a further important role by modifying state practices incrementally, such that a crisis is diverted or delayed. Such patterns of incremental change do not overturn the existing normative framework of the regime; rather, norm entrepreneurs can stretch existing practices and normative understandings to incorporate deviant or new challenges.

Who, then, are norm entrepreneurs? The efforts of various entrepreneurs have become near ubiquitous within this literature, including such a range of actors as transnational advocacy networks (Risse 1999; Klotz 2002: 56), epistemic communities (Haas 1992), international organizations (IOs; Barnett and Finnemore 2004), and key international figures such as the United Nations Secretary-General (Rushton 2008). The traditional view of norm entrepreneurs is that they seek to convince states of the value of the norm. Supportive states can then become norm leaders, using their privileged status at the international level to persuade other states to adhere to the new norm (Finnemore and Sikkink 1998: 901–02; Coleman 2013: 166).

This account is problematic in three ways. First, much of this work has focused on identifying categories of different actors who may play the role of entrepreneur. Given the ubiquity of norm entrepreneurs, it may be conceptually richer to classify norm entrepreneurship as an activity that any international actor can engage in. Of course, this leads immediately to the problem of classifying what is unique about norm entrepreneurship as opposed to other activities. For Finnemore and Sikkink, it was the fact that the actor held strong notions about appropriate or desirable behavior (Finnemore and Sikkink 1998: 897). But others, such as Nadelmann (1990: 481), link norm entrepreneurship explicitly to "moral proselytism," to furthering a moral agenda. Focusing on the specific prescriptive or ethical content of the norm in question provides one way of defining norm entrepreneurship (see Crawford 2002: 95–98). But this leads directly to a critique made by Checkel (2012: 3) that "the failure to address norm entrepreneurship of a less feel-good sort is worrying."

This leads into the second issue. Given that they emerge into a contested normative environment, new norms must fit coherently with the existing normative environment to ensure their legitimacy (Florini 1996: 376; Percy 2008: 29). Entrepreneurs use framing – "the conscious strategic efforts by groups of people to fashion shared understandings of the world and of themselves that legitimate and motivate collective action" (McAdam et al. 1996: 6; Benford and Snow 2000: 614) – to advance their ideas and to position their preferred norm within this environment. However, the framing process can be highly contested, with different frames being deployed by different sets of actors (Payne 2001). This, Krebs and Jackson suggest, can trigger a framing contest. The ensuing rhetorical contestation is not meant to convince the other party of the rightness of a frame. Rather, it "consists of parties attempting to maneuver each other onto more favorable rhetorical terrain and thereby close off routes of acceptable rebuttal" vis-à-vis a third party (Krebs and Jackson 2007: 44–45).

Frames with resonance have a greater chance of being adopted. For a frame to be resonant, consequently, it needs to be empirically credible; it needs to be consistent with the actor's "articulated beliefs, claims, and actions"; and that actor needs to also be seen as credible (Benford and Snow 2000: 620). But it also needs to be salient with the audience to which the framing argument is being made and be cultural resonant (Benford and Snow 2000: 622). Thus, successful framing works by ensuring the new norm resonates with broader public understandings and with established normative practices (Finnemore and Sikkink 1998: 897; Crawford 2002: 102).

If we assume that one of the competitors in a framing contest is advancing a moral or ethical cause, then that suggests other competitors are potentially advancing arguments related only to their own self-interests or other factors. Not only does this prejudge contestations, but even "moral" or "good" entrepreneurs may pursue their interests while advancing a broader cause (Bob 2010; Carpenter 2010; 2011).

If norm entrepreneurship is not based in moral action, then what does drive it? Here, policy studies can help. Policy entrepreneurs "distinguish themselves through their desire to significantly change current ways of doing things in their area of interest" (Mintrom and Norman 2009: 650). As Kingdon (2002: 122) notes, they "could be in or out of government, in elected or appointed positions, in interest groups or research organizations. But their defining characteristic, much as in the case of a business entrepreneur is their willingness to invest their resources – time, energy, reputation, and sometimes money – in the hope of a future return." Here, then, the activity is not judged by the cause or by the assumption that only certain actors can undertake it. This also reflects Finnemore and Sikkink's (1998: 896–97) idea that norm entrepreneurs call attention to or create issues about which they have strong notions. Using this perspective, I define norm entrepreneurship as an activity or process through which actors are willing to devote considerable resources (material and/or ideational) in order to introduce, change, or replace international norms in their areas of interest.

Redefining norm entrepreneurship in such a way provides two further advantages. First, a range of actors in a succession of roles are needed to support and advocate for the new norm. Carpenter (2010: 209) notes that, within the human rights field, there are at least "two necessary phases of transnational issue emergence, either of which may fail to occur: issue definition by an entrepreneur and issue adoption by one or more human rights organizations." Campaigners need to convince key organizations – ones that, due to their structural position, are network hubs – of the salience of the issue. These organizations, consequently, have a distinct agenda vetting power (Carpenter 2011: 70) (Figure 2.1).

International
• States • Individuals • International Organizations • Transnational Advocacy Networks
Domestic

• Nongovernment/Extragovernment Organizations
• Governmental Actors
  ○ Elite decision makers
  ○ Judicial actors
  ○ Institutions (as veto players)

Figure 2.1 Potential norm entrepreneurs

The capacity of these actors to further norm creation leads to a more complex view of norm creation. Following initial issue identification, other actors can step in to further the norm adoption process. This leads to the second advantage of this modified definition: norm entrepreneurship is not only an activity engaged in at the international level. Rather, actors at both the international and domestic levels – ranging from domestic institutions, IOs, to states themselves – can play critical roles in blocking or supporting normative change from the early introduction of a new international norm through to its internalization.

The role of domestic institutions and domestic entrepreneurs

Domestic institutions, clearly, have an agenda vetting power when it comes to new international norms. Yet, the two most-cited norm emergence models – Finnemore and Sikkink's norm life cycle and Risse and Sikkink's (Risse and Sikkink 1999) spiral model – focus primarily on international processes rather than on domestic-level effects. For Finnemore and Sikkink (1998: 902), once the norm passes the threshold or tipping point in the life cycle, the domestic role drops out and "international and transnational norm influences become more important than domestic politics for effecting norm change." Elsewhere, I have critiqued this model with respect to institutionalized norms (see Betts and Orchard 2014). The domestic level, however, can also have powerful effects with respect to emerging norms.

In most cases, a new international norm needs first to be accepted within domestic discourse, then within domestic institutions (Cortell and Davis 2000: 70). This case is made easier when the new norm, as Risse and Sikkink note, resonates or fits "with existing collective understandings embedded in domestic institutions and political cultures"

(1999: 271; see also Checkel 1999; Sundstrom 2005: 420–24). Alternatively, it is also easier when there are no preexisting understandings at the domestic level (Thomas 2001: 8–15; see also Cortell and Davis 1996: 452).

Shifts in domestic institutions, Koh notes, create "symbolic structures, standard operating procedures, and other internal mechanisms to maintain habitual compliance." Once this has occurred, decision makers outside the institution may be forced to shift their own views "from a policy of violation to one of compliance" to avoid friction (Koh 1997: 2653–55; Sandholtz 2008b). This may require first gaining the support of institutional veto players or gatekeepers who have "sufficient power to block or at least delay policy change" (Busby 2010: 56; Tsebelis 2000: 442).

Changes in domestic institutions, such as the introduction of laws or standard operating procedures, provide a strong indication that a new norm has "achieved more than nominal domestic salience" (Cortell and Davis 2000: 70). If this does not occur, the international norm may be only weakly internalized within the state; as a behavior guide, states may rhetorically support it, but their domestic interests will take priority over the new norm (Cortell and Davis 2000: 71; Shannon 2000: 300–03). This significantly increases the risk of violation.

Domestic institutions are not simply forums, however. They can control both access and the agenda by creating different channels into the political system (Cortell and Davis 2000: 66). Institutions can also affect the possibility of change, as Milner and Keohane (1996: 21) note, by "freezing coalitions and policies into place. They do this by making the costs of changing these coalitions and policies very high." Thus, norm entrepreneurs may need to build "winning" coalitions or logroll (Risse-Kappen 1995: 16; Kaufmann and Pape 1999: 632) within these institutions to get their ideas accepted.

In introducing new norms, international norm entrepreneurs can draw on their own international sources of authority and legitimacy (Cronin and Hurd 2008) while building either direct connections with domestic institutions or undertaking other ways to mobilize domestic support (Cox 1969: 225; Kaufmann and Pape 1999: 632; Moravcsik 1999: 272). But, as Checkel (1999: 88–89) notes, in most cases, norm entrepreneurs need to be empowered in some way in the national arena by shifting the interests and preferences of a domestic agent or institution. This suggests that domestic norm entrepreneurs may also have a critical, if unheralded, role in introducing new international norms.

The domestic institutional environment provides an important level of variation in the two countries I primarily focus on, the United

Kingdom and the United States. The United Kingdom, with a fused executive and legislature, has a single institutional veto player, whereas the United States has many (Tsebelis 2002). As Busby notes, in the United Kingdom, the influence and views of a few individuals will be crucial in adopting or rejecting new international norms (2007: 254; see also King 1992: 220). In the United States, a larger number of veto players – including the U.S. Congress – with widely differing interests will need to be convinced, with the result that policy stasis is more common (Kingdon 2002).

The U.S. Congress can be expected to play a gatekeeper role, potentially blocking new international norms. However, it can also take on an independent leadership role by embracing new international norms. It has forced the executive branch to act in a number of cases, including promoting human rights and against apartheid South Africa (Klotz 1995: 109–10). Hence, in the United States, the adoption of new norms will be more contested due to two independent institutions – the executive and Congress – having direct influence over the process.[5] Once norms are internalized in domestic law, the judiciary may also play a role in preventing backsliding.

Refugee policy at the domestic level, not surprisingly, has been shaped by a number of norm entrepreneurs. In Britain, the executive, and in particular the Foreign Office, generally had the power to determine the country's approach to individual refugee flows, as well as to the broader normative understandings of the refugee regime. In the United States, by contrast, refugee policy has changed only sporadically and usually only through long-term efforts. This has not been due to a lack of norm entrepreneurs. Rather, at times, their activities have been blocked within the executive branch – the State Department played such a role throughout the interwar period – and by Congress. When American policies toward refugees were successfully framed within the national interest, by contrast, and in particular when the president assumed a norm entrepreneur role (see Gerhardt 2001), Congress has been more consistently supportive of new norms. By the same token, Congress has also played a role in ensuring that the executive branch continues to abide by accepted norms, particularly after the enactment of the 1980 Refugee Act. Thus, the domestic environment can dramatically affect a state's receptiveness to new international norms.

---

[5] This is not to diminish the fact that within the executives of both countries there may also be tensions and infighting (Risse-Kappen 1991: 487) that diminish the efficacy of norm entrepreneurs.

The role of international organizations

Since 1921, IOs have also played important and independent roles within successive refugee regimes. An IO is a formal entity – "an organization that has representatives from three or more states supporting a permanent secretariat to perform ongoing tasks related to a common purpose" (Barnett and Finnemore 2004: 177; Coleman 2007: 6). For rationalism, IOs can have some independent properties because their value outweighs their costs. Yet, as Abbott and Snidal (1998: 5) argue, they remain creatures of member states, who "can limit the autonomy of IOs, interfere with their operations, ignore their dictates, or restructure and dissolve them."

Constructivism sees IOs as possessing their own sources of authority, "the ability to induce deference in others" (Avant et al. 2010: 9). International organizations, Barnett and Finnemore note, generally pursue goals seen as desirable and legitimate (2004: 17–18; see also Barnett and Finnemore 2005: 162). They are bureaucracies with their own hierarchical, continuous, impersonal, and expert systems in place. Because of this, their powers go beyond regulation to constituting "the world as they devise new categories of problems to be governed and create new norms, interests, actors, and shared social tasks" (Barnett and Finnemore 2004: 17).

Although IOs have authority delegated to them from states, they also possess rational-legal authority due to their bureaucratic structures. Furthermore, they possess expert authority due to their detailed, specialized knowledge and moral authority based on their need to embody, serve, or protect a widely shared set of principles (Barnett and Finnemore 2004: 20–24). With this authority, IOs have the ability to deploy "discursive and institutional resources in order to get actors to defer judgement to them" (Barnett and Finnemore 2005: 169). But this authority can be lost. The (in)ability of the IO to achieve its goals, to serve interests, and to satisfactorily achieve the community's purposes all matter to its continued relevance (Barnett and Finnemore 2004: 168; Sandholtz 2008a: 140; Avant et al. 2010).

The United Nations High Commissioner for Refugees (UNHCR) fits this mold closely. It has authority delegated to it by states as a consequence of its Statute and the 1951 Refugee Convention, the 1967 Refugee Protocol, and a series of UN General Assembly resolutions. It has powerful moral authority, derived "from its mission to help protect refugees and from its standing as a humanitarian agency that acted in an impartial manner" (Barnett and Finnemore 2004: 73–74; see also Barnett 2001). And, for much of its history, it "has acted as a 'teacher' of refugee norms."

It has used a number of tactics, including "persuasion and socialization in order to hold states accountable to their previously stated policies or principles" (Loescher 2001: 5). Even so, much of this authority is based on the prior development of key norms reflecting how states should protect refugees. Thus, the UNHCR's success reflects a historical process of gradual norm development and accumulation.

Furthermore, not all IOs are created equal. An important level of variation occurs between the UNHCR and the previous IOs created to protect refugees, a long list that begins with the League of Nations High Commission for Refugees in 1921. Each of these had such nexi of independent authority, although they varied significantly. The institutional record prior to the UNHCR was decidedly mixed; most notably in the failure of IOs both inside and outside of the League of Nations to protect refugees fleeing Nazi Germany.

States, power, and norm diffusion

The final question is how new norms that are internalized by a few states diffuse across international society. On one level, norm diffusion reflects that "national policy choices are interdependent – that governments adopt new policies not in isolation but in response to what their counterparts in other countries are doing" (Simmons et al. 2006: 782). Equally, norm diffusion can be driven through socialization (Finnemore and Sikkink 1998: 901–02) and through shaming, as states become concerned over their international reputation should they not follow a new norm (Price 1998: 635; Johnstone 2005: 187).

Yet, such diffusion processes raise the specter of coercion in the adoption of new norms, especially when the focus is on great powers such as the United Kingdom and the United States. From a realist perspective, the use of coercion and material incentives is common in altering the positions of other states. This can occur through "manipulating the opportunities and constraints encountered by target countries, either directly or through the international and non-governmental organization (NGOs) they influence" (Simmons et al. 2006: 790). Ikenberry and Kupchan similarly note that hegemonic states can exercise power through material incentives, such as threats of punishment or promises of reward, to alter the political or economic incentives of other states. Even so, socialization provides an alternative, more diffuse form of power because the hegemon alters the substantive beliefs of leaders in other states. From this process, "acquiescence emerges from the diffusion of a set of normative ideals" (1990: 284). Socialization helps to make hegemony more durable and less costly than coercion alone and thus suits the hegemon's self-interests (Ikenberry and Kupchan 1990); it is therefore limited to an "elite strategy to induce value change in others, rather than as a ubiquitous feature of interaction in terms of which all identities and interests get produced and reproduced" (Wendt 1992: 403).

Generally, constructivists understand socialization as a process in which actors' attitudes are changed without either material or mental coercion (Johnston 2001; Flockhart 2006: 97). As Checkel (2005: 804) notes, socialization is "a process of inducting actors into the norms and rules of a given community. Its outcome is sustained compliance based on the internalization of these new rules." Material incentives may assist the initial socialization process (Checkel 2005: 809). However, their long-term use may denote problems. As Reus-Smit notes, when states have to resort either to coercion or to the provision of tangible benefits, regimes will suffer from either decay or crisis, and the actor or institution "must either adapt (by reconstituting the social bases of its legitimacy, or by investing more heavily in material practices of coercion or bribery) or face disempowerment" (2007: 158; see also Price 2007: 235). The costs associated with the latter steps are such that they cannot be continued indefinitely (Finnemore 2003: 147).

In one sense, this debate reflects alternative views of power in international relations. As opposed to the view of power as compellance (Weber 1947: 52), I follow Barnett and Duvall's (2005: 3) conceptualization of power as "the production, in and through social relations, of effects that shape the capacities of actors to determine their own circumstances and fate." This view focuses on the ability of an actor to undertake independent action, including through force but also through negotiation, persuasion, and argumentation (Risse 2000).

I argue that it is primarily through socialization rather than coercion or benefits that states have historically changed international norms concerning refugee protection. Coercive actions or threats were seldom used to gain adherence to new understandings and never after the 1830s. In fact, a more frequent issue was threats of war being leveled against those states advocating new norms due to perceptions that their refugee policies were too lenient. Similarly, the states advocating new normative understandings were often willing to provide economic incentives by subsidizing IOs. But such incentives cannot offer a complete explanation because these efforts were generally short-lived and associated directly with the state taking on a norm leadership role. Direct financial support tended to decline as other states became socialized to the new norms.

In summary, three separate types of norm entrepreneurs are influential in the norm emergence process: individuals and domestic institutions, IOs, and states. Within the state, it is important to consider the different roles that might be played by entrepreneurs within and outside of government who may face distinctly different access problems and constraints.

Conclusion

The aim of this chapter was to establish the explanatory framework I use to explain continuity and change in states' refugee policies. This required detailing the roles of both structures and agents. The first part of the chapter dealt with the role of fundamental institutions in both constituting states as actors in international society and problematizing refugees and creating a space in which a cooperative solution is possible. I then elaborated a view of regimes that focused on their linking ability between these institutions and individual norms. Regimes are important because they frame the scope of the problem and provide a guide to states on what constitutes normatively correct behavior within the issue area.

Regimes, although fairly stable, will be challenged by crises, in particular changes in the nature and numbers of refugees. Crisis events cause states to question the ideational basis for a regime, thus undermining its legitimacy. These events also cause states to seek alternative norms for guidance, and their policies following a crisis will be either to follow an attempt to preserve the status quo, to increase restrictionist policies, or to increase humanitarian policies.

In the last section, I argued that norm entrepreneurs play a critical role as agents in introducing new norms and gaining their widespread acceptance. If these norms challenge preexisting understandings, however, they are unlikely to be internalized without the concerted efforts of domestic entrepreneurs to overcome institutional biases. Once states have accepted the new norm, however, they can succeed in acting as norm entrepreneurs in their own right, socializing other states in international society.

3 Refugees and the emergence of international society

How did refugees become constituted as an international problem? Territorial asylum is an old concept, having first emerged with the Ancient Greek city states. Yet, as a form of practice, it disappeared under the Roman Empire, even while religious-based forms of asylum continued. The key points in the reemergence of territorial asylum were two events that occurred forty years apart. The first was the Peace of Westphalia in 1648, which ended the Thirty Years' War. As a means to end further religious conflict, the Peace introduced the concept of *jus emigrandi*: that individuals who faced religious persecution had the right to leave their own state and seek sanctuary elsewhere. This right to leave was not directly challenged by any state in the decades following the Peace.

This changed in 1685. When Louis XIV revoked the Edict of Nantes, he ended a century of toleration for the Huguenot Protestant population in France. He also acted in direct contradiction to the understandings created by the Peace by denying them a right of exit from France. This denial was ineffective – some 200,000 Huguenots fled France following the revocation. But, in their flight, the Huguenots triggered a crisis for other European states. The receiving states faced the question of how to respond to these refugees. Their decision was to create a novel form of state practice by according the Huguenot refugees unique status in the receiving states, including domestic legal protections. This change was a watershed event. Throughout the next century and a half, other religious refugees were similarly identified and accepted by states, although the forms of protection they received varied.

To understand the shift in practice that began with the Huguenot flight, it is necessary to consider how the emerging European-based international society of the time was constituted. Two fundamental institutions, territoriality and international law, shaped how the receiving states formulated their responses.

A notion of statehood rooted in territoriality was not easily reconciled with a concept of status for citizens who had chosen to flee their own state. In effect, territoriality meant that refugees, as a class of people, became framed as an international problem (beyond the responsibility of the state) rather than a domestic problem (within the state's responsibility). Furthermore, it meant that prior forms of asylum rooted in church sanctuary could no longer function because they challenged the state's basic prerogative to administer justice within its territory.

Defining refugees as an international problem did not by itself lead to a ready solution to the refugee problem. Instead, the development of international law over the century preceding the revocation of the Edit of Nantes was critical to this process. This process articulated the rights and responsibilities of states vis-à-vis each other, as well as in relation to their individual citizens, within a common international society. International legal scholars of the time sought to justify an emerging territorial notion of asylum that was rooted in classical rights of hospitality. These doctrines were reinterpreted into clear protections for refugees.

The test for this system was the flight of the Huguenots. It was here that other states put these ideas into practice. They accepted that France was wrong to prohibit exit, offered the Huguenots sanctuary for a mix of religious and economic reasons, and provided them an assortment of legal protections. But this was not a single incident. Other refugee flows over the late seventeenth and eighteenth centuries also conform broadly to this pattern, as summarized in Table 3.1. This suggests that these basic understandings of who refugees were and that other states needed to provide them with asylum began to take on normative properties.

Practices between 1648 and 1755 demonstrate the difference between states independently following a norm-governed understanding and states cooperating within a regime. In this case, states accepted that refugees had a right to leave their own states, a normative understanding that influenced state decisions. However, states saw no corresponding normative obligation to accept refugees. Refugees were welcomed, but throughout this period it was usually for religious or economic reasons. The willingness of receiving states to accept refugees depended greatly on the demographics of the group and domestic pressures within the receiving state. Thus, whereas territoriality and international law as institutions helped create a space in which refugees were treated as distinct from other migrants, this practice was significantly different from state practices in the nineteenth century, in which liberal conceptions of popular sovereignty provided a strong ideational basis for a true regime.

Refugees and the emergence of a new state system

Doctrines of asylum have both religious and political roots. Religious understandings point directly to the need to provide protection to

Table 3.1 *Refugee movements, 1648–1755*

Year	Group	Refugee Numbers	Source Country	Host Country	Fled Religious Persecution	Denied Exit	Expelled	Granted Protection in Domestic Law
1685	Huguenots	200,000	France	Brandenburg, other German states, Netherlands, England	Yes	Yes	No	Yes
1686	Waldensians	3,000	Piedmont	Switzerland	Yes	No	Yes	No
1709	Palatines	12,000	Palatine	England	Yes	Yes	No	No
1731	Salzburgers	20,000	Austria	Prussia	Yes	No	Yes	No
1744	Jews	20,000	Austria	Allowed to Return	Yes	No	Yes	No
1755	Acadians	12,000	Nova Scotia	Within British Empire	No	No	Yes	No

Sources: Norwood (1969: 52, 102–34); Scoville (1952a: 296–98); Weiss (1854: 80); Clark (1998: 1277–79); Dickinson (1967: 465–66); Knittle (1965); Walker (1992); De Zayas (1988: 16); O'Brien (1969: 13); and Faragher (2005: 374).

outsiders and the vulnerable. Thus, Plaut argues that the Old Testament of the Bible introduces "a principle of non-refoulement in the case of slaves," including those from outside Israel. The Qu'ran provides protections to strangers and even idolaters. In addition, both Buddhism and Hinduism accept a notion of refuge (Plaut 1995: 18–22; Price 2009: 26).

True religious asylum first emerged within the Greek city-state system. The ancient Greeks accepted the inviolability of some people travelling outside their city-state. In addition, they recognized the special nature of temples, which were viewed as sacred or magical (Price 2009: 26–27). By seeking temple sanctuary, individuals sought to place themselves out of secular control and under the protection of the gods. This was not automatic – as Rigsby (1997: 10) notes, "one who took refuge in a temple was required by the temple to undergo a kind of trial to determine whether his flight was 'just.' The god was not obliged to accept and protect every supplicant, only those who had a just claim."

In addition to religious sanctuary, the Greeks also possessed a rule-ordered system of political asylum, with cities commonly accepting those who had fled or been exiled due to their political views. Movement was frequent enough, McClelland (1996: 74) suggests, that citizenship was easily transferred between city-states. Even so, such asylum was not automatic but rather a right granted by the city. Once granted, it acted as a "defense to extradition, placing a fugitive beyond the requesting city's authoritative reach" (Price 2009: 28; Schuster 2002: 41–42). The ancient Greeks therefore recognized both religious and political forms of asylum.

However, although religious asylum prospered under the Roman Empire, political asylum disappeared because "it served no purpose for the state, because there were no separately recognized jurisdictions, and because the Emperor provided an overarching authority within his domain" (Schuster 2003: 68; Price 2009: 31–33). For territorial asylum to function, it requires a system of autonomous territorially defined "states," such as those found in Ancient Greece. Hierarchical systems, such as the Roman Empire, did not recognize territorial asylum because they did not recognize the existence of independent jurisdictions.

Following from Greek and Roman practice on religious sanctuary, in the medieval period Church-based asylum offered protection to anyone who sought sanctuary, irrespective of their action or crime. It was not until the twelfth century that Pope Gratian codified the ecclesiastical law of asylum and excluded certain crimes from its protection, such as assassination within the church and violation of the right of asylum itself (Sinha 1971: 12). However, the political system of the medieval period did not provide for political asylum. Like in the Roman Empire, the Church created a hierarchical system that was incompatible with territorial political asylum:

[A]t one and the same time, the church was both the primary protector and persecutor... Within the [Holy Roman] empire, the conditions for granting "territorial" asylum as granted by the modern state did not exist, nor could they do so until the development of territorial states. (Schuster 2002: 42–43)

For the sanctuary system to change, there needed to be a shift away from the decentralized and Church-dominated international structure of the medieval period.

The reemergence of territorial asylum was tied into the emergence of a system of autonomous territorial states. As states emerged and sought to claim "the exclusive and unhindered right of administration of justice," Sinha (1971: 12) argues, the doctrine of Church-based asylum was progressively challenged and ended across Europe. In some places, it was outlawed completely – in France, Louis XII abolished it in 1515, while the English Parliament ended it in 1625 (Sinha 1971: 12). In others, practice shifted from a full grant of asylum by the Church to considering "the individual's reasons for requesting asylum" (Price 2009: 34). Thus, as John Marshall, the fourth chief justice of the U.S. Supreme Court, noted "the jurisdiction of the nation within its own territory is necessarily exclusive and absolute. It is susceptible of no limitation not imposed by itself" (Raustiala 2009: 10). Ending Church-based asylum was part of the larger process of the state asserting autonomy vis-à-vis the universal Church.[1]

At the same time, though, the Church was no longer universal. The Wars of the Reformation and Counter-Reformation created large flows of religious refugees, including 100,000 Dutch Protestants fleeing the Netherlands during the revolt against Spain; 30,000 Calvinists fleeing from England during the reign of Mary I; and up to 240,000 Scots emigrating between 1600 and 1700 through expulsion or by choice (Sinha 1971: 18; Kamen 2000: 48–50). By some estimates, in the seventeenth century, Europe may have had as many as a million refugees (Sassen 1999: 11; Parker 2001: 6).

Despite their numbers, these movements of refugees were of little concern to the sovereigns of the period. Those who did offer succor had little protection against retaliation. One such example is Count Frederick of the Duchy of Württemberg, who harbored French Huguenot refugees following the St. Bartholomew's Day massacre in 1572. He justified their

---

[1] The Church did not easily accept this shift. As late as 1869, Sinha (1971: 13) notes, Pope Pius IX "declared that the sovereign pontiffs had the right to excommunicate the violators of the right of asylum." The right of asylum within Vatican City itself was ended only with the Italian Constitution of 1947.

acceptance by arguing that he "was only doing his Christian duty, that his compassion accorded with God's command to love and to treat others as we should wish to be treated if we were afflicted for our sins with exile" (Raitt 1983: 153). His hospitality was met by invasion in December 1587, led by the Duke of Lorraine and supported by Henry III of France. The Duke justified his invasion as punishment against Württemberg for supporting the French exiles, who had engaged in armed raids into Lorraine (Raitt 1983: 155). Accepting in these refugees had direct, negative consequences for Frederick and for Württemberg. Yet, within a century, such retaliatory actions would be considered unconscionable.

The emergence of a European state system brought about two critical changes. The emergence of "states" is frequently dated to the fourteenth century, with the creation of a single point of authority within the state independent from external forces (Strayer 1970: 9, 57; Philpott 1997: 29). With the shift, Ruggie (1993b: 151) notes, "parcelized and personalized authority" was consolidated into a single, public realm that allowed for fundamental spatial demarcations between the public and private and between the internal and external. No longer bound to the person of the sovereign, the state could acquire the "moral authority to back up its institutional structure and its theoretical legal supremacy" (Strayer 1970: 9; see also Tilly 1992; Ertman 1997). It was as these doctrines developed over the next three centuries that church-based asylum ended. And it was these doctrines that anchored the state in a territorial basis.

The second change was the emergence of a European-based international society. The Peace of Westphalia is often held as a marker of the end of this transition from the medieval to the modern concept of state. Its proponents argue that the Peace marks the point at which states recognized each other as sovereign, ending church claims to transnational political authority (Zacher 1992: 59; Lyons and Mastanduno 1995: 5) and public international law was divorced from a religious background (Gross 1948: 20; Hinsley 1967: 168). Most importantly, Philpott (2001: 89) argues that the Peace – and the end of the Thirty Years' War – marked when "political leaders had lost their religious zeal and ceased to contest religion as a political affair . . . religion ceased to be a casus belli."

The role of the Peace of Westphalia in creating the modern international system has been challenged (Reus-Smit 1999: 88; see also Krasner 1999: 20; Teschke 2003: 6; De Carvalho et al. 2011: 740). Although it may not have been "the key turning point in the development of the European sovereign-territorial state and state system" (Nexon 2009: 281), it is emblematic as one bridge in a complex transition between the early modern and modern periods. As Osiander notes, the negotiators at Westphalia could:

protect existing structures, but could not shape the system in their own right, reflect[ing] the fact that the international system was largely the product of historical contingencies. The international system was a transitional set of structures on the threshold between the defunct medieval system and the new "classical" European state system. (Osiander 1994: 72)

In essence, Westphalia allowed rulers to reestablish agreed principles of coexistence missing since the Reformation began and for the "embryonic emergence of norms of non-intervention and respect for religious liberties" (Phillips 2011: 143–45). It is just such a shift to a common set of goals and rules that marked the steady emergence of international society over the next two centuries (Jackson 2000: 11), and it was this system that gradually spread outward from Europe. New states engaged in deliberate mimicry, as political elites copied and emulated institutional forms that they perceived as successful (Spruyt 1994: 158; see also Meyer 1980; Hall and Ikenberry 1989: 39). But whereas the Peace may not be the marker of the birth of international society, it remains important to my account for one element within it which served to start a normative practice that recognized refugees as distinct from other migrants and as an international problem.

The Peace of Westphalia and the right of jus emigrandi

The Peace presaged a remarkable change in how states could treat their own populations. In the late fifteenth century, Spain was able to expel its Jewish population with no international repercussions because there were no norms governing expulsions (Rae, 2002: 301). By the middle of the seventeenth century, by contrast, states had begun to tread lightly in matters of religion, even when dealing with their own populations. The main reason for this, as Toulmin (1990: 91) has argued, was that no European state wanted "to see a general reopening of hostilities, but the earlier convulsions still produced aftershocks" after Westphalia. These states accepted as guiding principles "*stability* in and among the different sovereign nation-states, and *hierarchy* within the social structures of each individual state" (Toulmin 1990: 128; emphasis in original). With these views, Rae argues, came the beginnings of a society of states resting on shared norms:

Although by no means uncontested, the effort to articulate minimum standards of coexistence extending to internal behaviour distinguish this period from the lack of such standards in the late fifteenth century when the system was taking shape. (Rae, 2002: 219)

One of the core principles embodied within Westphalia and contributing to this stability was a simple mechanism to ensure orderly population movements between states of different religions: the notion of *jus emigrandi* or the right to leave one's state with one's property.

Westphalia was not the first agreement to attempt to solve religious war. A century before, the Peace of Augsburg (1555) had established the formula of *cuius regio, eius religio* ("whose the region, his the religion") with that goal. This precedent allowed rulers in Germany to determine whether their states would be either Lutheran or Catholic (Golden 1988: 8). To deal with subjects whose religion differed from that of their prince, Augsburg also introduced in article 24 a right of *jus emigrandi* within the German states for Lutherans and Catholics alike (Golden 1988: 17; see also Cavallar 2002: 205):

> In case our subjects whether belonging to the old religion or the Augsburg confession should intend leaving their homes with their wives and children in order to settle in another, they shall be hindered neither in the sale of their estates after due payment of the local taxes nor injured in their honour. (Reich 1905 [2004]: 232)[2]

A right of emigration was an important step forward: "The medieval heresy laws whereby the dissenter lost life and goods yielded to a new principle, the first fruits of toleration, however unripe" (Spitz 1956: 120).

Augsburg was not a perfect system. It deliberately excluded all of the Reformed Churches, recognizing only Catholicism and Lutheranism, and this contributed to the outbreak of the Thirty Years' War. Furthermore, the *jus emigrandi* was interpreted by some princes as a right to expel minorities (Asch 2000: 79). Even so, under Augsburg, "central Europe experienced more than sixty almost unbroken years of peace" (MacCulloch 2003: 275).

The Peace of Westphalia built on this foundation.[3] In particular, the Treaty of Osnabrück (which, along with the Treaty of Münster, made up the Peace) further articulated rights of toleration. It allowed for liberty of conscience and the right of minorities to practice their religion, educate children in schools of their religion, be free from discrimination, and have equal access to hospitals and alms houses (Article V 28 in Parry 1969: 228–29; see also Holsti 1991: 34; Rae 2002: 216–17).

---

[2] Elector Frederick of the Palatinate, ruling over a mixed territory, argued for this view: "he demanded freedom of worship for the estates and freedom of conscience for all subjects, assured by the right to emigrate," a view favored by other participants and a solution recommended years before by Luther himself (Spitz 1956: 120–21).

[3] There is dispute as to whether the *cuius regio, eius religio* formula was renewed. Golden (1988) argues that it was and that it was extended to Calvinism, which has been the consensus. More recently, Osiander has argued that the Peace of Westphalia abolished this concept in the Holy Roman Empire "and forbade the German princes to impose their religion on their subjects" (1994: 12; see also Krasner 1999: 79–80; De Carvalho et al. 2011).

But the drafters realized these protections would not be enough. In addition to toleration, they articulated a clear right to leave for those whose religion differed from that of the state. Thus, a member of a minority had the right to change their abode and preserve their property:

That if any Subject, who had not the publick or private Exercise of his Religion in the year 1624 or who, after the Publication of the Peace, shall have a mind to change his Religion, *or be willing to change his Abode or be order'd by the Lord of the Mannor to remove, he shall be at liberty to do it,* to keep or sell his Goods, and have them administer'd by his Relations, to visit them with all Freedom, and without any Letters of Passport, and to prosecute his Affairs, and make payment of his Debts, as often as shall be requifite. (Article V 29, in Parry 1969: 229; emphasis added)

People who wished to leave were given five years to do so, or three years if they chose to change their religion after the Peace, and they could not be hindered in any way:

It has likewise been agreed, that the Lord of the Territory *shall allow a space of time, not less than five years, for his Subjects to remove,* who had not the publick or private Exercise of their Religion in the said year... And as for those who shall change their Religion after the Publication of the Peace, there shall be a Term allow'd them, not less than three years, to withdraw themselves and remove, if they cannot obtain a longer; and whether they remove voluntarily, or by Constrain, Certificates of their Birth, Parentage, Freedom, Trade and morals shall be granted them without difficulty or scruple; nor shall they be oppress'd with unusual Reversals, or Decimation of the Goods they shall carry with them, above what is just and equitable; and far less shall any Stop or Hindrance be made, upon pretext of Servitude, or any other whatsoever to those who shall remove voluntarily. (Article V 30, in Parry 1969: 229–30; emphasis added; see also Ward 1906: 412; Krasner 1999: 80; Rae 2002: 217)[4]

The Peace thereby laid out a clear right of emigration and established long time periods for the *jus emigrandi* to be used. The rights granted by the Peace were not universally accepted. As Gross notes, "the principle of liberty of conscience was applied only incompletely and without reciprocity," and the provisions included were insufficient to ensure it. Even so, religious equality was part of the Peace as "an international guarantee" (Gross 1948: 22; see also Ward 1906: 416).[5]

Although the division in Christendom meant that there was no longer one universal religion, Bainton argued that rulers used practices such as

---

[4] Ward noted that there was some ambiguity present. One passage provided for toleration "but another seems to imply that, exceptions apart, the ruler may oblige such subjects to emigrate" (1906: 412).

[5] Such guarantees became commonplace in subsequent treaties (Gross 1948: 22–24; Krasner 1999: 77).

the *jus emigrandi* to conserve religious unity "in many miniatures." Through this approach, dissenters could be banished rather than killed:

The system of the union of church and state, of the fusion of religion and the community, was thus conserved by an exchange of populations, and that was the point at which the system of *cuius regio* enshrined liberty of a sort. Extermination was displaced by emigration. (Bainton 1941: 115)

A right of emigration, in other words, served to stabilize the nascent European state system and avoid the cataclysmic wars of religion that had dominated Europe for the previous century and a half.

International law and the role of the individual and the state

In the formative days of European society, international law was crucial in framing the individual's role toward the state and toward international society. It was in this period, Kennedy suggests, that "law emerges as an idea, independent of and responsive to sovereign will" (Kennedy 1988: 13). The international legal theorists of the time – Grotius, Pufendorf, and Vattel, among others – sought to emphasize the binding character of international law on both states and individuals (Korowicz 1956: 534; see also Krenz 1966: 96).

Hugo Grotius (1583–1645) was critical to this process in several respects. Grotius was forced to flee his native Holland in 1621 and remained in exile for much of the rest of his life. Although his *De Jure Belli ac Pacis* predates Westphalia by twenty years, it is often, in Vincent's words, "combined with the Peace of Westphalia to locate in the second quarter of the seventeenth century the origins of the modern state-system" (Vincent 1992: 244). It was also the writings of a refugee, one who had already established a European reputation and who may have been using it partly as "a bid for employment" (Roelofsen 1992: 123; Jeffery 2006: 13). It is unclear how much Grotius's personal circumstances influenced his writings, but certainly his situation was unique for his time. Personally invited to Paris by Louis XIII, he was offered a pension of 3,600 livres and taken under the King's "special protection" in 1623 (Reeves 1925; Jeffery 2006).

Grotius made a number of contributions to the emerging theory of international law. First, within his writings was the first description of a clear society of states, of a "community of those participating in the international legal order, whose fabric was interwoven with international law" (Koh 1997: 2606; see also Cavallar 2002: 150). Second, however, his conception of international law was not purely focused on states. For Grotius, Vincent argues, "the jus gentium consisted in the rules covering all relations taking place outside the bonds of municipal law – the relations of princes between themselves, certainly, but also any other relations that went beyond the boundary of the state" (Vincent 1992: 243–44; see also Kennedy 1988). In so doing, he sought (however problematically) to define rights of the individual against those of the state and against unlimited power (Lauterpacht 1946: 45).

How individual rights mattered vis-à-vis the state is clear in Grotius's approach to the issue of political asylum. Ordinary crimes, he argued, that "properly concern the community to which they belong, should be left to the states themselves and their rulers" (Grotius and Kelsey 1925: 526). For those criminals who fled the state, Grotius notes that the person fleeing should either be punished or "entrusted to the discretion of the party making the appeal. This latter course is rendition" (Grotius and Kelsey 1925: 527).

Grotius associated asylum with cases in which there is no crime. Asylum, he suggested, exists for those "who suffer from undeserved enmity, not those who have done something that is injurious to human society or other men" (Grotius and Kelsey 1925: 530). For Grotius, there was no clear right of asylum. The state continued to possess a legally recognized right of expulsion, particularly for those who violated the state's hospitality (see Kedar 1996: 172; Walters 2002). But he argued that people did have a right to leave their own state. Quoting both Tryphoninus (who stated that "each has the unrestricted right to choose his own state") and Cicero (who praised the law that "no one is forced to remain in a state against his will"), Grotius argued that "it is believed that people consent to the free withdrawal of their nationals, because from granting such liberty they may experience no less advantage than other countries... Thus the state has no legal claim against exiles" (Grotius and Kelsey 1925: 253–54; Carter 2001: 29).[6] This was an important shift. As Price notes, "asylum interfered with the internal affairs of another state. By granting asylum, a receiving state effectively acted as judge in a dispute between another state and one of its subjects" (Price 2009: 37).

The question of how states should approach questions of asylum remained an active one in legal thought for the next century. Samuel Pufendorf (1632–94) argued that by standards of reciprocity, "it would be inconsistent to exclude foreigners while demanding hospitality rights for one's own citizens" (Cavallar 2002: 202) except in cases of extreme

---

[6] This is a right that can be limited, Grotius suggests, if it is contrary to the interests of society (and thus large numbers cannot leave at once), if the individual has debts, or due to war (Grotius and Kelsey 1925: II.5.XXIV). Even so, Grahl-Madsen suggests that Grotius here established a clear doctrine of granting asylum to exiles (1966: 278).

necessity, such as famine (Pufendorf 1749: 253). For him, a sense of common humanity created an obligation to accept those expelled from their home countries. But he was also quick to note that those states that accepted foreigners generally did well from it:

Humanity, it is true, engages us to receive a small number of men expelled [sic] their home, not for their own demerit and crime, especially if they are eminent for wealth or industry, and not likely to disturb our religion, or our constitution. And thus we see many states to have risen to a great a flourishing height, chiefly by granting license to foreigners to come and settle amongst them; whereas others have been reduced to a low condition, by refuting this method of improvement. . . If on the whole, it appears that the persons deserve our favour and pity, and that no restraint lies on us from good reasons of state, it will be an act of humanity to confer such a benefit on them. (Pufendorf 1749: 253)

Pufendorf saw no problem in linking together state interest and common humanity in arguing for refugee acceptance although, like Grotius, he accepted that there was no obligation for the state to accept exiles.

Once accepted, foreigners create an obligation for the state. Particularly, Pufendorf argued "the Government tacitly engages to grant [them] security and protection, and the benefits of public justice" (Pufendorf 1749: 274). Therefore, they should not be expelled. Pufendorf, as Sibley and Elias noted, argued that "having once admitted strangers and foreign guests, to turn them out again, unless upon good reason, is usually censured as some degree at least of inhumanity" (Sibley and Elias 1906: 4–5). For both Grotius and Pufendorf, therefore, a common understanding of a greater society led states to accept refugees (except in extreme cases) and to not expel them.[7] Carter (2001: 44) notes that this was in no sense an "absolute obligation to grant asylum"; rather, it was an obligation tempered by prudence: "A ruler needed to consider whether admitting refugees – particularly in great numbers – would strain national resources or disrupt society." Even so, both Grotius and Pufendorf articulated norms of legitimate behavior for states, norms that included allowing people who faced persecution to leave their own state, with this state having no legal claim for their return, and that other states had a duty through common humanity to allow these refugees in.

The idea that the state needed to protect refugees once accepted extends into the Age of Enlightenment. Emer de Vattel (1714–64) argued that the state has the right to refuse entry for legitimate reasons, such as

---

[7] Sir Leoline Jenkins countered Grotius's argument by suggesting there is a *Droit du Renvoi*, a "Right of State to dismiss foreigners commorant [ordinarily residing] in her territories." Sibley and Elias note that this right had been exercised by Queen Elizabeth but had gone into disuse by 1674 (Sibley and Elias 1906: 4).

diseases, possible corruption of morals, and public disorder, but that once people are admitted, the sovereign has a duty to protect them (1852: 173, 183; see also Cavallar 2002: 314). However, Vattel also argues that there existed a *natural* right to emigrate, including if the society failed to discharge its obligations toward the citizen and "if the major part of the nation, or the sovereign who represents it, attempt to enact laws relative to matters in which the social compact cannot oblige every citizen to submission, those who are averse to these laws have a right to quit the society, and go settle elsewhere" (1852: 180–81; see also Whelan 1981: 649). Vattel also supported the idea that refugees may require protection from another sovereign against their own:

If the sovereign attempts to molest those who have a right to emigrate, he does them an injury; and the injured individuals may lawfully implore the protection of the power who is willing to receive them. Thus we have seen Frederic William, king of Prussia, grant his protection to the emigrant Protestants of Saltzburgh [sic]. (Vattel 1852: 182)

In the writings of Grotius, Pufendorf, and Vattel, we see the struggle between the particular interests of states and a universal humanitarian imperative involving who is entitled to asylum. As Schuster notes, a consensus is apparent: "refuge is to be offered to those in need and those who deserve it. Since the decision on who is deserving rests with the sovereign, the sovereign is naturally in a position to take account of the interests of his state when making this decision" (Schuster 2003: 76).[8] Although there was no right of asylum, for these authors, the state's reasons for restricting entrance were limited.

Exclusion, today, is seen as an attribute of sovereignty and territoriality, one that is "defended as an inherent power necessary for the self-preservation of the state." Such a view was upheld by the U.S. Supreme Court in a 1972 opinion that referred to "ancient principles of the international law of states" (Nafziger 1983: 804, 808). And yet such a view has little historical backing. If principles suggested anything during the seventeenth and eighteenth centuries, it was toward a practice of free

---

[8] Such views transcended legal theorists. Immanuel Kant (1724–1804) introduced the "right of hospitality" whereby a stranger can be refused (if it can be done without causing his destruction) but, once accepted, and "so long as he peacefully occupies his place, one may not treat him with hostility... They have it by virtue of their common possession ... of the surface of the earth" (Kant, cited in Benhabib 2005: 11). As Benhabib argues, Kant's view of hospitality "entails a moral claim with potential legal consequences in that the obligation of the receiving states to grant temporary residency to foreigners is anchored in a republican cosmopolitan order" (2005: 11–12). Even so, Cavallar (2002: 366) suggests that "Kant supports immigration only in those grave cases when the refugees would face certain destruction on returning to their own country."

movement, with "a qualified duty to admit aliens when they pose no danger to the public safety, security, general welfare, or essential institutions of a recipient state" (Nafziger 1983: 805; see also Cavallar 2002: 10). As I demonstrate later, it was these early legal notions of asylum and the duty of the state to offer protection that influenced states' willingness to allow entrance and offer protection to persecuted refugees, as well as their recognition of a clear right to leave.

Territoriality and international law provided the underlying justification for the creation of two norms. The first was the *jus emigrandi* negotiated by states in the Peace of Augsburg in 1555 and in the Peace of Westphalia in 1648. A right to leave, however, was ineffective without state willingness to accept and protect refugees. This was the core of Grotius's, Pufendorf's, and Vattel's arguments. This became state policy, however, only when one state – France under Louis XIV – violated the *jus emigrandi* and thereby forced other states to decide how to deal with a large and sustained religious refugee flow. The second norm that began to develop as a result of this crisis was that refugees should be provided with domestic legal protections.

The revocation of the Edict of Nantes and the development of legal protections

Out of Westphalia we see evolve a doctrine of religious toleration designed to prevent subsequent wars. Religious toleration, Krasner notes, "evolved out of both principled arguments about the illegitimacy of coerced beliefs and a recognition that religious strife could destroy political stability" (1999: 78). In this sense, Westphalia worked: after 1648, there was an abatement of religious conflict. A cornerstone of the Westphalian doctrine of toleration was the *jus emigrandi*, the right to leave. But Westphalia also allowed states to continue homogenization policies by expelling unwanted minorities, a pattern that continued well into the eighteenth century in Western and central Europe (Zolberg 1983; Rae 2002).

Religious toleration and the *jus emigrandi* marked a thin international normative order anchored in the Westphalian treaties and broader understandings of international law. The crucial test for this understanding came in 1685, when Louis XIV revoked the Edict of Nantes. This caused the flight of 200,000 French Huguenots, even while Louis imposed ineffective exit controls.[9]

---

[9] Estimates of the flow range from 60,000 to 2 million, but generally 200,000 refugees is the accepted figure (Norwood 1969: 52; see also Scoville 1952a: 296).

The Edict had been passed in 1598 by Henry IV. It ended the French Wars of Religion by ensuring that the Protestant religion would be protected. It established that the Huguenots were free to practice their religion, although only in areas they controlled. It also allowed for their admission to political posts; for them to use schools, hospitals, and charities; for them to print books; and for the establishment of mixed courts of Catholic and Protestant judges to adjudicate cases between adherents of the two religions. As a de facto peace agreement, it also established guarantees for the Huguenots: they were allowed to maintain troops in 200 towns within their jurisdiction, of which half were fortified (Tylor 1892: 8–9; Robinson 1904: 183–85; Holt 1995: 163–66).

Following Henry's assassination in 1610, however, the rights granted by the Edict were gradually circumscribed. This began with restrictions on the ability of Huguenots to hold office and educate their children in Protestant schools (Stankiewicz 1955: 82). In the mid-1660s, Louis XIV, who had already faced a revolt by the aristocracy in the Fronds early in his reign, moved to cement his authority in France by progressively restricting the rights of the Huguenots. Norwood (1969) suggests that Louis had been convinced by his advisers, including Mme. de Maintenon (his mistress and subsequently his secret morganatic wife), that the Protestant population had been reduced to a negligible size and that at little cost Louis could create religious unity in France, as well as increase his own power vis-à-vis the Church. A succession of restrictions were passed prior to 1685. These included the "voluntary" conversion of Protestant children as young as seven, the closure of Protestant churches, bans on entry into professions, and the quartering of troops in Protestant homes.

In 1685, the Revocation declared Protestantism illegal in France (Norwood 1969: 37–41; Golden 1988: 18). Exit was denied, on pain of forfeiture of all property and (for men) being sent to work on the galleys for life. As Torpey (2000: 21) notes, the denial of the right of exit represented an attempt by Louis XIV to assert his authority over emigration from France. The repercussions from this were substantial. Louis's revocation:

abrogated the *jus emigrandi* which had been granted to religious minorities in Germany under the Treaty of Osnabruck and had gained a status of regional norm... In the international arena, the Revocation was regarded as illegitimate and it had a "marked effect upon an international opinion growing increasingly hostile to French pretensions and the Bourbon methods." (Rae 2002: 218–19)

Following the Revocation, Huguenots resorted to subterfuges, bribery, and even an "underground railway" to escape France (Norwood 1969: 49–51; see also Anon. 1697).

Not only did the persecutions outrage the Protestant communities of Europe, but the Revocation was greeted unenthusiastically by many Catholics who feared a return to wars of religion (Doyle 1992: 201–02). Opponents of the Revocation proceeded to attack Louis in print and pamphlets. Moreover, whereas Louis had hoped to gain the Pope's approval, Innocent XI opposed the policy. He felt that Louis had acted for political rather than religious reasons and said that "we do not approve in any sense these forced conversions, which as a rule are not sincere."[10]

The persecutions were also condemned by other European countries. The flight of the Huguenots not only brought censure upon France, but also saw these refugees recognized by other states as requiring protections in law. Whereas earlier refugee flows had gone unnoticed by other states, the reaction to the Huguenots was different.

In the Protestant Germanic states, approximately 30,000 Huguenot refugees were received and welcomed by the outraged public (Wolf 1951: 36). Many of these states took the added step of providing clear legal recognition to the refugees. Friedrich Wilhelm, the Great Elector of Brandenburg, issued the Edict of Potsdam, which authorized the Huguenots to establish themselves in his territory. It also granted them a number of rights, including provision of assistance, free movement, and freedom of worship (Scoville 1952b: 399; Reaman 1963). The Landgrave of Hess-Cassel, in April 1685, proclaimed that all Huguenots would find a haven there and in December promulgated an Edict similar to that of Potsdam. The Duke of Brunswick and Lüneburg also accorded immigrants religious, civil, and economic freedom. In a number of these states, relief aid was also raised through public collections and from abroad (Scoville 1952b: 400).

The Netherlands was the other notable continental Protestant power. Like Brandenburg, it sought to provide a long-term home to the Huguenots and encouraged self-sustaining Huguenots to settle within its borders. Here, too, economic and security interests, such as the military knowledge brought by the refugees, help explain the state's acceptance of the Huguenots (Reaman 1963: 106). Although they welcomed the refugees, the Netherlands did not provide legal recognition until 1709, when the Estates-General of the United Provinces decreed that all "Protestant refugees 'shall be acknowledged and received for the future as our subjects; and they shall enjoy the right of Naturalization'" (Scoville 1952b: 329).

---

[10] "A recollection of statements expressed to the deputy of Holland, in the papers of Cardinal Filippo Gaulterio, nuncio at Paris" (cited in O'Brien 1930: 143).

The English had a history of welcoming the Huguenots from France, one that predated the Revocation, including granting inducements to Huguenot artisans to settle in England (Reaman 1963: 73). Following the Revocation, one nineteenth-century history noted that "England again became their chief asylum" and that Louis XIV "drove into exile by his mistaken policy, above 500,000 of the most useful and industrious inhabitants of France" (Burn 1846: 17). A succession of British monarchs – Charles II, James II (VII), William and Mary, and Anne – took steps to recognize the Huguenots and extend to them the protection of the Crown. As early as 1681, in response to earlier Huguenot flows, Charles II stated "that he held himself obliged... To comfort and support all such afflicted Protestants, who, by reason of the rigors and severities which were used towards them on account of their religion, should be forced to quit their native country, and should desire to shelter themselves under his Majesty's royal protection, for the preservation and free exercise of their religion."[11]

James II (VII) came to the throne early in 1685. Following the Revocation, James noted that:

[W]e have thought Our Selves obliged by the Laws of Civilian Charity, and common Bonds of humanity, to take [the French Protestants] their Deplorable Condition into Our Tender Care and Princely Compassion. And to this end we have resolved to receive into Our Gracious Protection as many of them as shall live in entire Conformity and orderly Submission to Our Government. (James II 1687)

James's actions were driven not by his own views but by public concern for the refugees. Scoville notes that James, who was Catholic, "was not very sympathetic [to the Huguenots]. Public sentiment, however, was so strongly in favour of the refugees that even he acknowledged to representatives from the French Court that he did not dare display openly his true feelings" (1952a: 299). The English public accepted that the Huguenots should not only be allowed to leave, but also be accommodated for both religious reasons and through the dictates of common humanity, an understanding that James did not feel powerful enough to violate.

Following the Glorious Revolution, William and Mary declared on April 25, 1689, that "all French Protestants that shall seek their refuge in our Kingdom shall not only have our Royal protection for themselves, [their] families, and estates, but we will also do our endeavour in all reasonable ways and means so to support, aid, and assist them" (Scoville 1952a: 299). However, legal recognition was long delayed.

---

[11] Statement by the King in Council at Hampton Court, July 28, 1681 (reprinted in Burn 1846: 20).

William sought to naturalize the refugees in 1689, following the practice of Brandenburg, but was unable to persuade Parliament to pass the bill (Scoville 1952a: 299).[12] It was only twenty years later that Queen Anne succeeded in passing an Act for Naturalizing Foreign Protestants, and that was repealed two years later by "a Parliament ever-jealous of its rights" (Grahl-Madsen 1966: 278–79).

The English government took tentative steps toward providing public relief, with the Crown undertaking a number of fundraising exercises[13] and Parliament establishing a rarely distributed fund of 15,000 pounds per year for relief of poor refugees (Scoville 1952a: 299–300). Even so, private efforts, particularly through churches, were dominant.[14] English practice toward the Huguenot refugees reflected some of the practices on the Continent. But it also reflected the division in domestic political institutions: while the Crown offered personal protections to the refugees, Parliament was unwilling to introduce stronger legal ones.

Finally, Switzerland received about 60,000 refugees between 1682 and 1720, of which approximately 25,000 stayed. The governments of Geneva, Bern, and Zurich all took the unusual step of providing relief to the refugees, and more than 10,000,000 florins were spent. However, these governments offered no permanent recognition, Scoville (1952b: 405–06) suggests, because of threats by Louis XIV to engage in economic and military sanctions. These concerns over the French reaction may explain the limited protections offered by Switzerland. However, a purely materialist explanation fails to account for why other states – such as the Germanic states – offered the refugees both leave to enter and legal protections.

Several important threads can be drawn out concerning the Huguenots. The first is that material interests (in particular economic motivations) as well as ideational motivations (in particular religious sympathies) were factors in the acceptance of these refugees. Thompson argues that "it was

---

[12] Weiss suggested that this, at least in part, may have been due to heavy bribes from France, as well as to William's own personal unpopularity and fears of augmenting the King's authority (Weiss 1854: 230).

[13] James II (VII) had allowed his Letters Patents to be used to raise funds from the general populace to support the Huguenots in England (James II 1687). William expanded on this practice, also allowing his Letters Patents to be used to gather alms for refugees in Switzerland and Germany (William III 1699). James II (VII) also created a separate fund to contribute 16,000 pounds per year to poor Huguenots, following the direction of Parliament. Although the record of this fund is unclear, it was still in existence in 1727, when it was cut in half (Burn 1846: 21–22).

[14] Huguenot churches established by earlier refugees were vital to these efforts, as was favorable public opinion, with collections being taken up in Anglican churches throughout England (Stoye 2000: 271). The total number of refugees who received assistance may have been between 40,000 and 50,000 (Scoville 1952a: 298).

economic interest very largely which led Holland to sympathize with the Huguenots" (Thompson 1908: 45). Others, however, suggest that Protestant fervor was successfully aligned with these economic interests (see Stoye 2000: 271). Other governments were impressed by the skills the Huguenots brought with them and as much by the economic consequences of this loss to France as their own gain. This was reflected in the moves toward toleration in a number of states during the eighteenth century, including England, Prussia, and the Austrian Empire (Doyle 1992: 202).

The second thread was that many European states saw in the flight of the Huguenots further evidence of Louis's hegemonic ambitions. This led to him being cast as "a monarch of Machiavellian intentions and a man willing to break agreements with violence" (Black 1990: 30). As Harris (1964: 103) notes, "his suppression of the Huguenots in 1685 struck fear into the heart of Protestant Europe" and contributed to a coalition forming against him. Louis lost valuable Protestant allies, including Brandenburg (Stoye 2000: 272). Concerns were raised over what Louis's actions might be following the end of the Truce of Ratisbon, which had ended the First Dutch War, and what the fate of the Spanish Empire might be upon the death of the sickly and heirless Charles II. This led in 1686 to the creation of the secret League of Augsburg, which included both Protestant and Catholic states and which received the adherence of the Pope (Harris 1964: 103–04).[15]

Louis does appear to have been aware of the possible consequences of his actions. He chose not to interfere with the rights of the Protestant population of Alsace, which was conquered by France during the Thirty Years' War. He used the technical argument that because it had been conquered following the introduction of the Edict of Nantes, the Revocation did not apply. Clark suggests that Louis was focused on geopolitical issues: "it was essential to preserving [control over Alsace] to honour commitments to Alsatians ... long-term guarantees were in the treaties of the Peace of Westphalia" (1998: 1277). Alsace may have been bound by the Peace of Westphalia; France, formally, was not. This suggests that Louis was aware of the growing ideational consensus in European society that supported religious toleration, but that he was not concerned over international reaction to the Revocation because he felt it was a domestic issue. He may have simply miscalculated how gravely his actions would be treated by the other European states. Certainly, the

---

[15] The Nine Years' War that followed was the greatest international conflict since the Thirty Years' War and marked the first time that Louis XIV faced armies that matched his own. The Peace of Ryswick, signed in 1697, saw him lose many of his gains from the previous twenty years (Doyle 1992: 271).

Revocation brought many disadvantages to France, and, on his death bed, Louis XIV attempted to excuse his actions (Harris 1964: 93; Clark 1998: 1276).

Finally, the third key point is that there was a clear movement to protect the Huguenots in law. As Grahl-Madsen notes, England's Naturalization Act, like Brandenburg's Edict of Potsdam (and the other forms of legal recognition), "was clearly an invitation to refugees to come and establish themselves in the Kingdom for the mutual benefit" (Grahl-Madsen 1966: 278–79).

Why did the Huguenots receive these legal protections? Economic self-interest in attracting migrants can explain the response to a degree. However, it does not explain why the monarchs of Europe decided to grant the Huguenots clear legal protections or why, in many cases, they rapidly granted citizenship and an array of benefits that involved clear economic costs. It also does not explain retroactive grants of protection by both Britain and the Netherlands years and decades after the Huguenot flight. In addition, an economic argument cannot explain the reaction of the Swiss, who were willing to grant temporary asylum to so many refugees but encouraged them to move on for fear of France. Why accommodate them at all in that case? Finally, economic justifications may provide a reason for some government assistance but not for the widespread public relief efforts or the private funds set up to assist the refugees as co-religious.

Rather, an additional element is needed: the stirrings of normative change. By 1685, Rae argues:

The international system had experienced some further normative development, though its normative structure remained quite thin... The Revocation and its consequences were widely condemned by European powers, reflecting that in the late seventeenth century such behaviour was regarded as illegitimate as it breached the minimal standards of coexistence that had been articulated at this time. (2002: 301)

These new normative standards were those articulated in the Peace of Westphalia, which established the grounds for religious toleration through such ideas as the *jus emigrandi* and *cuius regio, eius religio*, first enunciated at Augsburg. It was these same principles that Louis XIV violated some forty years later by prohibiting the Huguenots from emigrating.

Other states could have reacted to Louis's actions in three ways. The first was to assume Westphalia no longer mattered, ignore its principles of toleration, and begin anew persecuting their own religious minorities. This, however, would have undermined the stability created through Westphalia and would likely have seen a return to the wars of religion.

The second would have been to attempt to ignore the principles of sovereignty and intervene in France to prevent the persecutions. But this was unlikely for logistical reasons: France was the major power of the continent and would have taken a substantial – and difficult to create – alliance to defeat. Such an alliance emerged in the later years of Louis's reign, motivated by the Revocation, but its primary goal was to stop his hegemonic ambitions rather than to uphold minority rights (Kennedy 1989). The third course of action was the one adopted: accepting the refugees and offering them protection. This course of action both preserved European stability and avoided war.

Other religious refugees of the eighteenth century

For the remainder of the eighteenth century, the treatment of refugees by European states varied from the pattern laid down with the Huguenots. Most subsequent monarchs avoided Louis XIV's mistake in denying the Huguenots a right to exit. These refugee flows were also neither as numerous as the Huguenots nor were they treated as an international concern. In spite of these differences, the refugee groups were accepted – usually by individual states – and accorded practical, if not legal, protections.

The first of these flows involved a Protestant sect, the Waldensians, who had been long established in Piedmont. In 1686, Piedmont's ruler, the Duke of Savoy, issued an edict effectively banning the religion. This move was heavily influenced by Louis XIV; the Edict included a clear reference to the Revocation. As opposed to French practice, this Edict did give the Waldensians the right to leave the country, although within a space of only fifteen days. Approximately 3,000 refugees, many of whom had been imprisoned after an attempted revolt, were allowed to flee to Switzerland following extensive negotiations.[16] Because of the negotiations, the Swiss did not have the same fears that they had in accepting the Huguenot refugees. Consequently, the Swiss provided the refugees with relief and then gradually settled them in the different Protestant cantons. Other Waldensians moved on to Brandenburg, where they were welcomed like the Huguenots (Norwood 1969: 102–15; Clark 1998: 1277–79). In this case, however, this did not end the story. Three years later, the Waldensians invaded Savoy and successfully occupied their

---

[16] These were the survivors. Norwood notes that there were likely 12,000 Waldensians prior to the exile and that between 1,000 and 2,000 did convert but that "no complete record is available of the thousands who died in the persecutions or during the months of imprisonment" (Norwood 1969: 95).

ancestral territory. The following year, Savoy joined the alliance against Louis, ensuring the Waldensians' long-term protection. As such, they may well be the first successful militarized refugee group.

The next major flow was Protestant refugees from the Palatine, 13,000 of whom fled to England. These refugees claimed religious persecution as the cause of their flight. However, their flight was also motivated by conflict following Louis XIV's invasion of the Palatine in 1708, as well as by rumors that England would provide passage and free land in America (Knittle 1965: 6–8; Otterness 2004). The elector Palatine, concerned by the large population flows out of his territory, issued a decree "making it death and confiscation of goods for any of his subjects to quitt [sic] their native country" (Dickinson 1967: 467). It is unclear to what extent the order was enforced: at least two boats were seized on the Rhine River and the emigrants imprisoned (Knittle 1965: 53), but Cobb notes that "out of necessity, the departure of the emigrants, if not 'by night,' was unheralded" (1897: 59–60).[17]

The refugees arrived in poverty and were quickly provided with the Queen's charity[18] and subsequently with charitable donations raised under the Queen's name. The Whig government, fearing the long-term expense of supporting such a large group of refugees, encouraged the majority of the Palatines to move on to permanent settlements in the thirteen colonies, using on-migration as an effective relief valve. A minority of the refugees settled in England permanently or returned to Germany (Dickinson 1967).

With the Palatines, as with the Huguenots, material interests as well as humanitarian impulses factored in England's decision making. Daniel Defoe made the case for accepting the Palatines in the interests of commerce and of increasing England's population: it was in the interest of "the People of England, who liberally and with open Hearts and Hands contribute to the Subsistence of their distressed Protestant Brethren" (Defoe 1964 (1709): 9). And yet, with few skills, the Palatines did not

[17] This order also led to a diplomatic exchange, with the English agent at Frankfurt being told to assure the Elector that Queen Anne "is in no ways concerned in encouraging his people to leave their country . . . but . . . her Maty [sic] does not think it proper to make an apology where there is no complaint made by letter nor any ground for one" (Dickinson 1967: 467). Although Anne raised no complaint over the elector's actions, five days later, she authorized the transport of the Palatine refugees to England (Knittle 1965: 55).

[18] Amounting to nine pence per day for subsistence; lodgings were provided in London, as well as a camp set up on the Surrey side of the Thames. *The Supplement*, Issue 228, June 29, 1709. Others occupied warehouses, barns, and empty buildings (Cobb 1897: 79–80; Defoe 1964 [1709]: 32). Papers routinely published the Palatines' qualifications "for the information of such as are willing to employ them." See *London Gazette*, Issue 4556, July 2, 1709.

easily fit into the mold of the Huguenots. Moreover, this economic rationale was quickly attacked. The Tories mounted a propaganda campaign
designed to embarrass the government, one that focused on the poverty of
the Palatines and the need to do more to help people in England. One
English tradesman was quoted in a pamphlet saying that "I think our
Charity ought to begin at Home, both in Peace and War, before we extend
it to our Neighbours... The Palatines may be Poor enough, but their
coming hither can never make us rich" (Dickinson 1967: 473). Once the
Tories succeeded the Whigs in government, in 1710, they argued that
accepting the Palatines had been a mistake, "who understood no Trade or
Handicraft, yet rather chose to beg than labour; who besides infesting our
Streets, bred contagious Diseases, by which we lost in Natives, thrice the
Number of what we gained in Foreigners."[19] Thus, the new government
sought to counter arguments that it was in England's economic interests
to accept poor refugees. In the long run, economic rationales disappeared
from the English political discourse, which was reframed around the need
to protect refugees.

Another refugee flow showed the continued resonance of Westphalia.
The Prince-Archbishop of Salzburg, part of Austria, sought to expel the
Protestant population of his region in 1731 without following the provisions of the Peace. Even though the religious protections of Westphalia
did not apply to Austria, the Archbishop felt the need to provide a
justification for ignoring its requirements, suggesting that he accepted
its normative relevance. He argued that "all non-Catholic inhabitants
were *ipso facto* subversive rebels who did not come under the protection
of any treaty regulations and hence the three-year period of grace allowed
for disposition of property did not apply" (Norwood 1969: 129–30).
Emperor Charles VI, cautious over potential international reaction,
unsuccessfully urged the Archbishop to use restraint. Local troops forced
out about 20,000 Protestants, most of whom were accepted by Frederick
William I of Prussia, who invited them to settle on his eastern lands
(Norwood 1969: 128–34; Walker 1992).

In 1744, Austria figured again in an expulsion movement, with Maria
Theresa's decision to expel 20,000 Jews from Bohemia and Prague for
alleged pro-Russian sympathies (O'Brien 1969: 13; De Zayas 1988: 16).
The economic consequences of the decision were substantial: "The state
suffered a noticeable reduction of income. Everyone was harmed, nobody
benefited, nor could the sovereign be satisfied with the results of her hasty
and unjust order" (Friedlander, cited in Iggers and Iggers 1992: 35–36).

---

[19] The Examiner, no. 44, June 7, 1711 (cited in Dickinson 1967: 483).

This, combined with protests from other countries, secured an annulment of the order after a year (Norwood 1969: 26).

In all these cases, the refugees fled from religious persecution and were accommodated by other states. Other cases of displacement, Henckaerts (1995: 2) notes, "are categorized as internal relocation because, allegedly, they took place within national borders." These include the expulsion of the Acadians from Nova Scotia in 1755 for political reasons, where British authorities, "fearing that if the Acadians were repatriated to France or one or another of France's colonies they would return in arms to reclaim their homes ... ordered them dispersed to Great Britain's colonies" where most faced abject poverty (Faragher 2005: 374; see also Henckaerts 1995).

How these states provided protection to these different groups of refugees varied considerably. Only the Huguenots received protection through formal recognition in domestic law. But the Huguenots were a unique case: no other refugee flow over this period approached the size of the Huguenot migration. In addition, they were useful to the states they settled in: only with the Huguenots do we see a competition for minds and bodies. In other cases, the refugees were allowed to settle or encouraged (as with the Palatines) to move on to North America. These later refugee flows were small enough to be easily absorbed by a single state. Thus, they were welcomed routinely, even matter-of-factly. Brandenburg, and subsequently Prussia, through an explicit policy of encouraging immigration, received many of the different refugee groups of the eighteenth century. Similarly, England accepted refugees even when, as with the Palatines, they were poor and had few skills.

In these patterns of behavior, we can see some norm-governed understandings. First, the receiving states recognized that refugees had a unique status. Movements before the Huguenots, by contrast, merited no attention from the state, and they were not identified separately. Second, states accepted that refugees had a right of exit and to be accommodated elsewhere. Thus we see the universal condemnation of Louis XIV when he prohibited exit and England's quick decision to accept the Palatines when they were denied exit.

Yet, no clear regime existed. There was no concurrent responsibility to accept refugees: states, individually, decided whether or not they wished to accept refugees and provide for permanent settlement. The state response to each new crisis did not evolve in a cooperative fashion or within the context of a regime but individually and, as with the Huguenots, with a degree of competition. Furthermore, the response was rooted in domestically held norms, economic interests, and religious allegiances. Although this may simply be a result of a lack of cases, there is no clear evidence that the Catholic states held similar views. Rather, they tended to be responsible for the majority of refugee flows over this period.

There is another reason why no cooperative regime evolved over this period. Refugees were understood to be a transterritorial issue in that they were outside of their own state. However, they were not understood as a "problem" for the international system, one that required cooperation. The mere existence of refugees did not trigger a need for state cooperation for several reasons. With each major refugee flow in the eighteenth century, there was at least one state willing to accept the refugees. As well, these religious refugee flows were understood to be permanent. In only a few cases were refugees granted temporary status, most notably in the response of Switzerland to the Huguenots. Yet, even there, the refugees were granted protection until such time that they could travel on to other countries for permanent settlement. Similarly, in only two cases – the Waldensians and the Austrian Jews – do we see widespread returns to the state of origin. In the case of the Waldensians, return was brought about through armed force and a geopolitical realignment on the part of Piedmont, which allowed for their long-term accommodation. The Austrian Jews were assisted by outcry on the part of other European states.

Finally, there is one outlier case here; that of the Acadian expulsion. The Acadians were forced out due to political rather than religious reasons and were not allowed a full right of exit from the British Empire. And yet this can be explained by the exigencies of the ongoing war with France. Britain feared that the Acadian population, if returned to France, might rejoin the war.

Conclusion

Following the Peace of Westphalia, a thin normative order developed in Europe concerning refugees. The driver for this shift was that many states feared that religious persecution might restart the disastrous religious wars of the early seventeenth century. To preserve order within the nascent European society, states recognized that groups subject to religious persecution should be allowed to leave their own state and be accommodated elsewhere. This principle of a right to leave was enshrined in the Peace of Westphalia, as well as in the arguments of international legal theorists who encouraged states to accept refugees and offer them hospitality.

As is shown in the next chapter, the growth of a true regime required the notion of refugees to be reframed by the emergence of a clear doctrine of citizenship rights. And yet this earlier period, in which there was no regime, cannot be easily discounted. A thin pattern of normative-based practice is apparent. Following both the doctrines of international law and the Peace of Augsburg and Westphalia, states accepted that religious refugees possessed a right to leave their own state if persecuted and to be accommodated within another state. With the Huguenots, we see the start of a broader shift that saw refugee protection anchored in domestic law, a shift that became an entrenched normative practice in the nineteenth century.

4   The nineteenth century: a laissez-faire regime

State practice in the seventeenth and eighteenth centuries had been marked by a thin pattern of normative behavior, rooted in the need to allow refugees to leave their states of origin. However, other elements of practice, such as offering protection under domestic law and providing financial assistance, were neither universal nor consistently applied. State policies toward refugees changed dramatically in the nineteenth century, due to the emergence of a new form of asylum seeker – political refugees – and by the steady institutionalization of clear norms centered around the need to protect refugees.

The shift toward a laissez-faire regime occurred for two reasons. The first was that the American and French Revolutions led to a redefinition of citizenship and the state–citizen relationship. Doctrines of popular sovereignty replaced dynastic sovereignty. These revolutions, and the rights gained by the citizens of America and France, ensured that states increasingly derived their domestic and international legitimacy from the consent of the governed (Haddad 2003: 304, see also Zolberg et al. 1989: 9). This new basis for legitimacy informed the common practices between states at the international level. In states unwilling to accord their population a role in governance, citizens sought to claim these rights. Where these claims were unsuccessful, and particularly after failed revolutions, these citizens often sought to flee. In the nineteenth century, political refugees, also called exiles or émigrés, became commonplace.

These new movements of political refugees created three concerns for states that had not existed with previous movements of religious refugees. The first was that political refugees were more likely to seek temporary protection and plan to return to their own countries once the political winds were in their favor. This differed from earlier religious refugees who had mainly been permanent settlers. Political refugees therefore caused increased movement within the system. The second was the fear among states that these refugees, as political revolutionaries, might seek to challenge the institutions of the receiving state. The third concern was how states should respond to the increasing number of requests and demands

71

from countries of origin for the return of their citizens, particularly if the demands included threats of the use of force.

The focus of this chapter is on how norms concerning religious refugees were reinterpreted by states at the domestic level to also protect political refugees and the process by which states subsequently created a tacit regime at the international level to assist their cooperative efforts. What were initially ad hoc processes became basic norms of cooperation that stabilized state expectations toward refugees. These new norms also continued to meet the deeper goal of preserving order within international society by lowering the likelihood of conflict over refugees.

The first norm reflected the practice initiated by states in response to the Huguenot flight: refugee protection should be provided in domestic law. Whereas legislation introduced in both England and France began as processes to control inflows, over time, the goals of legislators in both countries shifted to providing clear protection to refugees. This change was reinforced by the increasingly sophisticated understandings of refugee protection held by the general public. Challenges to these understandings led to widespread protests. They contributed to the fall of Palmerston's first ministry in England and indirectly to the 1830 Revolution in France. Even in the United States, where there were no laws providing domestic legal protections to refugees, the government followed the European pattern by supporting unrestricted immigration and refusing to extradite any political refugees. As Price (2009: 25) notes, "in a world of open borders, asylum was needed only by those facing extradition; other persecuted people were admitted as migrants."

It was the growth of extradition practices that led to the development of the second norm of this regime: that refugees should not be returned to their own state, even if those refugees were accused of political crimes. Although this norm took time to develop, it was accepted practice within a core group of states – including the United States, Britain, France, and Belgium – by the middle of the century. These states then successfully transmitted this norm across international society through the use of bilateral extradition treaties. Their efforts triggered a norm cascade. By 1875, the nonextradition of political refugees was accepted as a universal practice. These developments are shown in Figure 4.1.

Even so, these practices remained restricted to the area perceived as "legitimate" international society. This society excluded the colonial territories, even those of England and France, and the governments of much of the world's population. No right to flee and seek refuge was accorded to individuals seeking to bring about political change in colonial territories. Thus, although protections were accorded to both political and religious refugees until the outbreak of the First World War, they were

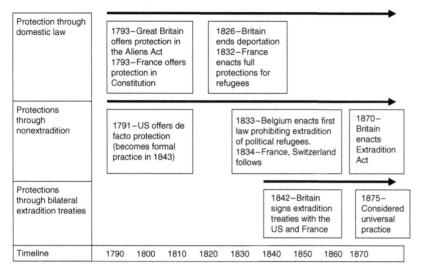

Figure 4.1 Refugee protections in the nineteenth century

entirely within the scope of European-based international society, including Europe, the United States, and Britain's dominions.

The flight from the American Revolution was the first event to produce large-scale emigration since the Huguenots. During and following the Revolution, some 60,000 loyalists and 15,000 black slaves fled elsewhere in the British empire (Jasanoff 2011: 6, 357–58). Although these migrants self-identified as refugees (Jasanoff 2011), they were atypical refugees because they continued to be British subjects and their flight was "tantamount to repatriation" either to Britain, to Upper and Lower Canada and Nova Scotia, or to its Caribbean colonies (Zolberg et al. 1989: 10; Baseler 1998).

It was the French Revolution that created the first major political refugee flow to other states, with a total of 129,000 émigrés fleeing the country. These included not only the clergy and nobility but, as the Revolution progressed, also political opponents of the successive ruling groups (Zolberg et al. 1989: 9). Other refugee flights from failed and successful revolutions were similarly accommodated. Such policies extended even to the refugees of the Revolutions of 1848, who were less sympathetically accepted due to fears that they might prove dangerous to the receiving states, as well as because of demands for their return.

Although flight from revolution was a major cause of displacement during this period (see Table 4.1), three other factors were also important,

Table 4.1 *Major refugee flows, 1776–1914*

Year	Source Country	Receiving Country	Number	Political or Religious Persecution
1776–89	United States	Great Britain	60,000–100,000	Political
1787	Netherlands	Germany, France	40,000	Political
1789	France	Great Britain, other European countries	129,000	Political
1820–21, 1831	Italy	Grand Duchy of Tuscany, France, Switzerland, Great Britain	Unknown	Political
1830	Poland	France	5,000–10,000	Political
Before 1848	Spain, Portugal, Italy, German states	France*	20,000	Political
1848	German, Italian states, Austrian empire	Switzerland, United States, Great Britain	15,000 4,000 sizable number	Political
1848	France	Great Britain, Belgium	45,000	Political
1863	Poland	Great Britain, Switzerland	Unknown	Political
1870	France	Germany	80,000	Political (expelled)
1870	Germany (Alsace-Lorraine)	France	130,000	Political
1870–1890s	Germany	Poland	1,000s	Political (expelled)
1870s–1890s	Turkey	Various	1,000s	Political
1880–1914	Russia	Great Britain, United States	2,500,000	Religious

1894–1906	France		1,600	Political (expelled as anarchists)
1890s	Macedonia (Turkey)	Bulgaria	100,000	Political
1897	Greece	Turkey	Unknown	Political/Religious
1900–1914	Russia	Germany	50,000	Political
1912–13	Balkans	Turkey	177,000	Political/Religious
1912–13	Turkey	Bulgaria	370,000	Political
1912–13	Macedonia	Bulgaria	15,000	Political
1912–13	Bulgaria (following occupation of Western Thrace)	Greece	70,000	Political
1913	Turkey	Bulgaria	50,000	Political
1913	Bulgaria	Turkey	50,000	Political

*Noiriel notes that in 1831, France was hosting 5,500 refugees: 2,867 Spaniards, 1,524 Italians, 964 Portuguese, 21 Poles, and 1 Prussian refugee. In 1837, France was hosting 6,800: 5,282 Poles, 870 Spaniards, 568 Italians, and 14 German refugees (1991: 38).

Sources: Leslie 1956: 259; Zolberg et al. 1989: 8–16; Noiriel 1991; Marrus 2002: 14–50; Burgess 2008).

particularly in the latter half of the century. One factor was territorial change following conflict. This produced large-scale refugee movements between Germany and France in 1871 and large and sustained flows between Turkey, the Balkans, Bulgaria, and Greece as the Ottoman Empire slowly collapsed. The second was religious persecution of Jews in Russia and Eastern Europe. Between 1880 and 1914, some 2.5 million Jews became refugees due to repression and harsh living conditions. Although this Jewish emigration triggered a tightening of borders in Western Europe, the vast majority of the refugees were able to migrate to the United States. The third factor was the emergence of anarchism that, although creating few refugees, contributed to increased suspicions of refugees and migrants. By the 1890s, these three factors brought about domestic legislative changes that began to close off open migration for refugees.

This chapter begins by sketching out the development of the doctrine of popular, rather than dynastic, sovereignty as a new fundamental institution. The following section then provides a brief overview of the refugee flows over this period, the reasons for them, and the state response, before moving on to detail the normative shift in domestic and bilateral laws. This latter section focuses on the cases of British and American policy, while briefly examining the continental view through the policies of France and Belgium. The chapter ends with two events that challenged this consensus: the flight of Eastern European Jews and the rise of anarchism.

The emergence of popular sovereignty

The revolutions of the eighteenth century fundamentally reshaped the linkages between the citizen and the state. This shift was caused by the steady evolution of doctrines of popular sovereignty, which based sovereignty "in the political will or consent of the population of a territory, rather than its ruler or government" (Jackson 1999b: 22; see also Mayall 1990: 2; Mayall 2000: 42–49). The evolution of popular sovereignty both undermined "ideological and material foundations of dynastic rule" and tied legitimate state action to the "augmentation of individuals' purposes and potentialities" (Reus-Smit 1999: 122).

Equally important to this domestic shift in concepts of sovereignty was a change in the state system, which was rebuilt over time "around the popular principle, deriving both its domestic and international legitimacy from the claims and consent of the governed" (Haddad 2003: 304; see also Zolberg et al. 1989: 9). Citizenship, as Brubaker has noted, was rooted in the international state system. It "was not the product of the internal development of the modern state. Rather it emerged from the dynamics of interstate relations within a geographically compact, culturally consolidated, economically unified, and politically (loosely) integrated state system" (Brubaker 1992: 69–70). This emergence of the idea of citizenship was a process bound up in the expansion of the state and its territorial redefinition (Giddens 1985: 210; see also Habermas 1994: 21).

Citizens became the source of state legitimacy. John Locke suggested that the state acquired legitimacy from its citizens: "the community put power into hands they think fit" (Locke 1993: 184). Legitimacy exemplified a bond between citizen and state that must be renewed through support by the people, based on a government pursuing "higher" and "nobler" purposes (Dahl 1982: 16, 52). But this process of citizens conferring legitimacy on the state occurs only over a long period. In Tilly's (1992: 102) view, citizenship emerged through a series of asymmetrical bargains "hammered out by rulers and ruled in the course of their struggles over the means of state action, especially the making of war."

The shift toward the concept of popular sovereignty was driven by both the American and French Revolutions because they "changed the basis of 'belonging' to a political unit by making it dependent on membership of a sovereign people. . . Participation as a citizen was the mark of true membership" (Dummett and Nicol 1990: 81). The American Revolution created a new form of consent-based citizenship that blended civic republican notions of citizenship with the liberal traditions of the Enlightenment (Klusmeyer 1996: 41; Jackson 1999b: 22). As Kettner has argued, "Americans came to see that citizenship must begin with an act of individual choice. Every man had to have the right to decide whether to be a citizen or an alien" (1978: 208).

The French Revolution directly fused citizenship with the nation-state (Tilly 1996: 225; Faulks 2000: 8). The core change was the transformation of subjects into citizens who assumed a public role: "Rather than passive subjects of an absolute monarch, the French were to become active participants in the public life of the nation. . . '[C]itoyen' became a central symbol of the Revolution" (Sewell 1988: 106). Individual rights and freedoms, Soysal (1994: 17) suggests, were codified "as attributes of national citizenship, thus linking the individual and the nation-state." Consent factored heavily in this process. As Klusmeyer argues, the French Constitution of 1791 "based French citizenship on a consensual expression of allegiance, which an individual demonstrated through the choice of holding residence in France and pledging a civic oath" (1996: 54). The consent of citizens to rule provided a clear alternative legitimating principle for states in international society, one that undermined the foundation of dynastic legitimacy and "ushered in the modern international system" (Bukovansky 1999: 197).

The introduction of this notion of consent is critical to how states approached refugee asylum during this period. As Arendt noted, new doctrines of human rights embodied in documents such as the American Constitution, the French Constitution (1793), and the Declaration of the Rights of Man were:

meant to be a much-needed protection in the new era where individuals were no longer secure... [T]hroughout the nineteenth century, the consensus of opinion was that human rights had to be invoked whenever individuals needed protection against the new sovereignty of the state and the new arbitrariness of society. (Arendt 1966: 291)

Consent was a check against the expansion of the state into the lives of the governed.

The French Revolution had created a new class of fugitive: the political revolutionary forced to flee their own state. Other states, accepting that flight was a valid alternative to revolution where consent was not possible, welcomed them. As Oppenheim (1920: 515) noted, "Great Britain, and the other free countries, felt in honour bound not to surrender such exiled patriots to the persecution of their Governments, but to grant them an asylum."

Such an argument challenges common views that protection was more often provided through benign neglect or through the inability of states to police their borders. Barnett (2002) suggests that each state reacted on an entirely ad hoc basis and remained in territorial isolation, whereas Marrus (2002: 22) notes that "preventing [the refugees'] entry into countries of refuge or tracking them down once they had arrived was practically impossible; even if they had wanted to eject foreigners, authorities would have been hard pressed to do so."

However, as I argued in Chapter 3, states had the capacity to expel elements of their own populations in the seventeenth and eighteenth centuries, and this ability continued into the nineteenth century. Expulsions stopped because, as Zolberg suggests, "the most undesirable had been eliminated – by way of their departure or gradual assimilation into the mainstream – but mainly because of the eventual generalization of rule of law" (1983: 34; see also Rae 2002). The absence of religious persecution became "the hallmark of 'civilized' states" (Zolberg et al. 1989: 9).

The presence of open migration does not indicate an absence of regulation and therefore state capacity, but that most states were not focused on stopping migration. As Fahrmeir, Faron, and Weil argue:

regulation was not designed to (and in any case could not) put a stop to migration. States took an active interest in "their" emigrants and in the immigrants who crossed their borders, and used various means of classifying international migrants as "desirable" or "undesirable"... regulations of cross-border travel were imposed in a variety of ways by a great number of different agencies... [influenced by] often short-term, political and economic considerations. (2003: 2)

States did have common goals with respect to their migration policies. The first was a commitment to international order by preventing aliens from disturbing public order within states. Disturbances, as Caestecker (2003: 121) argues, "had a political connotation; subversive aliens had to be expelled. What subversion implied, was, of course, subject to change." Thus, governments were willing to accept in refugees provided they did not challenge the domestic peace – activities outside of the host state were not seen as an issue. The second goal was to prevent the destitute from gaining entrance. Destitute aliens, rather than being considered refugees, were often seen by the state as criminals because begging and vagrancy were crimes in most of Europe. States used migration controls as a way to restrict the entry of the poor and to remove them in the event that they did cross a state's frontiers. Expulsion policies tended to focus largely on "those aliens who were not able to secure themselves a livelihood in the host country" (Caestecker 2003: 122).

The third goal was social stability. Emigration was a useful tool to allow elements of the population to leave who might otherwise challenge the social status quo. As Dowty has noted, it:

contributed to social stability. Emigration helps explain how Europe managed to survive a period of such wrenching social and economic changes with so few internal convulsions. America served as a safety valve. The exit of so many activists and potential revolutionaries probably facilitated the political accommodation of those left behind. (1987: 50; see also Hirschman 1981: 226–27)

These goals also contributed to the emergence of coherent refugee policy, ensuring that refugees be allowed to leave their own states and be accommodated elsewhere provided their activities remained inside the law of the host state. And yet, in all three states that I focus on in this chapter – Britain, the United States, and France – these policies took decades to first emerge in a coherent fashion in the domestic sphere and to then contribute to the development of clear international norms.

The evolution of norms and state policy

Policy change in both the United States and France was triggered by revolutionary ideology and the primacy of individual rights. In Britain, policy was also framed within a similar view of rights, although it was tempered by concerns about domestic unrest and enemy agent-led insurrection. All three states accepted clear normative understandings based in their understandings of territoriality, international law, and popular sovereignty concerning refugees: they accepted that refugees were a unique group who should be allowed to leave their own state and be accommodated elsewhere. The policy dynamics whereby these normative understandings were operationalized by individual states varied. Britain and France provided strong protections in domestic law, whereas the United States provided de facto protection through strong policies of nonextradition. In all three cases, these processes were driven by public sentiment at the domestic level that reflected strong support for refugee protection. When governments violated this pattern (as all three did at different times), they faced widespread domestic public unrest and changed subsequent policy.

Domestic law, along with widely institutionalized normative understandings, was one mechanism of refugee protection. The other important method was through extradition law (Goodwin-Gill and McAdam 2007; Burgess 2008: 120–21), which provided a mechanism whereby normative understandings were transmitted across European society.[1] Nonextradition was tied to protection because of the "well-founded apprehension that to surrender political criminals would surely amount to delivering them to their summary execution or, in any event, to the risk of being tried and punished by tribunals coloured by political passion" (Garcia-Mora 1962: 1226).

Extradition was reshaped in the nineteenth century. Before the French Revolution, it focused almost exclusively on those who were sought on political grounds and was provided for reasons of amity and interest: "sovereigns obliged one another by surrendering those persons who most likely affected the stability of their political order of the requesting state" (Bassiouni 1974: 4). But this was an exceptional practice, focusing only on the most serious of crimes against the state or sovereign. Common criminals were not perceived as a public danger and were not worth pursuing beyond the state's borders (Wijngaert 1980: 5).

The French Revolution was the origin of the idea of nonextradition for political "crimes." Britain and other liberal democratic states felt a clear obligation to not surrender exiled patriots (Oppenheim and Roxburgh 1920: 512, 515). The political offender, rather than being a threat to their sovereign and one who needed to be returned, became "a precursor and a

---

[1] Extradition in current practice "means a formal process through which a person is surrendered by one state to another by virtue of a treaty, reciprocity, or comity as between the respective states" (Bassiouni 1974: 2).

representative of modern and the most highly developed political ideas. . . the refusal of extradition for such offences became a principle of the law of extradition" (Schultz 1970: 15). Thus, extradition law, although tied to international efforts to suppress crime, also provided protection for those accused of political crimes and contributed to nascent understandings of human rights (Garcia-Mora 1962: 1228; Bassiouni 1974: 4–5). Nonextradition became part of the larger liberal democratic project (Radzinowicz and Hood 1979: 1421; Gilbert 1991: 115), and bilateral extradition law was used to transmit this new normative understanding across international society.

This section focuses on how shared understandings initially emerged at the domestic level in Britain, the United States, and France and how these states then acted as norm entrepreneurs within broader international society. In addition to these three states, Belgium introduced, in 1833, the first domestic law to explicitly ban the extradition of political refugees, and it also requires a separate mention as an important norm initiator in its own right. In all four states, the methods and processes by which these shared understandings emerged differed considerably. However, in all four, change was brought about through a mixture of governmental norm entrepreneurs working at the domestic level and pressure from broader public support for refugee protection. It is to these individual histories that I now turn.

The Alien Acts and open access: The policies of Great Britain

Throughout the nineteenth century, Great Britain welcomed political refugees, but did not offer them unfettered access. Beginning in 1793, the British government sought to regulate entry and to deport unwanted individuals. It was only over time and through significant pressure at the domestic level that the government gradually established clear protections for political refugees. These protections were based in domestic law, in particular the lack of a legal power of deportation from 1826 until 1905.

The origins of these protections lay in the government response to the refugee crisis brought on by the French Revolution. As we have seen, the British government had previously accepted religious refugees and was equally forthright in accepting loyalists fleeing the American Revolution. It was quick to welcome the émigré flow from France, prompted, as Carpenter notes, "by a sense of duty, honour and obligation to support those whose position was in sympathy with their own" (1999: xv). Thus, similar political views helped to ensure the accommodation of the Revolution's refugees in Britain, just as similar religious views had helped the Huguenots a century before.

Initially, the British response was universalist. They sheltered all émigrés who fled, without concern for their religious or political position (Schuster 2003: 78). This policy of asylum "was maintained, not by law, but by the absence of laws" (Porter 1979: 3). Even so, welcome rapidly turned into fear within the British public as the Revolution moved toward more extreme positions. The British government began to worry that the revolutionary government might send undesirables to Britain, including insurrectionists who might pose as émigrés in order to overthrow the British government. Even though there was no concrete evidence for these views, concerns led to significant support for aliens legislation in order to provide an element of control over who was entering (Dummett and Nicol 1990: 83; Carpenter 1999: 35–36; Stevens 2004: 18–19). The "laissez-faire, laissez-passer entrance policy" (Schuster 2003: 78), which had provided access not only to the émigrés, but also to the Huguenots and Palatines before them, was set aside in favor of domestic control through legislation.

The 1793 Aliens Act[2] was the first major statute enacted in Britain governing the status of aliens. The Act itself was draconian in that it provided the government not only the power to refuse aliens entry – although with a right of appeal within six days – but also required arriving aliens to provide port officers with a written declaration that included name, rank or occupation, and details on their place of residence in Great Britain (Plender 1988: 64).[3] In proposing the Act, the government had given little thought to the émigrés: its main concern was not to keep aliens out but rather to identify and restrict subversives (Dummett and Nicol 1990: 83). Even so, the Act gave the government unfettered power to restrict émigré entrance. As Stevens notes, "the wide powers in the Act – refusal to disembark, fines, expulsion, and capital punishment – could prevent individuals in genuine need of a safe haven from being granted asylum" (2004: 20; see also Sibley and Elias 1906: 37–42).

Because of these restrictions, the Act was challenged both in Parliament and by the broader public. Successive Alien Acts first introduced and then expanded the rights of refugees under British law. The 1798 Aliens Act[4] established the first clear protection for refugees from France, although it

---

[2] An Act for Establishing Regulations respecting Aliens arriving in this Kingdom, or resident therein in certain Cafes, 1793, 33 Geo. 3, c. IV. Article X. United Kingdom National Archives, Public Records Office (PRO) Foreign Office Records (FO) 83/294 (General Refugees Aliens 1782–1868).

[3] The Aliens Office created to administer it was lenient in enforcing these provisions (see Carpenter 1999: 39).

[4] An Act for Establishing Regulations Respecting Aliens, 1798, 38 Geo. 3 c.77.

was tempered by concerns over sovereignty and the potential security risk posed by the refugees. In its preamble, the Act noted:

and whereas the refuge and asylum which on grounds of humanity and justice, have been granted to persons flying from the oppression and tyranny exercised in France ... may ... be abused by persons coming to this kingdom for purposes dangerous to the interests and safety thereof... [I]t is therefore necessary to make further provisions for the safety of this kingdom with respect to aliens, and particularly to the end that a just distinction may be made between persons who either really seek refuge and asylum from oppression and tyranny ... and persons who ... have or shall come to ... this kingdom with hostile purposes. (Stevens 2004: 21)

As Stevens notes, this protection was introduced as a right of asylum for those refugees in Britain. However, although the rights of refugees were acknowledged in the preamble, these rights were offset by concerns over potential abuses of process, and no further mention was made of either refuge or asylum. Thus, refugees continued to be lumped within the broader aliens category: "the term 'aliens' continued to be applied to all non-British subjects, whatever their motivation for entry" (Stevens 2004: 21).

The Alien Acts also introduced a right for the state to deport unwanted aliens. The right was used most often between 1793 and 1800, at the height of the French Revolution, and resulted in the banishment of 436 aliens, including Charles Maurice de Talleyrand-Périgord, who would go on to become the chief French negotiator at the Congress of Vienna. As the European situation stabilized, not only did the number of aliens deported decline – from 1801 to 1815, 218 aliens were removed, and from 1816 to 1823, only 17 – but domestic opposition also increased as the power to expel was broadened to include "mere suspicion" (Sibley and Elias 1906: 38 fn). With the end of the Napoleonic wars, public sentiment ran against the Act.[5] Opposition to the measure also had political overtones. The Whig opposition supported the removal of a right of expulsion primarily because the reasons for its enactment – the issues around the French Revolution – had ceased. This view won the day. Increasingly, refugees were seen to be "expatriated friends of liberty to overthrow their tyrants at home" and, consequently, the refugees gained champions (Porter 1979: 68). Under the 1826 Registration of Aliens Act[6] and its successor, the 1836 Aliens Registration Act,[7] the British government had no power to deport aliens (Stevens 2004: 21–23).

---

[5] An editorial noted in 1824, "the Alien Act is a disgrace to the law of England and is supported in the House of Commons by arguments as unworthy of enlightened assembly, as the measure itself is of a free people." Editorial, *The Times of London*, March 25, 1824, 2.

[6] An Act for the Registration of Aliens, 1826, 7 Geo. 4 c. 54. Article X. PRO FO 83/294 (General Refugees Aliens 1782–1868).

[7] An Act for the Registration of Aliens, 1836, 6 & 7 Will. 4 c.11.

In 1848, a new Aliens Act[8] was enacted in response to the unease created by the European revolutions. In principle, it gave the government the power to expel any alien, including a refugee (Stevens 2004: 27–28). In practice, however, this power was never enacted in the two-year lifespan of the Act (Porter 1979: 3). Thus, the period between 1823 and 1906 represented a golden period for refugees in British domestic law: Porter finds that, in this period, "no refugee who came to Britain was ever denied entry, or expelled" (1979: 8). Restrictions on the rights of refugees were only justified by extraordinary circumstances, such as the French Revolution. In normal times, the British public did not think it proper "that governments should have any powers at all to exclude or expel aliens, except under extradition treaties for crimes committed abroad" (Porter 1979: 3). Consequently, the protections that Britain offered to a smaller number of refugees in the nineteenth century were significantly stronger than current practice.

Tied inexorably to this process was recognition by the British government of the nonextraditable nature of people charged with political crimes. This notion grew slowly. The first clear statement of this policy was in 1802, when Lord Hawkesbury, the secretary of state, noted (following demands by the French government that some émigrés be returned):

His majesty has no desire that they should continue to reside in this country, if they are disposed . . . to quit it; but he feels it to be inconsistent with his honour, and his sense of justice, to withdraw from them the rights of hospitality, as long as they conduct themselves peaceably. . . But the French government must have formed a most erroneous judgment of the British nation, and of the character of its government, if they have been taught to expect that any representation of a foreign power will ever induce them to consent to a violation of those rights on which the liberties of the people of this country are founded. (Hawkesbury, cited in Stevens 2004: 22)

This statement is all the more powerful because the British denial was one of the causes of the breakdown of the Treaty of Amiens and the restart of the Napoleonic wars (Wijngaert 1980: 10).

Yet, at least within the government, this concept was not clearly entrenched. In 1799, the British government demanded the return of two Irish rebels who had sought refuge in Hamburg, one of whom was a naturalised Frenchman. In spite of Napoleon Bonaparte calling the extradition a "gross abuse of hospitality," the free city complied. The British government faced little domestic criticism over its actions (Schuster 2003: 78–79).[9]

---

[8] Aliens Act, 1848, 11 & 12 Vict. c. 20.
[9] At least one of the rebels, Napper Tandy, was subsequently acquitted by British courts (Lewis 1859: 48).

In 1815, by contrast, the public reaction was different. That year, the Governor of Gibraltar extradited a number of rebels to Spain. His actions caused storms of protest in Britain, as well as parliamentary scorn. Sir James Mackintosh, a Whig Member of Parliament and a noted legal authority, "declared before ... Parliament that no nation should be allowed to refuse asylum to political refugees: 'Shall a British General perpetrate a violation of the right of supplicant strangers at which an Arab sheikh would have shuddered'" (Wijngaert 1980: 11). Mackintosh further argued that "though nations may often agree mutually to give up persons charged with the common offences against all human society, civilized States afford an inviolable asylum to political emigrants" (cited in Lewis 1859: 43).

This is considered by both contemporary and nineteenth-century legal scholars to be a watershed moment. Lewis suggests that Mackintosh "thus defined the approved practice of civilized nations with respect to the surrender of political refugees" (1859: 43). Oppenheim notes that "public opinion in free countries began gradually to revolt against such extradition, and Great Britain was its first opponent" (1920: 513). As Wijngaert similarly notes, "from this and many other interpellations in Parliament, it appeared that English public opinion was clearly opposed to the extradition of political refugees" (1980: 11). Most notably, the debate in the House of Commons appears to have permanently shifted government policy. A year after this incident, Lord Castlereagh, then foreign secretary, "declared that there could be no greater abuse of the law than by allowing it to be the instrument of inflicting punishment on foreigners who had committed political crimes only" (cited in Oppenheim and Roxburgh 1920: 513; see also Kellett 1986: 4).

Although such a view might have been anchored in British policy, it was not yet clear in law. This latter process began through a colonial decision. In 1829, a thief from Vermont tried to prevent his extradition by arguing to the King's Bench sitting in Montreal that it was being done for political reasons. The court agreed that extradition could not be undertaken for political crimes, arguing that "offences of a political nature, arising out of revolutionary principles, excited in any government" were different (*Rex v. Ball*, cited in American Jurist 1829: 301). The authority:

of the state to which the accused has fled may well be extended to protect rather than deliver [the political fugitive] up to his accusers, and this upon a wise and humane policy, because the voice of justice cannot always be heard amidst the rage of revolution, or when the sovereign and subject are at open variance respecting their political rights, and therefore no state will ever be induced to deliver men up to destruction. (*Rex v. Ball*, cited in American Jurist 1829: 302; see also Pyle 2001: 81)[10]

Pyle notes that this is the first "judicial acknowledgement that an exception to extradition for 'political offences' was appropriate... [I]t implicitly reserved the right to [refuse to grant extradition] if the executive did not refuse surrender first" (2001: 81).

By the 1850s, not only was there an entrenched notion of Britain's right to grant asylum and that Britain need not surrender political fugitives, but the British government also recognized the right of other states to do likewise. This, a major shift from fifty years earlier, received a forceful articulation by Lord Palmerston, then foreign secretary, after Russia and Austria demanded the expulsion of refugees from Turkey in 1851:

> If there is one rule which more than another has been observed in modern times by all independent states, both great and small, of the civilised world, it is the rule not to deliver up refugees unless the state is bound to do so by the positive obligations of a treaty; and Her Majesty's government believes that such treaty engagements are few, if indeed any such exist. The laws of hospitality, the dictates of humanity, the general feelings of humankind forbid such surrenders; and any independent government which of its own free will were to make such a surrender would be universally and deservedly stigmatised as degraded and dishonoured. (cited in Schuster 2003: 95 fn. 66; see also Lewis 1859: 47)[11]

This statement is often cited as "the definitive defence of a state's right to refuse to extradite" (Schuster 2003: 79). It not only provides a clear perspective on British policy at the time, but it also takes two important stances. The first reflects the principle of asylum not just for reasons of sovereignty but also for reasons of a common humanity: Britain could not turn the refugees over because it would challenge this basic notion. Second, the statement is applied not only to Britain, as was the case during the French Revolution, but is seen as an obligation on all "civilised" countries.[12] This view was generally inviolable.[13]

---

[10] The case was not a formal extradition case, but was over whether the government of Lower Canada could expel the defendant back to Vermont. The court found that political offences did not apply and that the prisoner "came into this province under suspicious circumstances, charged with a felony; as an alien his conduct did not merit protection" (American Jurist 1829: 309–10; Pyle 2001: 347).

[11] Correspondence respecting refugees from Hungary within the Turkish dominions presented to Parliament, February 28, 1851 (cited in Schuster 2003: 95 fn. 66; see Lewis 1859: 47).

[12] This statement was consistent with British Consular practice during this period. See "Memorandum Relative to the Grant of Asylum to Refugees in HM's Legations and Consulates," May 1870, PRO FO 881/1764, 1–2.

[13] Schuster suggests, however, that this statement was primarily used "to put a humanitarian gloss on what was a self-interested policy. It was written when material and ideal interests coincided" (Schuster 2003: 79–80). Using several mid-nineteenth-century German sources, she argues that within two years Britain was accused of violating this principle by

Britain's view on this issue not only challenged the prevailing notions within continental European society, but it also directly struck at Britain's security interests. Following the 1848 Revolutions, states throughout Europe demanded the return of revolutionary agitators. British policy was at odds with other European states because the government extended refugee protections to all refugees, regardless of the reason for flight. Britain had redefined how refugees should be normatively perceived.

European opinion concerning British refugee policy was divided between those who saw Britain's lax standards as deliberate policy to subvert or ruin the other states and those who believed that, although Britain's policy was not malicious, it was wrong "because it was unneighbourly, inconsistent with friendly diplomatic relations, and contrary to what was called 'the law of nations'" (Porter 1979: 51). States that fell within this latter category generally approved of refugee protections but saw the 1848 Revolutions as a unique event in which those rights should be set aside. Thus, the French envoy argued that there was clear evidence of a "continued conspiracy on the part of revolutionary committees organized by the political refugees in London against all the Governments of Europe, and particularly against France."[14] Similarly, Louis Napoleon stated to Lord Malmesbury in 1853 (who had just stepped down as foreign secretary) that the British failed "to make sufficient allowance for the Revolution of 1848, which prostrated the country and was felt by all Frenchmen to be only the forerunner of the Reign of Terror" (cited in Porter 1979: 51).[15]

Perhaps most dramatically, this policy in 1851 and again in 1853 saw the British government fearful of war. Lord Clarendon, the foreign secretary, argued in 1853 that "there is a project now under consideration for excluding us from the continent – moreover that we are known to be a defenceless state and that the time is now come for putting us down as a nuisance."[16] These fears "gave many British statesmen and diplomats a whiff of a war they all dreaded" (Porter 1979: 60). Yet in neither case did the British government alter its policy to mollify the other states. These tensions declined by the end of the 1850s as many refugees either left

demanding those "who engaged in subversive machinations against His Majesty's government should not be granted asylum" (Schuster 2003: 80). This may refer to Irish rebels, who by 1866, the British government "regarded as mere criminals, and whose extradition from foreign lands it did not want blocked by applications of the political offence exception" (Pyle 2001: 87).

[14] Count Alexandre Walewski (French Envoy to Great Britain) to Viscount Palmerston, October 29, 1851, PRO FO83/294 Correspondence on the Foreign Refugees in London.

[15] Malmesbury's response says a lot about British policy, that "'as we knew that half of them were rascals we should be very glad to get rid of them'; but the fact was that they could not" (Porter 1979: 143).

[16] Clarendon to Westmoreland, March 2, 1853 (cited in Porter 1979: 60). War did break out that October, but the Crimean War saw Britain and France allied against Russia.

following amnesties granted in their home countries or moved on to the United States. Some 1,500 refugees were secretly assisted with British government money to resettle (Porter 1979: 17, 160).

Oddly, it was the last major tension, the so-called "Orsini Affair" of 1858, that caused the British government enough concern that it attempted to change the open migration policy. Felice Orsini, an Italian revolutionary who had spent time in Britain as a political refugee, attempted to kill Napoleon III in Paris. Although Orsini and his accomplices were captured, and he was eventually sentenced to the guillotine, the problem for the British government was that the bombs had been made by Orsini and his collaborators in Birmingham. This led to criticisms of Britain for having accepted Orsini:

the continentals had always claimed that by harbouring Mazzini [an Italian radical] and [other refugees] Britain's policy of asylum was bound to lead, some time or other, to an eventuality like this. Britain had always claimed in reply that the continent's fears were exaggerated. The Orsini plot seemed to prove that they were not... Morally Britain was suddenly pushed on to the defensive. (Porter 1979: 172; see also Burgess 2008: 121)[17]

The plot led the British to fear war with France. Hyperbolic suggestions were made within the Cabinet that they might have to surrender India in order to save themselves.[18]

In reaction to French demands for a stricter policy, Prime Minister Palmerston moved not to alter protections for refugees but instead to propose a new Conspiracy to Murder Bill. The Bill would have increased the penalties and chances of conviction for international conspirators in Britain. This included, of course, conspiracies led by refugees. Popular opposition to the Bill was substantial, however. Not only was it seen as Britain caving to French pressure, but it challenged the traditional conception of refugee protection. The Bill was defeated in the House, and the defeat brought down Palmerston's government (Porter 1979; Kellett 1986: 6). This demonstrates the impressive salience the British public felt toward these normative understandings.

Domestic protections for refugees in Britain were rooted in the notion of nonextradition for political events. Even though this was a widespread

---

[17] Interestingly, two years earlier, another assassination attempt directed at Napoleon III – by two French brothers who placed an explosive on a rail line – produced a similar crisis for Belgium, where the plotters fled. France demanded their extradition, but the Belgian Court of Appeal refused because the act was political (Kellett 1986: 6). The French government subsequently withdrew the demand (De Hart 1886: 186).

[18] Seymour to Clarendon, January 18, 1858, PRO FO 7/538. Porter notes it is likely Lord Clarendon, the foreign secretary, "was at fault on this occasion, and that things were not as black as he believed" (1979: 173).

view, the government was slow to create bilateral treaties with other countries or to enshrine this right within domestic law. In 1842, an extradition convention was signed between Britain and France and established that fugitives would be turned over only if "the laws of the country where the fugitive or person so accused, shall be found, would justify his apprehension and commitment for trial, if the crime had been there committed."[19] A similar statement was included in an extradition treaty signed between Britain and the United States the same year.[20] In both cases, the protection was implicit through the mechanism of explicitly delineating that only certain crimes would allow for extradition (Kellett 1986: 5).

In 1870, the Attorney-General for England and Wales, John T. Coleridge, noted there was a deep reluctance to negotiate more treaties because the government "might be required to surrender political offenders, and violate the right of political asylum always afforded here to political refugees."[21] That year, to resolve this issue, the House of Commons created a comprehensive statute to cover all future extradition treaties. The 1870 Extradition Act[22] clearly established a political offence exemption:

A fugitive criminal shall not be surrendered if the offence in respect of which his surrender is demanded is one of political character, or if he prove to the satisfaction of the police magistrate or the court ... or to the Secretary of the State, that the requisition for his surrender has in fact been made a view to try or punish him for an offence of a political character. (cited in Garcia-Mora 1962: 1240)

This clause had two important elements. The first was to establish that those accused of offences of a political nature would not be returned. The second element was rooted in the prohibition of surrender for crimes in which the request was contaminated by partisan political motives (Pyle 2001: 92). States, in other words, could not cloak a political extradition request by charging the person with criminal acts. Following this change, the British government went on to sign thirty-seven treaties before the outbreak of the First World War (see Table 4.2 for a comprehensive list).

---

[19] Convention for the Mutual Surrender of Persons Fugitive from Justice, Article I. March 13, 1842, PRO FO 83/294 (General Refugees Aliens 1782–1868).

[20] A Treaty to settle and define the Boundaries between the Possessions of Her Britannick [sic] Majesty in North America and the Territories of the United States, October 13, 1842, Article X, PRO FO 83/294 (General Refugees Aliens 1782–1868). Prior to this, the first and only extradition treaty signed by the United States was the Jay Treaty, signed with Great Britain in 1794, which is discussed later.

[21] *Hansard, Parliamentary Debates*, Third Series, vol. 202 (1870), c. 301 (cited in Pyle 2001: 84).

[22] Extradition Act, 1870, 33 & 34 Vict. c. 52.

Table 4.2 *Britain's bilateral extradition treaties or conventions, 1843–1914 (year of original signature)*

Country	Initial Date Signed	Country	Initial Date Signed	Country	Initial Date Signed
Argentina	1889	Guatemala	1885	Paraguay	1908
Austria	1873	Haiti	1874	Peru	1904
Belgium	1872	Hungary	1873	Portugal	1878
Bolivia	1892	Iceland	1873	Romania	1893
Chile	1897	Italy	1873	San Marino	1899
Colombia	1888	Liberia	1892	Thailand (Siam)	1883
Cuba	1904	Luxembourg	1880	Spain	1878
Denmark	1873	Mexico	1886	South Africa★	1880
Ecuador	1880	Monaco	1891	Switzerland	1874
El Salvador	1881	Netherlands	1874	Tonga	1882
France	1843	Nicaragua	1905	USA	1843
Germany	1872	Norway	1873	Uruguay	1884
Greece	1910	Panama	1906	Yugoslavia	1900

★Orange Free State Only.
Source: British Foreign and Commonwealth Office Bilateral Commonwealth Treaties. www.fco.gov.uk

Where was the line drawn between ordinary crimes and political acts? This was tested in the Castioni case of 1890, in which the court agreed with an expansive definition that even criminal acts, provided they occurred during political disturbances, could not be used to justify extradition.[23] This case informed American practice on the issue as well. As Garcia-Mora (1962: 1245) notes, the American policy on extradition "is historically traceable to the Castioni case and, thus, is grounded on the incidence test of English law."

The 1890s saw Britain begin to tighten its immigration policies. This was due to the growing mass migration of Eastern European Jews. As Cesarani

[23] The case came before the British House of Lords as *In re Castioni*. Castioni's extradition was requested by the Swiss government, which alleged that during a political insurrection he had murdered a member of the state council of a Swiss canton, but the court ruled Castioni's actions were tied to the political insurrection and hence non-extraditable (Garcia-Mora 1962: 1240; see also Green 1962: 330; Kellett 1986: 16). This decision provided the definition of a political offence in British law until a 1973 case, *R. v. Governor of Pentonville Prison, ex parte Cheng* (1973), which added the requirement that the offence had to be political toward the requesting state (Gilbert 1983: 643).

(1992: 28) argues, with this immigration, "the concept of the alien became a touchstone for the elaboration of the values of British society and political culture. They were an object on which to project anxieties as well as aspirations." Racial theories of the day, along with widespread anti-Semitism, propelled a movement against alien immigration. Politicians campaigned on claims that "aliens brought crime and vice into the metropolis, and making use of populist prejudice which claimed that the Jewish immigrants were dirty, diseased, criminal and of poor physique" (Dummett and Nicol 1990: 100). Furthermore, anti-immigration campaigners claimed (with little support) that immigration into Britain was growing exponentially. As Gainer notes, the *Whitechapel Almanac*, published by the Conservative Party, "claimed in 1903 that immigration in the preceding decade had amounted to 429,298 – nearly double the number the Census had recorded two years earlier" (1972: 10–11).[24] Similarly, in 1889, a House of Commons Select Committee on the issue found that alien numbers not only were not alarming but that no new legislation was necessary (Wray 2006: 309). These pressures were heightened by long-term economic decline in Britain, and high unemployment reduced demands for migrants to provide labor (Schuster 2003: 82). A combination of domestic social pressure and economic decline winnowed down support for open immigration. The debate became framed within Parliament in these stark terms of racism and economic fears.

The Conservative government under Arthur Balfour sought to end the pressure by creating a Royal Commission on Aliens in 1903, anticipating that its findings "would kill the question once and for all" (Gainer 1972: 183). Although the Commission found that claims the immigrants suffered from ill-health and poor hygiene were unfounded, it did recommend the reintroduction of controls to limit certain categories of immigrants, especially those from Eastern Europe (Dummett and Nicol 1990: 102; Hansen and King 2000: 397). But controls were not so easily legislated. During 1904, several bills failed (Hansen and King 2000: 398; Wray 2006: 310–11). A new Aliens Act[25] was passed in 1905 only by offering significant concessions to opponents both in the Liberal opposition as well as within the Conservative party itself on the right of asylum. These concessions included a clear exemption if the immigrant faced persecution due to religious or political beliefs:

[I]n the case of an immigrant who proves that he is seeking admission to this country solely to avoid prosecution or punishment on religious or political

[24] Jewish immigration represented only a small amount of total immigration – between 1881 and 1914, around 150,000 Jews settled in Britain (Wray 2006: 308).
[25] Aliens Act, 1905, 5 Edw. 7 c.13.

grounds or for an offence of a political character, or persecution, involving danger of imprisonment or danger to life or limb, on account of religious belief, leave to land shall not be refused merely of want of means, or the probability of his becoming a charge on the rates. (Stevens 2004: 39; see also Vincenzi 1985)

As Balfour argued, "there was no difference of opinion in the House as to the desirability of admitting aliens into this country who were genuinely driven out (Landa 1911: 264). But, as worded, this passage shifted from the Victorian notion of an automatic right of asylum to one that now "was a matter of discretion" (Porter 1979: 218).

The government was dissolved within days of the Act passing, and the Liberal party won the December 1905 election decisively. However, the new government made no effort to repeal the Act. As Gainer (1972: 209–10) argues, once the Act was passed, "the Liberal consensus of opposition to it began to erode and the anti-alien faction to increase... [T]he principle having been admitted ... that the nation had a right to control the immigration of undesirables, there could only be a practical argument, and none in principle, for admitting any immigrants at all."

The new government's commitment to refugee protection was variable. Home Secretary Herbert Gladstone provided an instruction that "in all cases in which immigrants, coming from the parts of the Continent which are at present in a disturbed condition, allege that they are flying from political and religious persecution, the benefit of the doubt ... will be allowed" (Landa 1911: 223). But, as Landa noted, the instruction left the individual immigration boards created to administer the Act with "an entirely free hand in the matter" (Landa 1911: 224) while the Home Office itself did little to support the instruction (Pellew 1989: 375–76). The result was that few political refugees were admitted – 505 in 1906, falling to 5 in 1910 (Landa 1911; Feldman 2003: 168), although this may reflect that applicants did not specifically request refugee status (Stevens 2004: 41).[26]

The 1905 Aliens Act, therefore, represented a major change in state practice. Although it included clear language on the right of asylum, entry was no longer automatic but rather subject both to bureaucratic decision making and growing restrictionist sentiment within the population. Furthermore, although concerns were raised about the Act itself – leading to modifications, including the right to a lawyer and to appeal the board's

---

[26] This was not based on all immigration to Britain – the Act required only steerage passengers to be processed, and only if on board ships with more than twenty passengers. In 1909, of 422,548 aliens arriving from the Continent, only 35,254 were actually inspected (Landa 1911: 232). Between 1906 and 1913, "7,594 aliens were finally refused the right to immigrate to Britain" (Pellew 1989: 384).

decision (although not to the courts) – there was little public outrage about the broader shift in policy. This was markedly different from the events of fifty years earlier.

The 1905 Act also presaged a more radical shift in policy. With the outbreak of the First World War, a new Aliens Restriction Act[27] was passed by Parliament in a single day in order to remove or detain spies.[28] The new Act gave the government sweeping powers to control and prohibit the entry of aliens, to require them to remain within certain areas, and to allow for their unhindered deportation (Dummett and Nicol 1990: 104–07; Schuster 2003: 82–83). This new Act formed the basis for all subsequent immigration legislation in the interwar period.

Refugee protection grounded in practice: The United States

The United States, like Great Britain, was an asylum haven for refugees during much of the nineteenth century. Unlike Britain, the newly independent United States made an explicit decision to neither control nor extradite political refugees. In part, this reflected revolutionary ideology and the traditions of colonial America. The new state, Hutchinson (1981: 521–22) notes, "in view of its own revolutionary origin ... had a natural sympathy for independence movements and was disposed to welcome the members of such movements who had to flee." Thus, upon seeking asylum, David Rittenhouse identified the new United States as "an asylum to the good, to the persecuted, and to the oppressed of other climes" (cited in Wood 2009: 46).

For almost a century after independence, the federal government exercised little control over immigration. In 1788, the Federation Congress made the decision to not extend federal authority into an area previously controlled by the individual states. Instead, it recommended that the individual states pass their own legislation, a tacit recognition of state jurisdiction over immigration (Hutchinson 1981: 11). Even here, the main concern was not migrants as a whole, but rather transportation of convicts and paupers.[29] But although a number of states passed legislation to prevent

---

[27] Aliens Restriction Act, 1914, 4 & 5 Geo. 5 c.12.

[28] Reginald McKenna, Home Secretary, in *Hansard Parliamentary Debates*, Fifth Series, vol. 65 (August 5, 1914). Concerns were raised over the "exceptional powers" granted to a single minister, but McKenna noted that "the Order would cease to have effect as soon as the war has ceased or a state of national danger or grave emergency no longer exists."

[29] Throughout the 1780s, Great Britain continued the practice of making informal arrangements with ship captains to unload passengers, generally Irish convicts, in U.S. ports. With no concrete evidence of British involvement, Congress could only ask that Great Britain restrain its subjects (Baseler 1998: 164–65).

the immigration of these groups – Connecticut, Georgia, Massachusetts, Pennsylvania, South Carolina, and Virginia – New York, the main port of entry, took no action until 1833 (Neuman 1993: 1841–83; Reimers 1998: 9–11; Neuman 2003: 107). Thus, the state legislation was as much about signaling that those states opposed "dumping" paupers and convicts as it was about effective immigration control (Neuman 1993: 1885).

The executive branch supported the practice of asylum by deliberately choosing not to create an extradition policy. In 1791, soon after assuming the presidency, George Washington asked Thomas Jefferson, then secretary of state, to examine the state's right to extradite. Jefferson argued that, without a treaty, there was no requirement:

England has no [extradition] convention with any nation, and their laws have given no power to their executive to surrender fugitives of any description; they are, accordingly, constantly refused, and hence England has been the asylum ... of the most atrocious offenders as well as the most innocent victims, who have been able to get there. The laws of the United States, like those of England, receive every fugitive, and no authority has been given to our executive to deliver them up.[30]

Jefferson further argued in 1792 that even in the event of a treaty, treason should be exempted because the legal codes of most nations:

Do not distinguish between acts against the Government and acts against the oppressions of the Government. The latter are virtues ... strugglers against tyranny have been the chief martyrs of treason laws in all countries. Reformation of government with our neighbours is as much wanting now, as reformation of religion is or ever was any where. We should not wish, then, to give up to the executioner the patriot who fails and flees to us.[31]

The new government followed Jefferson's advice.

These views, however, were tested with the federal government's first, and brief, foray into immigration legislation through the 1798 Alien and Sedition Acts under President John Adams.[32] These Acts were passed due to fears of war with France and growing anti-immigrant sentiment within the Federalist Party (Wood 2009: 247). The Acts, although not governing admission of aliens, granted the president and the executive branch the unfettered discretion to arrest and deport aliens seen to be dangerous to the peace and safety of the United States (Hutchinson 1981: 15; Neuman 1993: 1881).

---

[30] Thomas Jefferson to George Washington, November 7, 1791 (cited in Pyle 2001: 15).

[31] Thomas Jefferson, "Heads of Consideration on the establishment of Conventions between the United States and their neighbours, for the mutual delivery of fugitives from justice," *The American State Papers: Foreign Relations*, vol. I, 258.

[32] 1798 Naturalization Act, 1 Stat. 566; 1798 Enemies Act, 1 Stat. 570; 1798 Alien Friends Act, 1 Stat. 577.

Opposition to the 1798 Acts quickly emerged. Opponents argued that such broad ranging powers for the president challenged constitutionally entrenched freedoms. In addition, the Federalist Party was increasingly out of step with the popular and more favorable perception of immigrants. President Adams, although a Federalist himself, was reluctant to enforce the Acts. Thomas Jefferson labeled them "a most detestable thing . . . worthy of the 8th or 9th century" (Wood 2009: 249).[33]

Jefferson used the Acts as an election issue in 1800, arguing instead for a strict defence of the rights of refugees. In his view, America needed to return to a time when:

> no alien law existed. . . [E]very oppressed man was taught to believe, that here he would find an asylum from tyranny . . . that it should not depend on the will of any individual, however important and elevated . . . to force him from this asylum, and banish him without the intervention of a jury. (cited in Baseler 1998: 287–88)

Jefferson won the presidency, and the Jeffersonian Republicans took control of both Houses of Congress. With their victory, the Acts were allowed to expire after two years[34] (Hutchinson 1981: 15–16). Notably, due to President Adams's strict interpretation of the Act and the numbers of foreigners who left before the Act was enforced, "the Federalist government never actually deported a single alien under [its] auspices (Wood 2009: 260).

Following the failed experiment of the 1798 Acts, Congress took little active interest in immigration affairs for three-quarters of a century. As opposed to the British case, no laws were passed subsequently to identify and protect refugees. This reflected a policy of benign neglect, however, rather than a lack of support for refugees. In 1835 and again in 1850, Congress took action to grant land to needy refugees, noting that they differed from other groups because they had been compelled to leave their home states.[35]

---

[33] Wood recounts that Adams would later justify signing the bill to Jefferson on the grounds that "we were then at War with France: French Spies then swarmed in our Cities and in the Country. . . To check them was the design of this law. Was there ever a Government . . . which had not Authority to defend itself against Spies in its own Bosom?" (Wood 2009: 250)

[34] Hutchison notes that there were also partisan political tones over this, as there had been a few years previously over naturalization laws. The Federalists opposed immigration broadly because their Jeffersonian opponents attracted the support of many immigrants (Hutchinson 1981: 14; see also Baseler 1998: 255–85). The 1800 election effectively destroyed the power of the Federalists, who never again won the presidency.

[35] The first such grant was to some 235 Polish exiles, *Register of Debates, Senate, 23rd Congress, 1st Session.* "Exiles from Poland," May 9, 1833, 1721–22 (see also Hutchinson 1981: 24). As the House noted, the "reasons of their leaving their home . . . being totally different from those of any other people. They are compelled, by the utmost rigor and perfidy of the Russian government, to say farewell to their sweet home" *House of Representatives, 23rd Congress 1st Session.* "No. 1234 Application of the Polish Exiles

Such a view remained true throughout the latter half of the nineteenth century. The United States signed its first major extradition treaty with Great Britain in 1842,[36] although the primary concern was in regulating the border between the United States and Britain's Canadian territories. Prior to the treaty, the lack of federal authority in the area had led individual states to pass statutes allowing extradition: in 1822, the New York state legislature had authorized the governor to unilaterally surrender fugitives if the crimes alleged were punishable by imprisonment or death, although five years later, the legislature amended the statute to exclude treason. Other states, including Vermont, refused to extradite without a treaty, a state power that the U.S. courts recognized (Pyle 2001: 64–67).

The 1842 Extradition Treaty did not explicitly include a special protection for political fugitives.[37] Such ambiguity, however, underlined the existence of a clear understanding of who would and would not be included within the treaties. President Tyler argued that "in the careful and specific enumeration of crimes, the object has been to exclude all political offences" (cited in Pyle 2001: 74).[38] When the United States negotiated a similar treaty with France in 1843, it did include a provision expressly prohibiting surrender for "any crime or offence of a purely political character" (Pyle 2001: 74). In 1848, the government created a domestic extradition law in order to govern its extradition treaties. It was characterized as a measure to properly implement these two treaties. Even so, it was challenged in the Senate on due process grounds, and it passed only after assurances that the law would not allow for the surrender of political offenders. This remains the basic extradition statute of the United States (Pyle 2001: 98).[39]

Until 1875, consequently, refugees received two forms of protection in the United States: open immigration allowed them entrance, whereas

for a Grant of Land for Settlement," April 22, 1834, 141–42. In 1850, the Senate passed a similar resolution in favor of Hungarian refugees, noting that "a grant of public land should be made, upon the most liberal terms, to the Hungarian refugees now in this country" *Senate of the United States, 31st Congress, 1st Session*, "Resolution" February 5, 1850).

[36] The Jay Treaty was signed in 1794. It was allowed to expire, however, "because there was no legal specification of the procedures to be employed in carrying out extradition, including the respective roles of the federal executive and judiciary." The expiry also followed the high-profile extradition and subsequent execution of a British mutineer who may have held American citizenship (Neuman 2003: 109; see also Bassiouni 1974: 30; for a history of the Nash/Robbins extradition crisis, see Pyle 2001: 24–47).

[37] A Treaty to settle and define the Boundaries between the Possessions of Her Britannick [sic] Majesty in North America and the Territories of the United States, October 13, 1842, Article X. PRO FO 83/294 (General Refugees Aliens 1782–1868).

[38] Forty years later, Secretary of State Hamilton Fish noted that "the public sentiment of both countries made it unnecessary. Between the United States and Great Britain, it was not supposed, on either side, that guarantees were required of each other against a thing inherently impossible" (cited in Hyde 1914: 490).

[39] Extradition Act of 1848, 9 Stat. 302, 303 (1848).

extradition law protected them against return. But that year, attempts by California to restrict Chinese immigration through a series of state laws (Price 1974) resulted in a Supreme Court decision that its practices were unconstitutional.[40] This meant that immigration control was suddenly and decisively given to Congress.

Responding to both nativist concerns over cheap labor and integration issues, as well as to lobbying by groups that favored immigration regulation (Graham 2004), Congress enacted a series of Immigration Acts over the next twenty years. These were limited acts, focusing either on vice – such as excluding prostitutes and criminals – or race – particularly against Chinese migrants (Neuman 1993: 1834; Neuman 2003: 106; Reimers 2002: 360). Racial concerns culminated in the Chinese Exclusion Act of 1882,[41] which suspended the admission of Chinese laborers for ten years and was supported by the Supreme Court through a series of six "Chinese Exclusion Cases" between 1884 and 1893 (Dunne 2002: 120; Graham 2004: 11–12). These Acts did little to curtail overall migration. Although total numbers declined in the 1890s to 3.7 million from 5.2 million in the previous decade, they resurged with 8.8 million arrivals in the first decade of the new century (Graham 2004: 17).

Furthermore, throughout this period, Congress preserved a refugee exemption. The 1875 Immigration Act (the Page Law)[42] clearly stated that political offenders were to be admitted (Hutchinson 1981: 522). Seven years later, the 1882 Immigration Act[43] confirmed a right of asylum to "foreign convicts who have been convicted of political offences" (Sibley and Elias 1906: 25), whereas the 1891 Act[44] noted that "nothing . . . shall be construed to apply or to exclude persons convicted of a political offence" (Hutchinson 1981: 522). In fact, the only purely political restriction introduced before the First World War was in the 1903 Immigration Act,[45] which prohibited the entry of anarchists. This was a reaction to the assassination of President William McKinley (Zucker and Zucker 1987: 4–5). Consequently, humanitarian motives remained important, with the public

---

[40] U.S. Supreme Court, *Chy Lung v. Freeman*, 92 U.S. 275 (1875), http://supreme.justia.com/cases/federal/us/92/275/case.html, accessed December 12, 2012. Justice Miller, writing for the majority, noted "The passage of laws which concern the admission of citizens and subjects of foreign nations to our shores belongs to Congress, and not to the states," otherwise "the patriot, seeking out shores after an unsuccessful struggle against despotism in Europe or Asia, may be kept out because there his resistance has been adjudged a crime" (280–81).

[41] Chinese Exclusion Act, 1882, 22 Stat. 58 (1882).

[42] Page Law, 1875, 18 Stat. 477 (1875).

[43] Immigration Act, 1882, 22 Stat. 214 (1882).

[44] Immigration Act, 1891, 26 Stat. 1084 (1891).

[45] Immigration Act, 1903 (Anarchist Exclusion Act), 32 Stat. 1222 (1903).

being broadly sympathetic to Jews fleeing the Russian pogroms and Armenians fleeing massacres in the Ottoman Empire (Seller 1982: 149). There was a clear normative understanding accepted by the population at large, as well as by the government, that refugees needed to be offered protection.

Continental protections: France, Belgium, and other European states

Like the United States, France's refugee policies throughout the nineteenth century were framed by its revolutionary experience. The Ancien Régime had sought to control all movements both within and outside of the country through a complex system of passports and other documents (Torpey 2005: 75). The revolutionary state made a clear break with these practices, with the 1791 Constitution guaranteeing that the first "natural and civil right ... was that of the freedom 'to go, to remain, [and] to depart'" (Torpey 2005: 75). As Peuchat wrote in *Le Moniteur* in 1790, "to allow a man to travel is to allow him to do something that one has no right to deny: it is a social injustice" (Le Moniteur, vol. 5: 351–52, cited in Torpey 2000: 25).

But although movement within France was liberalized, similar freedoms for foreigners soon disappeared. The 1791 Constitution was in force for less than two years. The 1797 Loi Relative aux Passeports and the 1799 Constitution did explicitly define alien status; however, they also provided for strong controls over immigrants, including registration requirements and the ability for the state to expel aliens who disturbed the public order (Grahl-Madsen 1966: 280; Haddad 2003: 307; Torpey 2005: 77; Burgess 2008).

French law was also restrictive toward the émigrés. Throughout the Revolutionary and Napoleonic periods, they were restricted in their right to return, and during some periods they were actually condemned to death upon return (Oppenheim and Roxburgh 1920: 512; Carpenter 1999: xviii–xxiv). France also forced some other states to return émigrés, most notably Switzerland, which signed a treaty with France to extradite political offenders in 1798 (Pyle 2001: 80).

In the following decades, public opinion in France, like that in Great Britain and the United States, evolved to recognize the need to protect refugees. This was made clear during the Galotti incident of 1829. Giovanni Galotti, a Neapolitan officer who had fled to France following the restoration of the Bourbons in Naples, was extradited to Naples for a number of common crimes. This occurred only after assurances were received by the French government that he would not be prosecuted for political offences. Following his extradition, however, he was prosecuted for his participation in the 1820 Revolution and sentenced to death. France not only revoked its extradition decree and requested his return, but threatened to declare war when Naples refused (Deere 1933: 250; Wijngaert 1980: 11–12). As Wijngaert notes:

As a result of this pressure, the Neapolitans finally decided not to execute Galotti and in the fall of 1830 his penalty was commuted to exile. This case, however, had provoked such deep emotion in French public opinion that shortly after the incident the French Government declared that henceforth extradition of political offenders would no longer be requested or granted. (1980: 12)

This case, and the start of the Polish refugee exodus in 1832, triggered a need in the French government to codify in law the rights of refugees.

The result was the Loi Relative aux Etrangers Réfugiés Qui Résideront en France, passed on April 21, 1832. This law, as Grahl-Madsen notes, was pivotal because it offered the first definition of a refugee as "ceux qui résident en France sans la protection de leur gouvernement" (those who reside in France without the protection of their government). Thus, he argues "it would seem that here we have the origin of the notion that refugees are 'unprotected persons'" (1966: 280; see also Haddad 2003: 307). The law did empower French officials to assemble the exiles in certain cities and granted them broad powers of expulsion (Burgess 2008: 57) but, in practice, French authorities were lenient. They also supported destitute refugees through living allowances, which were codified in an 1848 law (Marrus 2002: 16). Therefore France, like Britain, ensured that refugee protections were codified in domestic law and was lenient in the law's application.

Other European states reached similar positions over time. A particularly interesting case is that of Belgium. As in Britain, the United States, and France, Belgium's citizens, and especially its liberal elites, were sympathetic toward refugees. Unlike these states, however, the Belgian government also had to worry about antagonizing its much larger neighbors (Caestecker 2000: 5–14). To prevent demands for refugee return, the Belgian government played a crucial role as a norm entrepreneur.

In 1833, Belgium enshrined in law the nonextradition of political refugees, no matter their country of origin (Grahl-Madsen 1966: 280). The law codified that refugees would not be returned to their countries of origin through an extradition process. It also shifted extradition law from a purely executive matter normally left in the hands of the sovereign to one that could be subjected to parliamentary conditions and oversight and to judicial control (Wijngaert 1980: 12). Thus, the Belgian law moved extradition away from the realm of policy and instead created it as an institution within international law (Deere 1933: 249). This set a precedent rapidly adopted by other states. France adopted similar legislation in 1834, the Netherlands and United States in 1849, Britain and Luxembourg in 1870, Japan in 1887, Switzerland in 1892, Norway in 1908, Russia in 1912, Sweden in 1913, and Germany in 1929 (Deere 1933: 247, 256; Bassiouni 1974: 371, 375).

Such practices were initially resisted by other European states. In the 1830s, the central and eastern European powers – Austria, Prussia, Russia, and the Germanic Confederation – reached an agreement to return all people charged with high treason, conspiracy, or participation in a revolt. The policy was unsustainable, however, because it prevented these states from signing extradition treaties with the states of Western Europe. In 1856, the Austro-Hungarian Empire became the first autocratic state to sign an extradition treaty that included a political crimes exception. The North German Federation and Russia both followed suit in the 1860s (Oppenheim and Roxburgh 1920: 514; Deere 1933: 247, 251; Pyle 2001: 82–83).

Equally important, over the same time period, these states relaxed previously strict anti-emigration policies. This movement, as Torpey notes, was both for practical reasons as well as for a broader acceptance of a liberal notion of citizenship: "In part, this shift was intended to provide a safety valve for social unrest, giving unhindered passage to those who were most troublesome to the authorities. Yet it also reflected the liberalism of the forces that spearheaded the Frankfurt parliament" of 1848 (2000: 75).

As opposition dwindled, it became common practice to enter political offence exceptions into all negotiated extradition treaties. By 1875, Bassiouni notes that almost every bilateral European extradition treaty contained an exception for political offences and that this practice continued well into the twentieth century as both a standard clause in extradition treaties and in the municipal laws of many states (Bassiouni 1974: 371). Consequently, a norm based on the understanding that refugees who faced political persecution in their own state should not be returned even upon the request of that state was clearly entrenched by the latter half of the nineteenth century.

A challenge to practice: The rise of anarchism

The political offence exemption had one weakness: states deliberately did not define precisely what a political offence was (Deere 1933: 247; Wijngaert 1980: 12–18; see also Jones 1941). Ambiguity here appears to have helped in ensuring that this practice was widely adopted because states could apply the exemption as liberally or as conservatively as they wished. As British Justice Lord Denman noted in 1890, it was not "necessary or desirable ... to put into language in the shape of an exhaustive definition exactly the whole state of things, or every state of things which might bring a particular case within the description of an offence of a political character" (cited in Schroeder 1919: 30–31). Therefore, the ad hoc pattern that developed was for individual states to note exceptions to the exemption. Belgium began this practice with an 1854 clause that listed attacking a foreign sovereign as not a political crime and therefore extraditable (Wijngaert 1980: 15–16).

This ad hoc practice was challenged by the rise of anarchism in the 1880s and 1890s. Widespread public fears quickly grew that anarchist refugees were responsible for fomenting terrorist acts and political assassinations in host countries (Gilbert 1991: 116; 1998: 210). This helped to feed already growing restrictionist sentiment throughout Europe and the United States. In response, states sought to establish anarchist acts as being outside of the standard political offence exception. With this shift, anarchists as a group were defined to be outside the exceptional normative obligations through which states understood their practices toward refugees. There was, however, no single policy on how to respond. Some states went so far as to expel anarchists entirely, whereas others, including the United States, prohibited entry of anarchists and those suspected of being anarchists (Marrus 2002: 26).

Anarchism brought about the first major multilateral initiative that dealt with refugees, albeit obliquely. To coordinate individual states' responses, in 1898, Italy sponsored an international conference of police and other officials. Although the conference focused primarily on improving police responses to the anarchist problem, a major point of contention was the question of extraditing anarchists. The conference eventually reached an agreement whereby anarchist crimes would be considered nonpolitical for the purposes of extradition. However, few states actually modified their domestic legislation to incorporate such a view (Jensen 1981: 329–30). Great Britain, Belgium, and Switzerland all refused to alter their asylum policies and refused to surrender suspected anarchists to their native countries on demand. As Marrus notes, "liberal states, at least, stood firm on the question of individual rights for refugees" (2002: 26).

Anarchism represented a major challenge to the normative understandings concerning refugees. Although nonextradition of political refugees had become universal practice, anarchism led to a distinct limitation grafted onto this norm: that assassination or attempted assassination of heads of state was beyond the set of actions that states would legitimately allow. Thus, by the end of the nineteenth century, a corollary to the norm of nonextradition had emerged: certain political crimes were considered to be so repugnant that individuals who committed them lost the right to claim refugee status.[46]

Conclusion

States in the nineteenth century held a consistent view of refugees as people fleeing political and religious persecution who should be allowed to leave their own states, who should be offered protection in domestic law, and who should not be returned. These states had an ideational conception of refugees and understood their behavior toward refugees to be bound by a set of norms. Understandings that began to emerge in the seventeenth and eighteenth centuries were shaped into a consistent and noncontradictory pattern of practice. Although accepting refugees remained the purview of individual states, clear notions of correct behavior toward refugees shaped the interactions of states within international society, founded in the basic rules established by the fundamental institutions of territoriality, international law, and popular sovereignty. As opposed to the earlier period, states no longer offered protections because it was in their economic or religious interests – in many cases, offering protection went against these interests. Rather, it was because offering protection was seen as the right thing to do. Hospitality and humanitarian duty required it.

These norms did not emerge instantaneously. Initially, states sometimes engaged in hypocritical patterns of behavior, such as Britain demanding the return of its own subjects while refusing to extradite refugees. As time passed, individual governments increasingly adopted normatively correct patterns of behavior. Two processes led to this. The first was that individuals within government argued that such behavior was required for state legitimacy and that this behavior was just. The second was that governments found their policies bound by the domestic population who would protest any deviance. But even this tactical commitment over time became a whole-hearted commitment to the norms.

These developments also reflected the existence of a regime, albeit one created through informal understandings. Multilateral negotiations, by

---

[46] Other crimes – including genocide, war crimes, and terrorism – were added as additional exceptions in the twentieth century (Wijngaert 1980: 15–16). As discussed in Chapter 6, the 1951 Refugee Convention precludes refugee status for anyone who has "committed a crime against peace, a war crime, or a crime against humanity . . . [or] has been guilty of acts contrary to the purposes and principles of the United Nations," Article 1 F.(a, c), *Convention Relating to the Status of Refugees.*

contrast, were almost nonexistent.[47] Even so, norms of refugee protection and nonextradition were transmitted across international society, cascading to the point that nonextradition of political refugees was considered to be a universal practice with only very limited exceptions based on anarchism. Legalization, therefore, served as the mechanism whereby states created common understandings and reached consensus patterns of behavior. Thus, Grahl-Madsen could argue that, by the beginning of the twentieth century, two cornerstones of modern international refugee law had already been laid:

> a realization of the broken bond between the individual and the government of his country of origin, resulting on the international plane in lack of protection; and institutionalization of asylum (which was considered an important aspect of public policy) by the evolution of restrictions on extradition and expulsion (allowing as a by-effect the application of internal measures in lieu of expulsion). (Grahl-Madsen 1966: 281)

Even so, tacit state cooperation required a system with small numbers of refugees. Although states had accepted that there were common normatively correct positions toward refugee protection, refugee admittance remained the responsibility of each individual state. Not only were there no burden-sharing mechanisms, but states could easily close their borders to unwanted refugees. Obligations to protect refugees in domestic law and to not extradite applied only once those refugees were within the state's territory.

As refugee numbers increased toward the end of the nineteenth century, as huge numbers of Jews sought to flee from Russia and Eastern Europe, and as states dealt with the fears of anarchism, state policies changed. Governments abandoned earlier notions of open entrance for refugees – although often over widespread protest – and relied instead on bureaucratic processing systems for refugee claimants and increased border restrictions. In spite of these changes, the regime did not break down because the United States, with its massive absorptive capacity and domestic impediments to introducing restrictionist legislation, continued to accept huge numbers of refugees. As is shown in the next chapter, once the United States moved to close its borders following the First World War, coupled with the massive refugee flows created by the war itself, the laissez-faire regime was no longer an effective guide to state policy.

---

[47] The exception to this is in Latin America, where the 1889 Treaty on International Penal Law, signed in Montevideo by five states, recognized in Article XVI that "Asylum is inviolable for those sought for political crimes" (cited in Riveles 1989: 146; see also Bassiouni 1974: 22).

5 The interwar refugee regime and the failure of international cooperation

Refugee protection in the nineteenth century had been marked by tacit cooperation among states, defined by domestic and bilateral legal protections and an acknowledged humanitarian duty to refugees who were within the state of asylum's territory. This tacit regime worked because refugee numbers were small and because open emigration was available, particularly to the United States.

By the end of the nineteenth century, fears of anarchism coupled with growing restrictionist sentiment triggered by unprecedented migratory flows were challenging this tacit regime. The regime collapsed after the First World War, when faced with enormous flows of refugees created by the Russian Revolution and other state realignments. Open immigration was redefined as a direct challenge to state sovereignty in both Europe and the United States. Not only did immigration control increase dramatically, but, in a break with earlier practices, legislation in the 1920s ignored refugees. Refugees, Kushner and Knox (1999: 43) note, "were classified and treated as aliens and therefore as fundamentally undesirable. Traditions of asylum, even if adhered to in state rhetoric, became next to meaningless in practice." Refugees were no longer differentiated from the broader category of migrants.

Thus, even as refugee numbers increased, traditional forms of protection within the state were being systematically dismantled. A solution to this crisis was constructed through the efforts of international norm entrepreneurs who redefined refugees as an international problem that could only be addressed through formal multilateral cooperation. This shift, Soguk (1999: 119) argues, was critical, not only in enabling "subsequent regime activities," but also by facilitating "the emergence and consolidation of an intergovernmental legal or formal refugee space as a field of statecraft." The nascent idea of multilateralism, embodied by the League of Nations, was used by these entrepreneurs to reframe refugee protection as a collective responsibility for states.

But the interwar period is a bleak history. States may have accepted the need for formal cooperation and international legal protection – two new

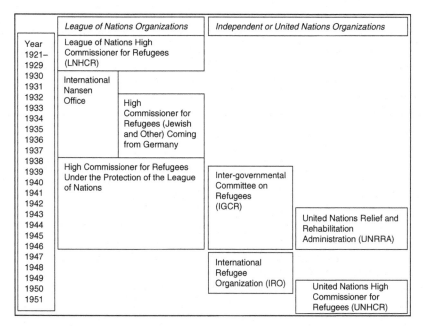

Figure 5.1 International organizations created to protect refugees, 1921–1951

norms that ameliorated the refugee crisis – but their actions at the international level were at odds with domestic preferences for strong immigration restrictions. Furthermore, states were leery of providing international organizations (IOs) with substantial autonomy, concerned that these organizations might challenge domestic restrictionist policies and create poorly defined obligations. Finally, state practices were also affected by the structure of the League itself – its rules of consensus meant that politics drove key decisions around which groups were accepted as refugees.

The result was that a succession of different IOs tasked with different responsibilities sought to offer refugees protection over the interwar period and into the immediate postwar period. No fewer than seven IOs were created and abolished prior to the creation of the United Nations High Commissioner for Refugees (UNHCR) in 1950 (see Figure 5.1). Multilateralism meant that, for the first time, a formal regime existed to provide refugees with protection anchored in international law. But significant constraints created by states meant that none of these IOs was entirely successful. The result was that the interwar regime was brittle, with little deep support by states. The regime could not be adapted to respond to new refugee crises, such as the rise of fascism and Nazi Germany.

This chapter begins with the efforts to create the League of Nations High Commissioner for Refugees (LNHCR) and the efforts of its first high commissioner, Fridthof Nansen, to institutionalize refugee protection between 1921 and 1930. It then explores the rise of domestic restrictionism and how this limited both refugee admission and protection. The final section discusses the failures by actors at both the international and domestic levels to fix this discordance and to prevent the unravelling of the interwar refugee regime.

The 1920s: Refugees become an international concern

Following the First World War, states faced an unparalleled refugee situation. The Russian Revolution alone displaced more than 1 million people (Simpson 1939; Torpey 2000: 124). Their numbers were too large to be ignored, but these refugees could neither return home nor be accommodated in a single sanctuary (Barnett 2002: 241–42). Governments faced their own reconstruction problems and "were ill-equipped for an influx of destitute people whose attitudes and dubious legal status made them a political problem" (Holborn 1975: 4–5). This was also not a short-term problem. Refugees became a part of the communal landscape of Europe as flows continued throughout the 1920s. These flows were by-products of the massive changes in the European state structure that had occurred with the war. One estimate suggests that Europe held 9.5 million refugees in 1926 (Marrus 2002: 51), although more concrete figures suggest around 3 million (see Table 5.1).

The Russian refugee crisis and the shift to formal multilateralism

The large flow of refugees created by the Russian Revolution arrived in states that were unprepared for a mass migration. A number of voluntary organizations had been created during the war to provide assistance to civilians and refugees, a role they continued to play after the war's end (Bicknell 1918: 33).[1] But refugees at the time were still perceived as a short-term problem; consequently, there were no efforts made to integrate or resettle them (Stoessinger 1956: 13; Grahl-Madsen 1983: 358). The results were paradoxical: "having kept so many refugees alive during the

---

[1] These included the Red Cross, the Quakers, and the Save the Children Fund, as well as dedicated refugee assistance organizations, including the American Committee for Relief in the Near East, the Armenian Relief Committee, the Lord Mayor's Fund, and Near East Relief. Assistance took on traditional forms, such as soup kitchens, emergency medical treatment, and orphanages. See Marrus (2002: 82–84).

Table 5.1 *Major refugee flows, 1921–1939*

Year	Nationality	Receiving Country	Number	League Recognition
1921 onward	Russians	France, Germany, Poland, Bulgaria, Romania, others	967,793 (1922 estimate)	Yes
1921	Hungarians	Hungary	234,000	No
1922	Italians	France, others	10,000	No
1922	Greek	Greece	900,000–1,200,000	No (assistance)
1923	Armenians	Various	320,000	Yes
1924	Bulgarians	Bulgaria	82,000–251,000	No
1923	Assyrians	Various	20,700 (1930)	Yes
1931	Polish	Various	8,632	No
1933 onward	Germans	France, Great Britain, United States	>154,000	Yes
1935	Saarlanders		8,000	Yes
1938	Austrian	France, Great Britain, United States	126,500	Yes
1938	Czechoslovakian		165,000	No
1939	Spanish	France	450,000	No
1939	Polish		440,000	No

Sources: League of Nations C.148.M.84.1922 [XIII] March 23, 1922; League of Nations C.249 1924 Russian Refugees – Report by Dr. Nansen; League of Nations A.27.1938 – International Assistance to Refugees. August 25, 1938, 5; Marrus (2002); Simpson (1939, 1940).

critical postwar period, the private organizations helped to maintain the pressure of refugee crises" (Marrus 2002: 82).

States similarly reacted in an ad hoc fashion, providing assistance to designated groups, which included the exiled remnants of the White Russian armies. Thus, the French government spent F150 million to provide assistance to the remnants of the army of General Pyotr Wrangel in Constantinople, while the British were supporting refugees in Egypt, Cyprus, and Serbia at a cost of £22,000 per month. The assumption was that the refugees would return home when counter-revolutionary efforts bore fruit. This meant that the refugees lacked a clear status, particularly after the Soviet government, in 1923, responded to emigration by sealing the border and removing all citizenship rights from those who had fled (Felshtinsky 1982: 328–40). As Torpey (2000: 124) notes, "by manipulating the legal status of its subjects, the Bolsheviks could punish from afar."

There was also no clear solution to this problem: bilateral negotiations were unsuccessful because of the refugees' lack of legal status, attempts to negotiate repatriation agreements with the Soviet Union were rebuffed due to a lack of trust, and the Eastern European hosts of the refugees were unwilling to accept responsibility for them (Holborn 1975: 4; Skran 1995: 89). Not only were these stateless refugees trapped in limbo, but as both the British and French governments began to back away from providing assistance, their positions were increasingly perilous. Many groups were close to starvation.[2] A crisis existed, and the states most directly involved with helping these refugees – France and Great Britain – could not foresee any form of long-term unilateral or bilateral solution.

Multilateralism provided an alternative. It created a sense of shared collective responsibility for the legal and political protection of refugees and allowed states to avoid the coordination problem they faced (see Ruggie 1992: 576–67). Although a multilateral regime can solve this cooperative dilemma, regime theory in this case does not adequately explain how states abandoned their earlier view of refugees as a domestic issue – in other words why the previous regime failed – and instead embraced a new understanding focused on formal international cooperation. In fact, there was no clear multilateral solution immediately following the war. When the League of Nations was formed, the refugee problem was not even discussed and "no machinery was therefore devised to deal with it" (UNHCR 1961: 3–4). For three years following the war, states continued to follow the core norms of the nineteenth-century regime – that refugees were the responsibility of individual states and that assistance should be provided by voluntary organizations – even though these were no longer effective.

Change occurred because of the interplay of two groups of norm entrepreneurs who offered an effective multilateral alternative. The first, the voluntary organizations led by Gustave Ador, the president of the International Committee of the Red Cross (ICRC),[3] directly lobbied the League and its membership. The second was the League of Nations secretariat, which lobbied its member states to accept an expanded mandate.

Ador argued that League intervention was vital to assist the more than 800,000 Russian refugees.[4] He successfully grafted the refugee issue onto

---

[2] A mission by the ICRC to Yugoslavia found many of the refugees "on the verge of starvation." Report from Brig. General C. B. Thomson, April 21, 1921, League of Nations Archives, Geneva (hereafter LNA), R1713/12381; Russian Refugees – Note by the Secretary-General, LNA, R1713/15001.

[3] Ador had unique access because the League's Covenant pledged it to cooperate with the Red Cross (Grahl-Madsen 1983: 358).

[4] Gustave Ador to League Secretary-General Eric Drummond, February 20, 1921, Reprinted as Council Document 11/111/69/10598, 2.

previous League successes, including "the repatriation of prisoners of war or the fight against typhus."[5] Ador also noted the international aspects of the problem: the lack of legal status for the Russian refugees; the need to repatriate, emigrate, or organize their employment; the need to provide relief; and the need to coordinate the activities of the various voluntary organizations.[6] By linking together the legal and humanitarian aspects of the problem, Ador's proposal helped to prompt a more positive response from the Council than a humanitarian appeal alone (Hathaway 1984: 351).

Ador's efforts were assisted by members of the League secretariat who also worked to convince the member states to accept the need for international cooperation. Philip Noel-Baker,[7] League Secretary-General Sir Eric Drummond's principal assistant, argued that "the problems connected with the refugees are insoluble except by international action" and that "the League might be able to accomplish something of real and great value if it managed to secure the international action required."[8] He also raised concerns that the voluntary societies would be unable to work together unless there was a strong outside authority to coordinate their efforts.[9] Noel-Baker and the League secretariat were able to exercise a great deal of influence in the creation of the LNHCR as a supposed "neutral broker," including conducting an unofficial search for the first high commissioner and asking for Council approval only after Fridthof Nansen had been convinced to take on the position (Skran 1995: 97–99).[10]

The arguments of these norm entrepreneurs presented states with a new set of policy options based on a modification of common normative understandings. States were persuaded that the refugee issue could be dealt with in a more effective manner if states were willing to surrender a degree of their sovereignty to a formal IO. The French delegation noted that "in this way the support of all civilized peoples would be gained for

---

[5] Gustave Ador to Eric Drummond, February 20, 1921, Council Document T6 11/111/69/ 10598. 4; Gustave Ador to Eric Drummond March 17, 1921, Reprinted as Ibid.

[6] Letter from Gustave Ador to the President of the Council of the League of Nations, June 15, 1921, LNA R1713/13314 (Dossier 12319); see also Frick Cramer, Principal of the International Red Cross Committee to Sir Eric Drummond, January 12, 1921, Council Document C512/10311/8822.

[7] Baker went on to advise Nansen. Following the Second World War, he served in Clement Atlee's cabinet. He was awarded the 1959 Nobel Peace Prize for his efforts on global disarmament.

[8] "Memorandum on the Possible Action of the League in Connection with Russian Refugees" 3–4 (nd) Philip Noel-Baker Archives, Churchill College, University of Cambridge (hereafter NBKR) 4/450.

[9] Letter from Baker to Lodge, August 17, 1921 NBKR 4/450.

[10] Nansen was chosen because he had already successfully negotiated the return of some 1.25 million Russian prisoners of war, overcoming a diplomatic crisis due to the ongoing Allied blockade and interventions in Russia (Marrus 2002: 88–91).

this humanitarian work, and their unanimity would be a proof that no private political aim was being pursued."[11] The British government argued the problem needed to be settled by international methods.[12] Only the Swedish government suggested that the voluntary organizations were the best method of helping refugees.[13]

Once state support was secured, the League Council created the new "High Commissioner on Behalf of the League in Connection with the Problem of Russian Refugees in Europe" (henceforth LNHCR), headed by Nansen. However, although the Council endorsed the need for an organization, it was quick to warn that the League itself "could accept no responsibility for the relief, maintenance, or settlement of the refugees" (Walters 1960: 187). The League would limit its support to administrative expenses (Simpson 1939: 192; see also McDonald 1944: 208–09), and assistance was expected to come from private agencies (Marrus 2002: 89; see also Holborn 1975: 7).

An important step forward had been taken: no longer would individual states be completely responsible for refugees. Rather, they would coordinate their actions through an IO. However, the League's hesitancy to provide the LNHCR with resources reveals that states remained wedded to the idea that voluntary organizations could provide adequate material support to the refugees.

Equally, the League member states sought to limit their direct obligations to refugees, assisted by the LNHCR's lack of formal legal status within the Covenant (Walters 1960: 187). Rather than a universal mandate for refugee protection, they accepted a responsibility only for "political and legal protection of certain classes of refugees" (Simpson 1939: 192), a limitation that existed throughout the interwar period. Not only did this allow the League members as a whole to control which groups were granted refugee status, but individual states could also decide to opt out from the legal arrangements that were granted to designated refugee groups. Member states were also leery that a powerful LNHCR might challenge their efforts to curtail immigration. "In these circumstances," as Walters notes, "it was not surprising that no efficient and well-defined organization was ever built up" (1960: 188–89; see also Marrus 2002: 110–12).

---

[11] Jean Gout to Drummond, April 11, 1921, Council Document C. 126.M.72.1921 VII. 3 The ICRC successfully lobbied the French government to adopt this position. See Rapport de M. Slavic concenant son activité a Paris du 1 au 8 Mai 1921, LNA R1713/12606.

[12] May 17, 1921, PRO FO 371 6867/N5827/38/38.

[13] Wrangel to Drummond, June 17, 1921, Council Document C. 126.M.72.1921 VII, 29.

States accepted that a formal regime was necessary, but they limited its scope and its role in providing assistance. Although Nansen successfully overcame some of these limitations, the member states and the League itself significantly weakened the ability of the LNHCR and its successor organizations to actually provide a long-term solution to the refugee problem.

The League of Nations High Commissioner for Refugees

Nansen was the prototypical norm entrepreneur (Roversi 2003: 24). Many of the League successes with refugees during the 1920s were because of his determined personality and force of will. His initial role with the Russian refugees was limited to "repatriation if possible, resettlement in countries of refuge or other areas, if necessary" (Stoessinger 1956: 16; see also League of Nations 1930: 269). Beyond establishing a new norm around the international legal status of refugees, Nansen steadily broadened the scope of how applicable norms were understood by member states. On a number of occasions, he persuaded states to expand the organizational and legal scope of the regime to incorporate other refugee groups. He also demonstrated to states how effective the LNHCR could be in an operational role.[14]

Nansen's first success was to create a solution for the Russian refugees' legal status. At a Conference in August 1921, he proposed that the refugees be granted the provision of passports or equivalent identity papers. The Conference adopted this as a recommendation with little debate (League of Nations 1930: 269). These "Nansen Passports" not only granted the refugees a legal identity but also marked the beginnings of international refugee law.

Nansen's main hurdle was to find a long-term solution first to the Russian refugee problem, then to other, newer refugee flows. Some flows, including Greek and Turkish refugees created by the Greco-Turkish war in 1923, were solved by host states adopting widespread naturalization policies (Adams 1939: 28). Refugees who shared an ethnic connection with the populations of their host states, like the Greeks, were quickly naturalized and received legal protection at the domestic level. Here, the main problem was ensuring assistance rather than protection.

---

[14] Nansen was a unique individual, a polar explorer, scientist, public figure, and diplomat. During the early part of the twentieth century, he served as Norway's first ambassador to Great Britain and to the League following its creation. He also received the 1922 Nobel Peace Prize for his repatriation efforts. As Marrus notes, Nansen "was universally admired and respected, believed to be 'above politics'" (2002: 87).

However, groups that lacked ethnic connections to their host states could not rely on mass naturalization. These included the Russians, Armenians, and, subsequently, the Jews. These groups counted only on the sufferance of host states. Nor was seeking naturalization elsewhere feasible. In Western Europe, mass naturalization was no longer practiced. In Eastern Europe, the lack of a shared ethnic identity was problematic because these states aimed to create ethnic homogeneity (Skran 1995: 103). As Haddad notes, these states used "population transfer and exchange aimed to bring about a better fit between political boundaries and ethnicity" (2008: 120; see also Soguk 1999: 114–15). Although the LNHCR assumed responsibility for both types of refugees, there was no ready long-term solution for these latter groups.

The LNHCR's lack of resources also reduced its effectiveness. Nansen argued that the League's stringency meant that he "was obliged to consider in the first place the measures which [he] could take without undue expenditure."[15] This was in spite of the LNHCR's proven record of cost-efficient solutions: for example, the British government had been prepared to give Yugoslavia £400,000–500,000 to take responsibility for 5,000 White Russian refugees. The group was successfully resettled by the LNHCR for £70,000.[16]

To overcome its limited resources, Nansen structured the LNHCR in a novel fashion. Its permanent staff in the early 1920s included only six people (Johnson 1938).[17] Instead, Nansen relied heavily on the existing voluntary organizations by setting up two consultative mechanisms. The first was a special joint committee of the voluntary relief organizations to raise funds to assist refugees (Johnson 1938: 159; Holborn 1975: 7).[18] The second was a network of in-country representatives, usually employed by the voluntary agencies, to serve as conduits to individual governments and to gather information on refugee numbers.[19] In this way, Nansen tied the LNHCR's operations into domestic constituencies. The LNHCR became "a clearing house for information, to fit the individual efforts into a general plan and to present it to the League of Nations" (Holborn 1939: 125).

---

[15] League of Nations *Russian Refugees: General Report on the Work Accomplished up to March 15th 1922 by Dr. Fridtjof Nansen*, March 15, 1922, C.124.M.74 1922, 4.

[16] LNA R1715/28099 – Russian Refugees, 2.

[17] These included T. F. Johnson who served as assistant high commissioner and Philip Noel-Baker. It also included Viakun Quisling, a Norwegian who would go on to be the pro-Nazi prime minister of Norway during the Nazi occupation (Marrus 2002: 88).

[18] The Committee began with sixteen members, including the ICRC. *Official Journal* (May 1922), 387; League of Nations. *Russian Refugees: Report by the High Commissioner for Russian Refugees*, September 15, 1922 A.84.1822, 3.

[19] League of Nations *Official Journal* (May 1922), 3.

The LNHCR in operation

The LNHCR's direct connections to governments were critical when it dealt with specific refugee crises. The first challenge, in 1922, was the fate of a group of 25,000 Russian refugees who were in Constantinople, then under allied control. This group was the remains of General Wrangel's White Russian Army. The refugees were in danger of starvation, with the French government threatening to stop all assistance in order to disperse the Army and support its return to Russia and the American Red Cross having exhausted their relief funds (League of Nations 1930: 270; Robinson 2002). Nansen asked Sir Samuel Hoare, a British parliamentarian, to visit and comment on the situation in Constantinople (Housden 2010: 504). Hoare reported that the situation was a complex problem solvable only by "protracted effort and the general goodwill of everyone connected to it."[20] Nansen used this report to secure emergency relief for the refugees from the British[21] and then mobilized the voluntary organizations for extra assistance to evacuate the refugees (Housden 2010: 504–06).

Beyond the plight of those in Constantinople, Nansen argued for improved resettlement procedures for all Russian refugees:

When it is realized that practically every country in the world has stringent regulations against the admission of refugees and that most of the refugees themselves are practically destitute, some idea can be obtained of the diplomatic and financial difficulties which had to be overcome.[22]

When those arguments failed, he focused instead on voluntary repatriation as the best long-term solution for them (Long 2009: 137–38). The Soviet government was cooperative, granting the refugees an amnesty and allowing inspection teams to be sent by Nansen to examine the conditions of those who had repatriated. However, most refugees were unwilling to return (Marrus 2002: 95).[23] Negotiations with the Soviets also failed. Nansen was unsuccessful in negotiating a general repatriation agreement with them, and a specific initiative with Bulgaria failed when that

---

[20] Sir Samuel Hoare, "The League and the Russian Refugees in Constantinople" (nd), NBKR 4/472; see also Nansen to Secretary-General, LNA R1714/ 45/19787/12319. Hoare was a Member of Parliament at the time and became the British Secretary of State for Air later that year.

[21] PRO FO 371/N 12256.

[22] League of Nations "Russian Refugees: Report by Dr. Nansen," C.472.1923, 2.

[23] This led to the return of 6,000 refugees. "Russian Refugees – Memorandum summarizing the more important work by the High Commissioner," April 28, 1923, LNA R1715 28099/12319, 2–3; T. Johnson, "The Situation of Russian Refugees General Notes on the principal outstanding questions connected with the High Commissioner for Refugees," (nd) LNA R1715/ 31937/12319. See also Robinson (2002: 41).

government cut relations with the Soviet Union (Simpson 1939: 202; Grahl-Madsen 1983: 361–62). Even so, the pressure created by the refugee flows declined by the mid-1920s, with most refugees permanently accommodated in their host countries. France alone accepted 400,000 (Simpson 1939: 106; Marrus 2002: 95–96).

The advent of new refugee flows elsewhere gave Nansen the opportunity to show how successful the LNHCR could be in soliciting assistance for refugees and coordinating relief efforts. Following the Greco-Turkish War in 1922, Nansen successfully negotiated agreements to exchange 1.1 million Greek Orthodox Turkish nationals for 380,000 Greek Muslims. He later negotiated another transfer of 100,000 refugees between Greece and Bulgaria (Skran 1995: 43–44; Loescher 2001: 25). Although the Greek government naturalized the refugees, Greece had a population of only 5 million in 1920; consequently, these refugees made up a quarter of the Greek population. The Greek government lacked the resources to assist the refugees. Nansen took the lead in coordinating relief and lobbied the League to take more long-term action.[24] This led to the creation of two Commissions tasked to provide support to the refugees by raising international loans and to work toward integrating the refugees.[25] Nansen not only used the Greek crisis to expand his mandate beyond the Russian refugee problem, but he also successfully mobilized international support for the shift.

The Armenian situation was not so easily solved. The genocide occurring between 1915 and 1918 had left Armenians fearful of their role in a new Turkish state, and they began to flee the country in 1920. By 1924, 200,000 Armenians were scattered throughout Europe and the Middle East. Many were stateless (Simpson 1939: 33, 43; Skran 1995: 45). The League took responsibility for their protection in 1923 and negotiated a new legal arrangement in 1924, modeled on the Russian Arrangement (Marrus 2002: 81, 119).

By 1925, with existing refugee flows stabilized and repatriation not an option for most groups, Nansen saw resettlement as the best long-term solution for Europe's refugees.[26] However, European resettlement was

---

[24] The League Council formalized this but accepted no responsibility for the refugees. A.80 1922, in NBKR 4/30/26.

[25] The Greek Refugee Settlement Commission raised funds to shelter, feed, and care for the refugees. The Mixed Commission was created by the Lausanne Convention of 1923 to supervise the transfers.

[26] Nansen had foreseen this issue in 1922, noting in his report to the Council that the Russian refugees were better off in Western and Central Europe, "however hard their lot may be there, than it would for them to return to Russia." "Report submitted to the Council by Dr. Nansen," May 13, 1922, C.280. M.152.1922, 1–2.

not feasible; France was the only country willing to absorb immigrants on a large scale due to their casualties during the First World War (Simpson 1939: 203; Burgess 2008). Nansen instead lobbied to hand some responsibilities for refugees, especially the technical issues surrounding employment, settlement, and migration, to the International Labour Organization (ILO) (Grahl-Madsen 1983: 362; Skran 1995: 189). For the rest of the decade, the LNHCR focused on the legal and political questions surrounding refugees, while the ILO worked to find employment and settlement opportunities for the refugees. By 1930, the "High Commission estimated that there remained 180,000 unemployed Russian and Armenian refugees, presumably all others were adequately settled" (Marrus 2002: 112).

The epithet for the LNHCR came abruptly. In 1929, with the start of the Great Depression, the ILO's efforts became fruitless. All responsibilities were transferred back to the LNHCR. This process, however, was short-circuited by Nansen's death on May 13, 1930, which caused the League to create a weaker International Nansen Office rather than appoint a new high commissioner. Even so, as a leader and champion for refugee issues throughout the 1920s, Nansen's role as a norm entrepreneur cannot be underestimated. He had, Marrus (2002: 121) notes, "helped to cultivate a political will, however fragile, to do something about refugees."

The creation of the arrangement system

One of Nansen's accomplishments was to create a distinct legal formulation for the protection of refugees. The first Arrangement, for the Russian refugees, was negotiated among states in August 1921. It recommended that the refugees be provided with passports or equivalent identity papers. Fifty-one states agreed to recognize these documents.[27] These "Nansen Passports" marked the beginning of international refugee law and ensured that refugees were "the possessors of a legal and juridical status" (Holborn 1975: 10; see also Torpey 2000: 129). This status extended to any Russian claimants outside of Russia, thus not requiring them to prove they had fled persecution. However, the Arrangement recognized only Russian refugees. New Arrangements had to be negotiated for additional refugee groups, including Armenians (1924), and Assyrians, Assyro-Chaldeanians, and Turks (1928). Through this measure, Nansen

---

[27] Note for the Conference on Russian Refugees, LNA R1728/15883/15883; see also League of Nations (1930: 269); "Governmental Conference on Passports for Russian Refugees," Held at Geneva July 3rd to 5th 1922, C.R.R/C.I./P.V.1.(1), LNA 45/21588/15833.

effectively expanded the norm reflecting the need for international legal protection to groups in similar situations as the Russian refugees.

The Arrangement system meant that the League focused on a group or categorical approach as opposed to the individually based approach of the 1951 Refugee Convention. Someone who was outside of their country of origin and without the protection of their own government could receive refugee status, but only if their group had been recognized by the League (Goodwin-Gill and McAdam 2007: 17; see also Weis 1954: 194).

Individual states continued to have the prerogative of granting or denying admission to refugees, "and even those that granted asylum did not necessarily acknowledge any legal obligation to do so" (Loescher, 1993: 38–39). Similarly, the passports offered their bearers "no guarantee of (re) admission to the country that had issued the document" (Torpey 2000: 128). As Rubinstein (1936: 22) noted: "theoretically, these papers may be 'vised' to allow a refugee to enter a country to which he desires to go, but in practice visas are granted with reluctance, and are invariably refused unless the Nansen Certificate authorizes its owner to return to the country of original issue."

Furthermore, in 1926, Nansen was rebuffed for the first time when he tried to further extend the Arrangement system to include some additional 155,000 refugees (Holborn 1938; Hathaway 1984: 355). The limitation was justified for temporal reasons. As the League Council's rapporteur argued, "the mere fact that certain classes of persons are without the protection of any national Government is not sufficient to make them refugees." Instead, refugees were seen to be groups "who are in a condition analogous to that of Russian and Armenian refugees as a consequence of the war or events directly connected with the war."[28] This shift meant that the League member states were no longer willing to grant status to all groups of refugees Nansen identified. More importantly, it ensured that recognition was increasingly political (Goodwin-Gill and McAdam 2007: 17). Thus, refugees from fascist Italy were not recognized as such because the members of the League Council "were not willing to provoke Mussolini on such a comparatively minor issue" (Sjöberg 1991: 27). Similarly, from 1936 onward, refugees from the Spanish Civil War were not recognized.

The 1933 Refugee Convention, negotiated by the LNHCR's successor, the International Nansen Office, attempted to break this pattern. The Convention was a binding multilateral instrument that also introduced a principle of nonrefoulement, first raised the year before (Grahl-Madsen

---

[28] League of Nations *Official Journal* 1137–8 (1927) 8 (10), cited in Hathaway (1984: 355).

1966; Beck 1999: 603).[29] The Convention, like the previous Arrangements, had significant limitations. It applied only to groups of refugees who already had League of Nations protection. In addition, only sixteen states became a party to the treaty, and a number of the parties set strict reservations (Beck 1999).[30] A successor agreement, the 1938 Convention on Refugees Coming from Germany, also included a right of nonrefoulement. However, just seven countries signed this Convention, and it did not come into force before the outbreak of the Second World War (Skran 1995: 137).

The group-based definitional scheme and ease by which individual states could shirk responsibilities meant that the Arrangement system proved limited as growing numbers of refugees fled from Nazi Germany. In 1935, France championed refugees from the Saar being given their own Arrangement (Simpson 1939: 211; Stoessinger 1956: 36–37). The next year, a broader provisional arrangement was created. However, it applied exclusively to Germans and covered only those who had already emigrated. Even the stateless were excluded, an oversight corrected in the subsequent 1938 Convention (Hathaway 1984: 363–64).[31] Although these legal efforts remained rudimentary, covering only the main elements of a refugee's status and ratified by few states (Weis 1954: 154; see also Simpson 1939: 1), they did mark a forming consensus among states that a formal international legal framework was needed.

The domestic shift

British and American policies during this period underlined the growing contradiction between principles of humanitarianism and those of sovereignty and immigration restrictionism. Few states were willing to follow France, which focused on immigration as a way to recover from the First World War (Simpson 1939: 297; Marrus 2002: 113). In most states,

[29] In 1932, the League's Thirteenth Assembly urged to little effect that "governments [are] not to proceed to the expulsion of a refugee unless he has obtained permission to enter an adjoining country," League of Nations Nansen International Office for Refugees, A.19.1933 *Report of the Governing Body*, 1, 5.

[30] Low number of adherents reflected some states' unwillingness to be bound by an international convention. Britain, however, did not sign due to an erroneous translation that suggested a right of asylum (Beck 1999: 621) and for fears that the terms might extend to all refugees. Memorandum, August 9, 1935, PRO FO371 19677, W 5796/346/98. Britain signed in 1936 because it was "politically desirable to do so." Lord Cranborne, April 9, 1936, PRO FO 371 20480, W3188/172/98; see also (Sherman 1973: 44–45, 71).

[31] League of Nations, *Refugees Coming from Germany*, A.19.1936.XII 3–4; League of Nations, *Refugees Coming from Germany*, A.25.1938.XII, 1–2.

opponents argued that open immigration weakened state sovereignty. It was framed as a policy that allowed other states to flood the country with undesirables. Furthermore, in both countries, legislators broke with historical tradition by removing any unique legal distinction for refugees within the broader group of migrants. By doing this, legislators effectively shifted the burden of determining who constituted refugees away from the legislative and judicial branches and to the bureaucracy. The only key difference was that the United States sought to deliberately curtail immigration from certain regions, whereas Britain did not implement an overtly race-based immigration policy. Britain's purpose was to maintain the political unity of the Commonwealth (Fahrmeir 2003: 53), although in practice there was "an undeclared immigration policy whose clear intention was to keep out Asian and black settlers" (Spencer 1997: 8–9).[32]

The policies of Great Britain

Following the First World War, Britain continued the restrictive practice set by the 1905 Aliens' Act and the Aliens' Restriction Act of 1914. The 1914 Act had granted the government almost unfettered powers of control and deportation over aliens in light of the war. It limited those powers to a state of war, immanent national danger, or great emergency. In the new Aliens Restriction Act of 1919,[33] that limitation was removed and the powers granted by the 1914 Act were made permanent. The 1919 Act also repealed the 1905 Aliens Act and therefore abolished any right of appeal. It failed to mention refugees at all, nor did it accord them any special status under its provisions (Schuster 2003: 84–85; Stevens 2004: 53).

Arguments against this policy by MPs, such as Sir Donald Maclean pleading for the "'great and noble traditions of the past' to be upheld" and Colonel Wedgewood arguing against "persecution of the weak," were ignored. As Stevens notes, the majority followed the "extravagant and inaccurate assertions of Horatio Bottomley" who noted that Great Britain "had been the dumping ground for the refugees of the world for too long" (2004: 53–54).

---

[32] Other immigration countries used similar tactics. Canada introduced a head tax on all Chinese migrants in the Chinese Immigration Act of 1885 and banned their immigration entirely in the Chinese Immigration Act 1923, repealed only in 1947. The Australian Immigration Restriction Act of 1901 introduced a dictation test that was used to block the entry of Chinese and other South Asian migrants. The Act, although amended, remained in force until 1958.

[33] Aliens Restriction (Amendment) Act, 1919, 9 & 10 Geo. 5 c.92. Although elements of the Act remain in force, most were superseded only with the United Kingdom Immigration Act, 1971, c. 77.

Both Conservative and Labour governments declared "that Britain was not or was no longer a country of immigration" (Kushner and Knox 1999: 65). But they also sought to redefine what political asylum meant. At the end of the decade, the Labour Home Secretary, J. R. Clynes, argued to a Jewish delegation that "I must correct what is, I find, a widespread misapprehension. The 'right of asylum' in so far as it exists or ever existed is not a right attaching to an alien, but is a right of the Sovereign State to admit a refugee if it thinks fit to do so" (Clynes, cited in Kushner and Knox 1999: 64). Thus, refugees' status reverted to that of "alien," and they "were no longer viewed as warranting exceptional treatment" (Stevens 2004: 54).

The internationalist views of Britain in the nineteenth century had not entirely disappeared. Groups continued to campaign for more open and generous policies. But they were isolated. State support for restrictions, once established, granted the restrictionist movement a greater legitimacy and framed the debate (Kushner and Knox 1999: 65). All aliens – including refugees – were permitted to land only if they could support themselves or if they received a permit issued sparingly by the Ministry of Labour and National Service. The arbitrary power to grant or deny entrance rested with individual immigration officers and with ministerial discretion (Stevens 2004: 55). The effect of the Acts of 1914 and 1919 was to establish, as former Lord Chancellor Hailsham noted in 1969, "one of the least liberal and one of the most arbitrary systems of immigration law in the world" (cited in Stevens 2004: 55).

The United States and the quota laws

Throughout most of the interwar period, the United States took no formal actions in the international sphere to assist refugees. Part of this was driven by the isolationist policies of governments of the time. The United States declined to join the League of Nations and did not participate in the institutions created under League auspices.[34] However, isolationism alone does not explain the U.S. approach to refugees in the interwar period. Americans continued to see refugees as an issue of domestic responsibility in law and policy and felt that assistance should be provided exclusively through voluntary organizations. In its practice toward refugees, the United States was disconnected from the new norms that Nansen was advocating at the international level in Europe. Instead, it continued to follow the core norms of the nineteenth-century refugee regime.

---

[34] The Senate had rejected the Treaty of Versailles by a 38–53 vote on November 19, 1919.

Thus, when the United States government was approached by France in 1920 to provide refugee relief,[35] the government supported American voluntary associations in providing assistance, but it felt no direct responsibility for European refugees and argued that the European governments needed to bear the costs. As Herbert Hoover, then secretary of commerce, noted to the secretary of state, "it is my impression that America has done and is doing more than her share in this problem ... and it does appear to me that the European Governments have more obligation in this matter than they have so far admitted."[36]

The Greek exodus from Turkey in 1922 sharpened this attitude. Admiral Mark Bristol, the U.S. high commissioner for Constantinople, argued that:

the present disaster in Anatolia, with its appalling refugee situation and attendant suffering, is largely if not entirely due to the Allies. Now that it has arrived the Allies turn to the United States and apparently ... expect us to handle the disaster which they have brought about.

He recommended that the State Department "bring pressure to bear upon the Allies to make them realize their responsibility in sharing the enormous expense and burden of this work."[37] President Warren G. Harding supported this view, arguing in a statement that this was an emergency, but that the American Red Cross and the Near East Relief were "the logical instrumentalities through which this relief may be extended and it is a manifest duty that they should take care of the situation."[38]

Although the U.S. government was prepared to allow private organizations to provide assistance, it would not work within the League framework. The American ambassador to Greece specifically informed the Greek government that it was "impossible for American relief organizations to work under the supervision of Doctor Nansen."[39] This was in spite of the fact that Bristol felt Nansen's efforts were successful, writing to him: "I desire to take this occasion to congratulate you ... I feel that, if this

---

[35] Letter to Secretary of State Colby from J. J. Jusserand, Ambassador of the French Republic, December 27, 1920, United States National Archives and Records Administration State Department (hereafter NARA) Record Group (RG) 59 861.48/1337.

[36] Letter to Secretary of State Charles Evans Hughes from Herbert Hoover, May 3, 1921, NARA RG 59 861.48/1439.

[37] Bristol to Hughes, September 13, 1922, NARA RG 59 868.48/160, 2–4.

[38] Presidential Statement forwarded to the American High Commission, October 9, 1922, NARA RG 59 861.48/180a.

[39] Memorandum to Hughes from Caffery, Athens, October 13, 1922, NARA RG 59 868.48/215.

co-operation can continue, work will be brought to a successful and satisfactory conclusion."[40]

Domestically, in the interwar period, the Americans abandoned their early commitment to open migration.[41] The first major success for the nativist and anti-immigrant factions within Congress came with the 1917 Immigration Act[42] requiring all immigrants as a whole to prove their literacy, although the Act explicitly exempted religious refugees (Lewis and Schibsby 1939: 74).[43] This literacy requirement, designed to block migration from Southern Europe, had little effect on overall immigration levels, with immigration reaching 805,228 by 1921. Congress then introduced two new laws governing immigration as a "direct response to the specter of millions of destitute European war refugees seeking entry into the United States" (Ngai 2003: 10). The first, the 1921 Quota Law,[44] was a temporary measure to restrict immigration to 3 percent of the foreign-born persons of that nationality living in the United States in 1910, with no provision for refugees.[45] The second, the 1924 Immigration Act (the Johnson-Reed Act),[46] made the quota system permanent, limited the quota for each country to 2 percent plus 200 immigrants, shifted the base year from 1910 to 1890, and set the burden of proof for admissibility onto the immigrants themselves (Hutchinson 1981: 190, 194). With the introduction of the Act in 1924, immigration fell to around 300,000 per year.[47]

The Quota Acts represented a major victory for anti-immigration proponents. They had been ascendant since before the War. Now they gained additional support through fears that American workers were being adversely impacted by immigration, as well as by beliefs that "the United States was being overrun by radicals, the diseased, criminals and morally unfit immigrants and that too many Jews and Catholics were arriving" (Reimers 1998: 21–22).

Anti-immigrant forces, however, were only part of the explanation for this change. Equally important, especially in the Congressional debates,

---

[40] League of Nations "Russian Refugees: Report by Dr. Nansen" C.472.1923, 3.
[41] Prior to the First World War, immigration per year was around 1 million individuals. *U.S. Immigrants and Emigrants: 1820–1998*, in Sutch and Carter (2006).
[42] Immigration Act of 1917, 39 Stat. 874 (1917).
[43] Previous versions of the Act had been vetoed by Presidents Taft and Wilson. Wilson also vetoed this one, however, Congress overrode it (Hutchinson 1981: 167).
[44] Emergency Quota Law, 42 Stat. 5 (1921).
[45] The House bill included a clause that it would not apply to aliens who proved "they are seeking admission to the United States to avoid religious persecution," but it was removed in conference (Hutchinson 1981: 178–180).
[46] Immigration Act of 1924, 43 Stat. 153 (1924). It also established that grounds for exclusion would be determined by American Consuls abroad (Stewart 1982: 9).
[47] "U.S. Immigrants and Emigrants: 1820–1998," in Sutch and Carter (2006).

was a newfound concern for immigration's effects on American sovereignty (Skanks 2001). Senator Henry Cabot Lodge, for example, declared that immigration control "is perhaps the greater of fundamental sovereign rights. If a country can not say who shall come into the country, it has ceased to be a sovereign country, it has become a subject country."[48] Others argued that refugee admissions meant "any foreign country could force a minority group upon us that they did not happen to like by persecuting or mistreating them"[49] and that foreign governments' regulation of emigration violated U.S. sovereignty: "Foreign countries are today dictating the class of immigrants that the United States must accept."[50] These arguments undermined traditional openness toward refugees, with the result that no provision was made for their admittance in law.

These negative views of immigration and refugees were not universally held. Senator Bourke Cockran argued that without providing provision for refugees:

You will have the world reduced to this condition, that however desperate might be the peril, however frightful the persecution to which people of another country might be subjected, a fugitive from those dreadful countries would be sent back by the hand of our officers to expiate in his own person our renunciation of the principles of civilization which we were supposed to embody in the highest degree during all our existence.[51]

And yet views such as Cockran's were in the strong minority. The 1924 Immigration Act passed with a vote of 323 to 71 in the House and 62 to 6 in the Senate (Stewart 1982: 14).

The quota laws dominated U.S. refugee policy throughout the interwar period. Once the Quota Laws were passed, Congress was reluctant to deal with the issue again because "the large number of immigrant Americans and the civic ideal that the United States was a haven for the oppressed made the restrictions highly controversial" (Kraut et al. 1984: 7). But, as with Great Britain, legislative changes meant that the determination of whether refugees qualified for protections increasingly rested with the bureaucracy. With the start of the Great Depression, President Hoover and the State Department used new restrictions to directly target refugees.

---

[48] Henry Cabot Lodge (R-MA), *Congressional Record (CR)* v. 65 pt. 6 (68C/1S) April 14, 1924 (cited in Skanks, 2001: 41).

[49] Walter Newton (R-MN) *CR* v. 64, pt. 1 (67C/1S), December 13, 1922, 437 (cited in Skanks 2001: 43).

[50] Albert Vestal (R-IN), *CR* v. 65, pt.6 (68C/1S), April 2, 1924, 5443 (cited in Skanks 2001: 43).

[51] Bourke Cockran (D-NY), *CR* v. 61, pt. 1 (67C/1S), April 22, 1921, 585 (cited in Skanks 2001: 53).

1930–38: The League fails to take action

Nansen's death and the start of the Great Depression adversely affected international efforts to assist and protect refugees. With Nansen gone, League efforts dwindled in spite of attempts by voluntary organizations and individuals to preserve them. At the same time, the Great Depression accelerated domestic immigration restrictionism across Europe and North America.

Following Nansen's death, the League's refugee machinery began to break apart. Assuming that the major refugee problems had been dealt with, the League created a Nansen International Office for Refugees rather than appointing a new high commissioner. Not only was the Office created as a temporary organization, set to expire in 1938, but the League Council reserved for itself all final policy-making authority. It denied the Office all financial support except for basic administrative expenses (Simpson 1939: 210; Stoessinger 1956: 30; Grahl-Madsen 1983: 362–63).[52] The Office had little of the authority of the LNHCR and was unable to provide even basic support to new refugees (Stoessinger, 1956: 31).

The creation of the High Commissioner for Refugees from Germany

In 1933, the first year of Hitler's rule, some 60,000 people fled Germany. By September 1935, 80,000 refugees had left, with about 80 percent being Jewish. Few states would accept these refugees – as noted earlier, both the United States and Great Britain had removed traditional language from their immigration legislation supporting refugee asylum. Furthermore, most Western European countries treated Jewish refugees without valid visas as illegal entrants, and they were habitually expelled (Caestecker and Moore 2010: 223). As Caestecker and Moore note, although many countries offered some informal protection, "most Western European states failed to acknowledge anti-Semitic persecution as prima facie grounds for anything more than temporary protection" (Caestecker and Moore 2010: 226).

Given the unwillingness of individual countries to accommodate these refugees, some form of international cooperation was necessary. Unfortunately, this provoked a major crisis in the League because member states did not want to raise the issue for fear of offending Germany. As Marrus notes, here was:

---

[52] The Office's major accomplishment, the 1933 Refugee Convention, was an effort to consolidate refugee protection after the Nansen Office disappeared (Simpson 1939: 210).

the classic League of Nations dilemma: on the one hand, it seemed obvious that some international response was necessary as refugees streamed from Germany into neighbouring countries; on the other hand League delegations were extremely concerned not to interfere in the internal affairs of a member state or to criticize German policies too violently. (2002: 161; see also Skran 1995: 196–97)

Hobbled by its internal politics, the League failed to take action.

As in 1921, the voluntary organizations, led by Ernst Feilchenfeld of the American Jewish Congress, sought to improve the response. They proposed to the League that the Office of the High Commissioner be revived and its mandate expanded to include both the existing refugee flows and the German refugees. This, they felt, would emphasize its humanitarian rather than political nature. After considerable lobbying, the Netherlands was persuaded to formally propose this.[53] But the German delegation used the League consensus rule to undermine the proposal, winning major concessions that weakened the High Commission. Not only did the High Commission not receive funds from the League, but only from individual governments and private funds, it was also officially independent and not affiliated with the League (Stewart, 1982: 91–99). In spite of its victory in the negotiations, Germany withdrew from the League the following month. Its absence, however, continued to color discussions as member states hoped Germany might rejoin the organization.

James McDonald[54] was offered the post as the high commissioner for Refugees (Jewish and Other) Coming from Germany. His role was circumscribed. Due to the Commission's independence, he reported not to the League's Assembly, but rather to a new Governing Body, which then forwarded reports to individual states (Simpson 1939: 216; Stewart 1982: 99). The Governing Body included few refugee experts. It was staffed mainly by nondescript diplomats already stationed in Geneva "who knew little, cared little, and wanted to do as little as possible about the cause" (Bentwich 1962: 131). Even the exceptions – such as Lord Robert Cecil from Britain; Joseph Chamberlain, an American; and Senator Henry Berenger of France – still accepted the consensus that Europe as a whole could not

---

[53] Other governments were unwilling to take action (Norman Bentwich to Kohler, September 7, 1933, cited in Stewart, 1982: 95) with Britain fearful that one solution – emigration to Palestine – needed to be "strictly conditioned by what the country can absorb." Cabinet Committee on Aliens Restrictions, Report, April 7, 1933, PRO C.P. 96 (33); and Sherman (1973: 30–35). They were also concerned that Germany would view efforts "as an act of unwarranted interference, if not of hostility." Foreign Office to Home Office, May 20, 1933, PRO FO 371 16274 C4549/319/18. They eventually relented. Minute by Perowne, September 6, 1933, PRO FO 371 16757/C7866/6839/18.

[54] McDonald, an American, was the chairman of the board of the American Foreign Policy Association and had the confidence of the New York Jewish community (Simpson 1939: 216; Skran 1988: 289).

support further refugees. But although overseas migration was touted as a possibility, no state was prepared to finance it (Stewart, 1982: 119).

McDonald was further stymied by the lack of resources (Skran 1988: 290). He was provided with only a tiny organization and budget and yet had a huge two-fold task: to coordinate relief and settlement efforts and to negotiate with governments to facilitate travel and resettlement. As under Nansen, the main source of funds was from the voluntary organizations.[55]

By the end of 1935, frustrated with the lack of progress in negotiations and unwillingness within the League to consider more effective institutional arrangements, McDonald very publicly resigned. In his widely published resignation letter, he argued that "conditions in Germany which create refugees have developed so catastrophically that a reconsideration by the League of Nations of the entire situation is essential" (McDonald 1936: 5–12). His resignation helped shock "the League and shamed it into continuing the Nansen tradition of humanitarian assistance" (Skran 1988: 292–93; Marrus 2002: 161–66). Unfortunately, McDonald's successor was ill-equipped to take advantage of this.

A new League LNHCR

The Norwegian government, on the eve of McDonald's resignation, argued that the refugee problem needed to be revisited. After a debate within the League,[56] the issue was forestalled by the creation of a Committee of Experts.[57] This Committee's report raised two issues. Institutionally, it pointed out that the division between the Nansen Office and the High Commission was responsible for the failure to assist German refugees. It recommended the two be recombined. More

---

[55] McDonald approached a number of governments unsuccessfully, including Britain and the United States. Britain argued assistance was to be provided only from the voluntary organizations. Letter to the High Commissioner from O. G. Sargent, British Foreign Office, October 29, 1934, LNA C1609 No. 4 Great Britain; Foreign Office Memorandum on the attitude of HMG to the performance of refugee work by the League of Nations 1926–33, June 21, 1935, PRO FO 371 19677/W5796/356/98.

[56] Rapport du Sous-Comité Pour L'Assistance Internationale aux Réfugies 20 Septembre 1935 (A./VI/9 1935), LNA R5633 20A/20038/20038 II. The debate was divided between states wishing to liquidate the Nansen Office and those favoring a new refugee organization. Britain supported an international solution but not expanded relief or resettlement. Makins, "Refugees – Memorandum on the Refugee Question," September 1, 1936, PRO FO 371 W10548/172/98.

[57] The Committee had a limited mandate, including not proposing anything "which might prevent the eventual return of Germany to the League" and to not "arouse the suspicion of the Soviet Government." Observations Présentées par Sir Horace Rumbold (annexe) – Comité Pour L'Assistance Internationale aux Réfugies, Procès-Verbal (C.A.I.R./P.V.), 18 December 1935, LNA R5633/21365/20038.

broadly, the Committee also argued that the state response to the refugee problem was too limited. Instead, it called for all states to engage in burden-sharing and for permanent administrative, financial, and legal measures to deal with refugees.[58]

Unfortunately, the League's member states were unwilling to take such a large step. They chose instead a limited mission for the new high commissioner, one which would be confined "to seeking the assistance of Governments in order to find solutions for the problems raised in connection with the legal status of the refugees... The various tasks connected with the assistance of refugees are in the province of the private organizations."[59] Few changes were enacted except that the new high commissioner, Sir Neill Malcolm, did report to the League Council and Assembly (Simpson 1939: 217).[60] By refusing to consider the mandate of the Office or the issue of assistance, League members avoided the more difficult discussion of burden sharing. In so doing, the governments ignored any responsibility to fund the multilateral structure they had created or to alter their own restrictive policies.

An effective high commissioner could have fought this process. Malcolm could have used the still-influential weight of League support to lobby individual states directly. Unfortunately, Malcolm was not another Nansen. He chose to deliberately limit his role even beyond the restrictions that the League placed on him. He was concerned almost exclusively with individual refugees' "questions of legal and political protection, on which he ... effectively intervened with governments" (Simpson 1939: 216–18).[61] He refused all private money. Although he did establish a Liaison Committee to communicate with the voluntary organizations, he felt he was not bound by its advice or recommendations

[58] Ibid. 13–16.

[59] Rapporteur's comments on the Council Committee's conclusions, cited in Sir Neill Malcolm, "Refugees Coming From Germany: Report submitted to the Seventeenth Ordinary Session of the Assembly of the League of Nations," A.19.1936.XII, September 1, 1936, 2. States were concerned that a revived High Commission with broad powers could challenge restrictive immigration policies. Comments by Lord Cranborne, January 16, 1936, PRO FO 371 W445–172–98; Foreign Office Memorandum on Report of Committee on International Assistance to Refugees, January 16, 1936, PRO FO 371 W445–172–98; see also Sherman (1973: 67).

[60] Malcolm was a much-decorated retired British officer who had been the general officer commanding in Malaya but had no experience with refugees (Sherman 1973: 68; Stewart 1982: 231).

[61] Malcolm was effective at helping individual refugees through his direct intervention, including some 5,000 in 1938 alone. Sir Neill Malcolm "Refugees Coming from Germany: Report submitted to the Nineteenth Ordinary Session of the Assembly of the League of Nations," A.25.1938.XII, August 22, 1938. However, Norman Bentwick, secretary of the Liaison Committee, found Malcolm "devoid of initiatives and ideas." Bentwick to Warburg (cited in Stewart 1982: 232).

(Stewart 1982: 231–32). He also did not work with the Nansen Office. Thus, when the League did take some actions – such as authorizing a limited number of Nansen certificates for German refugees – the Office refused to assist Malcolm in processing them (Stoessinger 1956: 37–38).

Two years later, with the League facing the scheduled end of the Nansen Office even as refugee numbers grew dramatically, a lengthy debate concluded with a decision to recombine the Nansen Office and the high commissioner.[62] This new High Commissioner of the League of Nations for Refugees continued to focus on the political and legal protection of refugees. But, as part of an expanded mandate, the High Commission also had a role coordinating relief and assisting governments and private organizations in promoting emigration and permanent settlement.[63] In effect, due to the now-substantial pressures on the League, member states had recreated a High Commission that included the same attributes Nansen had fought to create a decade earlier.

The new high commissioner, Sir Herbert Emerson,[64] still had only limited authority and resources. The League assumed no legal or financial responsibility for his activities, and he was denied the power to enter into legal commitments on behalf of the League (Loescher 2001: 32). In effect, Marrus (2002: 166) notes, the main hope was that the office would be better able to process "the considerable paperwork associated with refugee conventions, coordinate humanitarian assistance and promote resettlement." Within the year, it was superseded by the non-League Inter-Governmental Committee for Refugees.

League efforts had been marked by such promise. Like much of the other work of the League, however, these efforts fell apart in the 1930s. Part of the problem was that, as Stoessinger has argued, League aspirations for universal state membership meant that refugee efforts would inevitably arouse

---

[62] Great Britain shifted its position on the issue and argued that a "single League body should be established to deal with both categories of refugees" (Sherman 1973: 81), although not without internal opposition from the Home Office (Cooper to Hayter, January 11, 1938, PRO FO 371/22525, W527/104/98). The Soviet delegation initially opposed a combination on grounds of cost, suggesting that "while political assistance ... might be entrusted to the League, the latter should not have to bear any costs in connexion with it" (Foreign Office Minute, The Refugee Question August 1, 1938, PRO FO 371/22532 W11768/104/98, 2). In the end, they abstained after receiving assurances that the organization would not bear Nansen's name, be temporary, and not employ refugees. Foreign Office Minute, The Refugee Question, August 1, 1938, PRO FO 371/22532 W11768/104/98, 3–5.

[63] League of Nations, "International Assistance to Refugees: Report submitted to the twentieth ordinary session of the Assembly of the League of Nations," A.18.1939.XII, July 24, 1938.

[64] Emerson was a veteran British civil servant about to retire from governing the Punjab (Marrus 2002: 166).

the hostility of some potential or current members of the League. All refugee efforts were "a source of political embarrassment to the League and the organization, in its work on behalf of the uprooted, was actually divided against itself" (Stoessinger 1956: 32–33). The outcome of the League's failure is stark. As Torpey notes, the unwillingness of states to accept in the refugees that Germany was producing, which otherwise would have provided a form of exit, may "ultimately have helped to push the Nazis toward extermination as the 'final solution' of the 'Jewish problem'" (2000: 135–36). Between 160,000 and 180,000 German Jews (out of a population of 522,000 in 1933) were unable to leave Germany before the outbreak of war and went on to die in the Holocaust.[65]

1938–39: The United States becomes involved

The election of Franklin Delano Roosevelt in 1932 suggested that the United States' long absence from international affairs might be at an end. Although he pledged that the United States would once again be a "good neighbor ... who respects his obligations and respects the sanctity of his agreements in and with a world of neighbors,"[66] this was not echoed by a shift in refugee or immigration policy. The 1924 Immigration Act had become a frame through which all debates around immigration occurred. No one, even refugee advocates, sought to alter the existing law for fear that Congress would pass even more restrictive laws.

With the outbreak of the Great Depression, domestic pressure for decreased immigration in the United States had been renewed and coupled with both wider isolationist sentiments and anti-Semitism, views that colored immigration discussions throughout the 1930s (Harwood 1986: 203).[67] President Herbert Hoover responded to this pressure by asking the State Department to examine current immigration law to further restrict immigration.[68] The State Department supported strictly applying a little-used provision of the 1917 Immigration Act that

---

[65] United States Holocaust Memorial Museum, "German Jews During the Holocaust, 1939–1945," www.ushmm.org/wlc/en/article.php?ModuleId=10005469.

[66] Franklin D. Roosevelt, "Inaugural Address," March 4, 1933, *The American Presidency Project*. www.presidency.ucsb.edu/ws/?pid=14473.

[67] One poll asked if "the persecution of the Jews in Europe has been their own fault" to which 48 percent of respondents answered partly and 10 percent answered entirely (Simon 1974: 96; see also Wyman 1985: 10–22).

[68] Herbert Hoover "The President's News Conference," September 9, 1930, *The American Presidency Project*. www.presidency.ucsb.edu/ws/?pid=22344. Hoover justified this change by arguing that "with the growth of democracy in foreign countries, political persecution has largely ceased. There is no longer a necessity for the United States to provide an asylum for those persecuted because of conscience" (cited in Zolberg 2006: 270).

those "likely to become a public charge" (the LPC clause) be refused entry (Kraut et al. 1984: 7; Reimers 1998: 23). The Department then issued a directive to its consular officers that they "will, before issuing a visa have to pass judgement *with particular care* on whether the applicant *may become a public charge* ... [I]f the consular officer believes that the applicant *may probably be a public charge at any time* ... he must refuse the visa."[69] Consuls were orally advised to limit immigration visas to no more than 10 percent of the legal quota (Kraut et al. 1984: 7).

The strict application of the LPC clause ensured that most refugees could not qualify for an immigration visa and could not enter the United States. The State Department controlled both the application and review processes. Thus, through "purely administrative means," State Department officials were able to create a staunchly restrictionist immigration policy within the existing legal framework (Zucker 2010: 156). The LPC clause was a particular problem for the German Jewish refugees because the Nazi regime forced them to surrender most of their property in order to emigrate.

Yet, when questioned, these same officials argued their actions followed the law and suggested, as Wilbur J. Carr, the assistant secretary of state for the Visa Division and Consular Affairs, did, that the Hoover decision could not be overturned except legislatively (Stewart 1982: 48–51). This was despite the fact that the president, let alone Congress, had taken no formal action. Anti-Semitism among senior officials within the Department played a role (Feingold 1970: 15, 134–35; see also Wyman 1985), as did the lack of strong leadership – Cordell Hull, who became secretary of state in 1933, had little knowledge of immigration affairs and did not challenge more experienced officers, such as Carr (Stewart 1982: 48).

The dilemma facing refugee advocates in the United States after 1930, consequently, was not the quota laws themselves, but rather the State Department's interpretation of the laws. For Carr, existing legislation meant "the question of asylum ... is removed from the problem, and no action would be deemed necessary" when processing visas.[70] The fact that an applicant had faced persecution was no longer a reason for admittance.

The Department had a great deal of sway over not only visas, but also over refugee policy in general. From the mid-1920s onward, it had refused to issue Nansen Passports to refugees.[71] The Department also declined to

[69] U.S. Department of State, 'Press Release,' September 13, 1930 (emphasis in original), cited in Zucker (2010: 155).
[70] Carr, "The Problem of Aliens Seeking Relief from Persecution in Germany," April 20, 1933, NARA RG 59 150.01/2110. 1–7; see also Zucker 2010: 157.
[71] Letter from the Acting Secretary of State to Drummond (nd), NARA RG 59 511.1 C1/7.

sign the 1933 Refugee Convention, replying to the League's secretary-general that "the status of all persons coming to the United States of America is fully defined by existing legislation and this Government therefore does not contemplate becoming a party to the draft Convention in question."[72] It also refused to accept substitute travel documents for aliens still in their own country who could not acquire passports.[73] Thus, the secretary of state noted to McDonald that little could be done within U.S. policy, adding that most aliens would be ineligible for visas in any case.[74]

The Department actively hindered the League's efforts as well. Because McDonald, as high commissioner, was technically independent of the League, the American government consented to be represented on its Governing Body by Dr. Joseph Chamberlain, an important step forward. However, because McDonald noted that he expected the dealings with individual refugees to be left "to the private organizations already functioning,"[75] the State Department felt no government contributions should be made to McDonald's High Commission. They stopped a contribution that had been personally guaranteed by Roosevelt by arguing it required Congressional approval.[76]

Opponents of these policies found themselves blocked by the Department. "Few bureaucrats," Breitman and Kraut (1987: 9) note, "were willing to consider the rescue of persecuted foreigners as compatible with the defence of the national interest." Even those who were willing to champion the cause, they add, "found themselves confined to the channels and bound by the procedures of the bureaucratic system." Frances Perkins, as the secretary of labor, had responsibility over immigration and naturalization issues. She sought to overturn the LPC clause by executive order and argued against other restrictions because "it was consistent with American traditions and policies to grant free entry to refugees." Yet, the State Department blocked her efforts (Kraut et al. 1984: 9, Zucker 2001).

---

[72] Letter to the American Minister, Bern, April 21, 1937, Enclosure: Note to Secretary-General of League of Nations, NARA RG 59 548.D 1/327.

[73] Memorandum by John Farr Simmons, Visa Division, March 3, 1934, NARA RG 59 548 D.1/100.

[74] Secretary of State to McDonald, April 28, 1934, NARA RG 59 D.1/127.

[75] Statement of James G. McDonald to the Governing Body December 3, 1933, NARA RG 59 548.D1/84; Joseph Chamberlain, "Meeting of the Governing Body of the High Commission for Refugees (Jewish and Other) Coming from Germany." December 28, 1933, NARA RG 59 548.D1/86, 7.

[76] Memorandum by Wilbur J. Carr, Assistant Secretary of State, December 18, 1934, NARA RG 59 D 1/194; Phillips, Under Secretary of State, to Joseph Chamberlain, January 21, 1935, NARA RG 59 548. D1/202.

New York Governor Herbert H. Lehman, Roosevelt's successor as governor, also appealed to the president to alter the policy of limiting immigration from Germany to 10 percent of the quota: "[McDonald's Office] ask that the immigration quota of German Jews to this country be increased from 2,500 to 5,000. This, of course, is almost a negligible number." Roosevelt rebuffed the appeal, replying that the Department was "continuing to make every effort to carry out the immigration duties placed upon them in a considerate and human manner. They are issuing considerably more immigration visas to German Jewish applicants at the present time than was the case last year."[77] Instead of taking action on the issue, Feingold (1970: 18) notes, "Roosevelt was content to let the State Department handle the refugee matter. He preferred to remain above the battle. . . It allowed the agency involved to absorb much of the pressure and ire that might otherwise be directed at the White House."

The first suggestions that Roosevelt's view might change were in August and September 1936, months before the election, when he issued a public statement supporting a Jewish homeland in Palestine and urged Britain to not limit Jewish immigration to Palestine (Kraut et al. 1984: 17).[78] But he took little formal action until the Austrian Anschluss on March 12, 1938, which resulted in nearly 50,000 Jews fleeing the country in the following six months (Caestecker and Moore 2010: 245). Faced with this, Roosevelt argued that "America could never return to the passive role she had been playing" (Stewart, 1982: 267). He ordered the Austrian and German quotas combined, to give Austrian Jews a greater chance to obtain a visa, and he publicly called for an international conference to address the refugee problem.

Roosevelt's shift had a number of reasons. Part of it was a humanitarian desire to help the "steady flow of prominent refugees whose calibre impressed him and whose personal misfortunes aroused his sympathy" (Feingold 1970: 23). As Roosevelt would subsequently note:

For centuries this country has always been the traditional haven of refuge for countless victims of religious and political persecution in other lands. . . It was

---

[77] Herbert Lehman to Roosevelt, November 1, 1935, Lehman Collections, Columbia University, Folder 1167; Roosevelt to Lehman, July 2, 1936, Ibid. Folder 1168.

[78] Although there is no evidence that Roosevelt communicated any policy change to the State Department, "careful observers could see which way he was leaning." Carr directed consular officers to pay more attention to the "unusual features present in the case of German Jewish refugees." A total of 6,978 individual visas had been issued under the German quota in 1936; in the following year, the number doubled to 12,532. In spite of the LPC clause, the sheer number of applications filled the 1939 German quota. Between June 1933 and June 1939, 74,858 visas were issued, although the quota law allowed more than double that number (Kraut et al. 1984: 17–19, 21, 24).

quite fitting, therefore, that the United States government should follow its traditional role and take the lead in calling and conducting the Evian meeting. (Roosevelt 1941: 170)

But increased domestic pressure, particularly from the American Jewish community who formed an important voting bloc, also played a role (Feingold 1970: 23–24; Bon Tempo 2008). So, too, did a shift within the State Department, which recognized that the refugee flows constituted a major long-term problem. As Assistant Secretary of State (and the former Consul-General in Berlin) George Messersmith noted in a memo to the Secretary:

in spite of the difficulties involved in doing anything constructive, I believe that the prospects for at least some definitely useful action are good... The problem remains a long range problem and one that is not susceptible of rapid solution nor of solution by any one country. It is a problem which will require cooperative action such as that planned by the new Committee.[79]

Within the American government, Roosevelt's decision to convene an international conference to address the refugee problem was greeted with "universal surprise." Although Roosevelt had raised the admission of political refugees at a cabinet meeting on March 18, 1938, "[Secretary of the Interior Harold] Ickes suggested a temporary amendment to the immigration laws if necessary but remembered that Vice-President John Nance Garner thought this impossible" (Stewart 1982: 273; see also Ickes 1955: 342–43). International cooperation through the League was unlikely to work – by 1938, its prestige had been fatally damaged, as was its ability to deal with humanitarian issues. The League had yet to combine the International Office and the High Commission, and its only response to the Anschluss was to add Austrian Jews to the 1936 Provisional Arrangement (Walters 1960; Skran 1995: 207).[80]

Little action could be expected from the European powers who remained focused on excluding immigrants. In France, the government had initially welcomed the German refugees and waived all visa requirements. But, by December 1933, facing middle-class protest over "unfair competition" from German refugees, the government reestablished the

---

[79] Messersmith to the Secretary of State, March 31, 1938, NARA RG 59 840.48 Refugees/84½.

[80] "Additional Protocol to the Provisional Arrangement and to the Convention concerning the Status of Refugees Coming from Germany," September 14, 1939. Only Britain, Denmark, and France signed it (France in 1945). The American government did invite Malcolm to the conference. Judge Hansson, the then-president of the International Office, attended the conference as the representative of Norway. The Secretary of State to the Ambassador in the United Kingdom (Kennedy), June 14, 1938, *Foreign Relations of the United States* (hereafter *FRUS*) 1938, vol. I. "General," 749.

visa requirement. Over the following two years, Conservative govern-ments tightened immigration legislation and removed all provisions for a separate refugee status (Maga 1982: 434; Burgess 2002; Caron 2010: 57–60). Even people with visas were no longer guaranteed entrance (Caron 2010: 61). Although a 1936 Decree under the Léon Blum Popular Front government ameliorated the situation, it "failed to bind the government with respect to future refugees" (Caron 2010: 63; Caestecker and Moore 2010: 229). The subsequent Conservative Daladier government, fearful that refugees could be a "Trojan Horse" of spies and subversives (Maga 1982: 434), reintroduced restrictions and increased the government's expulsionary powers with the decree law of May 2, 1938. Although in principle the legislation guaranteed a right to asylum, "these measures either remained a dead letter or were not imple-mented immediately" (Caron 2010: 68; see also Maga 1982: 435; Marrus 2002: 147). Other Western European states similarly reacted to the Anschluss by introducing restrictive visa policies and refusing them "to Germans and Austrians who they suspected of wanting to remain in the country," providing asylum to only a small minority of wealthy refugees (Caestecker and Moore 2010: 249–50).

British policy had also changed little from the 1920s. On February 21, 1933, when Joshua Wedgwood had asked Home Secretary John Gilmour if there would be "some relaxation of the Aliens Act to afford refuge to the Marxists from Germany," the secretary had replied that the "general principle on which the Aliens Order is administered is that aliens are only allowed to come in for residence if their settlement here is consonant with the interests of this country."[81]

The British government did grant German Jews two accommodations. The first was that, in lieu of supporting themselves, Jews on temporary visas could draw on assistance from the broader Jewish community (Sherman 1973; London 2000). The second was to modify Palestine's immigration procedures to allow for increased emigration there: "the Colonial Office estimated that, in 1933–6 alone, 32,754 German Jews had been admitted to Palestine" (London 2000: 42). By 1938, however, both of these accommodations had broken down. Following the Anschluss, Jewish organizations contacted the Home Office to intimate that "in view of the new situation in Austria they could not continue" providing charitable aid to the Jewish refugees (Romain 1999: 90). Adding to the problem, following the 1936 Arab Revolt, the British

---

[81] *Hansard Parliamentary Debates*, Fifth Series, vol. 274 (February 21, 1933), c. 1598.

government had decided to limit immigration to Palestine to 12,000 immigrants per year (Halamish 2010: 124).[82]

Thus, when Roosevelt called for a conference to be held in Evian, France, in July, to address the refugee problem, neither the French nor British governments were prepared to alter their own policies. The French government made it clear that it "could accept no further Austrian immigration, 'no matter how minimal it might be'" and that refugees without visas for other countries "were to be '*refouler* without mercy'" (Caron 2010: 67).

The British thought that the conference was primarily a way for the President to assuage his domestic constituencies (Feingold 1970: 29). But the conference, as R. M. Makins, the then-assistant adviser for League of Nations affairs at the Foreign Office, noted, could do a lot, even if the only result was the American government's previously announced combination of the German and Austrian quotas and reserving three-quarters of those places for refugees. The Foreign Office also hoped increased support for emigration might reduce pressure from "world Jewry" on Britain's Palestine policy.[83] However, the Treasury argued that financial assistance to refugees "was almost out of the question" because of the precedent it would create, and the Colonial Office noted that the colonies "were not in a position to make a serious contribution to the problem" (Sherman 1973: 103).

Most other governments were supportive of the conference. Poland's and Romania's applications to attend were rejected because they "volunteered to attend as 'refugee producer' countries and indicated a desire to assist the departure of their own Jewish minorities" (Skran 1995: 209).

The unwillingness of most states to support a major policy change meant that whereas the conference's goals were laudable, it was under distinct handicaps even before it began. Even in the conference invitations, the American government had noted that "any financing of the emergency emigration referred to would be undertaken by private organizations" and that no states would be obligated to provide support. Furthermore, "no country would be expected or asked to receive a greater number of immigrants than is permitted by its existing legislation."[84] The first point reflected the abiding norm of the time that all support for

---

[82] In May 1939, the McDonald White Paper established a quota of 75,000 immigrants to Palestine for the next five years, which included space for 25,000 refugees. See the *British White Paper of 1939*, http://avalon.law.yale.edu/20th_century/brwh1939.asp.

[83] Memorandum by R. M. Makins, "International Assistance to Refugees," May 23, 1938, PRO FO 371/21749 C5319/2289/18; see also Sherman 1973: 100–02.

[84] Department of State Press Release No. 142, March 24, 1938, NARA RG 59 840.48 Refugees/61.

refugees still needed to come from voluntary organizations. The second point existed to ensure public support within the United States that the quota laws would not be altered. The administration:

perceived too many drawbacks to initiatives to bring much larger numbers of Jews to the United States. Conflicting American priorities and political constraints, as well as diabolical Nazi exploitation of anti-Semitic sentiment abroad, prevented Washington from going beyond what the quota system already allowed. (Breitman and Kraut 1987: 56; see also Stewart 1982: 274–76)

Interestingly, the proposed program for the Evian Conference reflected an understanding of the basic norms of the regime similar to that of the European countries. There needed to be international legal protections for refugees and an IO mechanism to facilitate cooperation in protecting and handling the refugee population. Assistance, however, would remain within the private sphere. More problematically, the United States shared with France and Britain a view that any international effort to help the German refugees should not alter domestic policies.

Advocates such as Myron Taylor,[85] who served as the U.S. representative and the conference's president, felt that a more expansive approach was necessary. Taylor argued that the League's approach had failed and that the LNHCR as then-structured was simply too limited.[86] A new international organization, he suggested, "should not be restricted in its efforts to the narrower mandate of the proposed combined office of the High Commission. Instead, such an Inter-Governmental Commission . . . should be free to attack the problem on broad lines."[87]

But this path was rejected at the conference. Delegates justified their own policies and congratulated themselves on how much had already been done, while making sure that existing immigration policies were not discussed and little pressure was applied. As one Jewish participant noted, "the little that was achieved bore no relationship to the hopes that were aroused" (Marrus 2002: 171).

George Warren, who served as Taylor's advisor, similarly noted that Roosevelt "felt he had to do something to react to the Anschluss in Austria. He didn't know what else to do," but the President was

[85] Taylor had served as the chairman of the board of the U.S. Steel Corporation. Although he knew nothing about refugees, he was an effective participant at the Conference. McDonald was appointed as his deputy.

[86] Telegram from Taylor to the Secretary of State, July 7, 1938, NARA RG 59 840.48 Refugees/468, Sec 3.

[87] Ibid. Sec 4. See also PRO CAB 23–94 Cabinet 33(38). Meeting held on Wednesday, July 20, 1938, 6–7.

"terribly embarrassed because, having called the conference, he couldn't do anything about taking refugees into the United States himself."[88]

The major outcome of the conference was the creation of a new IO outside of the League,[89] the Inter-Governmental Committee on Refugees (IGCR), with George Rublee as its head. However, like the League organizations, the IGCR had only a limited mandate. Its primary role was to negotiate with the German government to allow refugees to take property with them when departing, something the League could not do (Marrus 2002), whereas the League itself would focus on refugees who had already fled Germany.[90]

There was some hope that the Nazi government would cooperate. The American ambassador to Germany noted that "in my conversations, the Germans have shown deep interest in the work of the Evian Committee . . . this decision would be to their own interest."[91] The British similarly concluded that the IGCR's main aim would be "to replace the disorderly and disorganized exodus of destitute refugees by a system of planned migration."[92] The key issue was that the refugees needed to be able to leave with their property. As Roosevelt noted to British Prime Minister Neville Chamberlain:

The German Government, in forcing these persons to leave its territory without funds and without property, cannot be unmindful of the fact that it is thereby imposing great burdens on her friendly neighbors and on other nations throughout the world who, for humanitarian considerations, are doing what they can to alleviate the lot of these people.[93]

Chamberlain concurred, replying that "it is our duty not only to do what we can to alleviate the lot of the refugees but still more to endeavour to bring about a realisation of the extent of the damage

---

[88] Richard McKinzie, "Oral History Interview with George L. Warren," November 10, 1972, Truman Library. Online: www.trumanlibrary.org/oralhist/warrengl.htm.

[89] A British proposal that it serve only in an advisory capacity to the League was rejected by the United States. See the Chargé in the United Kingdom (Johnson) to the Secretary of State, August 12, 1938, *FRUS* 1938, vol. I, 764.

[90] The Chargé in the United Kingdom (Johnson) to the Secretary of State, August 23, 1938, *FRUS* 1938, vol. I (General), 769–770; The Secretary of State to the Chargé in the United Kingdom (Johnson), August 24, 1938, *FRUS* 1938, vol. I, 771.

[91] Ambassador in Germany (Wilson) to the Secretary of State, July 10, 1938, *FRUS* 1938, vol. I, 754.

[92] "British Policy Regarding the Problem of Refugees: Draft Memorandum to the Prime Minister," November 9, 1938, in NBKR 4–574 (Refugees – Nansen Office), 3.

[93] Personal message from the President to the Prime Minister, enclosed in the Acting Secretary of State to the Ambassador in the United Kingdom (Kennedy) October 5, 1938, *FRUS* 1938, vol. I, 792.

caused to friendly international relations by the harsh treatment of German emigrants."[94] The American government saw international cooperation as the key way to solve the problem and assumed the Germans felt the same.[95] Certainly, some German officials confirmed such views – Foreign Minister Joachim von Ribbentrop noted that "from Germany's point of view there were advantages in the expedition of emigration."[96]

Unfortunately, negotiations proved fruitless. The one proposal attempted by Hjalmar Schacht, head of the Reichsbank, suggested that Germany would support the emigration of 150,000 Jews over three years financed by a quarter of Jewish property in Germany (valued at 1.5 billion reichsmarks) being placed in trust against an additional 1.5 billion raised by "international Jewry."[97] But the plan was categorically opposed by Jewish leaders in Paris, fearful that it would "lend an air of credulity to the idea there is such a thing as world Jewry" and by the State Department, which saw the plan "as asking the world to pay a ransom for the release of hostages in Germany."[98] Further negotiations stalled after Schacht's removal (Feingold 1970).[99] Rublee in turn resigned in April and was replaced by Emerson, who henceforth headed both the IGCR and served as League high commissioner.

The American position had changed dramatically in 1938. Roosevelt and the State Department became strongly supportive of a multilateral solution through the IGCR. But their policy actions remained limited. Domestically, the government allowed the combined German and Austrian quotas to be

---

[94] The British Prime Minister (Chamberlain) to President Roosevelt, enclosed in the British Ambassador (Lindsay) to the Secretary of State, October 7, 1938, *FRUS* 1938, vol. I, 794.

[95] The Ambassador in Germany (Wilson) to the Secretary of State, November 11, 1938, *FRUS* 1938, vol. I, 819.

[96] The Ambassador in Germany (Wilson) to the Secretary of State, November 15, 1938, *FRUS* 1938, vol. I, 824. In December, Gilbert, the American Chargé in Berlin, reported that in a private meeting Hermann Goering had disclosed "that Hitler had ... admitted that what had begun as a party policy had now developed into a 'problem' for Germany both internally and externally ... it was of course 'absurd' to expect these emigrants from Germany to leave completely lacking in funds." The Americans interpreted this as a further sign that opinion within the Reich government on the issue was divided. The Chargé in Germany (Gilbert) to the Secretary of State, December 9, 1938, *FRUS* 1938, vol. I, 864; see Feingold 1970: 46.

[97] The Chargé in the United Kingdom (Johnson) to the Secretary of State, December 15, 1938, *FRUS* 1938, vol. I, 873–74.

[98] The Chargé in the United Kingdom (Johnson) to the Secretary of State, December 18, 1938, *FRUS* 1938, vol. I, 876; the Secretary of State to the Chargé in the United Kingdom (Johnson), December 19, 1938, *FRUS* 1938, vol. I, 876.

[99] The Chargé in Germany (Gilbert) to the Secretary of State, January 20, 1939, *FRUS* 1939, vol. II (Cooperation with the Inter-Governmental Committee on Refugees), 71.

used,[100] but it made no effort to modify the existing quota legislation. Internationally, as Roosevelt argued to Taylor, they were fearful that any actions might increase refugee flows from other countries.[101] Furthermore, though, the United States remained bound by the lack of opportunities for resettlement to third countries – although options were discussed, such as the Dominican Republic and Angola, they proved chimerical.[102]

Neither the IGCR nor the American government were able to convince European states to accept more refugees – after Sudetenland was ceded to Germany, the French government offered the population of its erstwhile ally only 100 visas (Caron 2010: 68). George Warren, in a 1972 interview, noted the constraints that the IGCR faced:

> there were reasons for that and it wasn't a complete failure. It was toward the end of the depression. All the Latin-American countries, which might have been reception countries of resource, were having trouble by movements from the rural areas into cities – and serious unemployment. Our own Congress was very hostile to the idea of admitting any refugees. We tried to get the United Kingdom to provide some place of resettlement on the land. Everybody at that time thought that the only thing to do was to colonize them in agriculture.[103]

As Roosevelt wrote to Taylor, "this government's interest in efforts to bring about a solution of the problem is strong ... it must reluctantly be admitted that this Government's efforts to stimulate concrete action by other governments to meet the problem have been met at best by a luke-warm attitude."[104] Even once Roosevelt was committed to helping the German Jews, his unwillingness to challenge Congress and his inability to convince other governments to alter their domestic policies meant that his efforts were stillborn.

Conclusion

At the Evian Conference, states sought to create an IO that could assist the Jewish refugees. But its outcome – the IGCR – had too limited a mandate

---

[100] By November, the secretary of state could note that "the United States is now admitting from Germany approximately 27,000 persons per annum, without regard to race or religious belief, the maximum number permitted by law." The Secretary of State to the Minister in Honduras (Erwin), November 19, 1938, *FRUS* 1938, vol. I, 835.

[101] Message enclosed in the Secretary of State to the Ambassador in the United Kingdom (Kennedy), January 14, 1939, *FRUS* 1939, vol. II, 66.

[102] See Memorandum by Mr. Theodore C. Achilles, of the Division of European Affairs, for President Roosevelt, April 28, 1939, *FRUS* 1939, vol. II, 105–07.

[103] Richard McKinzie, "Oral History Interview with George L. Warren," November 10, 1972, Truman Library. Online: www.trumanlibrary.org/oralhist/warrengl.htm

[104] President Roosevelt to the Chairman of the American Delegation (Taylor), June 8, 1939, *FRUS* 1939, vol. II, 119–20.

to effectively help those refugees, focused as it was on negotiations with the German government. As the Second World War began, neither it, nor the LNHCR, played an effective role in protecting the refugees who sought to flee Europe. It was not until 1945 that states would again focus their activities on creating a multilateral refugee regime.

Even so, over the interwar period, formal multilateralism had become an entrenched norm of cooperation toward refugee protection. Although states would continue to create "temporary" organizations and seek to limit who qualified as refugees, they had accepted that refugees needed a collective solution. Similarly, the legal understandings created in this period remain important. The Nansen Passports, created as a way of providing basic protections to Russian refugees, grew into a broader Arrangement system covering other refugee groups. Although efforts to evolve the Arrangement system into a formal, binding international convention in 1933 failed, the legal understandings that existed within that convention created important precedents for new forms of legal protection following the Second World War, as documented in the next chapter.

But the interwar period also shows that strong support for multilateral organizations alone could not adequately protect refugees. These efforts – within the League and with the IGCR – failed because no states sought to alter their own domestic restrictionist legislation. Governments accepted that refugees needed protection; they did not yet accept that this responsibility meant they needed to alter their own domestic practices.

6   American leadership and the emergence of the postwar regime

The collapse of international cooperation following the Evian Conference of 1938 reverberated throughout the Second World War. Neutral states, including Portugal, Spain, Sweden, and Switzerland, accepted only a small number of refugees (Marrus 2002: 240–82). The Allies undertook minimal efforts, including the Bermuda Conference of 1943, but these were sops to public pressure, producing no concrete results. Most refugees were trapped in Nazi-occupied Europe. The public revelation of the Holocaust galvanized governments to "put human considerations above political ones" (Holborn 1956: 32, 365; see also Stoessinger 1956: 201–02). States accepted that the previous refugee regime had failed due to the lack of institutional support and domestic immigration policy change.

After the war, states faced a massive refugee and displaced person (DP) problem.[1] To provide relief, the wartime allies revived multilateral cooperation to provide assistance and repatriation efforts. They created a new international organization (IO), the United Nations Relief and Rehabilitation Agency (UNRRA).[2] The Inter-Governmental Committee on Refugees (IGCR), moribund during the war, received a new lease on life as a protection agency for those who could not be returned.

The question of refoulement became a source of contention among the Allies. At the Yalta Conference in 1945, they agreed to repatriate each other's citizens, by force if necessary. This commitment triggered an important normative shift with respect to nonrefoulement. Whereas a legal norm had been established in the 1933 Refugee Convention

---

[1] No legal definition existed of who constituted a DP, with Holian (2011: 3) suggesting it referred to "civilians found outside their countries of origin at the end of hostilities," while Salomon notes that a "DP may be defined as a person displaced by war but wishing to return to his home once the fighting is over. A refugee, on the other hand, may be defined as a person who has fled his home or native country and who does not wish to return" (1991: 39). Officials at the time used the terms interchangeably.

[2] Created in 1943, its name reflected the Allied "united nations" rather than the organization.

prohibiting nonrefoulement, it was widely ignored. In the year following Yalta, by contrast, the American government became convinced that refoulement constituted a violation of humanitarian principles. It sought to entrench this view as a new international norm. The UNRRA, tasked with repatriation, was no longer supported. The Americans instead supported a new IO, the International Refugee Organization (IRO). Although the Americans made substantial efforts to include the Soviet Union in this IO, they refused to compromise on the fundamental issue of forced repatriation. Led by the Americans, other states also recognized a norm of nonrefoulement and a broader humanitarian duty to assist refugees.

Within the American government, a critical role was played by President Harry S. Truman and members of the executive branch. Truman's concerns blended humanitarian and practical interests: he not only accepted that the United States had a moral commitment to refugees, he also felt that a long-term solution was necessary to prevent the large numbers of refugees from destabilizing Europe. Importantly, he realized that his efforts needed to play out within a two-level game. No solution was possible without the United States accepting sizable numbers of refugees. Implementing this solution required that Truman both overcome Congressional opposition and reframe how refugees were perceived domestically.

This chapter focuses on why a normative shift occurred at the domestic level within the United States in the postwar period and how this shift resulted in the American government providing leadership to entrench these understandings as norms at the international level. Its leadership resulted in the emergence of a strong regime. This outcome was not obvious: the lack of commitment by states to protecting refugees prior to and during the Second World War suggests much weaker alternatives were realistic possibilities. The evolution of a strong postwar regime from the remains of the weak interwar regime signals the key roles played by norm entrepreneurs who accepted that change was necessary.

The Second World War interregnum

The start of the Second World War heralded the collapse of international cooperation. In Britain, although the government provided support for refugee maintenance and re-emigration, it adopted stricter measures of entry (London 2000: 169–70). Britain assumed that the only refugees being released from Germany would be "persons whose entry into other countries was desired for reasons connected with the war."[3] This

---

[3] War Cabinet, Committee on the Refugee Problem, "Summary of Conclusions," September 25, 1939, PRO CAB 98/1.

assumption disregarded the fact that Nazi authorities did not prohibit Jewish emigration until the autumn of 1941 (London 2000: 175). A humanitarian-based admissions policy was set aside in favor of security: "the policy of not admitting refugees – alien or British – to the United Kingdom solely on humanitarian grounds was repeatedly affirmed at Cabinet level" (London 2000: 173).

The United States also increased restrictions. The State Department no longer accepted affidavits of financial support from relatives and instructed consular staff to withhold visas from applicants about whom they had any doubt (Peck 1980; Wyman 1985: 174; Zucker and Zucker 1987: 22). Consistent with previous practice, these actions were based on bureaucratic procedures rather than legislation. The State Department cited "the danger of subversion by immigrants, the 'fifth column' threat, as sufficient reason to reject a liberal refugee policy" (1987: 120).[4] Anti-Semitism, Breitman and Kraut argue, was no longer the main factor. Restrictions were instead driven by a "genuine concern that careless visa policy might endanger national security" even though fewer than one half of one percent of refugees were ever questioned, let alone charged with espionage or any other crime (Breitman and Kraut 1987: 123–24). Thus, George Warren, then serving with the State Department, notes:

Roosevelt's hands were completely tied by an overwhelming unwillingness in the Congress to admit refugees based partly on fear that the refugees would be fifth columnists. I don't think that fear was real, but there was no question about the attitude of Congress. Roosevelt's hands were tied. He did all he could in the situation.[5]

National security concerns also stymied efforts to rescue the Jews and other refugees in occupied Europe. By positioning rescue efforts within the more important rubric of winning the war, Hasian notes, "any massive rescue efforts seemed to be morally reprehensible, because they might prolong the war and create national divisions" (2003: 163). As Senator Scott Lucas argued: "Every day that you postpone bringing this war to a conclusion you take upon your hands the blood of American boys" (cited

---

[4] The president was swayed by these arguments, and public and Congressional sentiment continued to run in favor of restrictions (Dallek 1979: 444–45; Peck 1980: 368). Roosevelt argued that, although he was sympathetic to refugees, spying was a issue: "Now, of course, the refugee has got to be checked because, unfortunately, among the refugees there are some spies . . . not all of them are voluntary spies – it is a rather horrible story but in some of the other countries that refugees out of Germany have gone to, especially Jewish refugees, they have found a number of definitely proven spies" (June 5, 1940, Presidential Press Conference, cited in Breitman and Kraut 1987: 121–22).

[5] Richard McKinzie, "Oral History Interview with George L. Warren," November 10, 1972, Truman Library. Online: www.trumanlibrary.org/oralhist/warrengl.htm

in Breitman and Kraut 1987: 180). Such reasoning made sense if sensibly applied. However, as Breitman and Kraut argue, for both the American and British governments, it effectively became "an all-inclusive and elastic standard ... virtually any publicized assistance or attention to European Jews jeopardized some requisite of the war effort" (1987: 180). The effects of such arguments were to reinforce the status quo policies of limited immigration.

The Bermuda Conference and the re-emergence of the IGCR

Despite reluctance to take positive steps to help refugees, the British and American governments needed to respond to public opinion, which increasingly favored a more humanitarian approach. This was particularly pressing following the public declaration on December 17, 1942, by the Allied governments, that the Nazis were committing atrocities against the Jews.[6] This statement mobilized humanitarian domestic opinion in both countries and produced a new public consensus around the need to take action (Penkower 1988: 98; Karatani 2005: 527). The popular press also shifted their positions. A *New York Times* editorial argued that efforts needed to shift beyond "palliative [ones] which appear designed to assuage the conscience of the reluctant rescuers rather than to aid the victims" (cited in Lipstadt 1982: 66–67). This pressure led both governments to call a conference in Bermuda, to be held in April 1943 (Wasserstein 1979: 176–79).[7]

In Britain, this did not reflect a change in what remained a self-interested refugee policy. The British were unwilling to consider new immigration policies due to lack of transport and because the absorptive capacity of neutral countries in Europe was limited. They were also unwilling to open Palestine to immigration from "enemy" countries,

---

[6] The Allied Declaration affirmed the "solemn resolution" of those governments "to ensure that those responsible for these crimes [should] not escape retribution." Anthony Eden, Secretary of State for Foreign Affairs, in *Hansard Parliamentary Debates*, Fifth Series, vol. 385 (December 17, 1942), c. 2083.

[7] British Embassy to the Department of State "Aide Memoiré: Refugees from Nazi-Occupied Territory" January 20, 1943, *FRUS* 1943, vol. I "General," 134 (see also Penkower 1988: 98–101). The Foreign Office requested the conference because "public opinion has been rising to such a degree that the British Government can no longer remain dead to it." The Charge in the United Kingdom (Matthews) to the Secretary of State, February 20, 1943, *FRUS* 1943, vol. I 138. Hull later wrote to the American Ambassador in the United Kingdom, John Winant, that the State Department "has been under most severe pressure from persons both within and without the Government through a long succession of months." The Secretary of State to the Ambassador in the United Kingdom (Winant), December 27, 1943, *FRUS* 1943, vol. I, "Governmental Assistance to Persons Forced to Emigrate for Political or Racial Reasons," 398.

including refugees already in neutral countries.[8] The Americans acquiesced to a request to not raise the issue of Palestine in exchange for no discussion of the American quota laws. Instead, they planned to focus the conference on the role of the IGCR (Feingold 1970: 190–91; London 2000: 212).[9]

The British also feared a positive result from the conference would be detrimental and that, in time, the idea of rescue would be "shown up as illusionary."[10] Partially, it was believed that it would raise false hopes among refugee advocates. Also, amazingly, they feared that it might make the refugee problem worse if Germany or its satellites changed "over from the policy of extermination to one of extrusion, and aim as they did before the war at embarrassing other countries by flooding them with alien immigrants."[11] Therefore, focused on preventing more refugee flows, the government was unwilling to consider options that might have mitigated the effects of the Holocaust.[12] The British suggested only that the United States accept more refugees or approach the Latin American countries.[13]

Publicly, at least, the conference positioned itself as having laudable goals when it opened on April 19, 1943, the eve of Passover and the start of the Warsaw ghetto uprising. The American Chairman, Dr. Harold Dodds, argued that Nazi ideology had resulted "in a calculated policy of oppression and extermination. . . This created the necessity for all possible assistance to such helpless peoples" (cited in Blumenthal 2003). However, given the limited agenda – and British and American unwillingness to negotiate with Germany and other enemy states – the conference accomplished little beyond authorizing the IGCR to negotiate with Allied and neutral countries (London 2000: 217).[14] This was a low-cost

---

[8] British Embassy to the Department of State "Aide Memoiré: Refugees from Nazi-Occupied Territory" January 20, 1943, *FRUS* 1943, vol. I, 134–38.

[9] Memorandum, Afternoon Conference, April 21, 1943, NARA RG 59 State Lot File No. 52 D 408 Records relating to the IGCR, Box 3 Bermuda Conference, Bermuda Conference Minutes, 1.

[10] Randall Minute, April 16, 1943, PRO FO 371/36658 (cited in Wasserstein 1979: 189).

[11] British Embassy to the Department of State "Aide Memoiré: Refugees from Nazi-Occupied Territory" January 20, 1943, *FRUS* 1943, vol. I, 134.

[12] For further details on this, see Aronson (2004).

[13] Ibid. 134–38. Herbert Emerson was a lone voice against this policy, arguing that the 1942 declaration "if not followed by such action as practicable to save persons is a mockery." U.S. Embassy London to State Department, December 28, 1942, NARA RG 59 840.48 Refugees/3557.

[14] Confidential Memorandum for the Chairman, Morning Conference, April 20, 1943, NARA RG 59 State Lot File No. 52 D 408 Records relating to the Inter-Governmental Committee on Refugees, Box 3; Bermuda Conference, Bermuda Conference Minutes, 1–6, Morning Session, April 22, 1943. Ibid. Richard Law from the Foreign Office would

option to assuage domestic Jewish opinion because the IGCR already existed.[15] Britain and the United States accepted joint responsibility for all operational expenses on a case-by-case basis (Vernant 1953: 28).[16] As a show of Allied unity, membership in the IGCR was extended to the Soviet Union (Wasserstein 1979: 217).[17]

With this new role, the IGCR budget and staff was enlarged while Sir Herbert Emerson continued as director. But it was still a "political organization without a political mandate," unable to provide relief and with no independent authority. Instead, it primarily served a coordinating function between the British and American governments (Wasserstein 1979: 218–19; Marrus 2002: 286). As Vernant notes, had the "IGCR been given more funds and more practical support, it is possible that it might have done more even while the war was being fought; as things were, it was an instrument of which the member governments made only limited use" (1953: 28). Its most important role was to deflect pressure from the American and British governments to do more to assist refugees trapped in Europe (Sjöberg 1991: 236).[18] Even Emerson noted that the IGCR could do little until after the war.[19]

His view was prophetic. In 1944, the IGCR's mandate was extended to "all persons, wherever they may be, who, as the result of events in Europe, have had to leave, or may have to leave, their countries of residence because of the danger to their lives or liberties on account of their race, religion, or political beliefs" (Biehle 1947: 144). This expansion made the

later note that the conference was a "façade for inaction. We said the results of the conference were confidential ... but in fact there were no results that I can recall" (cited in Dallek 1979: 446).

[15] Secretary of State to Beck, April 21, 1943, *FRUS* 1943, vol. I, 156–57. Assistant Secretary of State Breckinridge Long argued that the IGCR was a way to "go through the motions of doing something about rescue without actually doing anything" (cited in Feingold 1970: 201).

[16] Taylor, then the U.S. delegate to the IGCR, argued that both governments needed to be "prepared to lead the way for the other governments and to make definite commitments regarding ... cost." Hull to Roosevelt, May 7, 1943; Roosevelt to Hull, May 14, 1943; Hull, Morgenthau and Stimson to Roosevelt, May 25, 1944, NARA RG 59 General Records of the Department of State Lot File No. 52 D 408, Records relating to the Inter-Governmental Committee on Refugees Box 2, IGC Relations with War Refugee Board Folder.

[17] The Ambassador in the United Kingdom (Winant) to the Secretary of State, October 14, 1943, *FRUS* 1943, vol. I, 213.

[18] For the American government, this did little to address the concerns of critics within the administration. After Treasury Secretary Henry Morgenthau and Henry Dexter White, the assistant secretary, complained directly to Roosevelt about the State Department's ongoing intransigence, arguing that "this Government had played a role that is little short of sickening" (White, cited in Wyman 2002: 47), Roosevelt ordered the War Refugee Board to be created as a domestic complement to the IGCR (Hurwitz 1991).

[19] Emerson to Sean Lester, Acting Secretary-General of the League of Nations "The Refugee Problem after the War," July 29, 1942, LNA R5637/20A/41400/X.

IGCR the "default" refugee organization, protecting war refugees, the remaining League refugees, and, for the first time, refugees from the Spanish Civil War (Weis 1954: 210; Sjöberg 1991: 153). The IGCR also led negotiations in October 1946 to create a new Arrangement to provide travel documents for refugees under its mandate, which remained in place until the entry into force of the 1951 Refugee Convention (Vernant 1953: 29; Weis 1954: 207; Holborn 1975: 18). Yet the IGCR remained resource starved and incapable of providing substantial assistance or resettlement opportunities to refugees (Chamberlain 1947: 87; Proudfoot 1957: 295–96).

The Allies, UNRRA, and the forced repatriation of DPs

Although the Allied governments did little to help the Jews, they were conscious of a looming refugee crisis that would follow the war. By the middle of 1943, it was estimated that, in Europe, some 21 million people had been displaced by the fighting or forcibly removed. Eight million of these had been taken to Germany or Austria, and another 8 million were displaced within their own countries (Woodbridge 1950: 469). In total, at least 40 million people were displaced by the war in Europe (see Table 6.1),[20] whereas an additional 12 million Japanese and 50 million Chinese citizens were estimated to be displaced in their own countries (Cohen 2011: 14–15).

The Allies made the assumption that most DPs would want to return to their own homes. Such unorganized, large-scale, and mass movement "would interfere with the war effort, spread disease, and increase social and economic confusion" (Woodbridge 1950: 469). The response to those movements would require significant logistical support and a clearly coordinated effort by military authorities, national governments, and private agencies. In November 1943, UNRRA was created to manage this response.[21] The United States provided the bulk of contributions ($2.8 billion of the $3.6 billion spent during UNRRA's mandate) in exchange for significant control (Saloman 1991: 48).[22] But UNRRA initially had little focus on people with refugee status; instead, the

---

[20] Higher figures exist. Kulischer (1949: 305) suggests that 55 million Europeans were displaced, whereas Cronin (2003: 164 fn) suggests 65 million.

[21] Forty-four countries joined UNRRA and were included in its Council. The Council met only six times, and most policy decisions were taken by the Central Committee, composed of China, the United States, the United Kingdom, and the Soviet Union. France and Canada were added in 1945 (Saloman 1991: 48; see also Fox 1950).

[22] All three of the UNRRA's directors were Americans. Herbert Lehman, former governor of New York state, had been serving as director of Foreign Relief and Rehabilitation

Table 6.1 *Forced movements in Europe during the Second World War*

Country	Displaced Outside Their Country	Escaped from German/ Soviet Territory	Total Outside Their Country	Displaced Within Their Country	Total
Baltic States	509,200	36,450	545,650	21,900	567,550
Belgium	1,048,000	22,000	1,070,000	50,000	1,120,000
Britain	13,700	0	13,700	7,078,000	7,091,700
Czechoslovakia	154,000	9,000	163,000	322,000	485,000
Denmark	500	19,000	19,500	25,000	44,500
Finland	0	131,000	131,000	468,800	599,800
France	320,000	125,000	445,000	4,790,000	5,235,000
Germany	930,000	0	930,000	5,750,000	6,680,000
Greece	60,000	70,000	130,000	100,000	230,000
Italy	109,000	13,000	122,000	0	122,000
Luxembourg	72,000	500	72,500	0	72,500
Netherlands	160,000	35,000	195,000	200,000	395,000
Norway	8,000	90,000	98,000	521,000	619,000
Poland	2,212,000	188,000	2,400,000	2,108,000	4,508,000
Rumania	507,900	0	507,900	651,900	1,159,800
Soviet Union	350,400	0	350,400	10,400,000	10,750,400
Yugoslavia	199,000	22,000	221,000	573,800	794,800
Total From All Countries	**6,653,700**	**760,950**	**7,414,650**	**33,060,400**	**40,475,050**

Sources: Proudfoot 1957; Woodbridge 1950: II: 498, III: 423,

organization assumed that the IGCR would work to resettle refugees. Rather, UNRRA had two different roles: to provide assistance to the civilian populations of liberated territories and to work with "appropriate government and military authorities" to secure the repatriation of DPs to their former countries (Woodbridge 1950: 471–74).[23]

Displaced person status was limited. The UNRRA was required to screen out war criminals. It also had to distinguish between DPs and the *Volksdeutsche*, ethnic Germans who had fled in the wake of the German retreat along the Eastern Front and who were denied aid (Vernant 1953: 30–32; Stoessinger 1956: 50). These limitations were driven by the Soviet

Operations for the State Department. After his resignation, Fiorello H. LaGuardia, the former mayor of New York City, took over. He resigned in 1947 and was replaced in turn by Major General Lowell Ward.

[23] See also the Adviser, War Areas Economic Division (Gilpatric), and the Adviser on Refugees and Displaced Persons (Warren) to the Assistant Secretary of State (Acheson), April 17, 1945, *FRUS* 1945, vol. II "General: Political and Economic Matters," 1156–57.

Union, which, in U.S. Under-Secretary of State Dean Acheson's view, felt UNRRA "existed to give prizes for fighting Hitler." Not only did the Soviets expect a substantial share of UNRRA relief, but they saw assistance to the displaced as a secondary priority (Acheson 1969: 69, 78–79).

The largest question was whether DPs and prisoners of war (POWs) who did not want to return home should be forcibly repatriated. At the Yalta Conference, in February 1945, President Roosevelt, British Prime Minister Churchill, and Soviet Premier Josef Stalin had negotiated agreements for the return of all POWs and civilians who had been forcibly deported to Germany, which concluded that "all Soviet citizens ...[be] handed over to the Soviet...authorities."[24] The result was that in the next two years, 5 million Soviet citizens were returned to the Soviet Union, many against their will. This agreement passed over strong opposition within the American government. Both Secretary of War Henry L. Stimson – who argued "before we deliver any to the Soviets I think we should be sure that we are not delivering them to execution or punishment" (cited in Elliott 1982: 37) – and Attorney General Francis Biddle opposed the move. Biddle linked the question of forcible repatriation back to the issue of asylum, saying he:

gravely question[ed] the legal basis or authority for surrendering the objecting individuals to representatives of the Soviet Government... Even if these men should be technically traitors to their own government, I think the time-honoured rule of asylum should be applied... It has been so applied in many cases of men who were firmly regarded as traitors or otherwise political criminals in their own country. (cited in Elliott 1982: 37)

The State Department had similar reservations, arguing that the agreement violated the 1929 Convention relating to the Treatment of Prisoners of War.[25]

These concerns were ignored. Secretary of State Edward Stettinius replied that "the consensus here is that it would be unwise to include questions relative to the protection of the Geneva Conference ...we believe that there will be serious delays in the release of our prisoners of war unless we reach prompt agreement."[26] The American delegation also

---

[24] "Agreement Relating to Prisoners of War and Civilians Liberated by Forces Operating Under Soviet Command and Forces Operating Under United States of America Command," FRUS 1945, "Conferences at Malta and Yalta," 985.

[25] The Acting Secretary of State (Grew) to the Secretary of State, February 7, 1945, FRUS 1945, "Conferences at Malta and Yalta," 697.

[26] The Secretary of State to the Acting Secretary of State (Grew), February 9, 1945, FRUS, 1945 "Conferences at Malta and Yalta," 757. Cordell Hull had resigned as secretary of state due to health reasons. Joseph Grew, the under secretary, "knew that Stettinius was a diplomatic novice and felt compelled to advise him on the repatriation issue" (Elliott

faced an existing precedent created by the British in 1942, when they began to return all Soviets who fell into their hands.[27] This precedent was reaffirmed and made into cabinet policy in 1944 (Elliott 1973: 267).[28] As Fleet Admiral William Leahy[29] argued: "since the British War Office, with Foreign Office concurrence, has agreed that all captured Soviet citizens should be returned to Soviet authorities without exception, 'from the military point of view … it is not advisable for the United States Government to proceed otherwise.'"[30] The result, Elliott (1973: 267) argues, was that "the Yalta delegation was ready to sacrifice the right of political asylum in order to 'reach prompt agreement on this question.'" In the face of war and the need to repatriate American and British POWs, moral concerns over forced repatriation were dismissed.

The subsequent agreement negotiated between the Supreme Headquarters, Allied Expeditionary Force (SHAEF) and the Soviet military, although silent on forced repatriation, noted that measures be taken "to complete this repatriation in the shortest possible time,"[31] including the use of force if necessary. The Joint Chiefs of Staff confirmed this, noting that "Soviet displaced persons will be repatriated regardless of their individual wishes."[32] The repatriation effort proceeded in earnest once the agreement was approved on May 22, 1945, with more than 2 million DPs transferred by the end of September (Proudfoot 1957: 210–11).

Opinion shifted rapidly within the U.S. military. As early as May, the decision was made to not return any Balts, Poles, or Ruthenians to the Soviet Union because the Americans had not recognized any territory changes as a result of the war. In addition, the Americans decided not to

---

1973: 267). Coupled with Stettinius's lack of experience was that Roosevelt tended "to heed more the advice of his military advisers than that of his political advisers" at the conference who were less aware of international law (Elliott 1973: 266).

[27] As the Foreign Office noted in June 1944: "In due course all those with whom the Soviet authorities desire to deal must be handed over to them, and we are not concerned with the fact that they may be shot or otherwise more harshly dealt with than they might be under English law" (cited in Bethell 1974: 7).

[28] United States Political Adviser on the Staff of the Supreme Allied Commander, Mediterranean Theatre (Kirk) to the Secretary of State, September 16, 1944, FRUS 1944, vol. IV, "Europe," 1250.

[29] Leahy was the chief of staff to the commander in chief of the Army and Navy, the precursor role to the chairman of the Joint Chiefs of Staff.

[30] Telegram, Admiral Leahy to the Secretary of State, November 2, 1944, FRUS 1944, vol. IV, 1262 fn 52.

[31] "Plan" Signed by K. D. Golubev on behalf of the Red Army and R. W. Barker on behalf of the U.S. Army (cited in Proudfoot 1957: 210).

[32] SHAEF Administrative Memorandum Number 39 (Revised April 16, 1945) Displaced Persons and Refugees in Germany, Paragraph 23 (c) (cited in Proudfoot 1957: 461 (Appendix B)).

transfer other Eastern Europeans into the Russian occupation zone.[33] Beyond this, the military on the ground interpreted the orders as broadly as possible. If a DP claimed he or she was not a Soviet citizen, he or she was not returned unless Soviet reparation officers could prove the DP's citizenship (Proudfoot 1957: 215–17). This was a reaction both to the extreme actions taken by Soviet repatriation officers, including kidnapping DPs in broad daylight (Marrus 2002: 317), and to the reactions of DPs to repatriation – suicides and attacks on Allied soldiers to prevent return were common (Elliott 1982: 87–92).

Pressure to change the policy of refoulement began to work its way through the American military and civilian bureaucracies. These efforts were helped by the fact that the massive repatriation effort had significantly lessened the economic burden of the DPs on the Allies and that most British and American POWs had now been returned (Marrus 2002: 317). Even so, the shift reflected a significant humanitarian change at the lower levels of government, one that was rapidly transmitted upward. By September 1945, General Eisenhower reversed his prior position, and, "reacting to a groundswell of opposition within the military, as well as to the dictates of his own conscience, requested the State Department to re-examine the whole question" (Elliott 1973: 272). In December, the military formally announced that transfers would be limited to Soviet soldiers and known collaborators.[34]

Within the State Department, Dean Acheson also questioned the policy because of evidence that few of the DPs were returning to their homes in the Soviet Union.[35] Acheson raised his concerns both with Secretary James F. Byrnes[36] and with President Truman, who supported shifting the policy (Elliott 1982: 109–12).[37] By 1947, in the clearest statement on

---

[33] Memorandum by the Chairman of the State-War-Navy Coordinating Committee (Dunn) to the Secretary of State, March 9, 1945, *FRUS* 1945, vol. V "Europe," 1075–77; the Ambassador in France (Caffery) to the Secretary of State, May 9, 1945, *FRUS* 1945, vol. II, 1156–57.

[34] Those Soviet citizens who voluntarily rendered aid and comfort to the enemy "should be repatriated without regard to their wishes and by force if necessary." Byrnes to Kirk, Political Adviser to the Supreme Allied Commander, Mediterranean Theatre, March 14, 1946, *FRUS* 1946, vol. V "The British Commonwealth, Western, and Central Europe," 152 (Elliott 1973: 273).

[35] The U.S. ambassador to the Soviet Union, Averill Harriman, had raised concerns that those being repatriated were being executed or sent into slave labor. He knew of only a single liberated Soviet citizen who had been repatriated and actually returned to his home. Harriman to the Secretary of State, June 11, 1945, *FRUS* 1945, "Europe" vol. II, 1097–98.

[36] Byrnes, a former senator and Supreme Court justice, succeeded Stettinius after a year in office. Byrnes was in turn replaced by George Marshall, who had served as general of the Army, in 1947.

[37] Byrnes to the United States Political Adviser for Germany, July 25, 1946. *FRUS* 1946, vol. V, 174–5

the issue, Secretary of State George Marshall noted that "any coercion of displaced persons under our jurisdiction would not be tolerated" (Marshall 1947). A provision on "withholding deportation" of any alien who would be subjected to "physical persecution" was introduced into U.S. domestic immigration law in the Subversive Activities Control Act of 1950. This predated the Refugee Convention (Fitzpatrick 1997: 5).

The American shift on the issue caught others flatfooted. The British government urged the Americans to reconsider this new interpretation.[38] Not only did they suggest that these Soviets were traitors and not worthy of protection, but they also argued that breaking the Yalta Agreement would set "an appalling precedent. It would also encourage the Soviet government to breach other clauses of the Yalta Agreement" (Bethell 1974: 186; see also de Zayas 2006: 86). Yet, the British military had held similar concerns to the Americans. Field Marshal Sir Harold Alexander, the supreme Allied Commander in Italy, stated in June 1945 that "so far I have refused to use force to repatriate Soviet citizens, although I am not strictly entitled to adopt this attitude" (cited in Bethell 1974: 178). It was only in June 1946 that the British policy formally shifted, when the cabinet approved a request from Foreign Secretary Ernest Bevin to adopt an exemption to refoulement for Polish soldiers who had fought for the Allies (Elliott 1982: 115; Kushner and Knox 1999: 222–23).[39]

The norm of nonrefoulement had growing resonance beyond the Allies. On February 20, 1946, Bethell (1974: 192) recounts, Pope Pius XII protested against "the repatriation of men against their will and the refusal of the right of asylum." The UNRRA also shifted its position in August 1945, with the Washington office suggesting its assistance efforts should include "political dissidents as well as post-war political refugees" (Stevens 2004: 121).[40] Not surprisingly, this UNRRA policy change was challenged by the Soviet Union, leading to a requirement that applicants for refugee status "establish 'concrete evidence' of persecution before being admitted to the care of UNRRA" (Hathaway 1984: 373–74). Finally, in 1946, the United Nations (UN) General Assembly

---

[38] "We are both mystified and alarmed by this statement which is of course quite contradictory to His Majesty's Government's policy" (cited in Bethell 1974: 182).

[39] Foreign Office Minute "Discussion with Soviet Delegates," August 4, 1945, PRO FO 51098/WR2336/1/48 (Elliott 1982: 114–16; Kushner and Knox 1999: 222–23).

[40] This caused a debate within the organization. The London office argued that it meant: "any inhabitant of a liberated area who wishes to leave his country for economic reasons qualifies for UNRRA care on what appears to us the purely fortuitous circumstance of internal displacement [if it occurred during the war]. This leaves the door wide open to political refugees of every kind." UNRRA Outgoing Cable No. 1675, February 9, 1946 (cited in Hathaway 1984: 373; see also Vernant 1953: 31).

recognized the "fundamental principle that no refugees with valid objections to returning to their countries of origin should be compelled to do so" (Goodwin-Gill and McAdam 2007: 424).[41]

Perhaps the clearest evidence of the lasting strength of this normative shift comes from the peace settlement negotiations around the Korean War. By June 1951, the negotiations had deadlocked over the issue of POW repatriation. Truman made a "very clear, unequivocal decision that he expressed to everybody there, that we were going to stand for voluntary repatriation, because that was the moral and the right thing to do."[42] Although this decision supported the broader politics of the Cold War – as Carruthers (2005: 917) notes, the United States hoped that the refusal of the POWs to return "would enunciate a clear message of free world superiority" – it was a decision taken at high cost. As Beisner (2006: 438) argues, "Truman's decision remains controversial, for as U.S. negotiators fenced with the Chinese, U.S. troops fought up and down Porkchop Hill and Heartbreak Ridge, suffering nearly half of their casualties." These debates shaped not only Truman and Acheson's views on forced repatriation, but also how they viewed refugees more generally.

The displaced persons question

The larger question that underlay the forced repatriation debate was how the Allies should respond to DPs and refugees as a group. SHAEF had operational responsibility for the DPs until it ceased functioning in July 1945. At that point, responsibility for their care was transferred to each of the states in control of the occupation zones, as agreed to at Yalta, and to UNRRA. By 1946, with neither Britain nor the United States sanctioning forced repatriation, UNRRA's policy allowed DPs and refugees to decide whether they wished to return to their home countries. The Soviets opposed this, arguing that halting repatriation would allow anticommunist groups a chance to coalesce and that assistance would discourage them from returning (Loescher and Scanlan 1986: 15; Kochavi 2001: 14–19).

These normative shifts and the division between the United States and Britain on the one hand and the Soviet Union on the other meant that the UNRRA had an untenable mandate. It was not designed for large numbers of refugees, nor could it effectively deal with divisions between the Allies. As Dean Acheson noted in his memoirs:

---

[41] UN General Assembly Resolution 8(I), February 12, 1946.

[42] Richard McKinzie, "Oral History Interview with U. Alexis Johnson," June 19, 1975, Truman Library. Online: www.trumanlibrary.org/oralhist/johnsona.htm#;70, 79. Johnson was the deputy assistant secretary of state for far Eastern affairs at the time.

to both Congress and the [Truman] Administration, internationally administered relief had been a failure. The staff obtainable had been weak and the leadership weaker... Due to rules built into the charter of UNRRA ... the great bulk of relief, largely supplied or paid for by the United States, went to Eastern Europe and was used by governments bitterly hostile to us to entrench themselves, contrary to agreements made at Yalta. (Acheson 1969: 201).

President Truman similarly argued that the UNRRA's role had been "negligibly small in Western Europe" and that "its purpose was not clearly defined" (Truman 1955: 466).

At the same time, most DPs and refugees remained in camps, primarily under American military control. Conditions varied dramatically.[43] Responding to concerns raised by Jewish leaders, Truman sent Earl G. Harrison on a mission to Europe to develop plans to "meet the needs of those who, for justifiable reasons, could not return to their countries of former residence" (Truman 1955: 311).[44] Harrison's report showed that the situation was far worse than Truman thought. Three months after the war had ended in Europe:

many Jewish displaced persons and other possibly non-repatriables are living under guard behind barbed-wire fences, in camps of several descriptions, (built by the Germans for slave-labourers and Jews) including some of the most notorious of the concentration camps, amidst crowded, frequently unsanitary and generally grim conditions, in complete idleness, with no opportunity, except surreptitiously, to communicate with the outside world.[45]

Clearly, they could not be kept in such conditions.

The Harrison report had a significant impact on key American decision makers. General Eisenhower argued that many of the issues Harrison raised had been changed and that many of the other problems were due

---

[43] Some units treated DPs in a humane fashion whereas others, notably the Third Army under General Patton, generally treated them as prisoners. In his diary, Patton noted that others "believe that the Displaced Person is a human being, which he is not, and this applies particularly to the Jews who are lower than animals" (George S. Patton, cited in Dinnerstein 1982: 16–17).

[44] Memo from Grew to Truman "Earl G. Harrison's mission to Europe on refugee matters," June 21, 1945, NARA RG59 Lot file No. 52 D408 Records relating to the Inter-Governmental Committee on Refugees, Box 1- Miscellaneous Subject File, 1942–46 Folder labeled IGC Earl G. Harrison. Harrison had formerly been the U.S. Commissioner of Immigration and was the American representative on the IGCR (Dinnerstein 1982: 34–35).

[45] Most damningly, Harrison wrote "we appear to be treating the Jews as the Nazis treated them except we do not exterminate them... One is led to wonder whether the German people, seeing this, are not supposing we are following or at least condoning Nazi policy." Report of Earl G. Harrison, August 1945, NARA RG 59 Lot file No. 52 D408 Records relating to the Inter-Governmental Committee on Refugees, Box 1- Miscellaneous Subject File, 1942–46 Folder labeled IGC Earl G. Harrison.

to the large-scale mass repatriation efforts.[46] Even so, Eisenhower took additional steps to improve the lot of the DPs, including adding an adviser for Jewish Affairs. He created separate assembly areas for Jews, as well as for all Poles and Balts, who were also not to be returned. Finally, he ensured rigorous enforcement of the existing rules. Increasingly, these populations were treated as distinct from the broader DP population, thereby recognizing that they were akin to refugees.

The Harrison report is a powerful example of the mechanism of persuasion: when informed of the conditions, Truman's views rapidly changed. In his memoirs, Truman (1955: 138) recounted that he found the report "a moving document. The misery it depicted could not be allowed to continue." Truman, however, also felt a deeper resonance with the experience of the Jewish refugees based on his own family's experience during the American Civil War. As he noted in a 1964 television interview,

I had some notion of what these people were going through who had to be moved from one place to another in order to have a home and I was very anxious that they would not and should have to go through the same sort of difficulties that the families in the War Between the States had to go through... Hitler had been murdering Jews right and left... It was a horrible thing. I saw it and I dream about it even to this day. On that account, the Jews needed some place where they could go.[47]

As Truman sought an international solution to the problem, he ignored the State Department bureaucracy. As he argued in his memoirs:

it seemed to me that they didn't care enough about what happened to the thousands of displaced persons who were involved. It was my feeling that it would be possible for us to watch out for the long-range interests of our country while at the same time helping these unfortunate victims of persecution to find a home. (Truman 1955: 69; see also Acheson 1969: 169–70)

Instead, Truman focused on following Harrison's recommendations.

For the Jewish refugees, Truman considered Palestine to be the ideal solution.[48] The President argued to British Prime Minister Clement Atlee that the Jewish DPs should be allowed to migrate to Palestine, referencing American public opinion in favor of such a move and suggesting that this

---

[46] Letter from General Eisenhower, Commanding General, U.S. Forces, European Theater to President Truman, October 8, 1945, NARA RG 59 Lot file No. 52 D408 Records relating to the Inter-Governmental Committee on Refugees, Box 1- Miscellaneous Subject File, 1942–46 Folder labeled Harrison Report.

[47] "At War with the Experts," Episode 6, *Decision: The Conflicts of Harry S. Truman*, November 1964. Online: www.c-spanvideo.org/program/197078-1.

[48] "Report of Earl G. Harrison," NARA RG 59 Lot file No. 52 D408 Records relating to the Inter-Governmental Committee on Refugees, Box 1- Miscellaneous Subject File, 1942–46 Folder labeled Harrison Report.

could provide for a more stable Europe. However, this was not purely a strategic argument; Truman also provided a moral dimension, suggesting that "no claim is more meritorious than that of the groups who for so many years have known persecution and enslavement."[49] Even so, the British remained unconvinced, fearful of Arab reaction, and suggested that the matter be referred to the UN.[50]

Truman acquiesced to working with the British to find alternative resettlement opportunities (Dinnerstein 1982: 73–74). Truman noted that "it was my attitude that America could not stand by while the victims of Hitler's racial madness were denied the opportunities to build new lives. Neither, however, did I want to see a political structure imposed on the Near East that would result in conflict" (Truman 1955: II 140). His instincts on this point were correct: once the state of Israel was founded in 1948, much of the DP population in Europe immigrated there (Cohen 1990: xi).

In the short term, the DP situation remained critical, especially as emigration from the Eastern bloc began to increase (Loescher and Scanlan 1986: 7). If the DPs could not be returned, another solution was to cut off aid and close the camps. Field Marshal Bernard L. Montgomery, commander in chief of the British Zone in Germany, suggested that the British adopt a policy that any DPs who had not returned by April 1, 1945, be "taken out of his camp and set to work as a civilian in Germany living on German rations and under conditions parallel to Germans" (Kochavi 2001: 20). General Joseph T. McNarney, in command of the American zone, similarly argued in favor of discontinuing aid and assistance to the DPs, although this did not include the persecuted (Kochavi 2001: 21). His fears, reflected both by the War Department and by Byrnes, was that the U.S. government would be placed in the position of indefinitely financing the camps.[51] The UNRRA opposed the move, with Herbert Lehman arguing to Byrnes that such unilateral action would undermine the organization with its member states and damage separate efforts within the UN.[52]

The policy shift was blocked on normative grounds. In Britain, the Foreign Office argued that such actions would effectively become a form

---

[49] Truman to Attlee, August 31, 1945, *FRUS* 1945, vol. VIII "The Near East and Africa," 737–38.

[50] Attlee to Truman, September 16, 1945, *FRUS* 1945, vol. VIII, 740–41.

[51] Memorandum by the Secretary of State to President Truman, April 12, 1946, *FRUS* 1946, vol. V, 153 (Kochavi 2001: 23–24).

[52] Lehman to Byrnes, February 28, 1946, Lehman Collections, Columbia University, Folder 181.

of forced repatriation and contrary to British policy.[53] Within the United States, Acheson argued to Truman that the United States should "continue the present liberal policy so long as it is consistent with maintenance of satisfactory conditions among the Jewish displaced persons in Germany and Austria."[54] Truman supported Acheson, cancelling Byrnes's order and suggesting that the UN General Assembly should address the issue first.[55]

The United States and Great Britain had chosen to not accept policy solutions – forced repatriation and camp closures – that would have been the easiest way to end the DP situations. These would have violated the norms of the emerging regime, particularly nonrefoulement. But this left both countries without a clear solution to the DP problem. Not only were there more than a million DPs who would not be repatriated,[56] but the numbers were growing through both Jewish emigration from the East and from the *Volksdeutsche* movement. By December 1946, the battle lines were drawn. Because the American government had little ability to reshape the UNRRA's policies, the decision was made to terminate the IO and create a new organization within the UN.[57]

The American domestic shift: President Truman as domestic entrepreneur

By 1946, President Truman recognized that the only solution to the DP problem was through international cooperation within the UN, a view anchored in the American recognition of its "predominant global position and concomitant responsibilities [which were] likely to predispose the Executive towards more overt recognition of its international obligations to these displaced persons" (Charlton et al. 1988: 242). Coupled to this was the recognition that prewar efforts had been shamefully inadequate (Aleinkoff and Martin 1985: 620–21 fn).

---

[53] MacKillop to Gottlieb, December 22, 1945, PRO FO 371/51128/WR3682.

[54] Memorandum by the Acting Secretary of State (Acheson) to President Truman, May 2, 1946. *FRUS* 1946, vol. V, 156.

[55] The Secretary of State to the Secretary of War (Patterson), April 23, 1946, *FRUS* 1946, vol. V, 155. Truman was not being entirely altruistic here – as he wrote to Byrnes, "the Poles in this country and the Catholic Church are simply going to have a spasm if we close out these camps" (cited in Cohen 2011: 36).

[56] In May 1946, the UNRRA polled the DPs in the three occupation zones: 82 percent of those polled were opposed to returning home (Holian 2011: 83–84).

[57] As Lehman wrote, "there are clearly major political differences between certain of the great powers concerned and UNRRA[']s destiny is being fitted into the pattern." Telegram to Robert Jackson, August 10, 1946, Lehman Collections, Columbia University, Folder 642, 8.

The main lesson from the interwar period was that little could be done without changes at the domestic level. Roosevelt had been unwilling "to press the case for greater immigration," fearful that clashing with Congress on the issue would undermine foreign affairs more broadly (Dallek 1979: 446). Truman did not have the same concerns, and, in 1946–48, he effectively framed the refugee issue within the broader looming confrontation with the Soviets. His administration, Zolberg notes, saw the DP problem as a "threat to the social and economic stability of a strategically crucial region . . . the solution required some form of international resettlement, which would necessarily involve admission to the United States" (1995: 123). Truman converted the issue from one of immigration into "an aspect of the emerging Cold War, and thus providing a new basis for conservative support" (Loescher and Scanlan 1986: 14–15). In this regard, Truman sought to securitize refugee entrance into the United States by treating refugees from the Soviet bloc as a referent object that was existentially threatened (Buzan et al. 1998: 36).

But Truman was not just acting strategically – as his statements show, he believed that the United States also had a moral commitment to these refugees. Thus, he played an important role as a norm entrepreneur, using strategic and security considerations to reframe domestic understandings of refugee protection. His directive of December 22, 1945 declared that "common decency and the fundamental comradeship of human beings require us to see that our established immigration quotas are used to reduce human suffering" (cited in Loescher and Scanlan 1986: 5–6). In his 1946 State of the Union address, he urged Congress "to find ways whereby we can fulfill our responsibilities to these thousands of homeless and suffering refugees of all faiths" (cited in Loescher and Scanlan 1986: 14). And he took executive action to allocate unused immigration quotas to the displaced – by 1948, 40,000 DPs had thereby been admitted to the United States (Charlton et al. 1988: 243).

His arguments faced a restrictionist Congress. It took sustained effort on the part of both the Truman administration and domestic voluntary organizations to ensure legal changes.[58] The more active refugee groups, including the American Council on Judaism and the American Jewish Committee, deliberately played down Jewish claims to limit anti-Semitism and included Jewish refugee claims within the broader DP category (Loescher and Scanlan 1986: 9). In spite of these efforts,

---

[58] The views of the State Department changed with more activist leadership following Byrnes's departure. Secretary of State George C. Marshall advocated that the United States "admit a substantial number of these people as immigrants" and that Congress needed to take a "prompt decision and action" (Marshall, cited in Genizi 1993: 75).

Congress remained intransigent, dominated by restrictionist Republicans and Southern Democrats.

By January 1948, Truman restated a "desire that our country afford sanctuary to a substantial number of the men, women and children who lost their homes and all they held dear during years of persecution in the Old World" (Truman, cited in Genizi 1993: 78). His actions, along with ongoing lobbying efforts, led to the Displaced Persons Act of 1948,[59] which provided the first clear distinction between ordinary migrants and refugees since the Quota Laws, while also recognizing that DPs had a status akin to refugees. However, it allowed only 200,000 DPs to be admitted over two years.[60] Furthermore, it restricted admittance to those who were in camps on December 22, 1945. Although Truman signed the legislation, he noted his reluctance, arguing the bill "discriminates in callous fashion against displaced persons of the Jewish faith... [M]ost of the Jewish displaced persons now in those areas arrived there after December 22, 1945, and hence are denied a chance to come to the United States under this bill. By this device more than 90 percent of the remaining Jewish displaced persons are definitely excluded... The bill also excludes many displaced persons of the Catholic faith who deserve admission."[61]

The frame that most effectively resonated with Congress was the securitization of the refugee issue through association with the increasing tensions of the Cold War. By the early 1950s, Congress sought to place restrictions on any assistance to organizations that might aid the Eastern bloc (Holborn 1975: 59). Congressional rhetoric, however, was also moving in favor of accepting more refugees. Even those who had supported the strict 1948 Displaced Persons Act, such as Senator Alexander Wiley, argued that "if we revise this law speedily and equitably, it will be a real inspiration for all free people. It will be an ideological weapon in our ideological war against the forces of darkness, the forces of communist tyranny."[62]

Viewing refugees in this way created new security concerns, however, that progressively trumped open refugee admission policies and

---

[59] Displaced Persons Act of 1948, 62 Stat. 1009 (1948).

[60] The Act allowed quotas for subsequent years to be mortgaged for DPs. But "the results were ludicrous. By 1951 the Latvian quota had been mortgaged to the year 2255, the Estonian to 2130, and the Lithuanian to 2079" (Zucker and Zucker 1987: 28–29; see also Dinnerstein 1982: 182).

[61] Harry S. Truman, "Statement by the President Upon Signing the Displaced Persons Act," June 25, 1948, *The American Presidency Project*. www.presidency.ucsb.edu/ws/?pid=12942; Anthony Levieros "Truman to Deliver Congress Message in Person Tuesday," *The New York Times*, July 22, 1948, 1, 19 (see also Truman 1955: II 208).

[62] Alexander Wiley (R-WI) (cited in Loescher and Scanlan 1986: 24; see also Charlton et al. 1988: 247).

humanitarian concerns. The Internal Security Act of 1950[63] gave the American government increased authority to screen aliens and exclude subversives, including anyone who had belonged to the Communist Party. The Act was enacted over Truman's veto, who argued that "under this bill the government would lose the limited authority it now has to offer asylum in our country as the great incentive to such defection."[64] The Immigration and Nationality Act of 1952[65] was similarly restrictive, retaining the quota system. Once again, Truman's veto was overridden by a Democratic-led Congress in spite of his argument that "we do not need to be protected against immigrants from these countries; on the contrary, we want to stretch out a helping hand" (Bennett 1966: 130).

Framing the refugee problem as a Cold War issue ensured Congressional acceptance for the humanitarian policies of the Truman administration. From 1945 on, the United States was far more accepting of refugees than it had been either during the Second World War or during the interwar period. Yet, as discussed in Chapter 8, the Cold War frame would have lasting consequences beyond Truman's presidency for American refugee policy.

The regime begins to crystallize: The creation of the IRO

At the international level, by 1946, the United States, along with Great Britain, had accepted that DPs and refugees needed to be handled by a new IO. The existing institutional structure was rapidly unraveling. Not only was UNRRA winding down, but so too was the League of Nations High Commissioner for Refugees (LNHCR), still nominally protecting its prewar refugee caseload. Thus, LNHCR refugees, as well as nonrepatriable DPs and refugees under UNRRA, would soon be left without any form of international protection. The Norwegian government raised the question of a new refugee IO at the UN negotiations in San Francisco.[66] Herbert Emerson, as the director of both the LNHCR and the IGCR, raised his own concerns over the status of the nonrepatriable DPs with the British government.[67] Although there was broad agreement that a

---

[63] The Internal Security Act of 1950, 64 Stat. 993 (1950).
[64] "Internal Security Act of 1950 – Veto Message of the President of the United States," *CR*, September 22, 1950, 15631.
[65] The Immigration and Nationality Act of 1952, 182 Stat. 66 (1952).
[66] IGCR, *Minutes of the Fifth Plenary Session* (cited in Holborn 1956: 29).
[67] Cabinet Committee on the Reception and Accommodation of Refugees "Draft minutes of a meeting of the Committee held . . . on Friday 15th June, 1945," PRO FO 371/51095 WR1879/1/48, 3.

replacement IO was necessary, the form it would take remained unclear. This reflected the growing normative divide between the United States and Britain on the one hand, and the Soviet Union on the other.

Resettlement or repatriation: A normative divide

The United States' primary problem in the postwar period was how to handle the Soviet Union. During 1945 and early 1946, the Americans made substantial efforts to compromise on major issues with the Soviet Union as a necessary international partner.[68] In the year-long negotiations over the creation of the International Refugee Organization (IRO), however, the American government would not surrender on a key point: forced repatriation.

The initial American proposal focused on concentrating all efforts in the IGCR and moving it into the UN.[69] This had the advantage, the State Department felt, of requiring minimal negotiations with the Soviets because the organization already existed, and the question of forced repatriation could be sidestepped.[70] This move failed, however, not because of intransigence by the Soviets, but rather by the British.

Why did this occur? Although the British government continued to accept the need for an international regime, it was increasingly fixated on the potential costs of any options. The Cabinet Committee on the Reception and Accommodation of Refugees[71] worried that continued use of the IGCR would continue to divide all relief expenses equally between the British and the Americans. Consequently, the British viewed any suggestion of expanding the IGCR's role, such as providing relief to nonrepatriable DPs, with deep suspicion.[72]

---

[68] 1946 was a year in flux for U.S. policy toward the Soviet Union, as it shifted from ally to enemy. Truman was not interested in accommodating the Russians, but "strong counter-vailing forces kept the President from implementing this policy consistently during his first year in office" (Gaddis 2000: 199–200; see also Truman 1955: I 261, 552; Acheson 1969: 151, 195).

[69] Mr. Coppock to Mr. Wilcox "Refugee Problems," January 8, 1946, NARA RG 59 501. BD Refugees 1–846.

[70] "Refugees" Report attached to Ibid.

[71] The Committee's objectives were: to "i) to save money; ii) to avoid having large numbers of refugees left on our hands, and; iii) to ease the pressure on Palestine." Cabinet Committee on the Reception and Accommodation of Refugees "Draft minutes of a meeting of the Committee held ... on Friday 15th June, 1945," PRO FO 371/51095 WR1879/1/48.

[72] The Committee went on to argue that if the IGCR was used, "it would be essential to reorganize that body, and in particular get its financial structure placed on a proper international contractual basis." Non-Repatriable Refugee: Memorandum by the Minister of Education, Acting Chairman of the Cabinet Committee on the Reception and Accommodation of Refugees, June 19, 1945, PRO FO 371 51095/WE1911/1/48; see

In lieu of the IGCR, the British saw the UN as the perfect alternative. It was a body that could ensure that "every country realizes its responsibilities and takes its fair share of the burden," something that neither the UNRRA nor the IGCR could do. The IGCR, in particular, "is too small and limited in scope, and lacks any solid international basis."[73] An organization created within the UN Economic and Social Council (ECOSOC) had, they argued, better access to funds as part of the UN budget and "would give the new organization the full authority of the United Nations and the advantage of the support of public opinion."[74] Finally, the British government dismissed American concerns over forced repatriation by arguing that a strong enough majority already existed in the UN to block the Soviet Union and its allies.[75] Consequently, they raised the issue within the General Assembly in London in January 1946, without either consulting or gaining support from the Americans.[76]

The American delegation felt that the British were being short sighted and that they wanted "to put the refugee work directly under ECOSOC mainly in order to shift part of the financial burden to other countries."[77] The Americans accepted, however, that the IGCR could not continue if the British were opposed. With reservations, they proposed to instead create a new specialized agency within the UN.[78] Britain, too, moved toward a more conciliatory position, fearful that a failure of negotiations

also Ambassador Gallman to the Secretary of State, April 16, 1946, NARA RG 59 501. BD Refugees 4–1646; Note by MacKillop, January 22, 1946, PRO FO371 57700/WR193/6/48.

[73] "Problem of Non-Repatriable Refugees," January 8, 1946, PRO FO371 57700/WR136/6/48; for the American reaction to this, see Acting Secretary of State (Acheson) to George Warren, April 4, 1946, NARA RG 59 501.BD Refugees 5–426.

[74] Memorandum, British Embassy to the Department of State, May 13, 1946, FRUS 1946, vol. V, 159, 161–63; Coppock to Wilcox, January 8, 1946, NARA RG 59 501.BD Refugees/1–846.

[75] Foreign Office message to the Secretary of State, Enclosure to Makins to Wood, May 20, 1946, FRUS 1946, vol. V. 165; Makins to Rendel, January 14, 1946, PRO FO371 57700/WR193/6/48.

[76] "Paper on refugees for UNO assembly," Foreign Office Minute (Mr. Mackilliop), January 4, 1946, PRO FO 371 57700/WR67/648. See also Cohen (2011: 14–15). Durward Sandifer, a member of the U.S. delegation, noted that "One problem we had was to try to find out what the policy of the British Government was. We didn't know." Richard McKinzie "Oral History Interview with Durward V. Sandifer," March 15 and May 29, 1973, Truman Library, www.trumanlibrary.org/oralhist/sandifer.htm, 73.

[77] Mr. Coppock to Mr. Wilcox "Refugee Problems," January 8, 1946, NARA RG 59 501. BD Refugees 1–846. Not surprisingly, the British found they were having "difficulty in getting our point of view accepted by the representatives of the State Department." Note by Rendel, January 3, 1946, PRO FO 371/WR 180/6/48.

[78] Primarily, they did not trust the effectiveness of an agency within the UN, with Acheson suggesting to George Warren, leading the U.S. delegation, that he should note "the lack of confidence of this government in the potential effectiveness of a new agency consisting of all the member governments of the United Nations to be created to deal with the problem de novo." Acting Secretary of State (Acheson) to George Warren, April 4, 1946, NARA

would block any form of multilateral solution. A bilateral alternative, they worried, "would be unable to undertake half the duties ... required of a refugee agency."[79]

The American–Soviet divide

Following the decision to create a UN-based organization, the major point of debate coalesced around the question of forced repatriation. Neither the Americans nor the European allies, although prepared to discuss repatriation, were willing to engage in forced returns. This reflected the strength of the emerging norm of nonrefoulement. Instead, they focused on resettlement as the only long-term solution to the camps in Germany, a solution necessary to avoid instability in Europe. The British government argued that these refugees "constituted an immense international problem of concern to all members,"[80] whereas Eleanor Roosevelt, the U.S. delegate, emphasized the need for international action "in the interest of humanity and social stability."[81]

The Soviet Union and its allies favored repatriation of all refugees, regardless of their wishes.[82] Their arguments had three dimensions. The first was that the Eastern bloc, as opposed to the West, did not see this as a question of humanitarianism; rather, it was seen as principally a domestic concern involving their own citizens. Those who did not wish to return were likely "hostile elements," war criminals, and traitors who "must be silenced"[83] and who had "decided to displace themselves of their own free

RG 59 501.BD Refugees 5–426; No title, Two pages marked "Secret" attached to NARA RG 59 501.BD Refugees/ 5–746. "Refugees," January 1946, PRO FO371 57700/WR136/6/48, 4. They were also concerned that the process to create a new agency would take too long. Gallman to Secretary of State, April 16, 1946. NARA RG 59 501.BD Refugees 4–1646.

[79] "Refugees," January 24, 1946, PRO FO371 57700/WR293/6/48.

[80] Philip Noel-Baker, Committee 3 Summary Record, January 28, 1946. In United Nations *Journal* No. 18 Supplement No. 3 A/C.3/11. 8 This view was supported by other states. See, for example, Statement by Mr. Sassen (Netherlands), Committee 3 Summary Record, January 30, 1946. In Ibid.

[81] Committee 3, January 28, 1946, E/REF/1.7. See also Richard McKinzie "Oral History Interview with Durward V. Sandifer," March 15 and May 29, 1973, Truman Library, www.trumanlibrary.org/oralhist/sandifer.htm, 71–73.

[82] Unofficially, as they told a member of the American delegation: "we are aware that some displaced persons who are not criminals or traitors will not wish to return to their countries because they do not like their governments. We do not ask that they shall be forced to return. . . But we cannot agree that they should receive international assistance to resettle or that they should be the concern of an international organization" (Penrose 1951: 147).

[83] Statement by Mr. Bajan (Ukrainian SSR) Committee 3 Summary Record, February 1, 1946, United Nations *Journal* No. 12 Supplement No. 3 A/C.3/19.

will at the end of the war."[84] Given this, "there was now no reason why displaced persons who had fled the Axis countries should not return home"[85] and "no permanent international machinery was necessary, therefore, to organize assistance"[86] (see also Holborn 1956: 31).

At a broader level, the Soviet Union was also offering a normative challenge to the traditional ties between citizen and state. The Soviet government felt that "the tie between a state and its citizens was an exclusive one, and individuals could not simply 'opt out' and choose a new nationality," thus challenging the fundamental notion of asylum. The West's proposals were "at best an affront to state sovereignty and at worst a deliberate attempt to undermine the authority of the state within the refugees' countries of origin" (Cronin 2003: 168). Thus, although Roosevelt argued in favor of the right of the individual to free choice, Vishinsky, the Soviet delegate, argued of the paramount authority of the state over its nationals, even those outside of the state's borders (Ristelhueber 1951: 180; Holborn 1975: 28).

The American delegation responded to Soviet concerns by offering a compromise on the language associated with repatriation, which the Soviets found acceptable. Resettlement would not be explicitly raised, and the international community was entrusted to make every effort to encourage repatriation. The Americans, however, did require a guarantee that refugees would not be forcibly returned (Ristelhueber 1951: 180–81; Holborn 1956: 32; Proudfoot 1957: 399).[87]

This agreement moved the negotiations on to a Special Committee on Refugees and Displaced Persons, tasked with writing the new organization's constitution.[88] Here, the Soviets were crafty negotiators. As E. F. Penrose, a member of the U.S. delegation, noted:

---

[84] Statement by Ales Bebler, Yugoslav delegate. Committee 3 Summary Record, January 28, 1946, United Nations *Journal* No. 18 Supplement No. 3 A/C.3/11.

[85] Ibid.

[86] Statement by Mr. Arutinian (USSR) Committee 3 Summary Record, February 4, 1946, United Nations *Journal* No. 22 Supplement No. 3 A/C.3/19. If an IO was necessary, the Soviet Union "stressed that [the] new organization should be temporary, independent and specialized and have a very loose relationship to ECOSOC." Harriman to the Secretary of State (Telegram), May 7, 1946, NARA RG 59 501.BD Refugees/ 5–746.

[87] Byrnes acknowledged that the U.S. position adopted "acceptable features" of both the Yugoslav and Soviet proposals for it to pass. Byrnes to Consular Officers, February 14, 1946, *FRUS* 1946, vol. V 135–136; Resolution adopted by the General Assembly on February 12, 1946 (Doc A/45).

[88] Once again, efforts were made to compromise (Marrus 2002: 341), with the British delegation being ordered by Cabinet to take "special care ... not to damage relations with other United Nations by pressing views too hard or too strongly." "Refugee Question," Memo by MacKillop, April 30, 1946, PRO FO371 57706/6/48, 2.

It was difficult to defeat once and for all a specific proposal that seemed to endanger the rights of refugees. No sooner had one proposal been disposed of than another was put forward on a different part of the agenda which, if it did not reopen all the dangers of the first, threatened partially to undermine the decision already reached. (1951: 152)

The negotiated definition – which included both refugees and DPs – reflected these divisions, using both individual- and group-based elements as well as strict exclusions.[89] Refugees had to be outside of their own country and had to have been victims of the Nazi or fascist regimes, Spanish Republicans, or people considered refugees by the League.[90] Victims of Nazi persecution, including the Jews, were also included if they had not been resettled. Displaced persons included persons who had not been individually persecuted but who had been compelled to undertake forced labor or had been deported for racial, religious, or political reasons and were within or outside of their own country.

Neither form of status was automatic. Rather, it was granted by the IRO only if the DPs could not be repatriated or had expressed "valid objections: against being returned on the basis of persecution or fear of persecution because of race, religion, nationality, or political opinion, provided that these were not in conflict with the principles of the UN.[91] Thus, by considering the individual's expectations of persecution, and by limiting temporally refugee and DP status to before the IRO constitution's ratification, the IRO definition foreshadowed the 1951 Refugee Convention (Marrus 2002: 342; see also Sadruddin 1976: 5).

Thus, like the IGCR before it, the IRO was able to accord legal and political protection to the DPs and refugees under its mandate (Saloman 1991: 53).[92] But the valid objections criterion was constrained in that it applied only to specified categories of people. In addition, refugees and

---

[89] United Nations, "Report of the Special Committee on Refugees and Displaced Persons," E/REF/ 75, 29.

[90] The Soviet Union would accept this definition long after the end of the IRO. As Ginsburgs (1957: 357–58) notes, because it established that flight was caused by fascism and because the Soviet Union was not a fascist state, by this logic those who fled from it were "not genuine political refugees."

[91] Constitution for the International Refugee Organization, Annex 1, Part I, Section A-C. Soviet citizens concerned that they might be repatriated were quick to assume new national identities. Thus, in July 1948, the IRO officially found 1,452 Soviet DPs in its camp. Guesstimates among IRO officials, however, ranged as high as 1 million Soviet DPs (Fischer 1949: 8).

[92] Although protection activities were provided for in the IRO Constitution, nowhere was a precise definition of such activities provided. In the statute creating the Office of the UNHCR, the term used instead was "international protection," with a more comprehensive definition of activities (Weis 1954: 211).

DPs could be excluded from protection due to one of the definition's cessation clauses, which included:

refugees returning to their country of origin, acquiring a new nationality, becoming firmly established, unreasonably refusing to accept IRO repatriation or resettlement proposals, failing to make a substantial effort towards earning a living when able to do so or otherwise exploiting the IRO. (Hathaway 1984: 374–76)[93]

The definition was both complex and unwieldy. Yet, by mid-1947, as Hathaway (1984: 376) notes, it "was the only effective international standard" as the IRO took over the responsibilities of the UNRRA, the IGCR, and the League HCR.

Per the agreement reached between the United States and the Soviet Union, the IRO's mandate focused exclusively on repatriation:

a) To facilitate the return to their countries of origin of those persons who desire to return;

b) To facilitate the re-establishment in the reception countries, whether temporary or permanent, of non-repatriable persons or families, and, subject to certain reservations, to facilitate the carrying out of schemes for group settlement in these countries.[94]

To ensure this occurred quickly, and to minimize costs, a deadline of June 30, 1950 was imposed on its mandate (Ristelhueber 1951: 220).

Even with this compromised definition and after a year of negotiations, the Soviets refused to join the organization.[95] They voted against it at the UN, along with Poland, Ukraine, Byelorussia, and Yugoslavia. As Eleanor Roosevelt would later note, "this vote meant that the Western nations would have to worry about the ultimate fate of the refugees for a long, long time but it was a victory well worthwhile" (cited in Cohen 2011: 27). Yet the compromises and the lack of communist bloc support were widely seen to have crippled the organization. The IRO, Rees (1953: 267) argued, "emerged as an organization to which no communist government adhered and which was saddled with a definition of a refugee which was narrow, partial and in specific instances discriminatory and unjust." Other writers of the period were similarly critical. Ristelhueber argued because of the negotiations "a humanitarian organization … took on a political character which was to become even more marked" (1951: 180; see also Reston 1947: 102). Penrose (1951: 164–65) suggested that "the

---

[93] The *Volksdeutsch* were also excluded and became the responsibility of the German and Austrian authorities (Stoessinger 1956: 87).

[94] "Report of the Special Committee on Refugees and Displaced Persons," 31.

[95] Thirty-five states signed and eighteen states ratified the Constitution of the International Refugee Organization. United Nations, "Multilateral Treaties Deposited with the Secretary General, Status as at 31 December 2001," ST/LEG/SER.E/20, vol. 1, 329.

Russians meant what they said, that they sincerely desired that a temporary international body should be set up. . . But their efforts so to restrict its scope were frustrated and they decided . . . that they preferred to remain outside it."

The IRO in operation

As the League HCR showed, once an IO is established, the organization can work to expand its mandate. Once operational, the staff of the IRO quickly accepted that repatriation was simply not possible and focused exclusively on resettlement. However, they had two major constraints. The negotiations had taken so long that the organization did not come into formal existence until August 1948,[96] with barely two years to operate. This was in spite of strong U.S. efforts to expand the IRO's membership and get its Constitution to enter into force.[97] Many potential members feared the substantial financial commitments required for the organization, given its limited European focus (Malin 1947: 453–54; Saloman 1991: 52).

Although the IRO had to deal with the cumbersome eligibility process laid out in its Constitution, its focus on resettlement was helped by two major changes: President Truman successfully forced Congress to move away from its strict restrictionist policies with the passing of the Displaced Persons Act in 1948, and an independent state of Israel was created that same year.[98] Thus, in its five years of operations, the IRO successfully resettled more than 1 million refugees (see Figure 6.1).

For the first time, a refugee agency had access to substantial resources. During its existence, the IRO spent almost $430,000,000, with the American contribution to the organization exceeding $250,000,000. It had a staff of more than 2,600 by 1949, as well as thirty-nine chartered ships (Vernant 1953: 33–38; Saloman 1991: 52–53). It not only

[96] Because the UNRRA discontinued care of the DP population on June 30, 1947, the Preparatory Commission of the IRO (PCIRO) ran administrative operations during this period (Vernant 1953: 34).

[97] The Truman Administration urged Congress to ratify the Constitution as vital for the Cold War effort. Secretary of State Marshall argued that to turn the DPs "back to the Germans would be to perpetuate grave tensions and an ever present threat of internal conflict" and that the IRO would reduce the expenditures the United States faced from $130 million to $73 million. As Loescher and Scanlan note, "the pro-Western bent of the IRO was presented as one of its major assets and, not incidentally, as a way of distinguishing it from UNRRA" (Loescher and Scanlan 1986: 18). IRO membership passed as a joint resolution as public law 146, 61 Stat. 214.

[98] The IRO did not resettle refugees to Palestine prior to the creation of Israel, arguing that they could not be responsible for fostering movements into an area where there is a state of war or armed truce (Rucker 1949: 70).

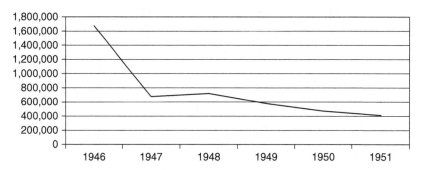

Figure 6.1 Refugees within the International Refugee Organization (IRO)'s mandate, 1946–1950. In 1946, 1,676,000 refugees were transferred from the Intergovernmental Committee on Refugees and the League of Nations to the IRO.

developed more efficient methods for providing basic services to refugees, including food, shelter, and medical care, but it also created a resettlement program on a massive scale. As Holborn notes "the success of the IRO was proof that such a machine could be built and made to work through international cooperation" (1975: 35; see also Proudfoot 1957: 407). The IRO's work demonstrated that an IO could provide significant assistance to refugees. Moreover, the IRO's membership and resources suggested a developing sense of "collective responsibility" for refugees, even those beyond a state's borders (Holborn 1975: 32; see also Cronin 2003: 169).

The IRO's structure provided its directors-general – all American – with significant autonomy. They had complete control over the large administrative apparatus and the power to evolve their own policies, control their own personnel, and distribute their own supplies and resources. As Proudfoot (1957: 407) notes, the zonal authorities in Germany, "far from being in a position to dictate to the IRO, came to depend on it in the hope that its resettlement program might solve the intractable refugee problem."

The creation of the hard core

Although the IRO's overall resettlement operations were successful, a remaining "hard core" of sick, disabled, infirm, and elderly refugees was created. These included Holocaust survivors who were discriminated against both on physical-condition grounds but also due to lingering anti-Semitism (Cohen 2011: 115). States saw the IRO refugees through a standard migration lens (Stoessinger 1956: 139–40; Hans and Suhrke 1997: 86). Patrick Malin, the former vice-president of the IGCR, argued that the receiving states sought to claim international support while being "overridingly reluctant to expose themselves to external interference in their sovereign rights . . . and the fear that membership in an international refugee organization will be interpreted as a moral obligation to receive refugees as immigrants" (Malin 1947: 444).

The IRO's efforts to correct this, including a fair share plan that would require receiving countries to accept a quota of the physically handicapped, sick, and aged refugees, failed because governments were unwilling to alter their own domestic legislation or to accept a quota determined by the IRO council (Holborn 1956: 483). Thus, the ability of the IRO to independently alter policies was limited. In 1949, the IRO instead offered increased subsidies to countries in an effort to resettle the hard core before the termination of the organization – ranging from $500 for the elderly to $1,000 for those with tuberculosis. It also began building old-age homes, hospitals, and other institutions in Germany to provide a permanent home for these refugees (Holborn 1956: 486–91). As Sir Arthur Rucker, the deputy director-general noted, "everything depends on whether the countries will in fact take refugees in sufficient generous form to leave us only with a small 'hard core'" (1949: 70). These efforts were unsuccessful – even as its mandate was extended until February 28, 1952, the organization accepted that the hard core might be permanent.

American resistance to the organization

At the same time, the American government was unhappy with the IRO. Publicly, it argued that it cost too much money. As George Warren noted in 1951, "the IRO has cost my Government a tremendous sum of money. The organization was not established to function indefinitely and the time has now come to attempt solutions to the problem through bilateral negotiations."[99] Although the expectation had been that a majority of UN members would also join the organization, by 1952 only eighteen countries had made contributions (see Table 6.2).

But the issue of funding provided cover for deeper U.S. misgivings about the IRO and the role of the UN. Parts of these misgivings were

---

[99] IRO Doc. GC/257/Rev. 1, November 8, 1951 (cited in Stoessinger 1956: 154). He was, however, willing to concede that the refugee situation did remain "so grave in terms of human suffering that they call for urgent consideration by the United Nations." UN Doc A/1948, November 10, 1951 (cited in Stoessinger 1956: 154).

Table 6.2 *Contributions made by member governments to the International Refugee Organization (IRO)*

Member Governments	Accumulated Totals, July 1, 1947–February 7, 1952, Contributions Due and Received
Australia	$9,194,156
Belgium	$5,262,255
Canada	$18,164,167
China	$13,591,513
Denmark	$2,491,948
Dominican Republic	$209,826
France	$21,652,462
Guatemala	$209,926
Iceland	$75,272
Italy	$8,290,709
Luxembourg	$147,002
Netherlands	$4,766,750
New Zealand	$2,299,784
Norway	$2,299,784
Switzerland	$4,033,698
United Kingdom	$76,218,086
United States	$237,116,355
Total Contributions Due	$406,867,295
Unpaid Contributions	$8,270,493
Contributions from UNRRA	$15,140,541
Contributions from IGCR	$517,326
Total Contributions Received	$414,254,669

Source: Holborn 1956: 122–23. Figures in 1952 U.S. dollars.

based on concerns over how the U.S. government would be perceived by refugees from the communist world. Following the Prague Coup of 1948, the IRO expanded its operations to include the Czechoslovakians as refugees. Donald Kingsley, the IRO director-general, noted that "as a result of the changes in the political scene after 1948, the organization liberalized the interpretation of its own definitions to fall into line with a wider conception of a refugee" (Cohen 2011: 46).

Yet the State Department, for one, was not impressed with the IRO's efforts. As Marshall argued, the IRO's assistance fell "far short of a reasonable minimum standard of care for those who have so valiantly resisted the political forces to which their country eventually succumbed. The public interest in these refugees is extensive and growing, and it appears inconsistent with the publicly stated policies of the democratic countries represented."[100] Furthermore, the American government feared the poor conditions in the IRO camps would discredit their efforts among noncommunist elements: "If amnesty is followed by voluntary return to [Czechoslovakia] of any considerable number of refugees as result of inadequate conditions, [the] US position would suffer in countries where efforts being made to encourage resistance to Communism."[101]

More broadly, the U.S. interest in protecting refugees was increasingly in tension with its efforts to disengage from the UN and with how to respond to new refugee flows from communist states. Will Clayton, the assistant secretary of state, noted "we must avoid getting into another UNRRA. The United States must run this show" (Clayton, cited in Acheson 1969: 231). The hard core, they felt, was a European problem that no longer required U.S. support:

The burden of caring for indigents among the residual refugees should not fall so heavily on any one country as to justify international assistance funds. Congress has made it clear that it does not propose to appropriate funds annually hereafter to cover United States contributions to such a fund.[102]

Instead of supporting the continuation of the IRO or creating a new UN agency, the Americans favored organizations "outside the UN for such activities and to restrict the role of the UN in handling such problems" (Holborn 1975: 59; Cronin 2003: 169), with the American government no longer continuing "large-scale financial contributions through a multilateral organization" (Saloman 1991). American leadership had led to a strong IO, yet within four years they questioned whether any organization within the UN could adequately protect refugees.

Conclusion

The immediate postwar period represented a time of transition. Prior normative understandings, including that refugees required international cooperation and internationally entrenched legal rights, continued to be followed. During the war, refugee admissions and rescue policies in both Britain and the United States were severely truncated by security

---

[100] Marshall to Robert Murphy, U.S. Political Adviser for Germany, June 25, 1948, NARA RG 59 501.MA/6–1148.

[101] Ibid. The United States abrogated the date restriction so that the IRO could assist Czechoslovakian refugees. See W. Hallam Tuck, Executive Secretary, PCIRO to General Lucius Clay, Commanding General, EUCOM, September 13, 1948, NARA RG 59 501.MA/9–2948 (see also Cohen 2011: 51–53).

[102] "Refugees and Stateless Persons," FRUS 1950, vol. II, "The United Nations, the Western Hemisphere," 539–40.

concerns. These states, however, continued to provide a basic level of protection, and the IGCR continued to function. Although much of both states' actions were merely rhetorical in nature and designed to respond to public opinion, they did lay a foundation for the postwar era.

A new norm of nonrefoulement emerged during this period out of the U.S. experience with the forced repatriation of millions of Soviet citizens. Solutions to the postwar refugee and DP problem, consequently, were debated within a limited policy environment. Actions such as returning the refugees to the East or even closing the camps in Germany were no longer accepted as legitimate courses of action by the American government. This caused them to argue not only that international cooperation was necessary, but also that a new IO, the IRO, was needed to ensure the repatriation and resettlement of these refugees. The negotiations around this organization were critical. They showed that whereas the United States sought to compromise with the Soviet Union, it refused to surrender on the critical point of forced returns, suggesting the importance that the American government attributed to this new norm. Although it resulted in a weaker IO with a limited mandate, it also entrenched a norm that had been ignored after the creation of the 1933 and 1938 Conventions, one that would be re-ratified with the 1951 Convention.

Assistance was a more complicated matter. The Americans were willing, first with the IGCR and the UNRRA and then with the IRO, to accept a substantial part of the financial burden for assisting and resettling refugees even while other Allies, notably the British, backed away from such undertakings. As U.S. policies shifted away from the UN, however, so did their support for IOs within its purview. They allowed the IRO to die and, as we see in the next chapter, provided little support to the UNHCR.

At this stage, a coherent regime was emerging, based in states accepting a collective responsibility for refugees and enshrined in IOs, the provision of assistance, and doctrines of nonrefoulement. Multilateralism formed the basis for international cooperation; international law provided the mechanism to ensure refugee protection. These fundamental institutions provided the prism through which states saw the refugee problem and contributed greatly to the institutional solution adopted.

Yet the regime was incomplete. Most of the understandings embodied within it were simply that: understandings with no international legal significance. In addition, the institutional structures created were significantly supported by the United States. As their focus moved away from the UN, it was unclear if the regime would continue and how new refugees would be protected. There also remained the issue of the Second World War refugee hard core. The IRO had been successful, but it had been unable to significantly alter states' preferences toward resettlement. A realist perspective would suggest that the regime would be transformed or replaced as hegemonic interest wanted. A neoliberal perspective would suggest that the regime might continue if its benefits continued to outweigh its costs. As we see in the next chapter, European and American views were divided on how to proceed. The Americans succeeded in creating a weak successor organization – the UNHCR – and yet the organization prospered in spite of a limited mandate due to its independent sources of moral and expert authority. Thus, the UNHCR would redefine how states perceived the refugee problem, expanding its own legal and operational role, as well as providing a global basis to the international refugee regime.

7 The norm entrepreneurship of the United Nations High Commissioner for Refugees

In the immediate postwar period (1946–50), American leadership helped to create a new refugee regime based around the International Refugee Organization (IRO). This regime was centered on protecting refugees displaced in Europe by the Second World War. As Cold War tensions mounted, however, institutional control became the main concern for the American government. This was impossible within the United Nations (UN), given the Soviet presence. Instead, starting in 1950, the United States worked outside the UN to create organizations over which the Soviets would have no voice – the Intergovernmental Committee for European Migration (ICEM) and the U.S. Escapee Program (USEP).

The American position was unsustainable however. Its European allies preferred a UN-based international organization (IO), the United Nations High Commissioner for Refugees (UNHCR), to replace the IRO. The negotiations around the UNHCR, and around the terms of the 1951 Refugee Convention, demonstrate that the Americans and Europeans held similar normative viewpoints around refugee protection. The main points of debate, rather, were on two questions of institutional design. The first was whether the UNHCR should be an assistance organization like the IRO before it or focus exclusively on legal protections for refugees. The second was how refugees should be defined, which affected both the scope of the UNHCR and who would be covered within the 1951 Convention.

Although the American government was unable to block the UNHCR from being created, the strong humanitarian assistance precedents created with the UNRRA and the IRO were abandoned; the UNHCR was created as a weak organization with only a limited Eurocentric mandate. Yet the UNHCR succeeded in spite of these limitations. This occurred for three reasons. The first was that neither of the organizations the United States created proved to be effective at protecting refugees. The second was that the UNHCR demonstrated that it could be an effective assistance organization within the politics of the Cold War. It fulfilled U.S. objectives while maintaining its neutrality. Finally, it also slowly created its own

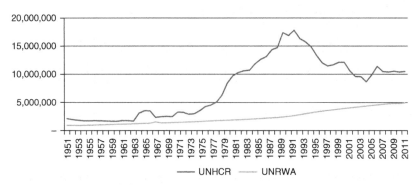

Figure 7.1 Total refugees by organization, 1951–2012.
Sources: United Nations High Commissioner for Refugees, www.unhcr. org/statistics/; Report of the Commissioner-General of the United Nations Relief and Works Agency for Palestine Refugees in the Near East A/35/13 (June 30, 1980), Annually 1981–2007. Reports from 1996 available at: www.un.org/unrwa/publications/index.html; reports prior to that date available at United Nations Information System on the Question of Palestine, www.unispal.un.org; 2007 onward from UNRWA Statistics website: www.unrwa.org/etemplate.php?id=253.

sources of authority as both an expert and moral actor (Loescher 2001; Barnett and Finnemore 2004). By the 1960s, the UNHCR was positioned to respond to the global growth of refugees and shift the regime away from its previous Europe-centered focus by arguing that the agency held a responsibility to refugees everywhere. Its success came at a cost, however. By the late 1980s, as refugee numbers grew dramatically (see Figure 7.1), the UNHCR's role in the regime was challenged by states that sought to control the agency's activities and limit its autonomy.

The creation of UNHCR

By 1949, the IRO's scheduled end the following year was in sight. In spite of its accomplishments, the organization had left two major unresolved issues. The first was that it had been unable to end the problem of the refugee "hard core." The second was that the IRO had made no changes to international law with respect to refugees beyond the cumbersome definition offered within its own Constitution and that had only eighteen ratifications. This meant that refugees remained legally protected by a diverse mixture of interwar Conventions (particularly those of 1933 and 1938) that had few ratifications and by the London Convention of 1946, which provided for access to travel documents. There was no clear definition of who qualified for refugee status, nor what the rights of refugees were.

A UN study on the issue of statelessness that year argued that although refugee protection could be improved in the short term by states ratifying the interwar Conventions, in the long term, both a new convention and new "permanent international machinery" were necessary to protect refugees (United Nations 1949: 73–74).[1] This report provided an opening for those who argued that the refugee question needed to be reexamined.[2] J. Donald Kingsley, the IRO director-general, argued that the refugee "situation demanded a new organization corresponding to the facts" because refugees would lose protection once the IRO shut down (Holborn 1975: 38–39). Similarly, John Peters Humphrey, the director of the Human Rights Division within the UN, noted that a new refugee convention would be pointless without a new organization to police it:

> In fact, experience had shown two things, first that a convention *without* an "international duly authorized watchdog" looking after its generalization and implementation might soon fall into disuse; two, that the field of intervention by an international agency empowered with the exercise of legal *and* political protection was infinitely larger than the sector of the field covered by conventional measures.[3]

At the same time, new displacements demonstrated the fallacy of hopes that the refugee problem would end with the resettlement of the Second World War-era refugees. The partition of India between 1947 and 1951 led to the displacement of 14 million people; the Korean War (1950–53) created almost 7 million refugees; whereas the 1948 Arab–Israeli War led to the displacement of 700,000 Palestinians. The IRO had no mandate to help any of these refugee groups. In the latter two cases, the General Assembly responded to the crises by creating ad hoc agencies: the United Nations Korean Reconstruction Agency and the United Nations

---

[1] As UN Secretary-General Trygve Lie noted, these efforts would work only through international negotiation: "No Government will be willing to take the first step in this direction for fear of being the only one to improve the status of stateless persons, thus causing an influx of them into its territory." United Nations, Ad Hoc Committee on Statelessness and Related Problems, Status of Refugees and Stateless Persons – Memorandum by the Secretary-General, January 3, 1950, E/AC.32/2.

[2] The stateless refugees were not forgotten; rather, the decision was made to draft two Conventions: one for refugees and one for the stateless, which was adopted in 1954. Ad Hoc Committee on Statelessness and Related Problems, 5th Meeting, January 18, 1950, E/AC.32/SR.5.

[3] "Notes on Meeting with Dr. Humphreys [sic] on Statelessness," April 23, 1948, Paul Weis Archives, Refugee Studies Centre, University of Oxford (hereafter PWA), PW/PR/IRO/5/2 (italics in original). See also "Memorandum on the Legal Position of the Hard Core" nd, PWA PW/PR/HRC/REF/1.

Relief Works Agency (UNRWA) (Stoessinger 1956: 159–61; Zolberg et al. 1989: 129–33; Saloman 1991: 231–32). Each of these relied heavily on American support (Loescher 2001: 64). Even in Europe, by 1951, refugees were entering West Germany at a rate of 15,000 a month. Once the IRO shut down, these refugees would have to rely solely on the West German government and various German voluntary organizations (Stoessinger 1956: 162–63). Continuing the IRO was not an option because of American opposition. UN Secretary-General Trygve Lie, supported by the French and Belgian governments, proposed three alternatives: the UN assuming direct responsibility, establishing a new specialized agency, or creating a new High Commissioner's Office under UN control (Saloman 1991: 219).[4]

Negotiations for a new institutional framework

As opposed to the IRO debate four years earlier, the main divisions around the creation of the UNHCR and a new convention were primarily between the United States and the countries of Western Europe. The Soviet Union and its allies argued against the need for a new IO, but their voices were marginalized within the debate. The Soviet delegate argued that "it is impossible to agree that persons unwilling to avail themselves of the protection of the country of their nationality should be regarded as 'refugees'. . . since they refuse to accept assistance from the government of the country of which they are nationals."[5]

There were broad areas of consensus between the United States and the European countries, reflecting now-entrenched normative understandings. All Western states accepted that "the primary function of a new international refugee organization should be to provide international protection to refugees" (Holborn 1975: 62; see also Gallagher 1989: 580). Not only did multilateral cooperation remain an important norm of the

---

[4] The Americans thought the proposal was done to reiterate the two countries' "well known apprehension over: a) being saddled with a hard core when the IRO closed down; and b) possible infiltration into their countries of refugees and DPs from Germany as a result of cutting off care." Troutman to the Secretary of State, June 30, 1949, NARA RG 59 501. MA/6-3049, 2.

[5] Mr. Soldatov (USSR), *GAOR*, 325th Meeting, December 14, 1950, 671. Soviet bloc delegates also argued that the West was deliberately keeping the refugee problem alive, with Mr. Altman of Poland noting "some delegations were making every effort to prolong [the refugee problem's] existence indefinitely" and the Czechoslovakian delegate arguing that it was now a political rather than a humanitarian issue. UN *General Assembly Official Records* (hereafter *GAOR*) 324th Meeting, November 22, 1950 (A/C.3/SR.324), 332; 325th Meeting November 24, 1950 (A/C.3/SR.325), 334–340; Mr. Klimov (USSR) *Ad Hoc Committee on Refugees and Stateless Persons*, Summary Record, 1st meeting, January 16, 1950, E/AC.32/SR.1.

regime; so, too, did the need to provide legal protection, reflected in the need for a new convention. Instead, the main debates were over the UNHCR's institutional scope and over how broadly or narrowly refugee status should be defined and what rights refugees should be granted. The negotiations were separate processes, with the UNHCR debates occurring within the UN Economic and Social Council (ECOSOC) and the General Assembly's Third Committee, while the convention was negotiated by an ad hoc committee struck by ECOSOC.[6] However, they involved many of the same people, same views, and same debates.

Scope of the organization

The scope of the organization was a critical question: was it to deal exclusively with refugees, or should so-called internal refugees also fall within its mandate? As the Australian delegate noted in the General Assembly, "all [member states] were aware of the refugee problem in the Near East, in Greece, in India, Pakistan, and other parts of the world. Some of those problems were being handled by special organs of the United Nations, but it might well be that in the future the General Assembly might wish to hand certain residual functions to the High Commissioner."[7]

Here, the United States staked its position clearly, arguing for the UNHCR to inherit responsibility for the existing IRO hard core alone. As Eleanor Roosevelt argued, these "internal refugee situations" were "separate problems of a different character, in which no question of protection of the persons concerned was involved ... but those problems should not be confused with the problem before the General Assembly, namely, the provision of protection for those outside their own countries, who lacked the protection of a Government and who required asylum and status."[8] Thus, we see the United States returning to the idea of refugee status held in the nineteenth century: an individual who was no longer protected by their own state. Internal refugees, whom today we would call *internally displaced persons*, did not qualify because they remained within their own state and therefore theoretically continued to have its protection. This claim was accepted, and internal refugees were not discussed again within the debates. Furthermore, as the negotiations

[6] ECOSOC Resolution 248(IX)B of August 8, 1949.
[7] Mr. Makin (Australia), *GAOR*, 264th Meeting, December 2, 1949, 479–80.
[8] Eleanor Roosevelt (United States of America), *GAOR*, 264th Meeting, December 2, 1949, 473.

proceeded, they focused on European refugees, with the result that other refugee groups were similarly removed from the discussion.[9]

The United States also saw the UNHCR exclusively as a legal protection organization rather than an assistance organization. Roosevelt warned against an "increasing tendency to drive the United Nations into the field of international relief and to use its organs as the source and center of expanding appeals for relief funds."[10] This shift in the American position occurred primarily because the country no longer saw the remaining refugees in Europe as a destabilizing crisis. The U.S. government felt that new refugee flows from the communist world and other migrants could be accommodated within the Escapee Program and the ICEM. The Cold War, Loescher, Betts, and Milner note, meant that "American leaders considered refugee policy as too important to US national security interests to permit the United Nations overall control" (2008: 20).

The European position, although varied, generally favored an organization with a broad scope and an operational role. The French and Benelux delegations argued that the UNHCR should be a strong, permanent, and multipurpose organization. This view had wide support, including from the German and Austrian governments (neither of which yet had a voice at the UN), as well as from non-European states such as India, Pakistan, and Brazil, which foresaw the need for the UNHCR to provide assistance. Britain occupied the middle ground, arguing that the primary responsibility for refugees should lie with the host states. Many of these positions were fluid: during the debates, the British delegation moved to favor an organization with broader powers, whereas the French delegation limited its calls for a powerful agency (Holborn 1975: 63–64; Loescher 2001: 44).

The Americans were not successful in limiting the mandate of the UNHCR to legal protection. This failure points to the limitations of a hegemonic role in an international society bound by an existing set of normative understandings. In addition, it indicates the independent capacity of IOs to create and manage their own autonomy.

---

[9] The European focus was in part due to the fact that although eighty invitations had been sent out, few non-European states attended the negotiations (Goodwin-Gill and McAdam 2007: 36).

[10] Eleanor Roosevelt (United States of America) *GAOR* 262nd Meeting, November 14, 1949 (A/C.3/SR.262). The delegation was advised to argue to restrict UN activities "to provision of legal protection with respect to civil status of refugees and DPs who have not acquired citizenship in countries of resettlement." No other functions "such as administration of [international] financial assistance to refugees" were envisaged. Acheson to USUN, August 11, 1949, NARA RG 59 501.MA/8-549.

Three questions dominated the debates about how the UNHCR would be structured: (1) the relationship of the agency to the UN, (2) the lifespan of the agency, and (3) whether it should be an operational agency. The relationship of the UNHCR to the UN dealt directly with the issue of its independence: should the agency be placed within the existing framework of the Secretariat, or should an independent high commissioner be directly responsible to the General Assembly? The U.S. delegation, preferring a high commissioner appointed by the secretary-general, referred the matter to Secretary-General Lie (Holborn 1975: 66).[11] This backfired, with Lie arguing that the high commissioner should "enjoy a special status within the UN" and also "possess the degree of independence and prestige which would seem to be required for the effective performance of his functions."[12]

As a mechanism to ensure this level of independence and prestige, Robert Rochefort, the French delegate, argued that the high commissioner should be directly elected: the role needed "an eminent international personality... The task was to find another Dr. Nansen."[13] In spite of arguments made by the American delegation that the high commissioner would need to work closely with the secretary-general and should be appointed by him, the French delegation's position prevailed (Holborn 1975: 61).

With regard to the agency's lifespan, the American delegation once again argued in favor of a limited mandate. This reflected their belief that the UNHCR should only be concerned with the remaining IRO refugee caseload and have no role once those refugees were resettled. Thus, the agency could be disbanded after three years. But this position failed to provide a mechanism to deal with new refugee flows, particularly those from outside the communist world. Donald Kingsley, the IRO's director-general, argued that this was a major problem for the IRO, with its temporary nature making it impossible to complete the task of providing protection to resettled refugees (Holborn 1975: 68), a view supported by the French delegation.[14] These arguments were also persuasive, and the General Assembly accepted that even if the agency's mandate was

---

[11] Mr. Kotschnig (United States of America), Ibid. 622; see also Saloman (1991: 219).

[12] United Nations, "Refugees and Stateless Persons," Report of the Secretary-General, A/C.3/527, October 26, 1949; see also Sadruddin (1976: 42–43).

[13] Mr. Rochefort (France), 326th Meeting of ECOSOC, August 6, 1949, ECOSOC Official Records, 1950, 617–20. Privately, Rochefort argued that this would suit American interests, because using the Secretariat increased the likelihood of the USSR "insisting on representation on the staff... with consequent danger of misuse of information." Alvin Roseman to George Warren, September 15, 1949, NARA RG 59 501.MA/8-1749.

[14] Mr. Rochefort (France) *GAOR*, 264th Meeting, December 2, 1949, 477.

limited to providing legal protection, it would need to function for more than three years (Holborn 1975: 67). However, the General Assembly hedged the question by adopting language that allowed for a review of the agency's work in 1953 and a vote on the renewal of its mandate.[15]

The final issue was over the agency's mandate, particularly whether it should have an operational role. The American delegation's position focused on ending the existing refugee problem and assumed that the UNHCR's remit would be confined to the "hard core" of refugees remaining from the Second World War (Goedhart 1955). They were also concerned that the Western European countries were trying to limit their own burdens by multilateralizing the financial aspect:

the Western European Governments, accustomed since 1945 to have indigent refugees on their territories cared for out of international funds, are now reluctant upon the termination of IRO to resume unilateral care... The United States Government holds the opposite view: that the caring for indigents among the residual refugees should not fall so heavily on any one country as to justify international assistance funds.[16]

The European view, particularly that of the French delegation, was that the UNHCR providing assistance to refugees was as important as legal protection. This view had historical weight – both the UNRRA and the IRO provided assistance and had significant financial resources.

Initially, the European goal of a broad mandate carried.[17] During the General Assembly debate, however, the American delegation successfully introduced an amendment that required General Assembly approval as a precondition for all appeals for voluntary contributions. The result of this was that the UNHCR had direct access to only a small administrative annual budget (Loescher 2001: 44).

Defining refugees

In addition to deciding on the structure of the UNHCR, the negotiators also had to define who was eligible for refugee status. This concept had to

[15] General Assembly Resolution 319 (IV) Refugees and Stateless Persons, December 3, 1949, Article 5. The UNHCR's mandate was renewed every five years until 2004, when the General Assembly voted to abolish the temporal limitation. General Assembly Resolution 58/153: Implementing Actions proposed by the United Nations High Commissioner for Refugees to Strengthen the Capacity of his Office to carry out its Mandate, February 24, 2004.

[16] Additionally, "Congress has made it clear that it does not propose to appropriate funds annually hereafter to cover United States contributions to such a fund." Refugees and Stateless Persons: Problems of Assistance to Refugees, September 2, 1950, *FRUS* 1950, vol. II, 539–40.

[17] ECOSOC Resolution 248 (IX), August 1949.

be defined in two legal instruments: the UNHCR's statute and the Refugee Convention. These parallel processes had different goals. The UNHCR negotiations focused on international actions, whereas the Convention focused on national responsibility (Holborn 1975: 80). Since Convention negotiations were taking longer, simply defining refugees in the Statute by referring to the Convention, a British proposal, was unworkable. Two different definitions needed to be negotiated.

As with the negotiations around the UNHCR's mandate, the European states favored a broad approach to the definition of refugees. The British delegation felt that the only criteria should be whether "the potential refugee had no government to which he could turn for protection." They argued that the UN had accepted "the protection of all refugees, regardless of their place of origin or the date upon which they became refugees. Hence the High Commissioner's competence should extend throughout the world and to all refugees."[18] The French delegation similarly argued that international protection was a collective responsibility and that a broad refugee definition was "the very embodiment of the liberalism of the European countries."[19] Thus, they suggested that a refugee should be anyone who had fled "justifiable fear of persecution" by their state of origin.[20]

The American delegation favored a narrower, group-oriented definition.[21] Their main concern was how the UN would respond to future flows. As the State Department argued in opposition to a global definition:

Such a definition would commit the United Nations to the protection of unknown groups of refugees and divest the Assembly of its freedom of action to deal with new refugee situations which might arise in the future. These new refugee situations ... can always be added later to the competence of the High Commissioner by Assembly action.[22]

---

[18] Lord MacDonald (United Kingdom), *GAOR* 324th Meeting, November 22, 1950 (A/C.3/SR.324).330–1.

[19] Mr. Rochefort (France) Ad Hoc Committee on Refugees and Stateless Persons, 33rd meeting, August 14, 1950. E/AC.32/SR.33.

[20] The French definition was the only one that reflected Article 14 of the Universal Declaration of Human Rights (UDHR), which had been passed in 1948. "Ad Hoc Committee on Statelessness and Related Problems," France: Proposal for a Draft Convention, January 17, 1950, E/AC.32/L.3. It enshrined a "right to leave any country, including his own, and to return to his country" (Article 13.2) and established that "everyone has the right to seek and to enjoy in other countries asylum from persecution" (Article 14.1).

[21] Ad Hoc Committee on Statelessness and Related Problems, United States of America: Memorandum on the Definition Article of the Preliminary Draft Convention, January 18, 1950. E/AC.32/L.4; Louis Henkin (United States) Ad Hoc Committee on Refugees and Stateless Persons, 3rd meeting, January 26, 1950. E/AC.32/SR.3.

[22] "Refugees and Stateless Persons," September 9, 1950. *FRUS* 1950, vol. II. 542; see also statement by Eleanor Roosevelt (United States) *GAOR* 324th Meeting, November 22, 1950 (A/C.3/SR.324). 331.

Rochefort, the head of the French delegation, moved to support this latter view as the negotiations progressed, arguing that "never before had a definition so wide and generous, but also so dangerous for the receiving countries, been put forward for signature by governments" (cited in Bem 2004).

Countries from the developing world had more mixed views. They had concerns over financial repercussions from a broad definition, and therefore some supported a narrow, European-focused definition (Humphrey and Hobbins 1994: II: 10; Bem 2004). Others, however, saw a narrow definition as distinctly problematic. As the Brazilian delegate argued, the UN "could not discriminate among refugees. Such an attitude would be a clear violation of the basic principles of morality and justice."[23] The Mexican delegate, while noting that the high commissioner "should primarily concern himself with the refugees who had been assisted by the IRO," added that refugees and stateless persons living in other parts of the world could be added, "thus broadening the new agency's field of action."[24]

Although a group-based definition was the historical model, it was open to critique. Delegates were particularly concerned with the IRO's experiences, which had required a trained body of eligibility experts and a semijudicial tribunal to determine which refugees fell within its mandate. A universal definition, by contrast, would eliminate the need for such substantial legal machinery. Furthermore, the definition could easily be applied to new refugee groups (Holborn 1975: 77).

Once again, a compromise between the Americans and Europeans was reached. For both the Convention and the Statute, it was decided to include separate components referring to groups and individuals. The group-based component of the definition was the same in both the Statute and the Convention and included anyone recognized under the League's Arrangements and Convention or by the International Refugee Organization.[25]

The other part of the definition was universalist in scope and focused on individuals. Aspects of this part of the definition varied between the

---

[23] Mr. Freyre (Brazil) *GAOR*, 265th Meeting, December 3, 1949, 484.

[24] Mr. de Alba (Mexico) *GAOR*, 265th Meeting, December 3, 1949, 488.

[25] "Any person who has been considered a refugee under the Arrangements of 12 May 1926 and of 30 June 1928 or under the Conventions of 28 October 1933 and 10 February 1938, the Protocol of 14 September 1939 or the Constitution of the International Refugee Organization" Convention on the Status of Refugees, 1951, Art I(A)(1); Statute of the United Nations High Commissioner for Refugees, Art. 6(A)(i). The 1933 Convention had incorporated the Russian Arrangement of 1922 and the Armenian Arrangement of 1924.

Convention and the Statute (Goodwin-Gill and McAdam 2007). Under the wording of the Convention, the term "refugee" applied to persons who:

As a result of events occurring before 1 January 1951 and owing to well-founded fear of being persecuted for reasons of race, religion, nationality, membership of a particular social group or political opinion, is outside the country of his nationality and is unable or, owing to such fear, is unwilling to avail himself of the protection of that country; or who, not having a nationality and being outside the country of his former habitual residence as a result of such events, is unable or, owing to such fear, is unwilling to return to it.[26]

The Convention specified that states could adopt one of two definitions of the phrase "events occurring before 1 January 1951." It could refer only to events in Europe or, alternatively, to events occurring in Europe or elsewhere.[27] Because states could choose to limit their obligations, the Convention created an "instrument for the legal protection of European refugees" (Loescher 2001: 45). The definition shielded states "from open-ended commitments by narrowing the range of people who could claim refugee status and the rights they might possess" (Gallagher 1989: 581; Barnett and Finnemore 2004: 85).

In contrast, the definition in the UNHCR Statute did not limit the UNHCR's responsibilities for protecting refugees to only European refugees. Section 6 A(ii) of the Statute said that the mandate of the High Commissioner of UNHCR applied to:

Any person who, as a result of events occurring before 1 January 1951 and owing to well-founded fear of being persecuted for reasons of race, religion, nationality or political opinion, is outside the country of his nationality and is unable or, owing to such fear or for reasons other than personal convenience, is unwilling to avail himself of the protection of that country; or who, not having a nationality and being outside the country of his former habitual residence, is unable or, owing to such fear or for reasons other than personal convenience, is unwilling to return to it.[28]

Section 6 also contained an additional clause that further expanded the mandate of the high commissioner. Part B of the section covered persons who did not meet the criteria of Part A, and extended the mandate to:

Any other person who is outside the country of his nationality, or if he has no nationality, the country of his former habitual residence, because he has or had well-founded fear of persecution by reason of his race, religion, nationality or

---

[26] Convention on the Status of Refugees, 1951, Article 1(A)(2).

[27] Convention on the Status of Refugees, 1951, Article 1(B); see also Sadruddin 1976: 6. The Convention also excludes those who committed war crimes, crimes against humanity, serious nonpolitical crimes, or who are guilty of acts contrary to the purposes and principles of the UN (Sadruddin 1976: 6–7).

[28] Statute of the United Nations High Commissioner for Refugees, Chapter II, 6.A (ii).

political opinion and is unable or, because of such fear, is unwilling to avail himself of the protection of the government of the country of his nationality, or, if he has no nationality, to return to the country of his former habitual residence. (UNHCR Statute, Chapter II, 6.B)

Crucially, this part contained neither geographic nor temporal limitations.

The Statute definition was a victory for the universalist view. It allowed new refugees who met the criteria to be automatically included in the competence of the UNHCR, and also stated that the agency's competence would be broader than that stipulated in the Convention (Holborn 1975: 77–79; Loescher 2001: 45).

The American delegation supported a strong set of rights for refugees being introduced in the Convention. As George Warren noted:

The United States Government had an interest in assisting in every way possible to secure broad adherence to the convention, particularly on the part of European states, because the legal establishment of rights and privileges for refugees under the convention would regularize the position of refugees and thus contribute to peace and order in areas in which large numbers of refugees reside. (Warren 1951: 503)[29]

For the U.S. government, a strong convention was the best way to guarantee that the rights of refugees would be protected in asylum countries. Therefore, "it is essential that the convention be opened for signature at the earliest possible time and applied as broadly as possible."[30] These rights included rights to property, to access courts, of association, to employment, to housing, to education, to support and assistance, to freedom of movement, to identity papers, and to travel documents (Office of the United Nations High Commissioner for Refugees 2006).

In addition to the specific rights of refugees, the Convention established two clear legal norms. The first precluded punishment for illegal entry of persons in search of asylum (Farer 1995: 79). The second enshrined the right of nonrefoulement: "No Contracting State shall expel or return ('refouler') a refugee in any manner whatsoever to the frontiers of territories where his life or freedom would be threatened on account of his race, religion, nationality, membership of a particular social group or political opinion" (Article 33.1) The Drafting Committee "felt strongly that the [non-refoulement] principle ... was fundamental and that it

---

[29] This support did not extend to the United States actually signing the Convention at this time. "Draft Convention Relating to the Status of Refugees," September 9, 1950, *FRUS* 1950, vol. II, 545.

[30] "Draft Convention Relating to the Status of Refugees," September 9, 1950, *FRUS* 1950, vol. II. 545; Louis Henkin (United States Delegate) Ad Hoc Committee on Refugees and Stateless Persons, 33rd meeting, August 14, 1950. E/AC.32/SR.33; Henkin, February 23, 1950, E/AC.32/SR.26.

should not be impaired" (Weis 1995: 235; see also Goodwin-Gill and McAdam 2007: 204).

The nonrefoulement provision within the Convention has gone on to provide "a model and textual basis" for a number of other human rights treaties (Weissbrodt and Hortreiter 1999: 2). Thus, the Convention against Torture expressly prohibits the refoulement of a person to any state "where there are substantial grounds for believing that he would be in danger of being subjected to torture."[31] Not only is this principle nonderogable, but it is also wider than that of the 1951 Convention because it permits no exceptions (Gorlick 1999: 481–82; Goodwin-Gill and McAdam 2007: 301).

Both sets of negotiations made it clear that there was a level of normative consensus among states on both the need for clear refugee protections in international law and that some form of multilateral organization was needed to regulate these protections. Where this consensus evaporated was on the form of the organization. The Europeans wanted a strong and independent organization within the UN. The Americans, focusing their efforts outside the UN, wanted a limited organization focused exclusively on legal protection. There was also a difference on the level of responsibility that states were willing to assign to the UNHCR and the level they would take on themselves. States were willing to assign a broader responsibility for refugees to the UNHCR by introducing a definition in its Statute with no geographic or temporal limitation while limiting their own responsibility to an interpretable geographic limitation. As time passed, this independence was crucial in allowing the UNHCR to take on a much broader mandate than even its most supportive creators envisioned, as the American government became increasingly supportive of its role in refugee protection.

Other institutional mechanisms: The U.S. escapee program and the ICEM

American opposition to a strong UN refugee organization was driven by two concerns on the part of the Truman administration. One was the level of Soviet influence in the UN. The other reflected a lessened concern toward refugees. Although they remained a potential source of instability in Europe, both Truman and his successor, Dwight D. Eisenhower, had become concerned over larger population pressures in Western Europe. For Truman, refugees and escapees were adding "to the pressures of

---

[31] *Convention against Torture and Other Cruel, Inhuman or Degrading Treatment or Punishment,* 1984, Art.3

overpopulation in certain countries... Humanitarian considerations, as well as the national interest, require that we reassess our immigration policies in the light of these facts."[32] Similarly, for Eisenhower the "problem of population pressures" continued "to be a source of urgent concern in several friendly countries in Europe ... these refugees, escapees, and distressed people now constitute an economic and political threat of constantly growing magnitude."[33]

Whereas the UNHCR would provide legal protections to existing refugees, the United States created two new organizations, the USEP and the ICEM, to assist refugees fleeing the communist bloc and transport them onward to resettlement countries. The United States was thereby attempting to create a broader international migration regime, one anchored in no further than three formal organizations.

With the ICEM, first established in 1951,[34] the United States sought to create a natural successor to the IRO.[35] It would contribute the bulk of funds,[36] and the organization would be open to all noncommunist governments. The ICEM gained one immediate advantage over the UNHCR because many of the staff and the fleet of ships that had been controlled by the IRO were transferred over to the new organization (Vernant 1953: 46–47; Robbins 1956: 329–30). The ICEM was also provided with a broad purview to provide transfer arrangements to migrants, as well as to "refugees, displaced persons and other individuals in need of international migration services" with all arrangements

[32] "Statement by the President Upon Issuing Order Establishing a Commission on Immigration and Naturalization," September 4, 1952, *The American Presidency Project*. www.presidency.ucsb.edu/ws/?pid=14244.

[33] Dwight D. Eisenhower, "Letter to the President of the Senate and to the Speaker of the House of Representatives Recommending Emergency Legislation for the Admission of Refugees," April 22, 1953, *The American Presidency Project*. www.presidency.ucsb.edu/ws/?pid=9821.

[34] Like the IRO before it, the ICEM's constitution was not quickly ratified, taking until 1954 to come into force. Initially, it was referred to as Provisional Intergovernmental Committee for the Movement of Migrants from Europe (PICMME), with its name changing to the ICEM in 1952. The organization subsequently changed its name to the Intergovernmental Committee for Migration, then to the International Organization for Migration (IOM) in 1989.

[35] Richard McKinzie "Oral History Interview with Donald C. Blaisdell," October 29, 1973, and June 27, 1975, Truman Library, www.trumanlibrary.org/oralhist/blaisdel.htm, 214.

[36] The United States contributed $10,000,000 to its creation, and other member states were expected to contribute about $3,000,000. Warren to Hickerson, November 14, 1951, US NARA RG 59 398.18-BR/11-1451; Warren "Confidential Report on the Conference on Migration Held at Brussels," US NARA RG 59 398.18-BR/1-1752; Report on the Conference on Migration and on the First Session of the Provisional Intergovernmental Committee for the Movement of Migrants From Europe, January 17, 1952, *FRUS 1952–1954*, vol. I, 1573.

conforming "to the laws, regulations, and policies of the States concerned."[37]

The USEP had a narrower purview. As a national program, it was designed to directly aid refugees fleeing communist Europe. It "served American strategic interests without the burden of open-ended commitments to international agreements" (Cohen 2011: 152). The program was designed to improve the reception facilities for people escaping from the Eastern bloc. It was an effort, George Warren noted, to rebuild hope "among the refugees when they become aware that they are no longer forgotten by a free world preoccupied by other concerns" (Warren 1953: 84–85; see also Rees 1953: 295–97). However, the program also served the goal, as Secretary of State John Foster Dulles argued, of responding to "Communist propagandists [who] have exploited with telling effect the inadequate conditions and general neglect which greeted escapees upon their arrival in the West."[38] Similar concerns were raised by U.S.-based voluntary agencies. As Reinhold Niebuhr, then chairman of the International Rescue Committee, wrote to Herbert Lehman, "the escapees who risk their lives to come over to our side, are prepared to risk their lives again for the common cause of democracy. But if they are not given the feeling that they are wanted, that the Western world really cares about them, they inevitably lapse into frustration and despair, and their will to fight is weakened."[39]

Neither the ICEM nor the USEP played the roles initially intended for them. The ICEM was designed to transport both refugees and migrants, based on fears of population overcrowding and unemployment in Western Europe. As a transport agency, the ICEM played an important role in resettling immigrants and refugees from Europe. By March 1965, it had transported more than 1.3 million people, including some 600,000 European refugees (Holborn 1964: 336). And yet economic growth in the 1950s quickly employed the surplus European population, thereby removing the ICEM's primary purpose (Perruchoud 1989: 506).

The USEP was designed, as Carruthers (2005) notes, to handle a broader caseload of refugees than the Refugee Convention envisioned. This included escapees who elected to leave the communist bloc for any reason, rather than solely those who faced individualized persecution. Yet its geographic purview was narrower than the ICEM's and limited to

---

[37] Constitution of the International Organization for Migration (1954), Chapter I, Art. 1.1(b)., 1.3.

[38] The Secretary of State to Certain Diplomatic and Consular Offices, February 19, 1953, *FRUS* 1952–1954, "Eastern Europe; Soviet Union; Eastern Mediterranean," 185.

[39] Reinhold Niebuhr to Senator Herbert Lehman, April 23, 1952, Lehman Collections, Columbia University, Folder 1014, underlining in original.

Eastern Europe. This did not include Germany because Berlin was "already over-crowded with refugees from the Eastern zone."[40]

The USEP had strong Congressional support.[41] However, the 1950 Internal Security Act's restrictive provisions, which included preventing the entry into the United States of anyone who had belonged to the Communist Party, meant that few escapees could actually enter the United States. A 1955 *Harper's* article estimated that by April of that year, only 563 visas had been issued for escapees, whereas by 1956 one report found that more than 250,000 persons eligible for program assistance remained in West German and Austrian camps (Carruthers 2005: 929–30). Thus, its primary goal – to move escapees out of these camps – failed due to domestic immigration concerns. The Internal Security Act similarly limited the ICEM's efforts to move migrants into the United States. Furthermore, from 1954, Congress, under Public Law No. 665, restricted the ICEM from spending any U.S. funds to move migrants to the Western Hemisphere without security clearances.[42] Thus, domestic legislation limited the ability of U.S.-based organizations to resettle communist refugees to the United States.

Equally, by 1953, the State Department's view of the UN's response had shifted on two points. The first was that earlier concerns over Soviet interference in the UNHCR had proved unwarranted: "an advantage in having separate structures for the Specialized Agencies [through ECOSOC] is the fact that the USSR and the Satellites do not, as a general rule, take part. This has freed the agencies from some of the political difficulties we encounter in the UN."[43] At the same time, they understood that the duplication of services between the UNHCR and the ICEM had proved ineffective:

These agencies are carrying out significant functions which for our own political reasons we did not feel able to further through the UN... However ... their

[40] The Secretary of State to Certain Diplomatic and Consular Offices, February 19, 1953, *FRUS* 1952–1954, 186.

[41] Its funds came from the Kersten Amendment to the 1951 Mutual Security Act, which provided $100 million for escapees to form into "elements of the military forces supporting the North Atlantic Treaty Organization or for other purposes." Section 101(a)(1) of the Mutual Security Act of 1951. In itself, this legislation was highly controversial and led to Soviet arguments in the UN General Assembly that these aggressive acts contravened international law (Carruthers 2005: 919).

[42] Memorandum on the US Appropriations Rider Attached to US Public Law No. 665, Enclosure to The Director of the Intergovernmental Committee on European Migration (Gibson) to the Secretary of State, October 6, 1954, *FRUS* 1952–1954, vol. I, 1564; The Secretary of State to the Director of the Intergovernmental Committee for European Migration, November 16, 1954, *FRUS* 1952–1954, vol. I, 1654.

[43] Inter-Relations of International Organization in Non-Political Fields, undated, *FRUS* 1952–1954, "General United States- United Nations Relations," 168.

existence outside the UN structure makes it much more difficult to prevent competitive and uncoordinated action... [T]he competition among the ILO, the UN High Commissioner for Refugees, and ICEM concerning their respective policies and programs involving refugees and migration exemplifies the difficulty created by parallel and overlapping responsibilities.[44]

Faced with the failures of the ICEM and USEP to resettle communist refugees, the American government was more willing to accept an expanded UNHCR role.

The norm entrepreneurship of UNHCR

The UNHCR's start was not auspicious: although it had the support of European governments (particularly those with large numbers of refugees), neither superpower supported it. Its Statute established that the agency had two main goals: to provide international protection and to seek permanent solutions for the refugee problem. Like the IOs before it, it had three mechanisms to create permanent solutions to refugee problems: voluntary repatriation, assimilation through local integration, and resettlement (UNHCR 1971: 16–17).

Unlike the USEP or ICEM, the UNHCR did have an international legal mandate to protect those who could no longer count on the protection of their own state. It therefore possessed a strong moral authority. Yet, the UNHCR had little else. It was a temporary organization with no operational budget or ability to provide material assistance, and only a limited staff (UNHCR 1971: 13, 17). Gerrit Jan van Heuven Goedhart of the Netherlands was selected as its first high commissioner. Goedhart had been a refugee himself – as a leader in the Dutch resistance, he had fled to Britain after being targeted by the Nazis – and he had chaired the Third Committee discussions on both the Statute and the Convention and knew the spirit behind each clause (Loescher 2001: 50–51).[45] As Goedhart would later note, when appointed "I found three empty rooms and a secretary and had to start from scratch" (cited in UNHCR 1971: 28).

In spite of these limitations, the UNHCR succeeded by making itself invaluable as an authoritative actor that could quickly respond to new refugee situations, ensure refugee protection, and coordinate assistance. As an impartial UN agency, it was able to act in areas where the USEP or the ICEM could not because of the politics of the Cold War. Most importantly, though, its first four high commissioners understood the

---

[44] Ibid., 169.
[45] Goedhart picked as his deputy James Read, an American with little connection to the State Department. Warren to Hickerson, March 12, 1951, NARA RG 59 320.42/3-1551.

refugee problem in a significantly different light than did the states that had negotiated its creation. They recognized that the problem would be ongoing and global. Hence, the agency actively sought to move away from its Eurocentric origins to embrace the developing world and, in so doing, to redefine the refugee regime as universal in scope.

UNHCR becomes an assistance organization

Both Goedhart and his successor as high commissioner, Auguste Lindt, understood that legal protection alone would not meet the needs of the hard core refugees still in camps. Nor did such a limited mandate allow the agency to effectively respond to new refugee flows that both high commissioners understood would be inevitable (Read 1962: 10). Therefore, they focused on its role as an operational agency, designed to provide both protection and assistance to refugees.

Goedhart's first step was to ask the General Assembly for an emergency fund to provide limited relief to refugees still in camps, a request triggered by the plight of refugees in Hong Kong who faced starvation (UNHCR 1953; Stoessinger 1956: 166–67; UNHCR 1961: 25). The American delegation argued against it, with Eleanor Roosevelt noting that she "could not vote for the resolution which would set the precedent of authorizing the United Nations to collect funds for a rather indefinite program."[46] This opposition was based on the nature of the commitment, rather than its cost. During the same time, the American government had given more than $150 million for the UNRWA and around $75 million for the UN Korean Reconstruction Administration (Loescher 2001: 64). The European governments were more magnanimous, with the Norwegian delegation arguing in support of a voluntary fund, a position the General Assembly accepted (Stoessinger 1956: 167).[47] This was a small success. The fund could only be used for emergencies, and it was undersubscribed, with only fourteen governments contributing a total of $755,000, less than a third of the $3 million Goedhart sought (UNHCR 1971: 14; Soguk 1999: 172; Loescher 2001: 62–64).

The UNHCR, like its predecessors, instead looked for funds elsewhere and approached the Ford Foundation for money for local integration programs (Ford Foundation 1958: 17). These funds allowed many of

---

[46] Statement by Eleanor Roosevelt (cited in Stoessinger 1956: 166). See also Warren to Hickerson, March 12, 1951, NARA RG 59 320.42/3-1551. 2–3; Hickerson to Warren, March 12, 1951, NARA RG 59 320.42/3-1551.

[47] General Assembly Resolution 538 (VI)B Assistance to and protection to refugees, February 2, 1952.

the refugees to leave the camps – of the 130,000 refugees remaining in the "hard core" in 1952, all but 26,500 had been successfully resettled or reintegrated by 1959. But it also helped to encourage "governments, private sources, and the general public to take greater interest, moral and material, in furthering a solution of the refugee problem" (Ford Foundation 1958: 9). By 1958, the Emergency Fund had $17 million in contributions, $3 million of which came from private sources, a shift Goedhart referred to as a "peaceful chain reaction" (Read 1962: 17; UNHCR 1971: 62).

Goedhart used new refugee flows to further buttress the idea that the UNHCR was needed as an operational agency. By 1953, 48,000 refugees per month were fleeing into West Germany from the East. Goedhart proposed to use the unrestricted Ford Foundation grant to provide immediate housing relief to the refugees (UNHCR 1954: paragraph 5; see also Read 1962: 14–15). Its response helped to legitimize it as an assistance organization. And, for the first time "the US began to perceive UNHCR programs as being potentially useful in the ideological struggle between East and West" (Loescher 2001: 74). Perhaps the biggest recognition of the agency's success was the UNHCR being awarded the Nobel Peace Prize the following year (Stoessinger 1956: 168).

Although the UNHCR's response in West Germany had increased its visibility, a new crisis would make its reputation. On November 4, 1956, the Soviet Union invaded Hungary after the Nagy regime declared neutrality and made moves to leave the Warsaw Pact. By November 21, refugees were crossing into Austria at the rate of 7,000 per day, and by March 1957, Austria was hosting 171,000 refugees. Another 20,000 had gone to Yugoslavia (UNHCR 1961: 26; Loescher 2001: 82–83; Marrus 2002: 359).

The Austrian government had two main concerns. The first was that accepting the refugees might lead to Soviet attack. This fear was heightened after Moscow Radio alleged that Austria had violated its neutrality by allowing the United States to use Austrian territory to provide weapons and ammunition to the Hungarian refugees. The fear of attack was alleviated after both Britain and the United States said publicly that they would consider an attack on neutral Austria as an act of war. Although Austria was willing to accept in the refugees following this announcement, the government's second concern was that it lacked the resources to care for the refugees.[48] The Hungarian refugees demonstrated conclusively that

---

[48] The Austrian government made it clear to UNHCR officials that although it supported a liberal asylum policy, it would be unable to provide assistance after four to six months. Thus, part of the expense for new refugees would need to be borne by outside sources. Dr. V. A. M. Beermann, UNHCR Representative Vienna, to the High Commissioner, October 12, 1956, UNHCR Archives HCR/22/11/AUS [2]-184.

international cooperation and assistance was required and "that countries of first asylum cannot go it alone" (Rees 1957: 234; UNHCR 1957).

The UNHCR was asked by the General Assembly to organize international relief efforts. For the first time, the agency was specifically designated a lead agency under High Commissioner Lindt and coordinated the UN effort. Lindt had succeeded Goedhart in December, following Goedhart's death that July (UNHCR 1971: 69–71; Loescher 2001: 83–84). For the first time, too, the agency was able to resettle large numbers of refugees following favorable shifts in immigration legislation in the United States and other countries (Read 1962: 18). A total of 154,000 Hungarian refugees were eventually resettled, whereas 18,000 were voluntarily repatriated (UNHCR 1961: 26; Marrus 2002: 362).

The most important innovation in response to the Hungarian refugees was that the UNHCR devised a legal justification for its presence within the January 1, 1951, dateline set by the Refugee Convention. Paul Weis, the legal adviser to the high commissioner, argued that the departure of the refugees related to the establishment of the People's Republic of Hungary, which had occurred in 1947, and therefore that this new refugee exodus was "an after effect of this earlier political change."[49] This enabled the UNHCR to apply prima facie refugee status to all Hungarian refugees based on the assumption that they were fleeing persecutions, thereby avoiding individual refugee determination processes (Loescher 2001: 88).[50]

The Hungarian exodus allowed the UNHCR to demonstrate its operational abilities. Following the resolution of the crisis, the UNHCR was able to position itself as a gatekeeper and extend its authority outside the UN by establishing a coordinating group to manage emergency assistance. The American government supported this shift and advocated that all relief should be managed by the UNHCR (Loescher 2001: 84).[51] As Deputy High Commissioner James Read later wrote, the ICEM "and all the foreign private voluntary agencies helping to deal with the [Hungarian] influx were

[49] Paul Weis, "Eligibility of Refugees from Hungary," January 9, 1957, UNHCR Archives, HCR/22/1/HUNG. The American government confirmed that it accepted this. Dr. V. A. M. Beermann, UNHCR Representative Vienna, to the High Commissioner, October 17, 1956, UNHCR Archives HCR/22/11/AUS [2]- 185.

[50] With prima facie recognition, individuals can acquire refugee status without having to justify their fear of persecution based on the objective circumstances of mass displacement and the obvious refugee character of the individuals so affected (Durieux and McAdam 2004: 11).

[51] This was helped by a favorable American view of Lindt. J. W. Hanes to Dulles, "Your appointment at 11:45 with the United Nations High Commissioner for Refugees," November 15, 1957, NARA RG 59 320.42/11-1557.

allowed to operate only insofar as they were integral parts of the mission" (1962: 15).

The UNHCR was also able to expand its mandate with the acquiescence of the UN member states (Gordenker 1987: 35; Gallagher 1989: 582). In 1957, the General Assembly extended the UNHCR's role to include new emergencies, including those outside of Europe, with the permission of its newly created Executive Committee.[52] The General Assembly also authorized the high commissioner to make appeals for funds for any of these new emergencies, thus removing the requirement that the UNHCR first receive General Assembly approval (UNHCR 1961: 28; Loescher 2001: 89–90).[53]

In its first seven years in operation, therefore, the UNHCR successfully expanded its mandate and gained considerable autonomy. From a tiny Office with no operational mandate, it proved its capability not only for providing assistance to refugees, but also in coordinating the response to large-scale emergencies. Thus, the UNHCR had successfully expanded its scope of concern, the legal definition of refugees and their protection in international law, and its finances (Gordenker 1987: 35). Its "latitude to act – albeit with permission and encouragement of states – was significantly widened" (Gallagher 1989: 582).

The Good Offices protocol and moving into Africa

The UNHCR remained hobbled by the temporally and geographically limited Convention definition of refugee status under which it operated. Through the use of the "high commissioner's good offices," a notion created by Lindt, the agency was able to make a concerted effort to sidestep these limitations. The good offices formula allowed the UNHCR to assist refugees who did not fall within its Statute but where "the problem is such as to be of concern to the international

---

[52] The Executive Committee of the UNHCR was created in 1958 and replaced the United Nations Refugee Emergency Fund Executive Committee, which had in turn replaced an initial Advisory Committee. Composed of member states, its terms of reference include advising the high commissioner in the exercise of his function, to authorize the high commissioner to make appeals for funds, and to approve projects for refugee assistance. General Assembly Resolution A/RES/1166 (XII) "International assistance to refugees within the mandate of the United Nations High Commissioner for Refugees," November 26, 1957; General Assembly Resolution A/RES/1166 (XII), November 26, 1957.

[53] General Assembly Resolution A/RES/1166 (XII), November 26, 1957, Article 5 (d); "Statement Made by Mr. A. Lindt, United Nations High Commissioner, at the Opening Meeting of the Fourth Session of the UNREF Executive Committee," February 15, 1957, UNHCR Archives HCR/6/1/GEN-Protection General-56A.

community."[54] It also allowed the agency to undertake prima facie determinations of eligibility.[55]

The good offices formula was first used soon after the UNHCR's creation with respect to Chinese refugees in Hong Kong. With the communist victory in China in 1949, some 700,000 refugees fled into Hong Kong. The Chinese refugees did not easily fit into existing refugee definitions as a result of a political move by the British government. Britain, interested in developing a positive political relationship with the communist government, declared that most of these refugees were illegal immigrants subject to immediate expulsion (Mark 2007: 1148). Britain went so far as to deliberately not extend its ratification of the 1951 Refugee Convention to Hong Kong in order to avoid recognizing the Chinese as refugees.

The issue was further complicated because either of the two Chinas might "have been called upon to exercise protection" (Goodwin-Gill and McAdam 2007: 24). In 1952, the Republic of China (ROC) government, still occupying China's seat at the UN, claimed that the refugees were entitled to its protection as the official government of China, even though it accepted few for resettlement. But this meant that the governments that recognized the ROC saw the refugees as having state protection and therefore falling outside the UNHCR's mandate.[56]

Goedhart needed to find a solution in which the refugees would receive protection but that would not endanger the bilateral relationship between Britain and China. For the first time, he argued that the UNHCR had a worldwide mandate to assist refugees (Goedhart 1953) and would be prepared to deal with the situation in Hong Kong if given the authority and funds to do so. In 1954, an independent assessment was conducted by Edvard Hambro, of the International Court of Justice, who found that the refugees should be considered to be de facto under the UNHCR's mandate because the ROC could not effectively protect or resettle them (Hambro 1955; Read 1962: 19–20).

---

[54] UNGA Resolution 1167 (XII) "Chinese Refugees in Hong Kong," November 26, 1957; UNHCR, "Report of the United Nations High Commissioner for Refugees," A/3828/Rev.1, January 1, 1959.

[55] "Determination of Mandate Eligibility in Countries Where UNHCR acts on the Basis of 'Good Offices,'" Unsigned memorandum, ND, PWA PW/PR/HCR/REF/9. See also Goodwin-Gill and McAdam (2007: 24).

[56] "Report of US Delegation of 5th Session of HC Advisory Cmmt on Refs 6–10 December 1954," December 10, 1954, NARA RG 59 320.42/12-1054. 4; Ruth Bacon to Mr. McConaughy, February 6, 1957, NARA RG 59 320.42/2-657.

Even so, the issue remained alive for another three years until the British position changed[57] and the matter was referred to the General Assembly. Because the problem was a concern to the international community, in 1957, the General Assembly authorized the high commissioner "to use his good offices to encourage arrangements for contributions."[58] As Holborn notes, this decision defused the main dilemma, ensuring "the end desired – more aid for the Chinese refugees – without making any declaration as to the legal status of the refugees and thereby become embroiled in the perennially troublesome issue of the two Chinas" (1975: 436). The contributions raised were minor – only a few hundred thousand dollars (Read 1962: 21). However, the crisis allowed the UNHCR to expand its mandate to de facto refugees. In so doing, it overcame the opposition of Britain, a Great Power, to having people within its territory classified as refugees.

The good offices formula was also used successfully to deal with another refugee crisis involving a Great Power in 1957: the Algerian war of independence against France. Approximately 85,000 refugees had fled into Tunisia. The refugees faced miserable living conditions, and the Tunisian government requested material assistance from the UNHCR (Thomas 2002). Like Goedhart before him, Lindt felt that the UNHCR's mandate was worldwide (Read 1962: 21). The French government initially denied any UNHCR authority to provide assistance, arguing that Algeria was an integral part of France and that agency involvement might internationalize the crisis. Despite the French opposition, Lindt nevertheless sought to have the UNHCR play a role. This was at the expense of a potential rift not only in the international community, but also within the agency. Some UNHCR officials were opposed on political grounds. They argued that "it was politically impossible for UNHCR to declare the Algerians refugees, because such an action would imply that France . . . was persecuting some of its own subjects" (Loescher 2001: 99).

Lindt began by arguing to the American government that it was in its interest to support the UNHCR becoming involved. He suggested that by channeling support to the Algerian refugees through the agency, the United States could win goodwill with the African states and avoid

---

[57] In 1956, following the success of UNHCR's efforts in Hungary, the Hong Kong government saw international recognition of the problem as a way to raise the funds the British government was unwilling to provide (Mark 2007). See also Ambassador Whitney (London) to Secretary of State, September 4, 1957, NARA RG 59. 320.42/9-457.

[58] UN General Assembly Resolution, "Chinese Refugees in Hong Kong" (A/RES/1167 (XII), November 26, 1957. The UNHCR quickly acknowledged that the resolution did not "imply that Chinese refugees in Hong Kong are at present within the competence of this Office according to its Statute." James Read to the Secretary of State, February 12, 1958, NARA RG 59 320.42/2-1258.

damaging its relations with France. By contrast, Lindt noted, refusing to intervene would justify charges that the High Commission was for European refugees only.[59] Following a UNHCR mission to Tunisia, Lindt met with French Foreign Minister Christian Pineau and provided details of atrocities committed by French forces against Algerians. Pineau acknowledged the findings and, when Lindt said that the UNHCR would provide aid to Tunisia, Pineau noted that it was "okay, but don't make too much of a fuss" (Loescher 2001: 100).[60] Lindt carefully argued that the refugees were not a legal issue. The agency made no clear determination of refugee eligibility to avoid a crisis with the French government; instead, Lindt suggested that the agency was providing assistance to people who needed help (Read 1962: 25; Loescher 2001: 100). In December 1958, he received formal approval from the General Assembly to continue.[61] "The politics of good relations," Goodwin-Gill (2008: 27) writes, "prevailed over legal niceties and positions of principle, but also enabled UNHCR to expand into the developing world and to help new groups of refugees."

In 1959, the General Assembly formally removed the requirement that the UNHCR seek further authorizations to use the good offices protocol.[62] As Holborn notes, the agency's successes meant that the General Assembly was now "willing to turn to UNHCR whenever its services could be usefully applied in meeting the needs of new and different refugee groups" (1975: 437). Thereafter, as Goodwin-Gill and McAdam note, the language in the General Assembly changed, "became more composite and began to reflect the notion of refugees 'of concern' to UNHCR" (2007: 25). By 1968, one UNHCR official noted, "one may see that there is no longer a specific reference to the *mandate*, but to the notion of 'competence' or of 'concern,' which is undoubtedly more flexible."[63]

Lindt also sought to make the agency as apolitical as possible. This led him to propose amending the UNHCR's Statute in 1960 to remove "well-founded" from the phrase "well-founded fear of persecution" along with other amendments. "I believe that it would be highly desirable" he argued, "in order to make clear that a decision bringing a person, or group

---

[59] Gowen to Dulles, June 5, 1957, NARA RG 59 320.42/6-557.

[60] This represented a major shift in the French position. Previously, they argued that there should be no investigation at all of the refugee status of the Algerians. Gowen to Dulles, June 7, 1957, NARA RG 59 320.42/6-757. See also Villard to Secretary of State, July 31, 1959, NARA RG 59 320.42/7-3159.

[61] UN General Assembly Resolution 1286 "Refugees in Morocco and Tunisia," December 5, 1958, A/RES/1286 (XIII).

[62] UN General Assembly Resolution 1388 (XIV) "Report of the United Nations High Commissioner for Refugees," November 20, 1959, A/RES/1388 (XIV) Article 2.

[63] John Colmar, "Note on the Good Offices," April 2, 1968, UNHCR Archives HCR/1/1/71 "Good Offices" Policy- 6. 3 italics in original.

of persons, within the competence of this Office, does not constitute a censure or a political judgement on the conditions in the refugee's country of origin."[64] The United States by this point had a strong interest in amending the agency's statute, but it was not willing to support such a move, in part over concerns about whether this proposed change would be acceptable to the General Assembly. This reluctance was in spite of the U.S. view that if the changes were not passed that year with Lindt as high commissioner, "they might as well be shelved for the indefinite future."[65] It would take another seven years to amend the Convention, rather than the Statute.

The good offices protocol also provided an effective way for the UNHCR to expand its activities into Africa under Lindt's successor, Felix Schnyder. As Schnyder argued upon taking office in 1960, the good offices protocol was elastic enough to shift emphasis to groups "in other continents . . . to permit him, when asked, to bring effective aid to nearly any group of refugees provided there was sufficient interest and support on the part of the international community."[66]

Even so, Schnyder acknowledged that the UNHCR's efforts were dependent on continued state support: "We must realize that we are not more than an instrument of the international community. We must therefore make sure that governments will support us and provide the means, either directly or indirectly, for an action that can be carried out until its successful conclusion" (cited in UNHCR 1971: 102). Most importantly, the American government tacitly endorsed the expansion into Africa: "in an era in which the concept of collective action through the U.N. has acquired increased importance, it might appear detrimental to U.S. leadership to oppose what could be regarded as a historic trend."[67] It felt that the UNHCR's expanded operations remained "consistent with traditional United States refugee policy, to call attention to the fundamental responsibility of asylum countries for refugees in their territory."[68]

---

[64] Lindt [Read signed] to Wilcox, May 30, 1960, NARA RG 59 324.8411/5-3060 and attached "Report," May 24, 1960, HCR/R8/18.

[65] Wilcox to Lindt, July 12, 1960, NARA RG 59 324.8411/5-3060; Memorandum of Conversation "Meeting of June 8," June 15, 1960, NARA RG 59 324.8411/6-1560. 2,4.

[66] UNHCR Press Release, N. Ref. 638, February 1, 1961, cited in Loescher, Betts, and Milner (2008: 133).

[67] Despatch from the Mission in Geneva to the Department of State, April 6, 1961. *FRUS* vol. XXV, "Foreign Relations, 1961–1963," 685. See also Eisenhower to Lindt, in Ibid.

[68] Department of State Instruction "Possible Shift in Emphasis in Program of the United Nations High Commissioner for Refugees," April 24, 1961, NARA RG 59 324.8411/ 4-2461. See also Telegram Brown to Consul, Geneva, October 6, 1961, NARA RG 59 324.8411/9-3061.

But the expansion into Africa posed its own legal and assistance problems, particularly with regard to individual determinations of refugee status (See Sadruddin 1976: 11–13; Elie 2007: 10). The UNHCR's response was to increase the use of "collective prima facie eligibility" as a "more pragmatic and humane rather than legalistic approach to the refugee problem" (Sadruddin 1976: 48; see also UNHCR 1966: Appendix I). This enabled the UNHCR to provide protection en masse, and if individual determinations were needed, they could be undertaken later (Gordenker 1987: 39). But, clearly, the Refugee Convention needed to reflect this shift to a global focus.

Amending the Convention

By 1967, the UNHCR was questioning the utility of the good offices concept. To ensure that the high commissioner could respond quickly, it "had to remain vague... [T]he High Commissioner, to a great extent, has judged himself whether or not to deal with new refugee problems in various parts of the world."[69] Even with this operational flexibility, however, the Refugee Convention's definition remained distinctly limited, especially as refugee numbers expanded due to decolonization, political instability, and an increased number of violent conflicts (Capelli 1987: 28; Soguk 1999: 173).

Under Schnyder, the agency began a process to amend the Convention. His goal, Davies suggests, was not only to remove the geographic and dateline limitations from the Convention but also to create a definition applicable to a wider range of refugee situations, one that would provide for prima facie determination (2008: 704–08). A legal review endorsed this view. The review argued that the refugee problem was both universal and of indefinite duration and that "it was urgent for humanitarian reasons that refugees at present not covered by the Convention should be granted similar benefits by means" of a protocol to amend the Convention.[70] Given how contentious the debates over the Convention had been seventeen years prior, it is a mark of the regard in which the UNHCR was now held that few states raised concerns over this process.

[69] A. Rorholt to J. Colmar "Good Offices and their Use," May 18, 1967, UNHCR Archives HCR/1/1/71 "Good Offices" Policy-3.

[70] "Memorandum by the United Nations High Commissioner for Refugees on the Report of the Colloquium on Legal Aspects of Refugee Problems," September 23, 1965 (HCR/RS/31), Paul Weis Archives PW/PR/HCR/BSN/14/2, 2. A Protocol helped avoid a General Assembly debate of the Convention, grounded in the fear "that there remained a large number of governments resistant to the idea of accepting increased legal obligations, as they saw it, to an unforeseen number of potential refugees" (Davies 2008: 722).

Rather, apart from a few states that felt the protocol did not go far enough, they responded favorably (Davies 2008: 725–26).

The Protocol was submitted to the UN for ratification, and it entered into force in 1967 (Lewis 2005: 77).[71] Notably, the Protocol was structured so that states who acceded to it would also, in effect, be undertaking all the obligations of the 1951 Convention. States that had previously not signed the Convention, including the United States, now became party to both (Loescher 2001: 124).

Most significantly, the Protocol removed the previous geographic and temporal restrictions from the Convention, thereby universalizing the UNHCR's mandate (Helton 2000). This "eliminated the central anomaly between the Statute of UNHCR and the Refugee Convention – the Refugee Commissioner's simultaneous responsibility for refugees and the limitation of his authority" (Gallagher 1989: 583). With this change, the Convention gained "a more legitimate claim to universality" and a much wider global acceptance (Smyser 1987: 13). The 1967 Protocol represented a high point for the postwar refugee regime by universalizing the regime and removing its Eurocentric bias.

But even with this shift, the Convention's definitional limitations triggered a move toward more expansive regional law. In 1963, the Organization for African Unity (OAU)'s Liberation Committee recommended that "the OAU should assume direct responsibility for the refugees in Africa" (Milner 2009: 23; see also Arboleda 1991: 193) whereas, the following year, the OAU's Council of Ministers created a Commission on Refugee Problems in Africa to "investigate ways to deal with the political nature of the continent's refugee problems" (Loescher 2001: 125). The main goal initially, Sharpe finds, was to create a modified version of the Refugee Convention without a dateline and that was applicable to Africa (Sharpe 2011: 7–8).

There is no question that the OAU Convention as adopted proved a victory for the UNHCR (Loescher 2001: 125; see also Milner 2004: 13). The then-proposed Convention helped to drive the UNHCR's own efforts to amend the Refugee Convention under the 1967 Protocol (UNHCR 2000: 56). By working closely with the OAU to draft the text, UNHCR officials were able to make sure the text followed and advanced the existing rights contained in the Refugee Convention (Sharpe 2011). At the same time, the agency was able to prevent a separate organization being created, with the OAU Convention noting

---

[71] UN General Assembly "Proposed Measures to Extend the Personal Scope of the Convention Relating to the Status of Refugees," October 12, 1966 (A/AC.96/346), 8. Paul Weis Archives PW/PR/HCR/BSN/14/8.

explicitly that "member states shall co-operate with the office of United Nations High Commissioner for Refugees."[72]

The OAU Convention did not enter into force until 1969, delayed in part due to the negotiations around the Refugee Protocol. It provided a wider definition for refugees than either the UN Refugee Convention or Protocol, adding that:

The term "refugee" shall also apply to every person who, owing to external aggression, occupation, foreign domination or events seriously disturbing public order in either part or the whole of his country of origin or nationality, is compelled to leave his place of habitual residence in order to seek refuge in another place outside his country of origin or nationality.[73]

The OAU Convention made several other advances. It allowed individuals to acquire refugee status without having to justify their fear of persecution, reflecting the UNHCR's practice of prima facie recognition (Arboleda 1991: 194). It also placed a responsibility onto receiving states, noting that member states "shall use their best endeavours . . . to receive refugees" (Milner 2004: 6; Rwelamira 1989). The reasons for this expansive set of rights are debated. Rutinwa suggests that, at the time, "African countries readily admitted all those in search of security and safety, and refugees were hardly ever rejected at the frontier or returned to countries where they might face persecution or serious harm" (1999: 1). But Milner adds that state concerns over national security and their own domestic politics helped support an egalitarian view (Milner 2004: 10).[74]

UNHCR in the 1970s and 1980s

Following the adoption of the Protocol, the Convention's geographic and temporal limitations were no longer significant constraints on the UNHCR's activities. In Africa, it could rely on the broader regional definition in order to avoid individual determinations under the 1951 Convention. Elsewhere, the UNHCR increasingly made prima facie

[72] Ibid., Article VIII. The OAU Convention, however, failed to create either an implementary treaty body or a unique oversight authority (Sharpe 2011: 16).

[73] Organization for African Unity *Convention Governing the Specific Aspects of Refugee Problems in Africa*, Article II.

[74] The Cartagena Declaration on Refugees, adopted by ten Central American governments in 1984, also provided an enlarged refugee definition, one including those "who have fled their country because their lives, safety or freedom have been threatened by generalized violence, foreign aggression, internal conflicts, massive violation of human rights or other circumstances which have seriously disturbed public order." Cartagena Declaration on Refugees, November 22, 1984, OAS Doc. 0AE/Ser.L/V/II.66/doc.10, rev.1, Article 1. However, it was nonbinding and merely "confirmed customary legal rules for defining refugees" (Arboleda 1991: 187).

determinations on the character of refugee groups by virtue of their composition in light of the Statute and the Refugee Protocol definition, which allowed them to avoid individual determination processes (Guest 1991: 585–86; Jackson 1999a: 459–60). It was no longer necessary for the agency to devote energy to advocating for a broader mandate. Instead, the UNHCR's attention was focused on responding to mass refugee situations, including those in Afghanistan, Vietnam, Cambodia, Somalia, El Salvador, and Mozambique.

With little legal limitation on its activities and with continued donor support, the UNHCR expanded its activities in the developing world dramatically. The agency, which had spent $8.3 million per year at the beginning of the 1970s, spent $69 million in 1975 (Loescher 2001: 151). Schnyder's replacement, Prince Sadruddin Aga Khan,[75] who served as high commissioner from 1966 to 1978, set out a vision of the UNHCR's mandate that was markedly broad:

> The High Commissioner's Office could take action on behalf of large groups of people who may not all conform to the conventional definition of a refugee but are in a situation analogous to that of refugees. . . The reasoning behind this evolution would appear to be that cut off from their origins and scattered or brought together again by circumstances in one place, or another, these displaced persons clearly need some form of international assistance. (Sadruddin 1976: 49–50)

Under Sadruddin's tenure, the agency became global, an expansion that continued under his successor, Poul Hartling, who served from 1978 to 1985. By 1980, the UNHCR annual government contributions totaled $500 million as the agency grappled with new refugee flows, including those from Vietnam and the Soviet invasion of Afghanistan. With these substantial resources, the agency became increasingly assistance-orientated, running more and more programs by itself and offering greater services to refugees (Guest 1991: 590; Loescher 2001: 202).

Conclusion

By the mid-1970s, the postwar refugee regime was strong, with a clear concordance among its norms. As discussed here and in the preceding chapter, this development occurred for three reasons. The first was strong

---

[75] This appointment required careful negotiations with the United States, which felt that the position should go to an American but that "Prince Khan is 'western' in his orientation and would be acceptable to us if we could not arrange for the appointment of an American." Memorandum from the Director of the Office of International Administration, Bureau of International Organization Affairs (Westfall) to the Assistant Secretary (Cleveland), March 31, 1961, FRUS XXV, 674–76.

support for refugee protection due to a historical legacy: the failure to help German Jewish refugees prior to the Holocaust. The second was a direct link between humanitarian and national interests in the regime's creation that saw American support for a strong IO, the IRO, and the 1951 Refugee Convention. The third was that, although the American government initially sought to limit the role of the UNHCR as the IRO's replacement, by the late 1950s, it had accepted that the UNHCR's role was vital to protect refugees and to act as an effective response against the Soviet government. For the following two decades, the UNHCR was an effective international actor for refugee protection and helped to convince states to create a universal regime.

The UNHCR's success was not ordained. The agency that emerged through negotiations among states in 1950 was one with a limited mandate, scope, and no operational role. As with the League HCR, it is possible for IOs to dramatically alter how states perceive the regime. The UNHCR succeeded in expanding its role by proving its effectiveness as an assistance organization. The UNHCR also was able to reframe its own source of legal authority by removing the dateline and geographic restrictions from the 1951 Refugee Convention. Thus, the UNHCR played a key role as a norm entrepreneur by reframing the legal basis for refugee status and by shifting the focus of the regime away from its Eurocentric beginnings to encompass the world. Equally important, it established its own autonomy and independent sources of authority. This enabled it to react successfully to changes in the nature of refugee flows from the 1950s into the 1980s.

Unfortunately, the story does not end there. In the 1980s, refugee numbers began to substantially increase. Developed states adopted policies focused on restrictionism at the expense of fundamental refugee rights. The UNHCR's role was increasingly questioned. And, as the agency's expert authority became compromised, donor governments sought to minimize the agency's autonomy and to control its budget, even as the UNHCR sought to grapple with refugee flows in a changed world.

8   The non-entrée regime

The strong regime that formed in the postwar era remained effective into the 1980s. The United Nations High Commissioner for Refugees (UNHCR) and other norm entrepreneurs had built on an existing normative foundation established in previous regimes to ensure that the postwar regime was based on a clear definition of refugees enshrined in international law; a right by refugees to leave their own state and seek asylum elsewhere, as well as a right of non-refoulement; and a collective responsibility among states to provide refugees with protection and assistance. This regime successfully functioned through much of the Cold War era and survived significant changes in both the form and location of refugees.

This normative consensus unraveled in the early 1990s due to a change in the numbers and nature of refugee claimants. The refugee population had grown only gradually in the 1970s and early 1980s, but rose dramatically starting later in that decade. The total global number of refugee claimants doubled in size from 1980 to 1992 (see Figure 8.1). Not only were refugees fleeing in greater numbers, but the number of claimants reaching the developed world was also rising. Between 1989 and 1991, asylum claims in the United Kingdom climbed from 16,775 to 73,400 before falling to 32,300 the next year. In Germany, the numbers were even larger, with asylum claims climbing from 121,315 in 1989 to 256,112 in 1991, then 438,191 in 1992 (Chernoff 2005: 112–13).

The growth in global refugee numbers was fueled by a change in the nature of conflict, as civil wars became increasingly prevalent and long-lasting (Human Security Centre 2005: 22–23, Human Security Report Project 2012: chapter 5). Not all of these refugees fled state-based persecution. They also fled from causes not defined by the Refugee Convention, including persecution by non-state actors, situations of generalized violence, and state failure (see Dowty and Loescher 1996; Lischer 2005; Salehyan and Gleditsch 2006). This shift in the nature of conflict also triggered growing numbers of internally displaced persons (IDPs) as would-be refugees were contained within their own countries.

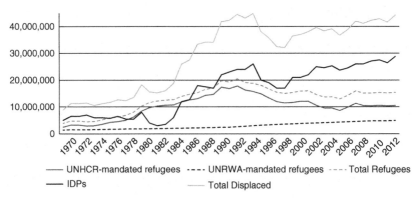

Figure 8.1 Total displaced persons, 1970–2012.
Sources: UNHCR data: www.unhcr.org/statistics/ (figures since 2007 include people in refugee-like situations and are not directly comparable); UNRWA data: Report of the Commissioner-General of the United Nations Relief and Works Agency for Palestine Refugees in the Near East, A/35/13, June 30, 1980, and Annually 1982–2007. Reports available at the UN Information System on the Question of Palestine, available at: www.unispal.un.org. Data for 1981 are missing and have been extrapolated from 1980 data based on annual growth rate of 2.2 percent. See BADIL *Annual Growth Rate of Registered Palestinian Refugees (1953–2000)*, www.badil.org/Statistics/ population/Statistics.htm. 2007 onward from UNRWA Statistics website: www.unrwa.org/etemplate.php?id=253; IDP Data: United States Committee for Refugees, *World Refugee Survey [Yearly 1997–2004]*, Washington D.C., U.S. Committee for Refugees; Internal Displacement Monitoring Centre, *Internal Displacement: Global Overview of Trends and Developments*, [Yearly 2004–12], Geneva, Norwegian Refugee Council, 2005–13; Norwegian Refugee Survey, *Internally Displaced Persons: A Global Survey*, London, Earthscan Publications, 1999, 28.

Shifts in displacement patterns reflect larger changes in the basic rules of international society. Decolonization granted independence for the first time to the majority of the world's peoples. But its dark side was to introduce governments that were unable or unwilling to support their own populations. These states no longer relied on domestic legitimacy or operated "an effective government," among the properties of statehood codified in the Montevideo Convention of 1933 (Grant 1999: 5–6). Rather, they survived by relying on superpower patronage and on the other material rewards available at the international level for recognized states (Jackson 1990: 8; Clapham 1996).

These refugees also no longer fit the mold developed through centuries of practice and framed in the postwar period by the flight from communism. As Chimni notes, "by producing the image of a 'normal' refugee – white, male, anti-communist – a clear message was sent to the population with regard to the '*new* asylum seeker': that asylum seekers were here for no good reason, that they abused hospitality, and that their numbers were too large. It merely confirmed xenophobia" (Chimni 1998: 357; see also Zolberg et al. 1989: 278).

In addition, with the slow end of the Cold War, one of the main drivers for the United States and its allies to accept refugees disappeared (Hathaway 1997: xix). With this disappeared a reason for indirect support to the UNHCR as an impartial organization that could protect refugees globally. The Soviet Union had demonstrated ongoing antipathy to the organization, and supporting the UNHCR had indirectly supported the political interests of the West. Without this driver, member states instead sought to restrict the UNHCR's budgetary and policy autonomy.

Combined, these factors triggered a crisis event and resulted in the formation of a new regime. Unlike previous regime shifts, there was no change in international organizations (IOs) or overarching legal framework: the UNHCR and the 1951 Refugee Convention both remained critical to the regime. The important shift, rather, was in *who qualified for protection* within the regime. This shift has had three components.

First, beginning in the 1980s, states began to push back against the previous expansive definition of who qualified for refugee status by narrowly interpreting the Refugee Convention and by introducing restrictions in domestic law. States legitimated these new deterrent policies by arguing that "a rising number of applicants for asylum . . . are not in genuine need of protection,"[1] by pointing to "the need to distinguish between 'genuine' and 'bogus' asylum seekers" (Vink and Meijerink 2003: 300), and by arguing that restrictive policies lead to a more efficient asylum system that helps "genuine asylum seekers and deters abusive claimants" (Home Office 1998: 1.8). More bleakly, these policies were also designed to make the costs of entry arbitrarily high for would-be asylum seekers, to criminalize them, and "to convince the electorate that the government is dealing effectively with the 'refugee problem'" (Hassan 2000: 185; see also Hathaway 1993).

It is important to note that these states were not and are not seeking to stop all refugees. Rather, as Gibney and Hansen suggest, these changes are meant to ensure that they receive "a manageable flow of asylum seekers and

[1] European Council "Resolution on Manifestly Unfounded Applications for Asylum," November 30, 1992.

refugees that is stable in that it does not fluctuate dramatically upwards over time" (2003: 14). For those who do not fall within the Convention definition, states do offer other forms of protection, such as leaves to stay on humanitarian grounds and temporary stays against removal (Duke et al. 1999: 106; Gibney 2004: 8). However, these low recognition rates for Convention refugees help to inflate the numbers of apparently "bogus" asylum seekers (Schuster 2003: 161). Thus, between 1996 and 2005, Britain accorded Convention status to 16.9 percent of asylum claimants, but accorded humanitarian status to an additional 32.8 percent of claimants (UNHCR 2006a: 161–62).

Second, beyond shifts in domestic policy, developed states also use a range of extraterritorial measures to prevent asylum seekers from accessing refugee determination processes (Gibney 2005: 4). These measures range from simple visa controls to safe third-country mechanisms to – at the extreme – wholesale interdiction at sea of refugees by the United States and Australia.

The increase in deterrent and extraterritorial measures has introduced a third component to how refugees are defined. This is a move to contain most refugees in their regions and even countries of origin in order to avoid incurring direct responsibilities toward them (Crisp 2003; Betts 2009: 12). This shift has seen long-term encampment of refugees in the developing world become the norm (Loescher and Milner 2005: 15–16; UNHCR 2006b). This shift has also resulted in the dramatic expansion of a separate category of forced migrant, IDPs, or those who have fled their own homes but remain within their own state.

These three changes have meant that the main property of the modern refugee regime is its restrictiveness: it has become a *non-entrée* regime for most of the world's refugees. As Helton noted, the international response to the refugee problem has evolved from one "of providing asylum in Western countries to containment of movement and humanitarian intervention to address the proximate causes of displacement in the states of origin of would-be refugees" (2002: 65–66).

Like with earlier regimes, a crisis event – the change in both numbers of refugees and the form of refugees – triggered a breakdown in the normative basis of the regime. However, even before the dramatic increase in the number of refugees with the end of the Cold War, these normative understandings were under pressure. Neither the United States nor the United Kingdom adopted the core normative understandings of the postwar regime they had created. Instead, both states sought to prioritize direct refugee admissions from communist countries while providing financial support to enable the UNHCR to deal with the larger refugee case load. The emergence of a norm for formal multilateral assistance allowed states to divorce their own policies from the broader functioning of the regime, a harbinger of future problems.

In this chapter, I trace out the slow changes in refugee protection policy in both the United States and the United Kingdom. The changes in these countries mark a broader shift in how the developed world responds to refugees. I then shift to explore the origins and development of a new, separate regime designed to protect IDPs, before concluding with the UNHCR's divided role in protecting forced migrants in the contemporary regime.

The United States and the Cold War frame

Although the United States played a key role in building the postwar refugee regime at the international level, domestically, these same norms were only weakly held. President Truman supported a strong Refugee Convention with a clear right of non-refoulement even as he sought to distance direct refugee assistance from the United Nations (UN) to organizations that the United States could better control. President Eisenhower's administration changed positions on the UNHCR, accepting that the UN agency could undertake operations American-supported IOs could not. Domestically, however, both presidents had significant difficulties gaining congressional acquiescence to their policies, with members fearful of the potential domestic costs of immigration and of refugee "inundation or subversion" (Morris 1985: 36).

Even after Eisenhower and his successors asserted independent executive control over the refugee issue (Tichenor 2002: 178), American policy was at odds with the international regime. It focused almost exclusively on accepting refugees from communist regimes while denying access to those fleeing persecution from right-wing or "allied" governments in Central America and the Caribbean (Loescher and Scanlan 1986: 70). This fit in directly with national priorities. Refugee outflows, Teitelbaum (1984: 439) argues, served "to embarrass and discredit adversary nations."[2] The UNHCR's existence allowed the American government to pursue a limited refugee policy focused on ideological movements (Avery 1983).

Executive dominance of refugee policy

In the 1950s, refugee migration into the United States remained limited under existing legislation. The 1952 Immigration and Nationality

---

[2] See also National Security Council "U.S. Policy on Defectors, Escapees, and Refugees from Communist Areas" NSC 5706, February 13, 1957.

(McCarran-Walter) Act[3] continued the immigration quota system established in the 1920s. Eisenhower, like Truman before him, initially sought
to alter immigration law generally to allow for refugee acceptance. The
president argued to the Senate that "these [European] refugees, escapees,
and distressed peoples now constitute an economic and political threat
of growing magnitude . . . [to] international political considerations" and
that a legislative solution was needed.[4] Congress passed the 1953 Refugee
Relief Act in response. However, almost all the 214,000 visas available
under this Act were limited to German, Italian, Dutch, and Greek applicants. Furthermore, stringent security measures – including pledges by
each applicant that they were not and had never been a communist
followed by exhaustive investigations – meant that two years after passage
of the Act only 21,000 visas had been issued (Bon Tempo 2008: chapter 2;
see also Zolberg 1995: 123–24).[5]

When confronted with the failed Hungarian uprising in 1956,
Eisenhower argued "our position of world leadership demands that . . . we
be in a position to grant" asylum to the Hungarians.[6] Yet, given the failures
of the 1953 Refugee Relief Act, he was predisposed to avoid a legislative
solution. Congressman Francis Walter (D-PA), one of the drafters of the
1952 Immigration Act, suggested that it allowed the attorney-general the
power to "parole" or temporarily release aliens for entry into the United
States without a visa (Markowitz 1973; Loescher and Scanlan 1986: 56).[7]

---

[3] The Immigration and Nationality Act of 1952, 182 Stat. 66 (1952).

[4] Dwight D. Eisenhower, "Letter to the President of the Senate and to the Speaker of the
House of Representatives Recommending Emergency Legislation for the Admission of
Refugees," April 22, 1953, *The American Presidency Project*. www.presidency.ucsb.edu/
ws/?pid=9821.

[5] Following White House pressure, acceptances increased dramatically and, by the end of
the program in 1956, 190,000 visas had been issued.

[6] Dwight D. Eisenhower, "Special Message to the Congress on Immigration Matters,"
January 31, 1957, *The American Presidency Project*. www.presidency.ucsb.edu/ws/?
pid=10967.

[7] The provision read that "the Attorney General may in his discretion parole into the United
States temporarily under such conditions as he may prescribe for emergent reasons or for
reasons deemed strictly in the public interest any alien applying for admission to the United
States," The Immigration and Nationality Act of 1952, 182 Stat. 66 (1952), Sec. 212 (d)(5).
The Act also established that "the Attorney General is authorized to withhold deportation of
any alien within the United States to any country in which in his opinion the alien would be
subject to physical persecution." Ibid., Sec 243 (h). In the 1965 Act, visas were extended to
aliens who faced "persecution or fear of persecution on account of race, religion, or political
opinion," whereas deportation was withheld for aliens facing "persecution on account of
race, religion, or political opinion." The Immigration and Nationality Act of 1965, 79 Stat.
911, Sec. 203(7), Sec 243(h). This difference in language, the Supreme Court has held,
means that the non-refoulement clause is narrower than the refugee admittance clause, even
following amendments introduced in the 1980 Refugee Act. See *INS v. Cardoza-Fonseca*,
480 U.S. 421 (1987) and Fitzpatrick (1997: 8).

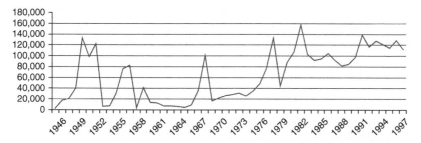

Figure 8.2 Refugee admissions to the United States, 1946–1997
Sources: Sutch and Carter (2006).

This was a limited admission: not only was the parole completely discretionary, but it provided no route for refugees so admitted to seek either permanent residency or citizenship (Bon Tempo 2008: 70).

Following the parole admittance of some 30,000 Hungarian refugees, Congressional support for this move disappeared both over security concerns and perceived executive branch usurpation of refugee affairs (Markowitz 1973: 55; Tichenor 2002: 203; Bon Tempo 2008: 83). Congress therefore sought to regularize the parole the following year, in the 1957 Refugee Escapee Act. A subsequent Act (the Hungarian Refugees Act of 1958) allowed the Hungarians to apply for permanent residency (Bon Tempo 2008: 83–84) but included strong security checks. This set a pattern in which Congress retroactively recognized parole admittances through legislation in order to grant the refugees a path to permanent residency.[8]

The failure to alter broader immigration legislation, however, meant that the use of the parole authority by the executive branch became commonplace for each new refugee flow from communist countries (see Figure 8.2). Thus, the quarter of a million refugees who fled Cuba between 1959 and 1962 were paroled as "fleeing from Communist oppression,"[9] a pattern President John F. Kennedy continued.[10]

---

[8] Such Acts included the Azores and Netherlands Act of 1958, the Refugee Relatives Act of 1959, the Fair Share Refugee Act of 1960, the Refugee Conditional Entrants Act of 1965, the Cuban Adjustment Act of 1966, the Indochinese Refugees Act of 1977, and the Refugee Parolees Act of 1978. For refugee numbers granted permanent residency under each act, see United States Immigration and Naturalization Service (1982: 99–100).

[9] Dwight D. Eisenhower, "Statement by the President on Releasing a Report on Cuban Refugee Problems," January 18, 1961, *The American Presidency Project.* www.presidency. ucsb.edu/ws/?pid=12097.

[10] John F. Kennedy, "Message to Chairman Khrushchev Concerning the Meaning of Events in Cuba," April 18, 1961, *The American Presidency Project.* www.presidency.ucsb. edu/ws/?pid=8070. The 1962 Migration and Refugee Assistance Act provided ongoing assistance to Cuban refugees and dedicated support to the UNHCR and the ICEM

The 1965 (Hart-Cellar) Immigration and Nationality Act[11] finally ended the quota system and the racial overtones of previous policy (Rudolph 2006: 57) and reserved 6 percent of all visas for aliens who had fled persecution. This was limited, however, to those from "any Communist or Communist-dominated country or area or ... from any country within the general area of the Middle East."[12] Furthermore, the small quota proved no match for the numbers fleeing the communist world. Thus, successive presidents returned to the use of the parole authority not only for the Cubans, but also for Soviet and Indochinese refugees. Between 1975 and 1979 alone, at least ten separate paroles were used to admit more than 300,000 Indochinese refugees (Loescher and Scanlan 1986: 75; Nackerud et al. 1999: 177, 183).

A Failed normative shift: The 1980 Refugee Act

A domestic refugee admissions system biased toward the communist world worked because there was no clear congruence between U.S. refugee policy and the Refugee Convention. The United States never ratified the Convention itself, and although it ratified the Protocol in 1968, this was primarily for international reasons. As President Lyndon Johnson argued, it was "decidedly in the interest of the United States to promote this United Nations effort to broaden the extension of asylum and status for those fleeing persecution."[13] Acceding to it, his administration felt, would "not affect the flow of refugees to the United States nor increase United States contributions for refugee assistance" and therefore did not require legislative changes.[14] Thus, the failure to amend domestic law, Fitzpatrick (1997: 6) notes, led to an awkward twelve-year period "in

(Holborn 1975: 572; Loescher and Scanlan 1986: 71; Zucker and Zucker 1987: 35), whereas the 1966 Cuban Adjustment Act provided permanent residency to any refugees who had arrived after 1958 and had remained in the United States for at least a year. Between 1960 and 1994, when laws were changed, the United States accepted a million refugees from Cuba.

[11] The Immigration and Nationality Act of 1965, 79 Stat. 911.   [12] Ibid., Sec. 203(7).

[13] Lyndon B. Johnson, "Special Message to the Senate Transmitting the Protocol Relating to the Status of Refugees," August 1, 1968, *The American Presidency Project*. www.presidency. ucsb.edu/ws/?pid=29058. This was also the prevalent view within the administration. Signing the Protocol, it was felt, would "highlight our continuing humanitarian concern with the problem of refugees, whatever their origin" and assist U.S. efforts to induce other countries "to implement more fully liberal asylum policies." Read to Rostow, December 4, 1967, NARA RG 59 REF 3 UNHCR; L. Murray and J. Belman, July 25, 1968 "Transmission to Senate of Protocol Relating to the Status of Refugees- ACTION MEMORANDUM," NARA RG 59 REF 3 UN, 4.

[14] Ibid., 4. See also the U.S. Supreme Court's decision in *Immigration and Naturalization Service v. Stevic*, 467 U.S. 407 (1984); and Fitzpatrick (1997: 5).

which compliance with the Protocol was left entirely to administrative discretion."

This shifted with the 1980 Refugee Act,[15] and particularly due to the role of Senator Edward Kennedy. Kennedy had served as the Senate floor manager for the 1965 Immigration Act and had tried since 1969 to pass legislation that would provide a more "humane method of allocating visas to applicants of all countries" (Kennedy 1970: 5).[16] In 1978, he became chairman of the Senate Judiciary Committee. In that capacity, he was able to gain executive support for a new refugee policy that introduced a humanitarian and universal outlook to refugee admissions (Kennedy 1981; Anker 1982: 90; Feen 1985: 107). As Dick Clark, President Carter's Coordinator for Refugee Affairs, argued to the Senate, refugee programs were based on a patchwork of legislation that was:

> inadequate to cope with the refugee problem we face today. It was originally designed to deal with people fleeing Communist regimes in Eastern Europe or repressive governments in the Middle East in the immediate post-war period and the early cold war years... The current law assumes that refugee problems are extraordinary occurrences. It provides for only a very limited number of refugees to enter the United States each year, on a conditional basis. (cited in Kennedy 1981: 145)

Kennedy's efforts were also helped by two other events. Popular interest in refugee admissions, particularly from Cambodia, had grown dramatically in the previous two years (Loescher and Scanlan 1986: 161). Furthermore, as the debates over the legislation began, the UNHCR held a successful conference that doubled the international resettlement opportunities for Vietnamese and other Indochinese refugees (Robinson 1998: 53–54). This helped to alleviate Congressional concern that the United States would be inundated by refugees and convinced Senator Strom Thurmond, among others, to vote in favor of the legislation (Kennedy 1981: 147).

The 1980 Act established a humanitarian basis for refugee admission: "The Congress declares that it is the historic policy of the United States to respond to the urgent needs of persons subject to persecution in their homelands, including . . . admission to this country of refugees of special humanitarian concern to the United States."[17] It introduced a definition of "refugee" identical to that of the Refugee Protocol, although it also included an additional clause allowing the president to specify that status to

---

[15] The Refugee Act of 1980, 94 Stat. 102 (1980).
[16] See also Senator Kennedy (D-Massachusetts) "Refugee Act of 1979," *Congressional Record* v. 125, March 13, 1979, 4881.
[17] The Refugee Act of 1980, 94 Stat. 102 (1980), Sec 101. (a).

a person remaining within his or her own country.[18] As the Supreme Court noted in a later decision "if one thing is clear from the legislative history of the new definition of 'refugee,' and indeed the entire 1980 Act, it is that one of Congress' primary purposes was to bring United States refugee law into conformance with the 1967 United Nations Protocol."[19]

The Act also normalized refugee admittance through three mechanisms: a "normal flow" quota of 50,000 refugees per year; a consultation process through which the president could admit an unlimited number of refugees based on humanitarian concerns or in the national interest; and an emergency clause that allowed for unlimited admissions without consultations. The consultation process was to include discussion of why "the proposed admission of refugees is justified by humanitarian concerns or grave humanitarian concerns or is otherwise in the national interest."[20] It also allowed for these refugees to apply for permanent residence.[21] Finally, it established that "the Attorney General shall not deport or return any alien ... to a country if the Attorney General determines that such alien's life or freedom would be threatened in such a country on account of race, religion, nationality, membership in a particular social group, or political opinion," thus bringing U.S. practice into accordance with the non-refoulement provision of the Protocol.[22]

The 50,000 per year quota was immediately insufficient. It was overwhelmed by the Mariel boatlift from Cuba in 1980, which saw some 130,000 refugees reach the United States. To complicate matters, the Carter administration refused to apply the Refugee Act to the boatlift claimants. It treated them instead as illegal migrants and subsequently exercised the parole authority again (Kennedy 1981: 152–55). Administration officials, Kennedy (1981: 154) notes, "asserted that Congress never intended the Act to accommodate large numbers of refugees arriving directly on our shores."

In spite of the boatlift, the Refugee Act appeared to have altered Congressional opinion. Senator Walter Huddleston (D-Kentucky) challenged the admissions process, arguing that the Act "created a vague open-ended admission process that has never come close to keeping refugee flows anywhere near the 50,000 per year normal flow ... we are running at over 300% of the so-called normal flow" (cited in Leibowitz 1983: 166). And yet Senator Alan Simpson (R-Wy), a staunch restrictionist and the chairman of the Senate Immigration Subcommittee, replied:

---

[18] Ibid., Sec 201 (a).
[19] *INS v. Cardoza-Fonseca*, 480 U.S. 421, 436 (1987) (cited in Fitzpatrick 1997: 6).
[20] The Refugee Act of 1980, 94 Stat. 102 (1980), Sec. 207 (a-b, e).
[21] Ibid., Sec. 201 (c) (2).   [22] Ibid., Sec. 202 (h) (1).

Refugees and immigrants are two distinct groups... [R]efugee policy is concerned with the United States accepting its fair share of persons who are fleeing persecution in their homeland. Both policies obviously have a humanitarian purpose, but the two groups should never be allowed to compete for admission. (cited in Leibowitz 1983: 166–67; see also LeMaster and Zall 1983: 470–72)

By bringing U.S. law into accordance with international standards and by reframing refugee admissions as a humanitarian process, the Act's proponents appeared to have shifted how refugee protection was perceived within the United States. This shift was short-lived, however, in spite of being implemented in domestic law. Following his victory over Jimmy Carter, the primary interest of President Ronald Reagan and his administration was shifting refugee admittance policies back to focusing on communist countries even as they sought to restrict and limit broader asylum claims. Rather than reinforcing a humanitarian basis for admissions, the Refugee Act had "left the executive branch, and specifically the White House, as the prime mover in refugee policymaking and failed to give Congress enough power to assert its prerogatives" (Bon Tempo 2008: 190).

The Refugee Act did give domestic civil society new abilities to challenge refugee policy through the Courts. Members of Congress also grew increasingly vigilant, especially when confronted with complicity in human rights abuses abroad (Loescher and Scanlan 1986; Tichenor 2002; Bon Tempo 2008). In spite of this, the Reagan administration was able to redefine U.S. refugee policy in ways that continue to resonate today through three methods: their use of the annual proposal system created by the Act, bureaucratic measures to deter and restrict asylum seekers, and the use of extraterritorial measures, particularly interdiction at sea.

The proposal system and the return of the communist bias

The Carter administration had established two precedents with its first and only annual proposal to Congress under the Act. The first was to dramatically exceed the normal flow quota, justifying it due to the urgent crisis in Indochina, where some 235,000 refugees were awaiting resettlement.[23] President Reagan continued the practice of proposing admissions above the "normal flow" provision of 50,000, although he set a lower quota of 140,000 in 1982 and continued to reduce proposed admissions to a low of 67,000 in 1986 (see Figure 8.3). The quotas also directly

---

[23] Office of the U.S. Coordinator for Refugee Affairs "Report to Congress: Proposed Refugee Admissions and Allocations for Fiscal Year 1981, September 1980," appendix to Committee on the Judiciary, House of Representatives, "Refugee admissions and resettlement program," September 24, 1980. http://catalog.hathitrust.org/Record/002755583.

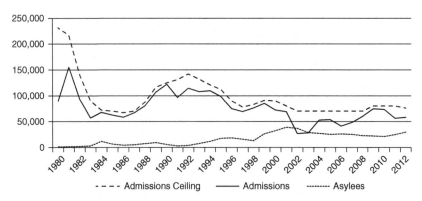

Figure 8.3 U.S. refugee admissions and asylee numbers, 1980–2012.
Sources: United States Immigration and Naturalization Service, *Statistical Yearbook* (1982, 1984, 1986, 1994, 1998); Department of Homeland Security, *Yearbook of Immigration Statistics*, 2006; Department of Homeland Security "Annual Flow Reports- Refugees and Asylees" (2007–12), www.dhs.gov/publications-0; Department of State, Bureau of Population, Refugees, and Migration, Refugee Admissions Statistics (2007–12), www.state.gov/j/prm/releases/statistics/index.htm, accessed March 29, 2013; U.S. Committee for Refugees, *Refugee Reports*, vol. XXVII, no. 1, February 2006, 15.

targeted communist countries, including the Soviet Union, Indochina, and other Eastern European countries. By contrast, countries in Africa, South and Central America, and the Middle East – irrespective of government type – received quotas of only a few thousand per region per year.[24]

The annual proposal system was not as unconstrained as the parole system had been. When Secretary of State Alexander Haig declared that all migrants from Vietnam, Laos, and Cambodia were refugees in 1981, the Department of Justice found the declaration to be illegal because "refugee status had to be decided on a case-by-case basis rather than by presuming a class of persons are refugees" (LeMaster and Zall 1983: 465; see also Feen 1985: 113–14). With the 1987 Nicaraguan Review Program, Attorney-General Edwin Meese sought to provide refugees from that country with an additional chance to apply for asylum even after rejection. This led to their approval rating soaring to 84 percent that year. However, the program was rescinded following a public backlash and strong Congressional scrutiny (Zucker and Zucker 1989: 361–63; García 2006: 115).

[24] U.S. Committee for Refugees, *Refugee Reports*, vol. XV, no. 12, December 31, 1994, 9; Bon Tempo 2008: 186–87.

These resettlement patterns have continued long after the end of the Reagan administration, and after the end of the Cold War, with a strong communist bias continuing to exist in U.S. domestic legislation. Most notably, the Lautenberg Amendment, introduced in the U.S. Senate in 1989, privileged the admittance of Jews, Evangelicals, and members of other religions in communist and formerly communist countries (Zucker and Zucker 1989; Beyer 1991). Between 1989 and 2003, some 470,000 people entered the United States under the Amendment, representing over 35 percent of total admissions (Vialet 1999; State Department 2004).

Other resettlement admissions, particularly those under the "special humanitarian concern" clause of the 1980 Refugee Act, have varied depending on presidential focus. During the 1990s, this was used frequently for countries where the United States had deployed troops (Gibney 2004: 160).[25] Since 2000, there has been a reorientation of U.S. refugee admittance policy toward accepting smaller numbers of refugees from a wider number of countries in an effort to resettle the most vulnerable populations. Under a new priority scheme introduced by President Barack Obama in 2010, the first priority for admission is given to people with compelling protection needs and who are referred by the UNHCR, designated nongovernmental organizations, or a U.S. embassy (Kerwin 2012: 5–6).[26]

Much as in the early years of the Cold War, security concerns have significantly affected refugee resettlement and asylum policy, particularly following the September 11, 2001, terrorist attacks. Legislative changes, including the USA Patriot Act of 2001[27] and the REAL ID Act of 2005,[28] expanded the grounds of inadmissibility due to terrorist activities, including providing even coerced material support. Asylum seekers are required to "demonstrate that their race, religion, nationality, membership in a social group, or political opinion represents 'a central reason' for the persecution they suffered or fear" (Kerwin 2005: 757; Human Rights First 2009; Kerwin 2012: 15). Stricter security checks and interagency vetting of materials has also meant that the actual numbers of resettled

---

[25] Such a pattern broke down in the 2000s. Between 2003 and 2007, only 2,074 Iraqi refugees were resettled before larger numbers were accepted in 2008 and 2009 (13,822 and 18,838, respectively). Similarly, only 1,366 Afghanis were resettled between 2007 and 2009 (Younes 2007; United States Department of Homeland Security 2010: 40).

[26] See U.S. Department of State, U.S. Department of Homeland Security, and U.S. Department of Health and Human Services, "Proposed Refugee Admissions for Fiscal Year 2011: Report to the Congress," 7–9, www.wrapsnet.org/Portals/1/Reports/ Admissions/Final%20Report%20to%20Congress%209-10.pdf; see also Bruno (2012).

[27] The Uniting and Strengthening America by Providing Appropriate Tools Required to Intercept and Obstruct Terrorism Act of 2001, 115 Stat. 272.

[28] REAL ID Act of 2005, 119 Stat. 302 (May 11, 2005).

refugees have fallen below the admissions quota in the last two years, to 56,424 in 2011 and 58,238 in 2012 against quotas of 80,000 and 76,000, respectively (see Figure 8.2).[29]

Within domestic American refugee policy, an effective refugee admissions policy emerged during the Cold War when the executive branch took control of the issue and isolated refugee admissions from broader immigration policies. Admissions, however, were always tempered by Congress' legislative role and particularly its security concerns. Efforts to broaden refugee admissions to reflect core humanitarian values failed with the reinterpretation of the 1980 Refugee Act by the Reagan administration. Recent bureaucratic initiatives by the Obama administration have similarly been affected by renewed security concerns over terrorism.

Extraterritorializing the refugee problem: American practice and beyond

Beyond resettlement policy, the 1980 Mariel boatlift heralded a shift in refugee admissions unanticipated by the Refugee Act's authors. This was that the United States was increasingly becoming a country of first asylum for refugees from Central America and the Caribbean (Meissner 1986: 61). Between 1980 and 1992, the United States received 629,000 asylum applications (McBride 1999: 5). Thus, the Reagan administration also sought to limit the numbers of asylum seekers entering into the United States.

To respond to these new influxes, Reagan argued that the United States needed "adequate legal authority to establish control over immigration: to enable us, when sudden influxes of foreigners occur, to decide to whom we grant the status of refugee or asylee."[30] Two years later, he raised the specter of uncontrolled refugee flows swamping the United States:

We must not listen to those who would disarm our friends and allow Central America to be turned into a string of anti-American Marxist dictatorships. The result could be a tidal wave of refugees – and this time they'll be "feet people" and not "boat people" – swarming into our country seeking safe haven from communist repression to our south. (Cannon 1983: A1)

---

[29] See U.S. Department of State, U.S. Department of Homeland Security, and U.S. Department of Health and Human Services, "Proposed Refugee Admissions for Fiscal Year 2012: Report to the Congress," iv, www.hsdl.org/?view&did=690218; and Human Rights First (2012: 15).

[30] Ronald Reagan, "Statement on United States Immigration and Refugee Policy," July 30, 1981, *The American Presidency Project*. www.presidency.ucsb.edu/ws/?pid=44128. Asylees are defined in the 1980 Refugee Act as individuals who satisfy the definition of refugee but are already present in the United States and therefore must undergo an asylum adjudication procedure (McBride 1999: 5).

This was a consistent theme within the Reagan administration, with Secretary of State George Shultz similarly differentiating the right to leave from a right of entrance: "International human rights standards recognize the right to emigrate and to return to one's country, but not to immigrate into any country of one's choosing. Standards and limits to immigration are determined by national decision and legislation" (cited in Beyer 1991: 38–39). Through such rhetoric, Reagan officials effectively "reversed the traditional rhetoric by implying that the spread of Communism poses a new immigration threat to the United States" (Loescher and Scanlan 1986: 192; Bon Tempo 2008: 187). With this shift, control and restrictionism became the administration's priority toward domestic asylum claimants.

There did remain a bias in favor of those fleeing leftist regimes. Between 1984 and 1990, for example, 26 percent of claims from Nicaragua were accepted, whereas only 2.6 percent of Salvadoran claims and 1.8 percent of Guatemalan claims were accepted (McBride 1999; García 2006: 90). The American government justified this unequal treatment by suggesting that "'conditions within El Salvador' were 'in no way comparable' to a civil war" and that most Salvadorans 'had emigrated for economic reasons'" (Elie 2008: 96; see also Bon Tempo 2008: 190). This was in spite of direct UNHCR criticisms of the returns: "it is difficult to escape the view that large numbers of Salvadorians would be exposed to serious danger in the event of their being returned."[31] Garcia (2006: 90) argues that one of the Reagan administration's concerns was sheer numbers in this case, with a "half-million Salvadorans believed to be in the country by 1983." Only in 1990, as part of a legal settlement, did the Bush administration agreed to grant asylum hearings for some 250,000 undocumented Guatemalans and Salvadorans (García 2006: 111–12; Rudolph 2006: 69).[32]

The main shift that the Reagan administration undertook, however, was to introduce the "extraterritorial application of refugee protection" for refugees fleeing from Haiti (Helton 1991: 2341). In so doing, they redefined the applicability of the norm of non-refoulement and made opaque the previously clear territorial responsibilities of the state at whose frontiers a refugee sought asylum. By shifting their own practices to intercept asylum seekers extraterritorially, they also created an important precedent for other countries – including Australia, Italy, and a proposed British

---

[31] UNHCR "Aide-Mémoire on Salvadorans in the United States," September 23, 1981, reprinted in *Refugee Survey Quarterly* 27(1), 165; Memorandum from the Regional Representative for Northern Latin America to Headquarters on "Forcible Return of Salvadorans from US" dated April 15, 1981; Folio 8 (cited in Elie 2007: 29).

[32] *American Baptist Churches v. Thornburgh*, 760 F. Supp. 796 (N.D. Cal. 1991). The lawsuit alleged that the Immigration and Naturalization Service had engaged in discriminatory treatment of nationals from both countries.

scheme – to apply their own extraterritorial measures to prevent would-be refugees from seeking asylum and to more tightly interpret the Refugee Convention's non-refoulement clause.

Wet foot, dry foot: American policy and the Caribbean exception

Haitian refugees began fleeing that country to the United States in the late 1950s, but had generally not been recognized as having valid persecution claims in spite of a flight pattern similar to that of Cuban refugees. Critics argued that the policies varied because the Haitian claimants were black and because they were fleeing from a U.S. ally, rather than a communist country (Loescher and Scanlan 1986: 80–81; Bon Tempo 2008: 113, 180). In 1980, however, this differential application of refugee policy within the United States became subject to challenge in the courts.[33]

In 1981, President Reagan took the additional step to target Haitian asylum seekers arriving by boat by declaring that illegal immigration by sea was a "continuing problem" for the United States, and he issued an interdiction order "to return the vessel and its passengers to the country from which it came" (Loescher and Scanlan 1986: 188–89; Martin 1990: 1250).[34] Although the executive order established that "no person who is a refugee will be returned without his consent," Helton noted that, over the next nine years, during which 21,461 Haitians were intercepted, "the Coast Guard permitted only six of these interdicted Haitians to seek asylum in the United States" (Helton 1991: 2341; see also Koh 1994: 140–41). Although the move survived domestic court challenges (Koh 1994: 142), the UNHCR was concerned about the precedent it created:

Whether or not the measures can be challenged from a legal point of view is not certain. . . The new interdiction measures could certainly constitute an undesirable precedent for other areas of the world (e.g. South East Asia) where UNHCR has sought to prevent asylum seekers being towed out to sea. (cited in Loescher and Scanlan 1986: 194)

In 1991, large numbers of Haitians began fleeing the country anew following a coup that removed President Jean-Bertrand Aristide. In the six months following a court order that prevented immediate repatriation, 34,000 Haitians were interdicted and sent to a screening facility established at the U.S. military base in Guantanamo Bay, Cuba. Some 10,500 were found to have a plausible asylum claim and sent to the United States

---

[33] *Haitian Refugee Center v. Civiletti*, 503 F. Supp. 442, 511–13 (S.D. Fla 1980).

[34] Ronald Reagan, "Executive Order 12324 – Interdiction of Illegal Aliens," September 29, 1981, *The American Presidency Project*. www.presidency.ucsb.edu /ws/?pid=44317.

(Koh 1994: 143–44; UNHCR 1997: 220). Facing a tough election, President George H. W. Bush expanded the interdiction policies started by Reagan through an executive order issued in May 1992. Prior orders had allowed Haitians who had been "screened-in" – deemed to have credible enough fears of political persecution to warrant an asylum hearing – to be detained off-shore rather than be granted entrance to the United States (Koh 1994: 143–44). This new order authorized "the Coast Guard to return all fleeing Haitians to Haiti without any process whatsoever" (Koh 1994: 146). Bush justified this by arguing that the non-refoulement provision of the Protocol did "not extend to persons located outside the territory of the United States."[35] Although President Bill Clinton challenged the direct return policy during the 1992 presidential campaign, he continued it once in office (Jones 1994; Rudolph 2006: 72).

This decision led to substantial litigation. In *Haitian Refugee Center v. Baker*, the Eleventh Circuit Court of Appeal found that because the refugees were beyond U.S. borders, they could not avail themselves of judicial review and that any claim under customary international law was meritless (Jones 1994: 115–17).

In a subsequent case, *Sale v. Haitian Centers Council, Inc.*,[36] the U.S. Supreme Court ruled 8 to 1 that Article 33 of the Refugee Convention (the non-refoulement article) did not have an extraterritorial effect (Jones 1994: 121; Koh 1994: 151). In dissent, Justice Blackmun argued that "what is extraordinary in this case is that the Executive, in disregard of the law, would take to the seas to intercept fleeing refugees and force them back to their persecutors – and that the Court would strain to sanction that conduct."[37] Along with the two prior decisions of *INS v. Cardoza-Fonseca*, and *INS v. Stevic*, Fitzpatrick (1997: 3) notes that this decision "unmoored US law from the international norms it was adopted to implement."[38] More fundamentally, UN High Commissioner for Refugees Sadako Ogata noted that "UNHCR considers the Court's decision a setback to modern international refugee law which has been developing for more than forty years."[39]

---

[35] George H. W. Bush "Executive Order 12807 – Interdiction of Illegal Aliens," May 24, 1992, *The American Presidency Project*. www.presidency.ucsb.edu/ws/?pid=23627.

[36] *Sale v. Haitian Centers Council, Inc.*, 509 U.S. 155 (1993).   [37] Ibid., 189.

[38] The Supreme Court has not reconsidered the issue. However, in the *Boumediene v. Bush* (553 U.S. 723) decision in 2008, the Court did rule that alleged enemy combatant detainees at Guantanamo Bay Naval Base do continue to possess rights under the U.S. Constitution, particularly to the writ of habeas corpus because the United States has practical sovereignty over Guantanamo. Farber (2010: 1009) notes that "by extension, if *Boumediene* does apply to all individuals at Guantanamo, then it should be applicable to the refugees as well."

[39] "UN High Commissioner for Refugees Responds to U.S. Supreme Court Decision in Sale v. Haitian Centers Council," *International Legal Materials* 32 (1993), 1215.

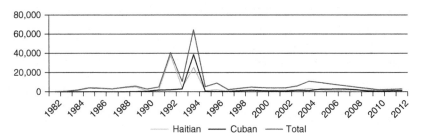

Figure 8.4 U.S. Coast Guard alien migrant interdiction.
Source: www.uscg.mil/hq/cg5/cg531/amio/FlowStats/FY.asp

The Clinton administration suspended direct returns in 1994 and negotiated with other Caribbean countries to conduct refugee status determinations on their territory with UNHCR monitoring (Legomsky 2006: 681). However, the use of Guantanamo Bay as a "safe haven" for Haitian and Cuban refugees continued (Morris 2003: 24). At the same time, and in a break with thirty years of practice, the Clinton administration began to intercept and detain Cuban migrants at sea, and these were also sent to Guantanamo Bay (Koh 1994; Nackerud et al. 1999: 187). In September 1994, the government reached an agreement with Cuba "to prevent unsafe departures using mainly persuasive means," though, as McBride notes, the policy "did not meet the needs of those who may have had a genuine fear of persecution, or uphold the USA's international obligations ... In effect, the US Government had reached agreement with another country to deny people their 'right to leave'" (1999: 6).

Interdiction continues to this day (see Figure 8.4). For interdicted Haitians, the only screening is the so-called *shout test*, under which an individual has to indicate a fear of persecution. Haitians are not advised of their right to request asylum, and translators are not required to be aboard Coast Guard ships (Frelick 2004; Legomsky 2006: 682–83). And beyond one mention by President Bush in 2004,[40] successive administrations have been careful to not acknowledge that many of the interdictees would have strong claims to refugee status if their claims were examined in the United States.

In 2002, President Bush reaffirmed the practice of interdiction, ordering the attorney general to:

---

[40] The president noted: "I have made it abundantly clear to the Coast Guard that we will turn back any refugee that attempts to reach our shore," George W. Bush, "Remarks Following Discussions with President Mikheil Saakashvili of Georgia and an Exchange with Reporters," February 25, 2004, *The American Presidency Project.* www.presidency. ucsb.edu/ws/?pid=62702.

maintain custody, at any location he deems appropriate, of any undocumented aliens ... who are interdicted or intercepted in the Caribbean region... [T]he Attorney General may conduct any screening of such aliens that he deems appropriate, including screening to determine whether such aliens should be returned to their country of origin or transit, or whether they are persons in need of protection who should not be returned without their consent.[41]

His administration also reframed the practice, with the INS publishing a notice which "concluded that illegal mass migration by sea threatened national security because it diverts the Coast Guard and other resources from their homeland security duties" (Wasem 2011: 6). More recently, the government has also argued that the policy is used "to discourage illegal and dangerous voyages by sea and to encourage future migrants to pursue safe and legal migration options."[42] Such arguments were used in 2010, following the January Port-au-Prince earthquake, with Homeland Security Secretary Janet Napolitano noting: "This is a very dangerous crossing. Lives are lost every time people try to make this crossing ... please do not have us divert our necessary rescue and relief efforts that are going into Haiti by trying to leave at this point" (Hsu 2010).

With U.S. interdiction at sea efforts, the American government has created a clear exception to the strong norm against refoulement. Beginning with the Reagan administration, Haitians and subsequently Cubans who have sought to enter the United States via the Caribbean do not receive the full asylum determination process accorded to asylum seekers who cross into the United States through a land border or an airport.

Britain, deterrence, and extraterritorial safe havens

As we have seen, the British government had been a strong supporter of refugee protection until the interwar period. Following the Second World War, its asylum policies went through no major changes from its practice in the interwar period. The 1920 Aliens Order, which had continued the restrictive processes adopted during the First World War, was not replaced until 1953 with a new Aliens Order. Even then, there was no mention made of the Refugee Convention, which Britain ratified in 1954, and discretion

---

[41] George W. Bush: "Executive Order 13276 – Delegation of Responsibilities Concerning Undocumented Aliens Interdicted or Intercepted in the Caribbean Region," November 15, 2002, *The American Presidency Project*. www.presidency.ucsb.edu/ws/?pid=61372.

[42] U.S. Immigration and Customs Enforcement "Fact Sheet: Guantanamo Bay Migrant Operations," July 23, 2004. http://web.archive.org/web/20070711063736/ www.ice.gov/pi/news/factsheets/072304gitmo.htm. Per Farber (2010: 990–91), this was deleted from the ICE's web page in 2009, despite its continued use of Guantanamo Bay for operations.

remained entirely with the Home Office (Stevens 2004: 70). It was not until 1971 that the Convention and Protocol were acknowledged in British domestic policy, and that was in a less binding statement of guiding principles for immigration admittance, the Immigration Rules, rather than in law (Gibney 2004: 114).

This is not to suggest that Britain ignored international norms with respect to refugee protection. As the under-secretary of state for the Home Department reassured the House in 1949: "It is still the practice, as always, not to send back to countries where they would be in danger of persecution people [who] ... are political refugees."[43] The British government accepted in 75,000 displaced persons (DPs) from the International Refugee Organization (IRO), although as "European Volunteer Workers" with only limited periods of admission rather than as refugees, 20,000 Hungarian refugees in 1956, and a steady stream of refugees from the communist world (Kushner and Knox 1999: 248; Schuster 2003: 135–38).

Like in the United States, however, the United Kingdom's refugee admission policies generally did not extend to noncommunist groups. Part of the issue for the British government was the Nationality Act of 1948, which had "invested some 800,000,000 subjects of the crumbling empire ... with the equal right of entry and settlement in Britain" (Joppke 1999: 101). The British government began introducing entrance requirements, including work vouchers for immigrants, in 1962. But when large numbers of East Asian Kenyans sought entrance, the government passed the Commonwealth Immigration Act (1968), which removed the right of these refugees to enter the territory of the state, even though they held British passports. The 1971 Immigration Act further gave the Home Office largely unrestrained powers to detain asylum seekers. These powers have been routinely used since the 1980s (Schuster and Solomos 1999: 59; see also Bloch 2002: 46; Stevens 2004: 77–78).

When Idi Amin expelled East Asian Africans from Uganda in 1972, the Conservative government accepted in 28,000 out of a total 50,000 refugees but persuaded other Commonwealth countries to share the rest of the burden. In 1974, Britain accepted 3,000 refugees from Chile following the coup against the Allende government, in part due to Labour sympathies to the former government. However, the new Conservative government was less willing to accept refugees from Vietnam. It accepted only 10,000 from Hong Kong and those only in the face of pressure from the UN (Schuster 2003: 141–42; Stevens 2004: 86).

---

[43] HC Deb, vol. 469, November 4, 1948, cols. 810–11, cited in Stevens (2004: 71).

With the end of the Cold War, Kenneth Baker, then home secretary, added to fears of mass immigration by warning that "there could be 7 million people seeking exit visas from Russia" (cited in Schuster 2003: 156). Domestically, a succession of new Immigration Acts – the Asylum and Immigration Appeals Act, 1993; the Asylum and Immigration Act, 1996; the Immigration and Asylum Act, 1999; and the Nationality, Immigration, and Asylum Act, 2002 – were passed under both Conservative and Labour governments. These Acts progressively limited asylum seekers' access to social services, employment, and asylum determination appeal processes while expanding detention practices (Bloch and Schuster 2002: 398; Schuster 2003: 149).

Therefore, although the British government continues to offer rhetorical support to the international refugee regime by framing its responsibility to "legitimate" refugees within the scope of the Refugee Convention,[44] at the domestic level, the focus is on preventing access to the British asylum system by asylum seekers. Even so, the basic norms of the refugee regime continue to hold sway. As Schuster notes, throughout this process, "none of the representatives of the different parties suggested that Britain cease to grant asylum. All agreed that the granting of asylum was the mark of a civilized and liberal state and that Britain had certain legal and humanitarian obligations" (2003: 146).

Deterrence is presented as justified because the government argues that most asylum seekers are not legitimate: thus, as the Conservative government argued in proposing the 1993 Act, the preservation of "civilized values" required immigration controls to be strengthened to ensure that they excluded economic migrants, even while it stated the primacy of the 1951 Convention over conflicting immigration rules for the first time. Thus, Kenneth Clarke, the home secretary, argued that: "we all willingly accept in this country the obligations laid on us by the 1951 Geneva Convention. We have a long and honourable tradition in the United Kingdom of offering political asylum to those who flee to this country."[45] Similarly, Home Secretary Michael Howard argued in 1995 that "the relentless rise in claims has outstripped the improvements in our ability to process them. By claiming asylum, those who have no basis to remain here can not only substantially prolong their stay, but gain access to benefits and housing at public expense."[46]

Critical to the shift in British policy has been language. As Kaye notes, "the frequent use of such terms as 'bogus,' 'phoney,' or 'economic migrant' socializes the readers [of the media] to think that the use of such terms is

---

[44] HC Deb, November 2, 1992, C. 21.   [45] HC Deb, November 2, 1992, C. 21.
[46] HC Deb, November 20, 1995, C. 335.

normal political discourse, and it also gives credence to the notion that 'bogus' refugees and asylum seekers represent a problem" (1998: 168). Asylum seekers are stigmatized in order to allow "politicians to justify limiting their responsibilities to such people" (Hassan 2000: 196).

The new Labour government, elected in 1997, quickly adopted similar positions to their predecessors. In July 1998, Home Secretary Jack Straw noted: "I am seeing a great growth of people abusing the asylum system simply to evade immigration control or because they are economic migrants in this country" (cited in Rudolph 2006: 191). The government made it clear that policy would not change: as a 1998 White Paper noted, "this government will not allow our controls to be abused with impunity" (Home Office 1998).

By the earlier 2000s, ongoing growth in the number of asylum claims – from 41,500 in 1997 to 103,080 in 2002 (UNHCR 2006a: 149) – and the perceived failure of domestic legislation led the British government to propose a radical reform. Domestically, the 2002 immigration White Paper continued to note the UK's support for a humanitarian asylum process (see Home Office 2002: 52). It framed policy reform as necessary given that asylum seekers were risking their lives to enter the UK illegally (Home Office 2002: 14, 48–49).

In 2003, the UK government proposed a shift to move processing asylum claims to "protected zones" outside of the European Union (EU) and thus into an extraterritorial space. The proposed plan argued that asylum seekers could have their claims processed within these zones. Those granted asylum could then be resettled in participating states. Those who were refused would be returned to their country of origin unless it was unsafe to do so, in which case they might be given temporary status in the EU. This approach, the UK argued, "could act as a deterrent to abuse of the asylum system, whilst preserving the right to protection for those who are genuinely entitled to it."[47] Home Secretary David Blunkett was explicit that these centers would be used as a deterrent, noting they would "rapidly reduce the number of economic immigrants using asylum applications as a migration route" (Migration News 2003).

The legality of the approach was unclear. The government argued that there "is no obligation under the 1951 Refugee Convention to process claims for asylum in the country of application."[48] Amnesty International critiqued it as an "attempt to circumvent important domestic and international legal instruments... [and contravene] the intent and purpose of the

---

[47] "United Kingdom concept paper on Zones of Protection," March 2003, www.parliament. the-stationery-office.co.uk/pa/ld200304/ldselect/ldeucom/74/7415.htm.
[48] Ibid.

right to seek and enjoy asylum" (Amnesty International 2003: 1). Its legality, however, was never tested. The approach did gain the support of other EU states, including the Netherlands and Denmark. However, it was not enough because a number of other states including Sweden, Germany, and France opposed the approach. This led to Britain withdrawing the proposal (UNHCR 2006b: 38).

Over the past three decades, there has been a concerted effort by the British government to restrict asylum seekers' ability to request asylum through domestic legislation. Although asylum seekers have been framed by the government as representing economic migrants seeking to abuse the advantages of a humanitarian-based refugee system, the government has been careful to not argue against the purpose of asylum itself. But efforts by the UK to introduce a comprehensive extraterritorial processing system to limit asylum seekers rights failed. As I argue in the next section, this is not because the EU does not accept extraterritorial provisions – these already exist in different forms, including through the safe third-country processes of the Dublin Conventions. Rather, the main point of dissension reflected different understandings of the norm of non-refoulement.

The growth of extraterritorial measures

European law establishes strong protections for refugee and asylum seekers. The Lisbon Treaty states that "the right to asylum shall be guaranteed with due respect for the rules" embodied within the Refugee Convention and Protocol.[49] Yet, whereas a range of EU Directives protect basic rights for asylum seekers, these are applied inconsistently across member states (Schuster 2011: 403).

Furthermore, at the extraterritorial level, a range of controls exist to limit the ability of asylum seekers to seek asylum. These include visa controls, designed as a mechanism to deny entry to those who might seek asylum (Neumayer 2005: 4). All EU countries except for Ireland and Great Britain refer to an identical list of countries whose inhabitants require a valid visa to cross external borders. The list included 132 countries in the 2001 regulation (Neumayer 2005: 5). Through carrier sanctions, introduced in the EU in the Schengen Implementing Convention, states levy fines on air, land, and sea carriers that bring foreign nationals without proper documentation to state territory and include both a financial penalty (which can

---

[49] Treaty of Lisbon, Art. 18. See also Guild and Garlick (2010: 65–66).

range as high as €10,000) and the ancillary costs of return (Collinson 1996: 80; UNHCR 2006b: 35).

Furthermore, under the Dublin and Dublin II Conventions (ratified in 1990 and 2003, respectively), asylum seekers must be examined by the first member state of the EU they reach and are therefore subject to return to that state without a determination process. Such "safe third-country" policies were designed to respond to the "problem of refugees and asylum seekers unlawfully leaving countries where they have already been granted protection or have had a genuine opportunity to seek such protection."[50] However, this effectively shifts responsibility for claim determination "from one Member State to another" (Garlick 2006: 602). Notably, Greece, one of the main entry points into the EU for asylum seekers, grants refugee status to only 2 percent of asylum claimants at the initial stage.[51] Furthermore, asylum seekers may also be sent to other "safe" third countries beyond the EU based on such simple standards as "if it has signed the 1951 Convention and the ECHR, and if it has an 'asylum procedure prescribed by law' – which does not necessarily equate to a system which functions in practice" (Garlick 2006: 613). Whereas the EU developed the safe third-country concept, other countries now have similar bilateral agreements, including the United States and Canada.[52]

Beyond this, Italy has moved to introduce a bilateral interdiction program. Between 2007 and 2009, Italy signed agreements with Libya that allowed the Italian Coast Guard to interdict and return vessels in international and Libyan waters without any screening process (Human Rights Watch 2009). The UNHCR, in May 2009, noted a number of procedural concerns:

it is likely that among them are people in need of international protection. . . [T]his incident makes a significant shift in policies by the Italian government and is a source of very serious concern. . . [I]n addition, Libya has not signed the 1951 Refugee Convention, and does not have a functioning national asylum system. (UNHCR 2009)

Other IOs also challenged the practices, including the Council of Europe Committee on the Prevention of Torture, which noted that Italy's policy "violated the principle of *non-refoulement*" and that "Italy was bound by

---

[50] European Commission "Resolution on a Harmonized Approach to Questions Concerning Host Third Countries," December 1, 1992.
[51] Appeals have a 35 percent recognition rate in Greece, but can take years (IRIN News 2012).
[52] Agreement between the Government of Canada and the Government of the United States of America for cooperation in the examination of refugee status claims from Nationals of third countries, December 5, 2002, www.cic.gc.ca/english/department/laws-policy/safe-third.asp, accessed May 7, 2011.

the principle of *non-refoulement* wherever it exercised its jurisdiction."[53] In its response, the Italian government argued that "no migrant, once on the Italian ships, expressed his/her intention to apply for asylum. . . . It is the opinion of Italian Authorities that, according to international and EU standards, there is no obligation during search and rescue operations to provide information on the possibility to apply for asylum."[54] The Italian government was making a claim similar to American practice: that the question of asylum did not apply outside of Italy's territorial waters.

In the case of *Hirsi Jamaa et al. v. Italy* in 2012,[55] however, the European Court of Human Rights found that Italy had violated the European Convention on Human Rights. The Court found that the case constituted "a case of extra-territorial exercise of jurisdiction by Italy capable of engaging that State's responsibility under the Convention" and that "the applicants were under the continuous and exclusive de jure and de facto control of the Italian authorities."[56] By returning the asylum seekers to Libya, Italy put them in a situation in which they were at risk of ill-treatment and at risk of secondary refoulement (Giuffré 2012; Hessbruegge 2012). This is a variation from the U.S. Supreme Court's *Sale* decision and establishes an ongoing state responsibility for asylum seekers even beyond a state's borders in Europe.

With respect to interdiction policies, the fundamental issue with the UK proposal and the U.S. and Italian practices is that they represent a core attack on the basic principle of asylum and non-refoulement. The UNHCR's position on interception practices has been that they violate non-refoulement. As the agency noted in its 2007 Note on International Protection:

Confronted with rising numbers of irregular arrivals, some States have resorted to undifferentiated interception practices resulting in *refoulement*. Many industrialized countries have increasingly "externalized" their border controls, including through interception in the territorial waters or territory of third States with the latters' permission and/or involvement. (UNHCR 2007a: 8)

---

[53] Council of Europe, "Report to the Italian Government on the visit to Italy carried out by the European Committee for the Prevention of Torture and Inhuman or Degrading Treatment or Punishment from 27 to 31 July 2009," CPT/Inf (2010) 14, www.cpt.coe.int/documents/ita/2010-inf-14-eng.pdf. 25.

[54] Council of Europe, "Response of the Italian Government to the Report of the European Committee for the Prevention of Torture and Inhuman or Degrading Treatment or Punishment on its visit to Italy from 27 to 31 July 2009," CPT/Inf (2010) 15, www.cpt.coe.int/documents/ita/2010-inf-15-eng.pdf. 9–10.

[55] *Hirsi Jamaa v. Italy*, App. No. 27765/09, European Court of Human Rights, February 23, 2012.

[56] Ibid., 78, 81.

Beyond refoulement, the UNHCR has noted that processing in extraterritorial camps introduces a range of practical concerns. This includes the question of whether the territorial state or the state who is financing the location bears legal responsibility for the processing (UNHCR 2006b: 39). The United States has avoided this issue by undertaking all processing either on American vessels or on de facto territory. The *Hirsi Jamaa* ruling removes this as an option for states within the EU.

The other state to introduce extraterritorial interdiction policies, Australia, has used a mixed approach to refugee processing, including using both Australia's own de facto territory and other states that accept the obligation for asylum processing in exchange for financial support. This mixed approach was developed under the so-called Pacific Solution, introduced by John Howard's Coalition government in 2001. Legislation excised large areas of the Australian coast and outer islands for immigration purposes. Interdicted asylum seekers were either housed on Christmas Island or transported to Papua New Guinea and the Pacific Island of Nauru for processing (Kneebone 2006: 697; Phillips and Spinks 2012: 13–14). Although the number of seaborne asylum seekers fell dramatically after the program's introduction – from 5,561 people to only 1 person the following year (Phillips and Spinks 2012: 18), asylum claims across the developed world fell in the same period. In 2005, the fifteen-member EU received 212,709 asylum applications – slightly over half the 394,973 applications it received in 2002 (UNHCR 2006c: 149). Furthermore, the Pacific Solution was limited and expensive. Of the 1,547 asylum seekers processed between 2002 and June 2007, 60 percent were found to be refugees and resettled, with two-thirds going to Australia. During this period, the Pacific Solution is estimated to have cost more than AUS$1 billion (Bem et al. 2007: 4, 55).

The Rudd Labor government ended the Pacific Solution in 2008 but continued to process "unauthorized" asylum seekers on Christmas Island and to detain them. Under Prime Minister Julia Gillard, Rudd's successor, the Australian government proposed in 2011 to reintroduce a regional processing arrangement following a steady increase of asylum seekers arriving by boat (from 2,726 in 2009 to 4,565 in 2011). The arrangement – which would have transferred 800 asylum seekers to Malaysia in exchange for 4,000 UNHCR-recognized refugees – was blocked by the Australian High Court in August 2011 (Lowes 2012).[57] Instead, Australia once again

---

[57] *Plaintiff M70/2011 v. Minister for Immigration and Citizenship and Another; Plaintiff M106 (by his litigation guardian, Plaintiff M70/2011) v. Minister for Immigration and Citizenship and Another (2011)* 122 HCA 32 (August 31, 2011). The Court ruled the arrangement violated Australian law because Malaysia had not signed the 1951 Refugee Convention, and the asylum seekers could be refouled by Malaysia to their own countries (Lowes 2012).

began transporting asylum seekers to Nauru and Papua New Guinea in August 2012.[58]

Throughout the developed world, the norms of the refugee regime have salience. These states remain committed to them. With respect to their domestic refugee policies, however, a critical area of variance lies with how these states interpret their normative obligation outside their territory – their responsibilities toward protecting all refugees. I have argued that these states do not seek to prevent asylum completely; rather, these states seek to limit the number of refugees they receive. How can they do this without actively violating the norms of the regime? They have used a mixture of deterrent policies and extraterritorial measures designed to prevent refugees from reaching the state's territory and establishing an asylum claim. Few states have gone so far as the United States, Australia, and Italy in introducing full interdiction programs. But all states in the developed world now use some measure of extraterritorial controls, including visa programs, carrier sanctions, and safe third-country legislation.

Extraterritorial practices vary across these states, which has led to variable understandings of how basic norms apply to refugee protection. Interdiction policies have undermined prior understandings of the norm of non-refoulement being applicable both within a state's borders and at its frontiers. Through their actions and attempted actions, the United States, Australia, Italy, and the United Kingdom have sought to provide a reinterpreted view of this norm, one that significantly reduces the prescriptive element embodied by it and the associated state responsibility. As the next section discusses, not only has this shift affected how the UNHCR operates, but it has also led to a substantial shift in how forced migration is understood and institutionalized in general.

The growth of forced migration and UNHCR's shifting role

Paralleling the development of the modern non-entrée regime has been the emergence of a new international regime, one designed to protect IDPs. Refugee status has always been defined on the absence of state protection and on the fact the refugee was outside of their country of origin. In the immediate postwar period, refugee numbers were far smaller than the category of "displaced persons" who, as Saloman (1991: 39) notes, were those displaced by war but willing to return home. The idea that some

---

[58] This followed the advice of a high-level government panel (Houston 2012: 43).

forms of protection might need to be extended to displaced persons within countries was discussed, and dismissed, during the 1951 Refugee Convention negotiations because they were perceived as being under the state's protection.

Because IDPs remain within their own state, they do not represent a similar transterritorial problem as refugees. Further, any international actions designed to protect IDPs directly challenge their own state's sovereignty. Thus, during the Cold War, IDPs were ignored. It was only with two international conferences – on the Plight of Refugees, Returnees, and Displaced Persons in Southern Africa in 1988 and the International Conference on Central American Refugees the following year – that they began receiving significant international attention. The profile of IDPs was further raised due to the Gulf War and its aftermath in 1991, which caused 1.5 million Kurds to flee into Iran and Turkey, while another million remained trapped in Iraq after Turkey closed its border. The American and British governments responded by launching a humanitarian intervention into Northern Iraq in order to defuse the crisis (OCHA Internal Displacement Unit 2003: 16; Orchard 2010c: 108–13). These separate events triggered widespread recognition that internal displacement was becoming a crisis that needed an international response.

Francis Deng, the first representative of the UN Secretary-General on Internally Displaced Persons, provided one way to navigate this issue. As an academic, he coined the notion of "sovereignty as responsibility": that, in order to be legitimate, governments must provide protection to their own people (Deng 1998: 3). But as a career diplomat, he was careful to couch internal displacement as a positive aspect of sovereignty that could lead to international assistance:

In my dialogue with governments ... the first five minutes with the head of state is crucial to assure them of my recognition of the problem as internal and therefore under state responsibility. Having emphasized my respect for their sovereignty, I quickly move on to present the positive interpretation of sovereignty and the supportive role of international cooperation. Once I establish a cordial climate, candid and constructive dialogue can follow with little or no constraint in the name of sovereignty. (Deng 2001: 145; see also Orchard 2010b: 291)

As part of his role, Deng was asked by the UN's Commission on Human Rights[59] to study the status of the internally displaced in international law and to find ways in which to improve protection and assistance for them. Thus, as with the earlier efforts to protect refugees, the primary

[59] Although the resolution (Commission on Human Rights 1993/95) passed unopposed, some states, including Sudan, voiced concerns over the issue of state sovereignty (Bagshaw 2005: 81).

focus was on anchoring the notion of IDP protection in law. The ensuing report[60] noted that there was substantial coverage for the internally displaced in existing international law but that there were also areas where existing law failed to provide sufficient protection:

> Some weaknesses relate to the need for an expressed right to not be unlawfully displaced, to have access to protection and assistance during displacement, and to enjoy a secure return and reintegration. There are also gaps in legal protection relating to personal documentation for the internally displaced or restitution or compensation for property lost during displacement. And although there is a general norm for freedom of movement, there is no explicit right to find refuge in a safe part of the country nor an explicit guarantee against forcible return of internally displaced persons to places of danger. (Cohen and Deng 1998: 74)

These findings were critical in convincing other international and nongovernmental organizations that some form of legal protections dedicated to IDPs were necessary. As Phuong (2004: 53) notes, organizations that "had previously opposed the creation of a new instrument . . . came to admit that the existence of such a protection gap nevertheless required some action."

Deng drafted a set of nonbinding Guiding Principles on Internal Displacement, which were introduced in 1998 through the UN Office for the Coordination of Affairs. The principles use as their foundation existing international human rights law, humanitarian law, and analogous refugee law to lay out the protections that IDPs are entitled to as citizens of their own state and as human beings (Cohen and Deng 1998: chapter 3). As Walter Kälin, the former representative of the secretary-general for the human rights of internally displaced persons, has argued:

> It is possible to cite a multitude of legal provisions for almost every principle. . . Because of that solid foundation, as well as the breadth of rights covered and the wide acceptance the Guiding Principles have found, it can persuasively be argued that they are the minimum international standard for the protection of internally displaced persons. (Kälin 2005: 29–30)

States have provided strong rhetorical support for the principles, and they have gained widespread international recognition. The 2005 UN World Summit Outcome Declaration recognized the principles as "an important international framework" for IDP protection (United Nations General Assembly 2005: para 132). The General Assembly, the Security Council, and the Commission on Human Rights/Human Rights Council have all acknowledged or recognized the principles (Orchard 2010b: 294), as have

---

[60] For a fuller discussion of the two legal studies that led to this report authored by Walter Kälin, a Swiss international law professor, see Weiss and Korn (2006: 57–60).

a range of regional and subregional organizations (Mooney 2005: 166). Opposition to the principles by all but a handful of states is nonexistent.[61]

Furthermore, the principles are being introduced into regional hard law, including through the 2006 Protocol on Protection and Assistance to Internally Displaced Persons[62] and the 2009 Convention for the Protection and Assistance of Internally Displaced Persons in Africa (the Kampala Convention), which was ratified in December 2012. This Convention deliberately replicates the normative structure introduced by the guiding principles (Abebe 2010: 42). It includes the principles' definition of IDPs, their established rights, and the need for states to cooperate with "international organizations and humanitarian agencies, civil society organizations and other relevant actors."

Protecting IDPs is a critical issue. But this emerging IDP protection regime poses challenges for the current refugee regime. By definition, IDPs represent people who could be refugees if they had been able and willing to leave their own state. Increasing the protections available to IDPs fits in with the broader containment agenda (Dubernet 2001). Furthermore, as I have argued, the cornerstone of refugee protection has been law. Yet, although it has been suggested that the growth of IDP protection complements refugee protection (Cohen 2006a), other commentators have been concerned that an extension of direct rights to IDPs is "detrimental to the traditional asylum option that is central to refugeehood" (Barutciski 1998: 11; Dubernet 2001). Thus, although there is centrally a degree of overlap between the two regimes, the effects of these developments remain ambiguous (Betts 2010: 22–23).

Furthermore, the growth of IDP numbers is linked to increased restrictions on asylum seekers and would-be refugees. But it is also linked to the increased number of civil wars as a proportion of conflicts and to deliberate displacement strategies undertaken by some states (Orchard 2010a). This suggests that the creation of an IDP regime reflects a broader humanitarian concern on the part of the international community: that IDPs require some form of protection because their own state cannot provide it.

---

[61] At the time the principles were created, several states, including China, Egypt, and Sudan, questioned their soft law origins (Cohen 2004). By contrast, in the most recent General Assembly debate on internally displaced persons, in 2009, the only country to obliquely critique them was Sudan, whose representative noted "his delegation would have preferred the draft resolution to refer to international instruments and did not consider itself bound by any language or definition that came from documents that had not been universally ratified." UN General Assembly Official Records, "Summary Record of the 42nd Meeting," November 12, 2009, p. 6, see also Orchard (2014).

[62] International Conference on the Great Lakes Region, "Protocol on Protection and Assistance to Internally Displaced Persons" (2006).

UNHCR and forced migrant protection

Increased restrictionism on the part of the developed world, alongside the dramatic growth in IDP numbers, has caused the UNHCR's role in the refugee regime to shift. The UNHCR's success as a norm entrepreneur was marked by its independence – established through its Statute and through ongoing General Assembly resolutions – and by its authority as a moral actor. In the mid-1980s, its position in the regime began to change. Developed states no longer granted it blanket authority over refugee matters (McDowall 1989: 181; Cunliffe 1995) As High Commissioner Poul Hartling (1985) cautioned: "states which have been champions of human rights are now finding it difficult to grant some of these basic rights to asylum seekers... Is it too much to ask that this small number of bona fide asylum-seekers ... should be received and treated in accordance with those international instruments and those humanitarian traditions?"

Under Hartling's successor, Jean-Pierre Hocke, who served from 1986 to 1989, the agency deliberately shifted its focus from protection to increased involvement in the countries of origin. In his view, the best possible solution was "to achieve voluntary repatriation under appropriate conditions" (Hocke 1989: 42, 44). But as the UNHCR's budget grew dramatically with this shift – by 27 percent between 1986 and 1989 – the Executive Committee moved to significantly reduce the agency's budgetary independence. Thorvald Stoltenberg, Hocke's replacement, who only served a year, noted that budgetary limitations had a "crippling effect [because] of the unstable and unpredictable nature of funding of our activities. Living almost on a month-to-month, sometimes week-to-week basis, is not only uneconomic – and may I say not very dignified – but it also makes the UNHCR a much less responsible and effective organization" (cited in Cunliffe 1995: 285).

The UNHCR has always relied on voluntary contributions. But in the post-Cold War period, these contributions were increasingly earmarked to specific programs, thus limiting the agency's operational effectiveness and raising concerns over its independence (Cunliffe 1995: 284; Vayrynen 2001: 164; Loescher et al. 2008). This financing has divided the UNHCR's role between policies advocated, and supported, by governments in the developed world and supporting those governments of the developing world that host the majority of refugees (Morris 1990: 46). At the same time, developed states increasingly justified the support they provide to the UNHCR as part of their contribution to the regime instead of offering resettlement opportunities.

Financial issues supported the UNHCR's shift away from being an agency of resettlement to one of repatriation. This was driven not only

by donor states, including its own Executive Committee, which encouraged this shift (UNHCR Executive Committee 1980; see also Goodwin-
Gill 1989), but also by the UNHCR itself as a reaction to the international
realities it was now operating within (for example, see UNHCR 1986).

The Bosnian War symbolized the dilemmas the UNHCR faced. During
the war, the UNHCR moved away from its traditional role and provided
humanitarian assistance not only to refugees, but also to IDPs and the
broader civilian population of Bosnia, who accounted for more than 40
percent of their case load (Weiss and Pasic 1997: 47). High Commissioner
Sadako Ogata, who served from 1991 to 1999, argued in support of this
shift:

If I, as the High Commissioner for Refugees, emphasize the right not to become a
refugee, it is because I know that the international protection that my Office, in
cooperation with countries of asylum, can offer to refugees is not an adequate
substitute for the protection that they should have received from their own
Governments in their own countries. The generosity of asylum countries cannot
fully replace the loss of a homeland or relieve the pain of exile. (Ogata 1993; see
also Frelick 1990)

The concept of a "right to remain," however, was problematic in three
ways. The first was that it fit in with a "hardening of views with respect to
the movement and admission of asylum seekers generally" (Goodwin-Gill
1996: 103). As Hathaway and Neve (1997: 136) note, "would-be refugees
may indeed have remained within their own states, but not because they
exercised a 'right to remain.' They had no option but to remain."

The second was its practical effect on the ground. Whereas Ogata
may have felt that assistance and protection could be combined, too
often, assistance was prioritized over protection. As one UNHCR field
officer was quoted, "it would compromise food deliveries if I made a
demarche" on human rights violations against minorities (Minear et al.
1994: 24–25). Furthermore, the UNHCR's role was seen as a way for
the international community to avoid other, more decisive, forms of action
(Andreas 2008: 13). Thus François Fouinat, the Coordinator of the
UNHCR Task Force, stated that "it is not simply that the UN's humanitarian efforts have become politicized; it is rather that we have been transformed into the only manifestation of international political will" (UNHCR
2000: 220).

An additional challenge was posed by the large numbers of refugees from
the former Yugoslavia and, subsequently, Kosovo. The major concern on
the part of both potential host countries in Europe and the UNHCR was
ensuring that these refugees could be offered protection without overwhelming the host state in question. The UNHCR argued that temporary
protection offered "a means of affording protection to persons involved in

large-scale movements that could otherwise overwhelm established procedures for the determination of refugee status."[63]

Temporary protection was not a new concept – it had been offered
to the Hungarian refugees in 1956. However, in applying it to Bosnia
and Kosovo, the UNHCR recast it as "an alternative to asylum and generally premised on the understanding that the 'exit strategy' would be
return rather than resettlement" (van Selm 2003: 83). Thus, the
UNHCR was seen as catering to fears by developed governments that
providing refugees with full rights might hamper their repatriation
(Roxström and Gibney 2003: 47). Not only did this introduce ambiguity
into the basic notion of who a refugee was according to the 1951
Convention (Fitzpatrick 2000: 281), but it was designed in the political
interests of the receiving states, rather than of the refugees themselves
(Roxström and Gibney 2003: 49; see also Hathaway and Neve 1997).
Although it may have been welcomed by states, Dennis McNamara
notes it also "kept refugees for years in temporary, albeit safe, limbo"
(cited in Gorlick 2003: 287 fn 14).

These issues point to a disjuncture between the UNHCR's role as an
agency for refugee protection and as a humanitarian agency. As Barutciski
argues, a focus on in-country humanitarian assistance not only left the
agency ill-prepared for its core and primary asylum protection duties, but
also politicized the agency. If it gives little deference to state sovereignty,
governments in the developing world have "legitimate reasons to fear its
presence" (2002: 368, 70; see also Roberts 1998: 382).

Currently, the UNHCR appears to be navigating a course between
these two opposing views. It is continuing its involvement in countries
of origin – in particular by expanding its role in providing protection and
assistance to IDPs – while renewing its focus on refugee protection.
Through this focus, the UNHCR can position itself as a broad-based
protection agency, thus once again seeking to establish its own moral
authority. Equally, by focusing on solutions to long-running refugee situations, it can once again reclaim legitimacy as an important global actor
through its performance. As Antonio Guterres, who became high commissioner in 2005, has argued:

Protecting, assisting and helping to provide solutions for refugees, stressing the
rights of stateless people and reducing statelessness are our core mandate. In
everything we do, we can never forget our mandate, and nothing will distract us
from it. . . We are a protection agency, and protection is at the centre of everything
we do. (Guterres 2007)

---

[63] UNHCR Background Note, Comprehensive Response to the Humanitarian Situation in
Former Yugoslavia, January 21, 1993 (cited in van Selm-Thorburn 1998: 36).

However, this does not necessarily limit the UNHCR to protecting only refugees. A continuing presence in states of origin to offer protection to IDPs is increasingly a vital part of its mandate (Orchard 2010b).[64] As a number of commentators have noted, other efforts to provide protection through interagency efforts have been at best ineffective and at worst complete failures (Mooney 2005; Cohen 2006b).

With the emergence of the "cluster approach" for humanitarian assistance within the UN in 2005, the UNHCR has been given a coordinating role as cluster lead for IDP protection, emergency shelter, camp management, and coordination. However, in a dramatic change from its policies in the 1990s, the UNHCR has argued that whereas its involvement in internal situations "could be seized upon to ground measures on a national, bilateral or regional basis to keep internally displaced or other persons otherwise seeking asylum in neighbouring countries strictly within national borders," it plans to systematically monitor all situations (UNHCR 2007b: 11).

Both the shifts in the refugee regime and the emergence of the parallel IDP regime have created tensions within the UNHCR as the primary agency assigned the role of protecting refugees. It has had little influence over state policy and has even been complicit in a shifting role toward containing would-be refugees in their countries of origin and in limiting refugee rights. This confusion within the agency, however, reflects the broader challenges that the refugee regime has faced over the past twenty years.

Conclusion: How effective is the modern refugee regime?

The non-entrée regime represents a transformation, rather than a wholesale replacement, of the postwar refugee regime. The same norms continue to hold sway, embodied in the 1951 Refugee Convention. States continue to accept the paramount importance of the right of refugees to seek asylum. Yet, the introduction of domestic restrictions and of extraterritorial controls by developed states has clearly affected that right. Furthermore, it has represented an attempt to redefine two key norms that have underpinned the regime. The first of these is the right of non-refoulement, in which interdiction policies and other measures are used to prevent would-be refugees from making an asylum claim. This normative change has meant both a lessening of the prescriptive power of the norm of

---

[64] See General Assembly Resolution 53/125 (1998).

non-refoulement and an attempt by states to lessen their direct responsibilities toward refugees.

The second challenge has been to the basic way in which refugees are defined. As we have seen, who was included within this definition gradually expanded over centuries. The Refugee Convention both reflected these long-term practices and enshrined a clear international legal definition of who refugees are. As patterns of displacement have shifted, states have been able to argue that large numbers of asylum seekers – still warranting protection – do not qualify as "Convention refugees." At the same time, efforts to contain refugees have led to the dramatic expansion in IDPs who also need forms of international legal protection. The UNHCR has been left trying to protect multiple groups of forced migrants, a situation that has undermined its core mandate.

The result of this is that the non-entrée regime is based on key norms that have undergone variable degrees of reinterpretation and hence are no longer commonly understood. This directly affects their compliance pull. Furthermore, these shifts have seen the expansion of a diffuse responsibility at the expense of direct responsibilities. States in the developed world feel that support for the UNHCR fulfils their obligations. They have sought to offload their responsibilities to that agency and to the developed world, which now bears a disproportionate responsibility toward providing asylum to the world's refugees.

9   Refugees and state cooperation
in international society

I began this book with a puzzle. Developed state practice toward refugees (and particularly asylum seekers) has shifted dramatically in the past quarter century, with a range of domestic legislation, bilateral and multilateral agreements, and extraterritorial controls used to limit opportunities to apply for asylum. Yet these states have not taken the obvious next step: to simply remove themselves from the refugee regime entirely. In fact, these same states are careful in their public rhetoric to continue to support the goals of the regime, in particularly its key element of providing asylum to refugees. In addition, these states continue to financially support the United Nations High Commissioner for Refugees (UNHCR), an international organization (IO) whose budget has continued to grow. Furthermore, although these restrictionist policies have dramatically altered the refugee regime, the core values that states continue to support were agreed to at a time when international society faced just as significant a crisis with larger numbers of refugees.

At the outset, I suggested that three arguments have been used to explain why states provide refugee protection: an interest-based approach, a collective interests-based approach, and a normative approach. I noted that I do not see these as competing explanations but rather cumulative ones; in other words, each argument provides a greater degree of depth and clarity. None of these arguments can explain refugee protection by itself.

The first argument focuses purely on state interests, primarily a subset of interests marked by sovereignty, security, and economics. It is linked to American practices toward refugees from communism during the Cold War. The argument there was that refugee protection was tied directly to interest calculation, and that, as the Cold War ended, the United States no longer needed to accept such refugees. Within this book, however, I have shown that this argument is unpersuasive in three ways.

First, by looking over the full history of refugee protection, in few other events are the role of interests as clearly at play. Economic motives did in part explain the acceptance of the Huguenots, but economic arguments explain neither why states chose to offer them legal protections, nor the retroactive grants of protection by both Britain and the Netherlands years and even decades after the Huguenot flight. With subsequent eighteenth-century flights – such as the Palatines – any economic rationale for accepting them was quickly proven false.

Second, the United States played a key role in building the postwar regime. But the goals of its chief architects – namely, President Truman – were primarily humanitarian in origin. Refugee protection was reframed as a Cold War security issue to gain Congressional support, which did have long-term effects. But, as I have documented, Truman was not motivated solely by the self-interest of the United States. Furthermore, Cold War politics certainly affected U.S. practice. It led to the American government's decision to not support the UNHCR and instead create IOs outside of the UN's purview. Yet, the United States still supported a broad set of refugee protections in the 1951 Refugee Convention. It was unwilling to compromise on the key norm of non-refoulement, even when it would have aided the negotiations around the International Refugee Organization (IRO) or would have helped to end the Korean War eighteen months early.

Third, it was not the end of the Cold War itself that led to a shift in how the developed world provided refugee protection, but rather an associated growth in the numbers of asylum seekers. Even here, the United States has never stopped refugee resettlement; although its policies continue to be biased toward postcommunist countries, this is more a legacy rather than a deliberate choice. American policies of interdiction at sea in the Caribbean do mark a major challenge to the norms of the postwar regime. This shift, however, dates to the Reagan administration and to subsequent shifts under George H. W. Bush and Bill Clinton. It is a limited reaction to the United States becoming a country of first asylum and facing growing numbers of Haitians and Cubans, not a reaction to the end of the Cold War.

The second argument focuses on the idea of collective interests. Here, the goals of stability and preserving the values and institutions of international society are both important factors. If this argument was a sufficient explanation, we could expect change based on the possibility that developed states have decided that either a lower overall level of refugee protection can fulfil these goals or that costs can be better redistributed. This would provide an explanation for changes within the refugee regime that did not lead to its wholesale abandonment.

Cost-based arguments are frequently used to justify narrowing or restricting asylum options. The United Kingdom justified its zones of protection proposal in 2003 in part by noting that "support for refugees is badly distributed, with asylum seekers who make it to Europe frequently receiving support and legal costs exceeding $10,000 per year, whereas the UNHCR spends an average of only $50 a year on each refugee."[1] One frequently cited figure suggests that developed states spent more than $10 billion to administer their asylum programs in 2003, whereas the UNHCR's budget that year was only $1.17 billion (Price 2009: 190). Restrictionism, however, rarely reduces financial expenditures. As noted in Chapter 8, over the course of five years, the Australian government's Pacific Solution is estimated to have cost more than AUS$1 billion to process 1,547 asylum seekers. By contrast, the total budget for refugee resettlement by the U.S. government in 2011, when it accepted 56,424 refugees, was approximately the same at $1.062 billion.[2]

Furthermore, limited opportunities for asylum in the developed world are one of the reasons internally displaced person (IDP) numbers have grown. Yet providing IDPs with protection and assistance is a significant and costly undertaking. In the case of Darfur, Sudan, for example, in 2012 – nine years after the outbreak of conflict – 1.4 million IDPs continued to receive international assistance and protection (through the UN Assistance Mission in Darfur) at an annual cost of almost $2 billion (UN General Assembly 2012; UN OCHA 2012).

Instead, to understand state practices toward refugee protection, I have argued that the mutually constitutive roles of structures and agents have played a key role. Importantly, the flight of the Huguenots in 1685 provided little indication that they would have lasting effects on state practice. Small decisions taken by individual states at the time of that crisis event – to recognize them as a distinct group, to let them in, and to offer them legal protections – continue to form the basis of how we understand refugee protection today. Over the next two centuries, these decisions slowly became international normative obligations. In this final chapter, I focus on the implications of this argument for both theory and policy. In particular, I show how these processes have functioned over time and review the important roles that both structures and actors have played within the international refugee issue area.

Explaining the existence of refugee protection

Fundamental institutions – including territoriality, international law, popular sovereignty, and multilateralism – provided the basic rules that states have followed to govern their behavior and assist cooperation.

---

[1] "United Kingdom concept paper on Zones of Protection," March 2003, www.parliament. the-stationery-office.co.uk/pa/ld200304/ldselect/ldeucom/74/7415.htm.

[2] U.S. Department of State, U.S. Department of Homeland Security, and U.S. Department of Health and Human Services, "Proposed Refugee Admissions for Fiscal Year 2012: Report to the Congress," 57, www.hsdl.org/?view&did=690218.

These institutions served to first problematize refugees as a transterritorial issue – a view not prevalent prior to the seventeenth century – and provided the political space in which state cooperation was possible to protect refugees.

These institutions have periodically changed. International law served to define the role of the sovereign and the citizen with respect to each other and to international society, then to define the similar role of the state. Popular sovereignty shifted the basis for the legitimacy of rule from the ruler to the population. Then, after the Second World War, it was expanded and redefined to incorporate a norm of sovereign equality. Multilateralism provided a way for states to better coordinate international cooperation. It also allowed for states to indirectly provide protection, then assistance, to refugees beyond their own borders. Finally, extraterritorial practices first helped to frame refugee protection, but then offered an alternative to states seeking to limit their own direct responsibilities to refugees.

Regimes served to link these fundamental institutions with individual issue-specific norms and, in so doing, provided a clear sense of the scope of international behavior and obligations with respect to refugees. Regimes thereby introduced regularity to state practices. I have argued that four independent regimes have functioned within the refugee issue area: the laissez-faire, informal regime of the nineteenth century; the interwar regime; the postwar regime; and, finally, since the end of the Cold War, the non-entrée regime. All four regimes have embodied different normative understandings and thus had different goals and purposes. The laissez-faire regime was based in the notion that individual states had a responsibility to not return refugees who entered their territory, and this understanding was framed by protections in domestic and bilateral extradition law. The interwar regime was based in the notion that certain groups of refugees required protections through formal multilateral cooperation, and this understanding was anchored in the creation of a succession of IOs and the gradual development of international law. The postwar regime was based in the notion that all refugees require protection and to not be returned to their own countries, with protection anchored in international law and in the ongoing efforts of the UNHCR. The non-entrée regime continues to support the notion that refugees require protection but is equally based in the use of extraterritorial measures to limit the direct responsibilities for developed states toward refugees.

Change within and between regimes has occurred as they have been challenged by crises that redefined the scope of the problem. Regime persistence relates directly to the regime's legitimacy. Legitimacy depends on its normative content, its ability to create shared understandings between actors, and whether it links these understandings to other structures in international society and at the domestic level. The first two regimes collapsed when they could no longer provide a linking mechanism between the international and domestic levels and between the norms of the regime and the broader norms and fundamental institutions of international society. The postwar regime did not similarly collapse but was transformed as states reinterpreted critical norms, including how refugees are identified and the role of non-refoulement.

The critical role of crisis events

One of the main arguments of this work has been that state policies over time tend to be stable, rooted in normative beliefs that become institutionalized within a regime. Crisis events disrupt this stability and trigger significant policy and normative change. I defined these events as instances of failure of existing policies triggered by a dramatic and sustained change in the nature and/or numbers of refugees seeking protection. These failures are public and significant enough that they cause states to question preexisting normative understandings and the purpose of the regime. Thus, reversion to the status quo is no longer feasible.

I have focused on six crisis events that led to significant normative change and either regime replacement or transformation. In Chapter 3, I showed that the Peace of Westphalia marked an important transition as individuals were provided with the right of *jus emigrandi* to leave their own state if their religion differed from that of their Prince. This doctrinal evolution occurred due to the interplay of two fundamental institutions: territoriality and international law. The flight of the Huguenots from France in 1685 marked a key crisis event: by forbidding their flight, Louis XIV violated this normative understanding. What had been a thin normative order was expanded to incorporate the principle that allowing refugees to emigrate was a hallmark of a legitimate state. Equally, states were willing to not only accommodate the Huguenot refugees, but to offer them protection in domestic law. This was a singular shift. Although few other refugee movements during this period were offered similar protections, individual states did seek to accommodate them for religious and economic reasons. Furthermore, the Huguenot crisis did not lead to state practice being institutionalized at the international level; states accepted no concurrent responsibility for refugees but rather accommodated them on a case by case basis.

A cooperative, albeit tacit, regime emerged only in the nineteenth century, following the French Revolution. The flight of the émigrés triggered a crisis event that forced states to consider the role of political, as well as religious, refugees. As Chapter 4 showed, this shift in practice had required the emergence of doctrines of popular sovereignty. This created a broader view that political as well as religious refugees should be granted asylum and that this was a duty for states in European society: hospitality and humanitarianism required it. Refugees were no longer accepted because of state interests; rather, in many cases, offering protection ran against these interests and on some occasions even risked war. As norms in international society, these doctrines first emerged in Great Britain, the United States, and France. In each state, decision makers and the domestic population accepted that accommodating refugees and not returning them to states where they might be persecuted was morally just. These states then successfully transmitted these new norms across European society through the mechanism of bilateral extradition treaties so that, by the 1870s, nonreturn (non-refoulement) of political fugitives was considered to be a universal practice. Legalization of refugee protection thereby served a crucial role as a mechanism to create and transmit shared understandings among states.

Such informal mechanisms worked as long as refugee numbers were relatively low and as long as open immigration remained a principle of the system. As Chapter 5 showed, during the interwar period, much larger numbers of refugees triggered by the Russian Revolution caused this informal regime to fail. Norm entrepreneurs at the international level responded to this crisis event by convincing states that an effective solution to the refugee problem was through formal multilateral cooperation and the entrenching of refugee protection in international rather than domestic law. This new formal regime provided a successful cooperative mechanism for states during the 1920s. At the same time, however, immigration control was being recast at the domestic level as an important aspect of state sovereignty. In the 1930s, the discordance between state support for the regime at the international level and domestic norms favoring restrictionism proved too much. In their efforts to assist the Jews fleeing from Nazi Germany, states were unwilling to provide a succession of IOs with strong mandates due to fears that the organizations might seek to challenge their domestic immigration policies. Equally, domestic decision makers who favored a humanitarian response to this crisis – including, from 1938 onward, Franklin Roosevelt – were unable to challenge the domestic restrictionist consensus.

The interwar period, although a failure for cooperative efforts to protect refugees, did create important norms. These norms reflected the need for states to cooperate through formal multilateral structures and to provide protections in international law. As Chapter 6 showed, this provided a basis for a new regime to emerge in the postwar period, driven by American leadership. The United States government, and Harry Truman in particular, committed to new cooperative efforts and were willing to provide significant support to these IOs. This was both because of concerns that the large refugee population might endanger European stability and for humanitarian reasons. Two separate events – the plight of refugees and displaced persons in European camps and the forced repatriation of millions of Soviet citizens – triggered this shift and recast the American government as a norm entrepreneur. Following it, while the American government sought to create an IO – the International Refugee Organization – in cooperation with the Soviet Union, it was unwilling to compromise on the crucial point of non-refoulement. The IRO, therefore, provided refugee protection primarily through resettlement activities supported in large part by the U.S. government. Equally, Truman fought to ensure that the United States also welcomed refugees at the domestic level. He succeeded in altering the position of Congress but only by securitizing refugees as a Cold War issue – a frame that continues to play a role today.

As the Cold War deepened, the United States sought to substitute IOs within the UN system for ones that it could create and control. This meant, as Chapter 7 showed, that the United States was unwilling to support the UNHCR. In spite of this lack of U.S. support, and in spite of a very limited and nonoperational mandate, the UNHCR prospered because of its moral and expert authority and because it proved its effectiveness as a protection- and assistance-oriented organization. At the international level, the UNHCR played a key role as a norm entrepreneur by reframing the legal basis for refugee status and by moving the regime away from its Eurocentric origins to encompass the world.

Yet, as Chapter 8 showed, refugee flows to the developed world triggered a new crisis event in the late 1980s and 1990s. This was coupled with the dramatic growth in numbers of a parallel forced migrant group, IDPs. Faced with this challenge, the UNHCR found its authority and autonomy challenged by states. As it pragmatically sought to cope with this changing environment, it began to focus less on refugee protection, with the result that it undermined the power of the 1951 Convention and the agency's sources of moral and expert authority.

At the same time, the United States and Great Britain have increasingly engaged in bifurcated policies, supporting the UNHCR and the international refugee regime at the international level while prioritizing national interests and immigration control at the domestic level. As both states grapple with their role in a globalized world, a humanitarian basis for their refugee policies has been allowed to drift. In particular, although both continue to reflect the key norms of the regime – support for multilateral cooperation, for refugee protection in international law, and for non-refoulement – they compromise these norms on a day-to-day basis through policies of refugee deterrence and extraterritorial processes, including interdiction at sea. These changes have created a new non-entrée regime. This regime, although based in the collective understandings of the postwar regime, has a weaker collective basis because of these issues. Although states in the developed world may provide rhetorical support for refugee protection and asylum, it is the UNHCR and the developing world that bear a disproportionate share of the regime's costs.

The role of norm entrepreneurship

Wholesale norm change and regime replacement occur following crisis events. Following such events, norm entrepreneurs played crucial roles in presenting new normative understandings at both the international and domestic levels. Critical to this process was their ability to successfully frame these new norms in ways that correspond to existing normative understandings and domestic structures. These efforts occurred at the international level (as in 1921) or at the domestic level (as in 1685 and during the nineteenth century) but worked best when efforts simultaneously occurred at the domestic and international levels (as between 1945 and 1951). Different types of norm entrepreneurs succeeded in bringing about change, whether individuals or nongovernmental organizations (NGOs) at the international level (Gustave Ador and the ICRC in 1921), IOs (the UNHCR's expansion of its mandate in the 1951–67 period), or domestic entrepreneurs able to work within domestic structures (most notably President Truman in the 1945–51 period).

This book highlights three critical issues. First, my findings reinforce recent arguments about the ability of IOs to not only reflect state interests but also, through independent sources of authority and legitimacy, to create new norms. Such an argument has already been made in terms of the UNHCR (Loescher 2001; Barnett and Finnemore 2004). Other IOs within this issue area, most notably the League of Nations High Commissioner for Refugees, played similar roles. However, not all IOs are created equally, with states frequently seeking to limit their scope and mandate. None of the League IOs during the 1930s, nor the Inter-Governmental Committee on Refugees, were able to introduce new norms or sway state practice. Hence, the external environment, international constraints, and how refugee protection is viewed at the domestic level in key states all affect an IO's ability to bring about practical and normative change.

Second, the role of norm entrepreneurs at the domestic level is a critical element to understanding the history of refugee protection. I challenged the view that these are moral actors and suggested that norm entrepreneurship should be viewed as an activity that anyone or any organization can engage in. I drew on the conception of policy entrepreneurs to provide an alternative to a moral basis and instead suggested that norm entrepreneurs are those who are willing to contribute considerable resources to the issues about which they have strong notions. Of particular importance is the need to disaggregate true entrepreneurs (those proposing new ideas) from other groups or states determined to ensure international adoption of norms they have committed to at the domestic level. I argued as well that a range of domestic institutions can play critical roles in either accepting or blocking the new norm. As states adopt new international normative understandings, they, too, can play an entrepreneurial role at the international level as norm leaders, seeking to convince other states to adopt new norms.

Furthermore, constructivist accounts have often ignored or limited the role that domestic institutions and norms play in affecting state internalization of new norms. Yet, whether new international norms are internalized within the state depends significantly on how they are interpreted and received by domestic institutions. International norms are most likely to be internalized when they either occupy a novel issue area or when they are successfully framed to fit with existing normative understandings at the international and domestic levels. When such salience does not exist, domestic institutions, particularly those with a veto power, can play critical roles in blocking new norms. Thus, one of the major failures of the United States in the 1930s was the inability of concerned norm entrepreneurs working within the Roosevelt administration to bring about a change in U.S. refugee policy. Conversely, Truman succeeded in shifting policy because he was able to reframe refugee protection as a security issue and thereby gain Congressional support.

Truman's efforts represent a third path for domestic norm introduction: active persuasion on the part of domestic norm entrepreneurs. This process can take years, and even strong rhetorical commitments to norms at the international level can be blocked or undermined by domestic institutions. But once norms introduced at the domestic level are internalized, the state can shift roles at the international level, becoming a norm leader that seeks to persuade states in favor of a normative position already accepted as correct by the state's domestic institutions and public.

The third issue is the role played by norms and other structures in helping to construct how states understood refugee protection. The first step was the recognition that refugees did have a right to leave their own state, recognized in international legal doctrines, in peace agreements (particularly Augsburg and Westphalia), and, following the Revocation of the Edict of Nantes, in state practice. From that point on, a growing set of norms identified how these individuals outside of their own states could be provided with protection. These norms recognized that individual states had a responsibility toward refugees who reached their frontiers, a responsibility that was subsequently transferred to the collective level through formal state negotiations. Crucial to this transition was recognition that individual states could not be expected to deal with large refugee flows by themselves. States accepted that there needed to be international cooperation facilitated by an institutional framework. Equally critical has been the role of law, accepted by states as the best mechanism to provide refugee protection. This occurred first at the domestic, then the bilateral, and finally the international level. As a corollary to international legal protection, states also accepted in the post-Second World War period that refugees should not be returned or refouled to states where they would be subject to persecution.

Not all these norm shifts were positive in their impacts on refugees. During some periods, most notably the 1920s and 1930s, norms reflecting restrictionism at the domestic level significantly curtailed the willingness of states to engage in refugee protection, causing international cooperation to unravel. This failure of international cooperation caused Nazi Germany to shift its policies toward the Jews and was one of the triggers for the Holocaust. New norms introduced since the end of the Cold War have focused on the regionalization and restriction of refugee movement and rights. Historically, states recognized refugees as those who fled state-based persecution, an understanding that remains the basis for the international regime. And yet, since the 1960s, refugee flows have increasingly included those fleeing persecution by non-state actors and situations of generalized violence, neither of which are adequately reflected in this view. Each new regime over this period, although it embodied a clear right to leave, also ensured that refugees had an obligation to *seek* asylum, not a right to automatically receive it. The introduction of the legal doctrine of non-refoulement meant that states had to provide such protections not only to refugees who were in their territories, but also to those who reached their frontiers. States were concerned that they might be subject to uncontrolled refugee flows; therefore, increased restrictions enabled them to limit their individual responsibility and, if refugee numbers grew too large, to count on the support of other states to deal with the problem.

By the same token, states balanced restrictiveness on the one hand with a willingness to accept, or to even encourage, refugee resettlement. This was clearest during the early decades of the Cold War, when Western states routinely accepted in large numbers of refugees from the communist world. It is less true today, as these same states seek not only to prevent entry of refugees (or, in the new parlance, asylum seekers) but also to restrict the numbers of refugees they resettle. Thus, since the 1980s, the vast majority of refugees remain in the developing world. These host states, lacking support from the developed world, are increasingly unwilling to engage in permanent resettlement. The result is that most refugees today are in limbo, trapped in camps with no solution to their plight in sight. The normative obligations accepted by states have been tempered by an increased focus on restrictionism and border controls, a switch that has undermined the basis of the regime rooted in a collective responsibility for refugees.

How states understand the normative obligations they have undertaken is affected by how they view their own responsibilities toward refugee protection. Is refugee protection understood as a responsibility of states to protect refugees within broader international principles of humanitarianism, or do states perceive refugees as a challenge to their sovereignty and national interests? Policies toward refugees have been most effective at providing protection when international norms governing refugee protection are in accordance with domestic understandings. Increased admittances of refugees and increased support at the international level, although it ensures better protection, may seem like a negative outcome for the states concerned. And yet it is not. It is during these times that the strongest regimes are created, when refugees are most effectively dealt with at the international level, and when states are confident not only in protecting their interests, but also in ensuring order in the international system. Conversely, restrictionism, although it may appear to better limit the state's obligations, has invariably led to the destabilization and weakening of the regime. In the long run, this triggers a new search for an effective solution, often requiring new structures and new IOs. Norms alone do not mean that state behavior will be consistent or that a state's identity will be shaped in a positive manner. For this to occur, rather, we require norm entrepreneurs who can serve as champions.

Diverting crisis events

Beyond these crisis events, however, I have also documented a number of moments that *could have become crises* in that they either represented a dramatic increase or change in form of refugee movements. These ranged from the 1848 revolutions, through the rise of anarchism, to the Armenian refugees of the interwar period, to the flight of the Hungarians in 1956. Why did these events not similarly challenge the existing regimes? Three different processes explain the ability of the regime to weather the crisis, based on both the regime's legitimacy and the concordance of the individual norms within it.

During the 1848 Revolutions and their aftermath, Britain's strong protections for refugees – their unwillingness to return anyone who sought asylum – was an outlier compared to the policies on the continent. Those states saw the Revolutions as exceptional, as a unique event that required previous rights to be set aside. Yet the British government was willing to stare down the threat of war rather than alter its policies. Even a tangential change in policy, such as the Palmerston government's proposal for a new Conspiracy to Murder Bill following the Orsini Affair, was enough to bring the government down. Here, the normative understandings embodied within the nineteenth-century's laissez-faire regime were so strong that government policy was suborned to the public will. No change occurred because, at the time, it was intolerable to the British public.

A second process of incremental change in practice is reflected in both the rise of anarchism in the late nineteenth century and in the response to the Armenian refugees in the early 1920s. Both of these were novel events. Anarchism claimed the lives of heads of states across Europe and in the United States. Refugees, particularly from Eastern Europe, were quickly labeled as anarchists and thus a threat. With respect to the Armenians, by 1924, 200,000 of them were scattered across Europe, having fled the genocide between 1915 and 1918 or otherwise fearful of their role within the new Turkish state. This was a group second in size only to the group fleeing the Russian Revolution. Yet, in both these cases, small changes brought them within the regime. In the case of anarchism, assassination or attempted assassination of heads of states was added to the political exemption established in the 1850s, thereby removing those individuals from the right to claim refugee status. With respect to the wider refugee population, however, few states were willing to modify their own legislation or return or surrender suspected anarchists without proof. With the Armenians, Fridthof Nansen simply argued that the League of Nations should take responsibility for them and a new Arrangement was drafted. The regime established to protect Russian refugees was expanded to incorporate them.

The third process saw existing normative understandings stretched to incorporate new issues.[3] The postwar regime had not been designed to respond to the flight of refugees from Hungary following the failed uprising in 1956, nor to deal with the longer term flow of refugees into Western Berlin starting in 1953. The Refugee Convention's dateline had clearly indicated refugees needed to have fled events prior to 1951, whereas the UNHCR had been designed to provide legal protection to refugees rather than assistance. And yet the UNHCR was able to stretch the norms of the

---

[3] This represents a variation on the concept of regime stretching. See Betts (2013:34–35).

regime in two ways. With respect to legal protection, Paul Weis, the legal adviser to the high commissioner, argued that the departure of the refugees was related to the establishment of the Hungarian People's Republic in 1947 and therefore was an after-effect of this earlier change. Stretching the refugee definition in this way served to bring first refugees from communism, then from conflicts in the developing world, into the refugee regime. Furthermore, the UNHCR was able to justify its effectiveness as an assistance organization, convincing the UN General Assembly (and, more importantly, the American government) to broaden its mandate to incorporate this role, following the IRO's precedent.

What all three of these processes suggest is that entrepreneurial leadership – whether by governments, individuals, or IOs – not only serves to advance new normative understandings, but also to protect them from challenges either by blocking change or by arguing in favor of incremental adjustments. The presence of norm entrepreneurs alone is not enough to prevent a crisis event from occurring – Roosevelt's leadership in creating the Evian Conference in 1938 failed to shift states' refugee policies. Having a ready-made alternative, however, and being able to apply it quickly can avoid states and other actors questioning their more deeply held normative understandings.

Whither the international refugee regime?

The non-entrée regime today is at a turning point. The stresses that have been building up within it – the divide between states and the focus on restrictionism rather than humanitarianism – are similar to those experienced by the interwar regime. That regime did not survive, and one of the consequences of its collapse was the Holocaust. There is hope on the horizon for the current regime. The UNHCR is once again actively arguing in favor of refugee protection. At the same time, states in the developed world, motivated by declining numbers of asylum seekers, are starting to limit some of their more restrictionist practices.

Significantly, throughout this history of regime change and adaptation, a strong foundation of normative understandings has remained, including the right of refugees to leave their own states, to be protected in international law, and to have protection and assistance provided by an IO. This provides support to arguments that suggest that many normative understandings are path dependent or sequence-based and that once new understandings are created and internalized by actors, it is difficult to alter them. Many of these norms today, like the concept of the right of leave, are so deeply sedimented within state practice that they are seldom, if ever, challenged.

Even as the state response to refugee protection, and the refugee problem itself, has grown more complex, states have continued a process of cooperation in order to ensure that refugees do receive some measure of protection. In this, state cooperation toward refugees marks an ongoing pattern of continuity and change that can only be understood by examining different structural elements of international society and the role played by agents working at the international and domestic levels.

Refugee protection continues to constitute an obligation for states in international society. Having fled their own states, having been persecuted, injured, and forced to abandon their home, property, and possessions, it is critical that refugees receive some form of protection. There are practical reasons to ensure that cooperation continues because, without it, refugees become a destabilizing force within international society. Equally critical is that states continue to accept this obligation because, without it, refugees cease to be protected and once again become faceless. If history is any judge, these obligations are not to be taken lightly. States have been too quick to forget this history. Refugees will be a major problem for the future, as they have been in the past and present.

References

Abbott, K. W., & Snidal, D. 1998. Why States Act through Formal International Organizations. *Journal of Conflict Resolution*, 42, 3–32.

Abebe, A. M. 2010. The African Union Convention on Internally Displaced Persons: Its Codification Background, Scope, and Enforcement Challenges. *Refugee Survey Quarterly*, 29, 28–57.

Acheson, D. 1969. *Present at the Creation: My Years in the State Department.* New York: W.W. Norton.

Adams, W. 1939. Extent and Nature of the World Refugee Problem. *Annals of the American Academy of Political and Social Science*, 203, 26–36.

Adler, E. 1997. Seizing the Middle Ground: Constructivism in World Politics. *European Journal of International Relations*, 3, 319–363.

Agnew, J., & Corbridge, S. 1995. *Mastering Space: Hegemony, Territory, and International Political Economy.* London: Routledge.

Aleinkoff, T. A., & Martin, D. A. 1985. *Immigration: Process and Policy.* St. Paul, Minn.: West Publishing.

Alter, K. J., & Meunier, S. 2009. The Politics of International Regime Complexity. *Perspectives on Politics*, 7, 13–24.

American Jurist. 1829. Fugitives from Justice. *American Jurist*, 1, 297–309.

Amnesty International. 2003. UK/EU/UNHCR Unlawful and Unworkable: Extra-Territorial Processing of Asylum Claims. Amnesty International.

Andreas, P. 2008. *Blue Helmets and Black Markets: The Business of Survival in the Siege of Sarajevo.* Ithaca, N.Y.: Cornell University Press.

Anker, D. 1982. The Refugee Act of 1980: An Historical Perspective. *In:* Tomasi, L. (ed.), *In Defense of the Alien.* New York: Centre for Migration Studies.

Anon. 1697. The Case of the Poor French Refugees. *Early English Books Online Ebook Collection, 1641–1700* [Online]. Available: Eebo.Chadwyck.Com.

Arboleda, E. 1991. Refugee Definition in Africa and Latin America: The Lessons of Pragmatism. *International Journal of Refugee Law*, 3, 185.

Arendt, H. 1966. *The Origins of Totalitarianism.* New York: Harcourt Brace & World.

Aronson, S. 2004. *Hitler, the Allies, and the Jews.* Cambridge: Cambridge University Press.

Asch, R. G. 2000. Religious Toleration, the Peace of Westphalia and the German Territorial Estates. *Parliaments, Estates & Representation*, 20, 75–89.

Atzili, B. 2007. When Good Fences Make Bad Neighbors: Fixed Borders, State Weakness, and International Conflict. *International Security*, 31, 139–173.

Avant, D. D., Finnemore, M., & Sell, S. K. 2010. Introduction: Who Governs the Globe? *In*: Avant, D. D., Finnemore, M., & Sell, S. K. (eds.), *Who Governs the Globe?* Cambridge: Cambridge University Press.

Avery, C. L. 1983. Refugee Status Decision Making: The Systems of Ten Countries. *Stanford Journal of International Law*, 19, 235–356.

Axelrod, R., & Keohane, R. O. 1985. Achieving Cooperation under Anarchy: Strategies and Institutions. *World Politics*, 38, 226–254.

Bagshaw, S. 2005. *Developing a Normative Framework for the Protection of Internally Displaced Persons*. Ardsley, N.Y.: Transnational Publishers.

Bainton, R. H. 1941. The Struggle for Religious Liberty. *Church History*, 10, 95–124.

Barnett, L. 2002. Global Governance and the Evolution of the International Refugee Regime. *International Journal of Refugee Law*, 14, 238–262.

Barnett, M., & Duvall, R. 2005. Power in Global Governance. *In*: Barnett, M., & Duvall, R. (eds.), *Power in Global Governance*. Cambridge: Cambridge University Press.

Barnett, M. N. 1996. Sovereignty, Nationalism and Regional Order in the Arab States System. *In*: Biersteker, T. J., & Weber, C. (eds.), *State Sovereignty as Social Construct*. Cambridge: Cambridge University Press.

2001. Humanitarianism with a Sovereign Face: UNHCR in the Global Undertow. *International Migration Review*, 35, 244–76.

Barnett, M. N., & Finnemore, M. 2004. *Rules for the World: International Organizations in Global Politics*. Ithaca, N.Y.: Cornell University Press.

2005. The Power of Liberal International Organizations. *In*: Barnett, M. N., & Duvall, R. (eds.), *Power in Global Governance*. Cambridge: Cambridge University Press.

Barutciski, M. 1998. Tensions between the Refugee Concept and the IDP Debate. *Forced Migration Review*, 3, 11–14.

2002. A Critical View on UNHCR's Mandate Dilemmas. *International Journal of Refugee Law*, 14, 365–381.

Baseler, M. C. 1998. *"Asylum for Mankind" America, 1607–1800*. Ithaca, N.Y.: Cornell University Press.

Bassiouni, M. C. 1974. *International Extradition and World Public Order*. Doobs Ferry, N.Y.: Oceana Publications Inc.

Beck, R. J. 1999. Britain and the 1933 Refugee Convention: National or State Sovereignty? *International Journal of Refugee Law*, 11, 597–624.

Beisner, R. L. 2006. *Dean Acheson: A Life in the Cold War*. Oxford: Oxford University Press.

Bell, S. 2011. Do We Really Need a New "Constructivist Institutionalism" to Explain Institutional Change? *British Journal of Political Science*, 41, 883–906.

Bem, K. 2004. The Coming of a "Blank Cheque" – Europe, the 1951 Convention, and the 1967 Protocol. *International Journal of Refugee Law*, 16, 609–627.

Bem, K., Field, N., & Maclellan, N. 2007. *A Price Too High: The Cost of Australia's Approach to Asylum Seekers*. Glebe: A Just Australia and Oxfam Australia.

Benford, R. D., & Snow, D. A. 2000. Framing Processes and Social Movements: An Overview and Assessment. *Annual Review of Sociology*, 26, 611–639.

Benhabib, S. 2005. Disaggregation of Citizenship Rights. *Parallax*, 11, 10–18.

Bennett, M. T. 1966. The Immigration and Nationality (Mccarran-Walter) Act of 1952, as Amended to 1965. *Annals of the American Academy of Political and Social Science*, 367, 127–136.

Bentwich, N. 1962. *My 77 Years: An Account of My Life and Times, 1883–1960.* London: Routledge.

Berger, T. U. 1996. Norms, Identity, and National Security in Germany and Japan. *In*: Katzenstein, P. (ed.), *The Culture of National Security.* New York: Columbia University Press.

Bernstein, S. 2000. Ideas, Social Structure and the Compromise of Liberal Environmentalism. *European Journal of International Relations*, 6, 464–512.

Bethell, N. 1974. *The Last Secret: The Delivery to Stalin of over Two Million Russians by Britain and the United States.* New York: Basic Books.

Betts, A. 2004. The International Relations of the "New" Extraterritorial Approaches to Refugee Protection: Explaining the Policy Initiatives of the UK Government and UNHCR. *Refuge: Canada's Journal on Refugees*, 22, 58–70.

2009. *Protection by Persuasion: International Cooperation in the Refugee Regime.* Ithaca, N.Y.: Cornell University Press.

2010. The Refugee Regime Complex. *Refugee Survey Quarterly*, 29, 12–37.

Betts, A. 2013. *Survival Migration: Failed Governance and the Crisis of Displacement.* Ithaca, N.Y.: Cornell University Press.

Betts, A., & Orchard, P. 2014. Introduction: The Normative Institutionalization-Implementation Gap. *In*: Betts, A., & Orchard, P. (eds.), *Implementation and World Politics: How International Norms Change Practice.* Oxford: Oxford University Press.

Beyer, G. A. 1991. The Evolving United States Response to Soviet Jewish Emigration. *International Journal of Refugee Law*, 3, 30–59.

Bicknell, E. P. 1918. Belgium and the Red Cross – a Partnership. *Annals of the American Academy of Political and Social Science*, 79, 23–39.

Biehle, M. 1947. Intergovernmental Committee on Refugees. *International Organization*, 1, 144–145.

Biersteker, T. J., & Weber, C. 1996. *The Social Construction of State Sovereignty.* Cambridge: Cambridge University Press.

Black, J. 1990. *The Rise of the European Powers, 1679–1793.* London: Edward Arnold.

Bloch, A. 2002. *The Migration and Settlement of Refugees in Britain.* Houndmills, UK: Palgrave Macmillan.

Bloch, A., & Schuster, L. 2002. Asylum and Welfare: Contemporary Debates. *Critical Social Policy*, 22, 393–414.

Blumenthal, E. 2003. The Bermuda Conference of 1943. *Penn History Review*, Spring 2003, 39–50.

Blyth, M. 2002. *Great Transformations: Economic Ideas and Institutional Change in the Twentieth Century.* Cambridge: Cambridge University Press.

Bob, C. 2010. Packing Heat: Pro-Gun Groups and the Governance of Small Arms. *In*: Avant, D. D., Finnemore, M., & Sell, S. K. (eds.), *Who Governs the Globe?* Cambridge: Cambridge University Press.

Bon Tempo, C. J. 2008. *Americans at the Gate: The United States and Refugees during the Cold War.* Princeton, N.J.: Princeton University Press.

Breitman, R., & Kraut, A. M. 1987. *American Refugee Policy and European Jewry, 1933–1945*. Bloomington: Indiana University Press.

Brubaker, R. 1992. *Citizenship and Nationhood in France and Germany*. Cambridge, Mass.: Harvard University Press.

Bruno, A. 2012. Refugee Admissions and Resettlement Policy. Washington D.C.: Congressional Research Service.

Bukovansky, M. 1999. The Altered State and the State of Nature – the French Revolution and International Politics. *Review of International Studies*, 25, 197–216.

Bull, H. 1966. Society and Anarchy in International Relations. *In*: Butterfield, H., & Wight, M. (eds.), *Diplomatic Investigations: Essays in the Theory of International Politics*. London: George Allen & Unwin Ltd.

2002. *The Anarchical Society: A Study of Order in World Politics*. New York: Columbia University Press.

Burgess, G. 2002. France and the German Refugee Crisis of 1933. *French History*, 16, 203–229.

2008. *Refuge in the Land of Liberty: France and Its Refugees, from the Revolution to the End of Asylum, 1787–1939*. Basingstoke, UK: Palgrave Macmillian.

Burn, J. S. 1846. *The History of the French, Walloon, Dutch, and Other Foreign Protestant Refugees Settled in England*. London: Longman, Brown, Green, and Longmans.

Busby, J. W. 2007. Bono Made Jesse Helms Cry: Jubilee 2000, Debt Relief, and Moral Action in International Politics. *International Studies Quarterly*, 51, 247–275.

2010. *Moral Movements and Foreign Policy*. Cambridge: Cambridge University Press.

Bush, G. W. 2002. *Executive Order Regarding Undocumented Aliens in the Caribbean Region*. [Online]. www.whitehouse.gov/news/releases/2002/11/20021115-10.html.

2004. President Bush Welcomes Georgian President Saakashvili to White House [Online]. www.whitehouse.gov/news/releases/2004/02/20040225-1.html

Butterfield, H., & Wight, M. 1966. *Diplomatic Investigations: Essays in the Theory of International Politics*. London: George Allen and Unwin Ltd.

Buzan, B. 2004. *From International to World Society? English School Theory and the Social Structure of Globalisation*. Cambridge: Cambridge University Press.

Buzan, B., Waever, O., & de Wilde, J. 1998. *Security: A New Framework for Analysis*. Boulder, Col.: Lynne Rienner.

Caestecker, F. 2000. *Alien Policy in Belgium, 1840–1940: The Creation of Guest Workers, Refugees, and Illegal Aliens*. New York: Berghahn Books.

2003. The Transformation of Nineteenth-Century West European Expulsion Policy, 1880–1914. *In*: Fahrmeir, A., Faron, O., & Weil, P. (eds.), *Migration Control in the North Atlantic World*. New York: Berghahn Books.

Caestecker, F., & Moore, B. 2010. *Refugees from Nazi Germany and the Liberal European States*. New York: Berghahn Books.

Cannon, L. 1983. Reagan Sees a Latin "Axis." *Washington Post*, June 21.

Capelli, F. 1987. UNHCR and the Plight of Refugees: International Protection and Solutions in a Changing World Context. *In*: Nash, A. E. (ed.), *Human*

Rights and the Protection of Refugees under International Law. Halifax: Institute for Research on Public Policy.

Caron, V. 2010. Unwilling Refuge: France and the Dilemma of Illegal Immigration, 1933–1939. *In*: Caestecker, F., & Moore, B. (eds.), *Refugees from Nazi Germany and the Liberal European States*. New York: Berghahn Books.

Carpenter, K. 1999. *Refugees of the French Revolution: Émigrés in London, 1789–1802*. London: Macmillan Press Ltd.

Carpenter, R. C. 2010. Governing the Global Agenda: "Gatekeepers" and "Issue Adoption" in Transnational Advocacy Networks. *In*: Avant, D. D., Finnemore, M., & Sell, S. K. (eds.), *Who Governs the Globe?* Cambridge: Cambridge University Press.

2011. Vetting the Advocacy Agenda: Network Centrality and the Paradox of Weapons Norms. *International Organization*, 65, 69–102.

Carruthers, S. L. 2005. Between Camps: Eastern Bloc "Escapees" and Cold War Borderlands. *American Quarterly* 57, 911–942.

Carter, A. 2001. *The Political Theory of Global Citizenship*. London: Routledge.

Cavallar, G. 2002. *The Rights of Strangers: Theories of International Hospitality, the Global Community, and Political Justice since Victoria*. London: Ashgate.

Cesarani, D. 1992. An Alien Concept? The Continuity of Anti-Alienism in British Society before 1940. *Immigrants & Minorities*, 11, 24–52.

Chamberlain, J. 1947. The Fate of Refugees and Displaced Persons. *Proceedings of the Academy of Political Science*, 22, 84–94.

Charlton, R., Farley, L., & Kaye, R. 1988. Identifying the Mainsprings of US Refugee and Asylum Policy: A Contextual Interpretation. *Journal of Refugee Studies*, 1, 237–259.

Checkel, J. T. 1997. *Ideas and International Political Change: Soviet/Russian Behavior and the End of the Cold War*. New Haven, Conn.: Yale University Press.

1998. The Constructivist Turn in International Relations Theory. *World Politics*, 50, 324–48.

1999. Norms, Institutions, and National Identity in Contemporary Europe. *International Studies Quarterly*, 43, 83–114.

2005. International Institutions and Socialization in Europe: Introduction and Framework. *International Organization*, 59, 801–826.

2008. Process Tracing. *In*: Klotz, A., & Prakash, D. (eds.), *Qualitative Methods in International Relations*. Houndmills, UK: Palgrave Macmillian.

2012. Norm Entrepreneurship: Theoretical and Methodological Challenges. *Workshop on the Evolution of International Norms and 'Norm Entrepreneurship': The Council of Europe in Comparative Perspective*. Oxford, UK: Wolfson College, Oxford University.

Chernoff, F. 2005. *Power of International Theory*. Milton Park: Routledge.

Chimni, B. S. 1998. The Geopolitics of Refugee Studies: A View from the South. *Journal of Refugee Studies*, 11, 350–374.

Clapham, C. S. 1996. *Africa and the International System: The Politics of State Survival*. Cambridge: Cambridge University Press.

Clark, S. 1998. International Competition and the Treatment of Minorities: Seventeenth-Century Cases and General Propositions. *American Journal of Sociology*, 103, 1267–1308.

Cobb, S. 1897. *The Story of the Palatines: An Episode in Colonial History*. New York: G. P. Putnam's Sons (reprint by University Microfilms International).

Cohen, G. D. 2011. *In War's Wake: Europe's Displaced Persons in the Postwar Order: Europe's Displaced Persons in the Postwar Order*. Oxford: Oxford University Press.

Cohen, M. D., March, J. G., & Olsen, J. P. 1972. A Garbage Can Model of Organizational Choice. *Administrative Science Quarterly*, 1–25.

Cohen, M. J. 1990. *Truman and Israel*. Berkeley: University of California Press.

Cohen, R. 2004. Some Reflections on National and International Responsibility in Situations of Internal Displacement. *In*: Mishra, O. (ed.), *Forced Migration in the South Asian Region: Displacement, Human Rights & Conflict Resolution*. New Delhi: Jadavpur University and Manak.

2006a. Developing an International System for Internally Displaced Persons. *International Studies Perspectives*, 7, 87–101.

2006b. Strengthening Protection of IDPs: The UN's Role. *Georgetown Journal of International Affairs*, Winter/Spring, 101–110.

Cohen, R., & Deng, F. M. 1998. *Masses in Flight: The Global Crisis of Internal Displacement*. Washington, D.C.: Brookings Institution Press.

Coleman, K. P. 2007. *International Organisations and Peace Enforcement: The Politics of International Legitimacy*. Cambridge: Cambridge University Press.

2013. Locating Norm Diplomacy: Venue Change in International Norm Negotiations. *European Journal of International Relations*, 19, 163–186.

Collinson, S. 1996. Visa Requirements, Carrier Sanctions, "Safe Third Countries" and "Readmission": The Development of an Asylum "Buffer Zone" in Europe. *Transactions of the Institute of British Geographers*, 21, 76–90.

Cortell, A. P., & Davis, J. W. J. 1996. How Do International Institutions Matter? The Domestic Impact of International Rules and Norms. *International Studies Quarterly*, 40, 451–478.

2000. Understanding the Domestic Impact of International Norms: A Research Agenda. *International Studies Review*, 21, 65–87.

Cox, R. W. 1969. The Executive Head: An Essay on Leadership in International Organization. *International Organization*, 23, 205–230.

Crawford, N. C. 2002. *Argument and Change in World Politics: Ethics, Decolonization, and Humanitarian Intervention*. Cambridge: Cambridge University Press.

Crisp, J. 2003. Refugees and the Global Politics of Asylum. *Political Quarterly*, 74, 75–87.

Cronin, B. 2003. *Institutions for the Common Good: International Protection Regimes in International Society*. Cambridge: Cambridge University Press.

Cronin, B., & Hurd, I. 2008. Introduction. *In*: Cronin, B., & Hurd, I. (eds.), *The UN Security Council and the Politics of International Authority*. London: Routledge.

Cunliffe, A. 1995. The Refugee Crises: A Study of the United Nations High Commission for Refugees. *Political Studies*, 43, 278–290.

Dahl, R. A. 1982. *Dilemmas of Pluralist Democracy: Autonomy Vs. Control*. New Haven, Conn.: Yale University Press.

Dallek, R. 1979. *Franklin D. Roosevelt and American Foreign Policy, 1932–1945*. New York: Oxford University Press.

Davies, S. E. 2008. Redundant or Essential? How Politics Shaped the Outcome of the 1967 Protocol. *International Journal of Refugee Law*, 19, 703–728.

De Carvalho, B., Leira, H., & Hobson, J. M. 2011. The Big Bangs of IR: The Myths That Your Teachers Still Tell You About 1648 and 1919. *Millennium-Journal of International Studies*, 39, 735–758.

De Hart, E. L. 1886. The Extradition of Political Offenders. *Law Quarterly*, 2, 177–187.

De Zayas, A.-M. 1988. A Historical Survey of Twentieth Century Expulsions. *In*: Bramwell, A. C. (ed.), *Refugees in the Age of Total War*. London: Unwin Hyman.

2006. *A Terrible Revenge: The Ethnic Cleansing of the East European Germans*. New York: Palgrave Macmillan.

Deere, L. L. 1933. Political Offenses in the Law and Practice of Extradition. *American Journal of International Law*, 27, 247–270.

Defoe, D. 1964 (1709). A Brief History of the Poor Palatine Refugees. *In*: Moore, J. R. (ed.), *Augustan Reprint Society*. Los Angeles: University of California.

Deng, F. M. 1998. Promoting Responsible Sovereignty in Africa. *In*: Deng, F. M., & Lyons, T. (eds.), *African Reckoning: A Quest for Good Governance*. Washington, D.C.: Brookings Institution.

2001. The Global Challenge of Internal Displacement. *Washington University Journal of Law and Policy*, 141–156.

Dessler, D. 1989. What's at Stake in the Agent-Structure Debate? *International Organization*, 43, 441–473.

Dickinson, H. T. 1967. The Poor Palatines and the Parties. *English Historical Review*, 82, 464–485.

Dinnerstein, L. 1982. *America and the Survivors of the Holocaust*. New York: Columbia University Press.

Donnelly, J. 1986. International Human Rights: A Regime Analysis. *International Organization*, 40.

2012. The Elements of the Structures of International Systems. *International Organization*, 66, 609–643.

Dowty, A. 1987. *Closed Borders: The Contemporary Assault on Freedom of Movement*. New Haven, Conn.: Yale University Press.

Dowty, A., & Loescher, G. 1996. Refugee Flows as Grounds for International Action. *International Security*, 21, 43–71.

Doyle, W. 1992. *The Old European Order 1660–1800*, Oxford: Oxford University Press.

Dubernet, C. 2001. *The International Containment of Displaced Persons: Humanitarian Spaces without Exit*, Aldershot, UK: Ashgate.

Duke, K., Sales, R., & Gregory, J. 1999. Refugee Resettlement in Europe. *In*: Bloch, A., & Levy, C. (eds.), *Refugees, Citizenship and Social Policy in Europe*. Houndmills, UK: Palgrave.

Dummett, A., & Nicol, A. 1990. *Subjects, Citizens, Aliens and Others: Nationality and Immigration Law*. London: Weidenfield and Nicolson.

Dunne, M. 2002. Asylum. *In*: Deconde, A., Burns, R. D., & Logevall, F. (eds.) *Encyclopedia of American Foreign Policy*. New York: Charles Scribner's Sons.

Dunne, T. 1998. *Inventing International Society: A History of the English School.* New York: St. Martin's Press.

Durieux, J.-F., & McAdam, J. 2004. Non-Refoulement through Time: The Case for a Derogation Clause to the Refugee Convention in Mass Influx Emergencies. *International Journal of Refugee Law*, 16, 4–24.

Elie, J. B. 2007. The UNHCR and the Cold War: A Documented Reflection on the UN Refugee Agency's Activities in the Bipolar Context. *The UNHCR and the Global Cold War, 1971–1984* [Online], Geneva: UNHCR/GIIS/GCSP.

———. 2008. "Protection Is the Art of Possible": Relations between UNHCR and the United States in the Early 1980s – the Case of Displaced Salvadorans. *Refugee Survey Quarterly*, 27, 89–103.

Elliott, M. 1973. The United States and Forced Repatriation of Soviet Citizens, 1944–47. *Political Science Quarterly*, 88, 253–275.

———. 1982. *Pawns of Yalta: Soviet Refugees and America's Role in Their Repatriation.* Urbana: University of Illinois Press.

Erskine, T. 2003. Making Sense of "Responsibility" in International Relations: Key Questions and Concepts. *In*: Erskine, T. (ed.), *Can Institutions Have Responsibilities*. Houndsmill, UK: Palgrave Macmillian.

Ertman, T. 1997. *Birth of the Leviathan: Building States and Regimes in Medieval and Early Modern Europe.* Cambridge: Cambridge University Press.

Evans, G. J., & Sahnoun, M. 2001. *The Responsibility to Protect: Report of the International Commission on Intervention and State Sovereignty.* Ottawa: IDRC.

Fahrmeir, A. 2003. Immigration and Immigration Policy in Britain from the Nineteenth to the Twentieth Centuries. *In*: Steinert, J.-D., & Weber-Newth, I. (eds.), *European Immigrants in Britain 1933–1950.* Munich: K.G. Saur.

Fahrmeir, A., Faron, O., & Weil, P. 2003. Introduction. *In*: Fahrmeir, A., Faron, O., & Weil, P. (eds.), *Migration Control in the North Atlantic World.* New York: Berghahn Books.

Faragher, J. M. 2005. *A Great and Noble Scheme: The Tragic Story of the Expulsion of the French Acadians from Their American Homeland.* New York: W.W. Norton & Co.

Farber, S. R. 2010. Forgotten at Guantánamo: The Boumediene Decision and Its Implications for Refugees at the Base under the Obama Administration. *California Law Review*, 98, 989.

Farer, T. J. 1995. How the International System Copes with Involuntary Migration: Norms, Institutions and State Practice. *Human Rights Quarterly*, 17: 72–100.

Faulks, K. 2000. *Citizenship.* London: Routledge.

Fearon, J., & Wendt, A. 2002. Rationalism V. Constructivism: A Skeptical View. *In*: Carlsnaes, W., Risse, T., & Simmons, B. A. (eds.), *Handbook of International Relations.* London: Sage.

Feen, R. H. 1985. Domestic and Foreign Policy Dilemmas in Contemporary US Refugee Policy. *In*: Ferris, E. G. (ed.), *Refugees and World Politics.* New York: Praeger.

Feingold, H. L. 1970. *The Politics of Rescue: The Roosevelt Administration and the Holocaust, 1938–1945.* New Brunswick, N.J.: Rutgers University Press.

Feldman, D. 2003. Was the Nineteenth Century a Golden Age for Immigrants? The Changing Articulation of National, Local and Voluntary Controls. *In*: Fahrmeir, A., Faron, O., & Weil, P. (eds.), *Migration Control in the North Atlantic World: The Evolution of State Practices in Europe and the United States from the French Revolution to the Inter-War Period*. Oxford: Berghahn Books.

Felshtinsky, Y. 1982. The Legal Foundations of the Immigration and Emigration Policy of the USSR, 1917–27. *Soviet Studies*, 34, 327–348.

Finnemore, M. 1996. *National Interests in International Society*. Ithaca, N.Y.: Cornell University Press.

2000. Are Legal Norms Distinctive? *New York University Journal of International Law and Policy*, 32, 699–705.

2003. *The Purpose of Intervention: Changing Beliefs About the Use of Force*. Ithaca, N.Y.: Cornell University Press.

Finnemore, M., & Sikkink, K. 1998. International Norm Dynamics and Political Change. *International Organization*, 52.

Fischer, G. 1949. The New Soviet Emigration. *Russian Review*, 8, 6–19.

Fitzgerald, K. 1996. *The Face of the Nation: Immigration, the State, and the National Identity*. Palo Alto, Calif.: Stanford University Press.

Fitzpatrick, J. 1997. The International Dimension of US Refugee Law. *Berkeley Journal of International Law*, 15, 1–26.

2000. Temporary Protection of Refugees: Elements of a Formalized Regime. *American Journal of International Law*, 94, 279–306.

Flockhart, T. 2006. "Complex Socialization:" A Framework for the Study of State Socialization. *European Journal of International Relations*, 12, 89–118.

Florini, A. 1996. The Evolution of International Norms. *International Studies Quarterly*, 40, 363–389.

Ford Foundation 1958. *Final Report on the Ford Foundation Program for Refugees, Primarily in Europe*. New York: Ford Foundation.

Fox, G. 1950. The Origins of UNRRA. *Political Science Quarterly*, 65, 561–584.

Franck, T. M. 1990. *The Power of Legitimacy among Nations*. New York: Oxford University Press.

Frelick, B. 1990. The Right of Return. *International Journal of Refugee Law*, 2, 442–447.

2004. Abundantly Clear: Refoulement. *Georgetown Immigration Law Journal*, 19, 245–276.

Frost, M. 1996. *Ethics in International Relations: A Constitutive Theory*. New York: Cambridge University Press.

Gaddis, J. L. 2000. *The United States and the Origins of the Cold War, 1941–1947*. New York: Columbia University Press.

Gainer, B. 1972. *The Alien Invasion: The Origins of the Aliens Act of 1905*. London: Heinemann Educational Books.

Gallagher, D. 1989. The Evolution of the International Refugee System. *International Migration Review*, 23, 579–598.

Garcia-Mora, M. 1962. The Nature of Political Offenses: A Knotty Problem of Extradition Law. *Virginia Law Review*, 48, 1226–1257.

García, M. C. 2006. *Seeking Refuge: Central American Migration to Mexico, the United States, and Canada*. Berkeley: University of California Press.

Garlick, M. 2006. The EU Discussions on Extraterritorial Processing: Solution or Conundrum? *International Journal of Refugee Law*, 18, 601–629.

Genizi, H. 1993. *America's Fair Share: The Admission and Resettlement of Displaced Persons, 1945–1952*. Detroit, Mich.: Wayne State University Press.

George, A. L., & Bennett, A. 2005. *Case Studies and Theory Development in the Social Sciences*. Cambridge: MIT Press.

Gerhardt, M. J. 2001. Norm Theory and the Future of the Federal Appointments Process. *Duke Law Journal*, 50, 1687–1715.

Gerth, H. H., & Mills, C. W. 1958. *From Max Weber: Essays in Sociology*. New York: Oxford University Press.

Gerring, J. 2004. What Is a Case Study and What Is It Good For? *American Political Science Review*, 98, 341–354.

Gibney, M. J. 2004. *The Ethics and Politics of Asylum: Liberal Democracy and the Response to Refugees*. Cambridge: Cambridge University Press.

2005. Beyond the Bounds of Responsibility: Western States and Measures to Prevent the Arrival of Refugees. *Global Migration Perspectives* [Online]. www.gcim.org. Geneva: Global Commission on International Migration.

Gibney, M. J., & Hansen, R. 2003. Asylum Policy in the West: Past Trends, Future Possibilities. Helsinki: United Nations University, World Institute for Development Economics Research.

Giddens, A. 1985. *The Nation-State and Violence*. Cambridge: Polity Press.

Gilbert, G. 1991. *Aspects of Extradition Law*. Dordrecht: Martinus Nijhoff.

1998. *Transnational Fugitive Offenders in International Law: Extradition and Other Mechanisms*. Leiden: Martinus Nijhoff.

Gilbert, G. S. 1983. Right of Asylum: A Change of Direction. *International and Comparative Law Quarterly*, 32, 633–650.

Gilpin, R. 1981. *War and Change in World Politics*. Cambridge: Cambridge University Press.

Ginsburgs, G. 1957. The Soviet Union and the Problem of Refugees and Displaced Persons 1917–1956. *American Journal of International Law*, 51, 325–361.

Giuffré, M. 2012. State Responsibility Beyond Borders: What Legal Basis for Italy's Push-Backs to Libya? *International Journal of Refugee Law*, 24, 692–734.

Glanville, L. 2006. Norms, Interests and Humanitarian Intervention. *Global Change, Peace & Security*, 18, 153–171.

Goedhart, G. J. v. H. 1953. *United Nations High Commissioner Explains His Policy at Press Conference Given by Swiss Aid to Europe, 19 February 1953* [Online]. www.Unhcr.Org/Admin/ADMIN/3ae68fba18.html.

1955. *Refugee Problems and Their Solutions: Address of the High Commissioner for Refugees at Oslo* [Online]. www.Unhcr.Org/Cgi-Bin/Texis/Vtx/Print?Tbl=ADMIN&Id=3ae68fb918.

Goertz, G. 2003. *International Norms and Decisionmaking: A Punctuated Equilibrium Model*. Lanham, Md.: Rowman & Littlefield.

Golden, R. M. 1988. *The Huguenot Connection: The Edict of Nantes, Its Revocation, and Early French Migration to South Carolina*. Dordrecht: Kluwer Academic.

Goldstein, J. 1989. The Impact of Ideas on Trade Policy: The Origins of US Agricultural and Manufacturing Policies. *International Organization*, 43, 31–71.

Gong, G. W. 1984. *The Standard of "Civilization" in International Society*. Oxford: Clarendon Press.

Goodwin-Gill, G. 1989. Voluntary Repatriation: Legal and Policy Issues. *In*: Loescher, G., & Monahan, L. (eds.), *Refugees and International Relations*. Oxford: Oxford University Press.

Goodwin-Gill, G. S. 1996. The Right to Leave, the Right to Remain, and the Question of a Right to Remain. *In*: Gowlland-Debbas, V. (ed.), *The Problem of Refugees in the Light of Contemporary International Law Issues*. The Hague: Martinus Nijhoff.

2007. Extraterritorial Processing of Claims to Asylum or Protection: The Legal Responsibilities of States and International Organisations. *University of Technology Sydney Law Review*, 9, 26–40.

2008. The Politics of Refugee Protection. *Refugee Survey Quarterly*, 27, 8.

Goodwin-Gill, G. S., & McAdam, J. 2007. *The Refugee in International Law*. Oxford: Oxford University Press.

Gordenker, L. 1987. *Refugees in International Politics*. London: Croom Helm.

Gorlick, B. 1999. The Convention and the Committee against Torture: A Complementary Protection Regime for Refugees. *International Journal of Refugee Law*, 11, 479–495.

2003. Refugee Protection in Troubled Times. *In*: Steiner, N., Gibney, M., & Loescher, G. (eds.), *Problems of Protection: The UNHCR, Refugees, and Human Rights*. New York: Routledge.

Graham, O. L. 2004. *Unguarded Gates: A History of America's Immigration Crisis* Lanham, Md.: Rowman & Littlefield.

Grahl-Madsen, A. 1966. The European Tradition of Asylum and the Development of Refugee Law. *Journal of Peace Research*, 3, 278–289.

1983. The League of Nations and the Refugees. *The League of Nations in Retrospect: Proceedings of the Symposium*. New York: United Nations Library, Walter de Gruyther.

Grant, T. D. 1999. *The Recognition of States: Law and Practice in Debate and Evolution*. Westport, Conn.: Praeger.

Green, L. 1962. Political Offences, War Crimes and Extradition. *International and Comparative Law Quarterly*, 11, 329–354.

Greenhill, K. M. 2010. *Weapons of Mass Migration: Forced Displacement, Coercion, and Foreign Policy*. Ithaca, N.Y.: Cornell University Press.

Gross, L. 1948. The Peace of Westphalia, 1648–1948. *American Journal of International Law*, 21, 20–41.

Grotius, H., & Kelsey, F. W. 1925. *The Law of War and Peace: De Jure Belli Ac Pacis, Libri Tres*. Indianapolis: Bobbs-Merrill.

Guest, I. 1991. The United Nations, the UNHCR, and Refugee Protection: A Non-Specialist Analysis. *International Journal of Refugee Law*, 3, 585–605.

Guild, E., & Garlick, M. 2010. Refugee Protection, Counter-Terrorism, and Exclusion in the European Union. *Refugee Survey Quarterly*, 29, 63–82.

Guterres, A. 2007. Closing Statement by Mr. António Guterres, United Nations High Commissioner for Refugees, at the Fifty-Eighth Session of the Executive Committee of the High Commissioner's Programme. Geneva: UNHCR. [Online] www.Unhcr.Org/Admin/ADMIN/47172a422.Html.

Guzzini, S. 2000. A Reconstruction of Constructivism in International Relations. *European Journal of International Relations*, 6, 147–182.

Haas, P. M. 1992. Introduction: Epistemic Communities and International Policy Coordination. *International Organization*, 46, 1–35.

Habermas, J. 1994. Citizenship and National Identity. *In*: Van Steenbergen, B. (ed.), *The Condition of Citizenship*. London: Sage Publications.

Haddad, E. 2003. The Refugee: The Individual between Sovereigns. *Global Society*, 17, 297–322.

  2008. *The Refugee in International Society: Between Sovereigns*. Cambridge: Cambridge University Press.

Haggard, S., & Simmons, B. A. 1987. Theories of International Regimes. *International Organization*, 41, 491–517.

Halamish, A. 2010. Palestine as a Destination for Jewish Immigrants and Refugees from Nazi Germany. *In*: Caestecker, F., & Moore, B. (eds.) *Refugees from Nazi Germany and the Liberal European States*. New York: Berghahn Books.

Hall, J. A., & Ikenberry, G. J. 1989. *The State*. Minneapolis: University of Minnesota Press.

Hall, P. A. 1993. Policy Paradigms, Social Learning, and the State: The Case of Economic Policymaking in Britain. *Comparative Politics*, 275–296.

Hambro, E. 1955. *The Problem of Chinese Refugees in Hong Kong; Report Submitted to the United Nations High Commissioner for Refugees, by Edvard Hambro, Chief of the Hong Kong Refugees Survey Mission*. Leiden: A.W. Sijthoff.

Hans, A., & Suhrke, A. 1997. Responsibility Sharing. *In*: Hathaway, J. C. (ed.), *Reconceiving International Refugee Law*. The Hague: Martinus Nijhoff.

Hansen, R., & King, D. 2000. Illiberalism and the New Politics of Asylum: Liberalism's Dark Side. *Political Quarterly*, 71, 396–403.

Harris, R. W. 1964. *Absolutism and Enlightenment*. London: Blanford Press.

Hartigan, K. 1992. Matching Humanitarian Norms with Cold, Hard Interests: The Making of Refugee Policies in Mexico and Honduras, 1980–89. *International Organization*, 46, 709–730.

Hartling, P. 1985. *Consultations on the Arrivals of Asylum Seekers and Refugees in Europe (Geneva, 28–31 May, 1985), Opening Statement by the United Nations High Commissioner for Refugees* [Online]. www.Unhcr.Org/Admin/ADMIN/ 3ae68fd028.Html.

Harwood, E. 1986. American Public Opinion and US Immigration Policy. *Annals of the American Academy of Political and Social Science*, 487, 201–212.

Hasenclever, A., Mayer, P., & Rittberger, V. 1997. *Theories of International Regimes*. Cambridge: Cambridge University Press.

Hasian, M. 2003. Franklin D. Roosevelt, the Holocaust, and Modernity's Rescue Rhetorics. *Communication Quarterly*, 51, 154–174.

Hass, P. M. 1992. Introduction: Epistemic Communities and International Policy Coordination. *International Organization*, 46, 1–35.

Hassan, L. 2000. Deterrence Measures and the Preservation of Asylum in the United Kingdom and United States. *Journal of Refugee Studies*, 13, 184–204.

Hathaway, J., & Neve, A. 1997. Making International Refugee Law Relevant Again: A Proposal for Collectivized and Solution-Oriented Protection. *Harvard Human Rights Journal*, 10, 115–211.

Hathaway, J. C. 1984. The Evolution of Refugee Status in International Law: 1920–1950. *International and Comparative Law Quarterly*, 33, 348–380.

1993. Harmonizing for Whom: The Devaluation of Refugee Protection in the Era of European Economic Integration. *Cornell International Law Journal*, 26, 719–736.

1997. *Reconceiving International Refugee Law*. Boston: M. Nijhoff.

Hawkins, D. 2004. Explaining Costly International Institutions: Persuasion and Enforceable Human Rights Norms. *International Studies Quarterly*, 48, 779–804.

Hay, C. 1999. Crisis and the Structural Transformation of the State: Interrogating the Process of Change. *British Journal of Politics & International Relations*, 1, 317–344.

2008. Constructivist Institutionalism. *In*: Rockman, B. A., Binder, S. A., & Rhodes, R. A. W. (eds.), *The Oxford Handbook of Political Institutions*. Oxford: Oxford University Press.

Helton, A. C. 1991. The Mandate of US Courts to Protect Aliens and Refugees under International Human Rights Law. *Yale Law Journal*, 2335–2346.

2000. Forced Displacement, Humanitarian Intervention, and Sovereignty. *SAIS Review*, 20, 61–86.

2002. *The Price of Indifference: Refugees and Humanitarian Action in the New Century*. Oxford: Oxford University Press.

2003. What Is Refugee Protection? A Question Revisited. *In*: Steiner, N., Gibney, M., & Loescher, G. (eds.), *Problems of Protection: The UNHCR, Refugees, and Human Rights*. New York: Routledge.

Henckaerts, J.-M. 1995. *Mass Expulsion in Modern International Law and Practice*. Leiden: Martinus Nijhoff.

Herbert Lehman Collections. Rare Book and Manuscript Library, Columbia University.

Herbst, J. I. 2000. *States and Power in Africa: Comparative Lessons in Authority and Control*. Princeton, N.J.: Princeton University Press.

Herz, J. H. 1957. Rise and Demise of the Territorial State. *World Politics*, 9, 473–493.

Hessbruegge, J. A. 2012. European Court of Human Rights Protects Migrants against "Push Back" Operations on the High Seas. *American Society of International Law Insights* [Online], 16. www.Asil.Org/Pdfs/Insights/Insight120417.Pdf (Accessed April 17, 2013.)

Hindess, B. 2000. Citizenship in the International Management of Populations. *American Behavioral Scientist*, 43, 1486–1497.

Hinsley, F. H. 1967. *Power and the Pursuit of Peace: Theory and Practice in the History of Relations between States*. Cambridge: Cambridge University Press.

Hirschman, A. O. 1981. Exit, Voice, and Loyalty: Further Reflections and a Survey of Recent Contributions. *In*: Hirschman, A. O. (ed.), *Essays in Trespassing: Economics to Politics to Beyond*. Cambridge: Cambridge University Press.

Hocke, J.-P. 1989. Beyond Humanitarianism: The Need for Political Will to Resolve Today's Refugee Problem. *In*: Loescher, G., & Monahan, L. (eds.), *Refugees and International Relations*. Oxford: Oxford University Press.

Holborn, L. W. 1938. The Legal Status of Political Refugees, 1920–1938. *American Journal of International Law*, 32, 680–703.

1939. The League of Nations and the Refugee Problem. *Annals of the American Academy of Political and Social Science*, 203, 124–135.

1956. *The International Refugee Organization: A Specialized Agency of the United Nations: Its History and Work, 1946–1952*. London: Oxford University Press.

1964. International Organizations for Migration of European Nationals and Refugees. *International Journal*, 20, 331–349.

1975. *Refugees, a Problem of Our Time: The Work of the United Nations High Commissioner for Refugees, 1951–1972*. Metuchen, N.J.: Scarecrow Press.

Holian, A. 2011. *Between National Socialism and Soviet Communism: Displaced Persons in Postwar Germany*. Ann Arbor: University of Michigan Press.

Holsti, K. J. 1991. *Peace and War: Armed Conflicts and International Order, 1648–1989*. Cambridge: Cambridge University Press.

2004. *Taming the Sovereigns: Institutional Change in International Politics*. New York: Cambridge University Press.

Holt, M. P. 1995. *The French Wars of Religion, 1562–1629*, Cambridge: Cambridge University Press.

Home Office. 1998. Fairer, Faster, and Firmer? A Modern Approach to Immigration and Asylum. London. [Online] www.Archive.Official-Documents.Co.Uk/Document/Cm40/4018/4018.Htm.

2002. Secure Borders, Safe Haven: Integration with Diversity in Modern Britain (White Paper). London: Home Office.

Housden, M. 2010. White Russians Crossing the Black Sea: Fridtjof Nansen, Constantinople and the First Modern Repatriation of Refugees Displaced by Civil Conflict, 1922–23. *Slavonic and East European Review*, 495–524.

Houston, A. 2012. *Report of the Expert Panel on Asylum Seekers*. Australian Government.

Howard, M. 2004. *Speech on Asylum and Immigration* [Online]. http://News.Bbc.Co.Uk/2/Hi/Uk_News/Politics/3679618.Stm (Accessed October 28, 2007.)

Hsu, S. S. 2010. Officials Try to Prevent Haitian Earthquake Refugees from Making Trek to U.S. *Washington Post*, Jan 18.

Hudson, A. 1998. Beyond the Borders: Globalisation, Sovereignty and Extra-Territoriality. *Geopolitics*, 3, 89–105.

Human Rights First. 2009. Denial and Delay: The Impact of the Immigration Law's "Terrorism Bars" on Asylum Seekers and Refugees in the United States. New York Human Rights First. [Online] www.Humanrightsfirst.Org.

2012. How to Repair the U.S. Asylum and Refugee Resettlement Systems New York: Human Rights First. [Online] www.Humanrightsfirst.Org/Wp-Content/Uploads/Pdf/Asylum_Blueprint.Pdf.

Human Rights Watch. 2009. *Pushed Back, Pushed Around: Italy's Forced Return of Boat Migrants and Asylum Seekers, Libya's Mistreatment of Migrants and Asylum Seekers*. New York: Human Rights Watch.

Human Security Centre. 2005. *Human Security Report: War and Peace in the 21st Century*. Oxford: Oxford University Press.

Human Security Report Project. 2012. *Human Security Report 2012: Sexual Violence, Education and War – Beyond the Mainstream Narrative.* Vancouver: Human Security Press.

Humphrey, J. P., & Hobbins, A. J. 1994. *On the Edge of Greatness the Diaries of John Humphrey, First Director of the United Nations Division of Human Rights Fontanus Monograph Series.* Montreal: McGill University Libraries.

Hurwitz, A. 1991. The Struggle over the Creation of the War Refugee Board (WRB). *Holocaust and Genocide Studies,* 6, 17–31.

Hutchinson, E. P. 1981. *Legislative History of American Immigration Policy 1798–1965.* Philadelphia: University of Pennsylvania Press.

Hyde, C. C. 1914. Notes on the Extradition Treaties of the United States. *American Journal of International Law,* 8, 487–514.

Ickes, H. L. 1955. *The Secret Diary of Harold L. Ickes.* London: Weidenfeld and Nicolson.

Iggers, W., & Iggers, W. A. 1992. *The Jews of Bohemia and Moravia: A Historical Reader.* Detroit, Mich.: Wayne State University Press.

Ikenberry, G. J., & Kupchan, C. A. 1990. Socialization and Hegemonic Power. *International Organization,* 44, 283–315.

IRIN News. 2012. Migration: Greece Failing Asylum Seekers. October 15.

Jackson, I. C. 1999a. *The Refugee Concept in Group Situations.* The Hague: Martinus Nijhoff.

Jackson, P. T. 2011. *The Conduct of Inquiry in International Relations: Philosophy of Science and Its Implications for the Study of World Politics.* Milton Park: Routledge.

Jackson, R. H. 1990. *Quasi-States: Sovereignty, International Relations, and the Third World.* Cambridge: Cambridge University Press.

1999b. Sovereignty in World Politics: A Glance at the Conceptual and Historical Landscape. *In:* Jackson, R. (ed.), *Sovereignty at the Millennium.* Oxford: Blackwell.

2000. *The Global Covenant: Human Conduct in a World of States.* Oxford: Oxford University Press.

James II. 1687. James the Second, by the Grace of God King of England, France and Ireland, Defender of the Faith, &C. [Electronic Resource]: To All and Singular Archbishops, Archdeacons, Deans, and Their Officials Parsons, Vicars, Curates, and All Other Spirit. In the Savoy [i.e. London]: Printed by Thomas Newcomb . . ., Early English Books Online Ebook Collection. [On-line].   http://eebo.chadwyck.com/search/full_rec? SOURCE=pgimages.cfg&ACTION=ByID&ID=V105013.

Jasanoff, M. 2011. *Liberty's Exiles: American Loyalists in the Revolutionary World.* New York: Knopf.

Jeffery, R. 2006. *Hugo Grotius in International Thought.* Houndsmill: Palgrave Macmillian.

Jensen, R. B. 1981. The International Anti-Anarchist Conference of 1898 and the Origins of Interpol. *Journal of Contemporary History,* 16, 323–347.

Jepperson, R., Wendt, A., & Katzenstein, P. 1996. Norms, Identity and Culture in National Security. *In:* Katzenstein, P. J. (ed.), *The Culture of National Security: Norms and Identities in World Politics.* New York: Columbia University Press.

Johnson, T. F. 1938. *International Tramps: From Chaos to Permanent World Peace.* London: Hutchison & Co.

Johnston, A. I. 2001. Treating International Institutions as Social Environments. *International Studies Quarterly,* 45, 487–515.

Johnstone, I. 2005. The Power of Interpretative Communities. *In*: Barnett, M., & Duvall, R. (eds.), *Power in Global Governance.* Cambridge: Cambridge University Press.

Jones, B. D., Baumgartner, F. R., & True, J. L. 1998. Policy Punctuations: US Budget Authority, 1947–1995. *Journal of Politics,* 60, 1–33.

Jones, J. 1941. Modern Developments in the Law of Extradition. *Transactions of the Grotius Society,* 27, 113–141.

Jones, T. D. 1994. Sale V. Haitian Centers Council, Inc. *American Journal of International Law,* 88, 114–126.

Joppke, C. 1998. Immigration Challenges the Nation-State. *In*: Joppke, C. (ed.), *Challenge to the Nation-State.* Oxford: Oxford University Press.

1999. *Immigration and the Nation-State: The United States, Germany, and Great Britain.* Oxford: Oxford University Press.

Kälin, W. 2005. The Guiding Principles on Internal Displacement as International Minimum Standard and Protection Tool. *Refugee Survey Quarterly,* 24, 27–36.

Kamen, H. 2000. *Early Modern European Society.* London: Routledge.

Karatani, R. 2005. How History Separated Refugee and Migrant Regimes: In Search of Their Institutional Origins. *International Journal of Refugee Law,* 17, 517–541.

Kaufmann, C. D., & Pape, R. A. 1999. Explaining Costly International Moral Action: Britain's Sixty-Year Campaign against the Atlantic Slave Trade. *International Organization,* 53, 631–668.

Kaye, R. 1998. Redefining the Refugee: The UK Media Portrayal of Asylum Seekers. *In*: Koser, K., & Lutz, H. (eds.), *The New Migration in Europe: Social Constructions and Social Realities.* Basingstoke, UK: Macmillan.

Kedar, B. Z. 1996. Expulsion as an Issue of World History. *Journal of World History,* 7, 165–180.

Keely, C. B. 1996. How Nation-States Create and Respond to Refugee Flows. *International Migration Review,* 30, 1046–1066.

2001. The International Refugee Regime(s): The End of the Cold War Matters. *International Migration Review,* 35, 303–314.

Keene, E. 2002. *Beyond the Anarchical Society: Grotius, Colonialism and Order in World Politics.* Cambridge: Cambridge University Press.

Kellett, M. 1986. Extradition – the Concept of the Political Offence. *Liverpool Law Review,* 8, 1–22.

Kennedy, D. 1988. A New Stream of International Law Scholarship. *Wisconsin International Law Journal,* 7, 1.

Kennedy, E. M. 1970. Immigration Law: Some Refinements and New Reforms. *International Migration Review,* 4, 4–10.

1981. Refugee Act of 1980. *International Migration Review,* 141–156.

Kennedy, P. M. 1989. *The Rise and Fall of the Great Powers: Economic Change and Military Conflict from 1500 to 2000.* New York: Vintage Books.

Keohane, R. O. 1980. The Theory of Hegemonic Stability and Changes in International Economic Regimes, 1967–77. *In*: Holsti, O., Siverson, R., & George, A. (eds.), *Change in the International System*. Boulder, Colo.: Westview Press.

1984. *After Hegemony: Cooperation and Discord in the World Political Economy*. Princeton, N.J.: Princeton University Press.

1988. International Institutions: Two Approaches. *International Studies Quarterly*, 32, 379–396.

1990. Multilateralism: An Agenda for Research. *International Journal*, 45, 731–64.

1993. The Analysis of International Regimes: Towards a European-American Research Programme. *Regime Theory and International Relations*, 23–45.

Keohane, R. O., & Nye, J. S. 1989. *Power and Interdependence*. Glenview, Ill.: Scott Foresman & Co.

Kerwin, D. 2005. The Use and Misuse of "National Security" Rationale in Crafting US Refugee and Immigration Policies. *International Journal of Refugee Law*, 17, 749.

2012. The Faltering US Refugee Protection System: Legal and Policy Responses to Refugees, Asylum-Seekers, and Others in Need of Protection. *Refugee Survey Quarterly*, 31, 1–33.

Kettner, J. H. 1978. *The Development of American Citizenship, 1608–1870*. Chapel Hill: University of North Carolina Press.

King, D. S. 1992. The Establishment of Work-Welfare Programs in the United States and Britain: Politics, Ideas, and Institutions. *In*: Steinmo, S., Thelen, K., & Longstreth, F. (eds.), *Structuring Politics: Historical Institutionalism in Comparative Analysis*. Cambridge: Cambridge University Press.

Kingdon, J. W. 2002. *Agendas, Alternatives, and Public Policies*. New York: Longman Publishing Group.

Klotz, A. 1995. *Norms in International Relations: The Struggle against Apartheid*. Ithaca, N.Y.: Cornell University Press.

2002. Transnational Activism and Global Transformations: The Anti-Apartheid and Abolitionist Experiences. *European Journal of International Relations*, 8, 49–76.

Klusmeyer, D. B. 1996. *Between Consent and Descent: Conceptions of Democratic Citizenship*. Washington, D.C.: Carnegie Endowment for International Peace.

Kneebone, S. 2006. The Pacific Plan: The Provision of 'Effective Protection'? *International Journal of Refugee Law*, 18, 696–721.

Knittle, W. A. 1965. *Early Eighteenth Century Palatine Emigration*. Baltimore: Genealogical Publishing Co.

Kochavi, A. J. 2001. *Post-Holocaust Politics: Britain, the United States, and Jewish Refugees, 1945–1948*. Chapel Hill: University of North Carolina Press.

Koh, H. H. 1994. America's Offshore Refugee Camps. *University of Richmond Law Review*, 29, 139–173.

1997. Why Do Nations Obey International Law? *Yale Law Journal*, 106, 2599–2659.

Korowicz, M. S. 1956. The Problem of the International Personality of Individuals. *American Journal of International Law*, 50, 533–562.

Koslowski, R., & Kratochwil, F. V. 1994. Understanding Change in International Politics: The Soviet Empire's Demise and the International System. *International Organization*, 48, 215–247.

Krasner, S. D. 1982a. Regimes and the Limits of Realism: Regimes as Autonomous Variables. *International Organization*, 36, 497–510.

1982b. Structural Causes and Regime Consequences: Regimes as Intervening Variables. *International Organization*, 36, 185–205.

1984. Approaches to the State: Alternative Conceptions and Historical Dynamics. *Comparative Politics*, 16, 223–246.

1999. *Sovereignty: Organized Hypocrisy*. Princeton, N.J.: Princeton University Press.

Kratochwil, F. V. 1989. *Rules, Norms, and Decisions: On the Conditions of Practical and Legal Reasoning in International Relations and Domestic Affairs*. Cambridge: Cambridge University Press.

Kraut, A. M., Breitman, R., & Imhoof, T. W. 1984. The State Department, the Labor Department, and the German Jewish Immigration, 1930–1940. *Journal of American Ethnic History*, 5–38.

Krebs, R. R., & Jackson, P. T. 2007. Twisting Tongues and Twisting Arms: The Power of Political Rhetoric. *European Journal of International Relations*, 13, 31.

Krenz, F. E. 1966. The Refugee as a Subject of International Law. *International and Comparative Law Quarterly*, 15, 90–116.

Krook, M. L., & True, J. 2012. Rethinking the Life Cycles of International Norms: The United Nations and the Global Promotion of Gender Equality. *European Journal of International Relations*, 18, 103–127.

Kulischer, E. M. 1949. Displaced Persons in the Modern World. *Annals of the American Academy of Political and Social Science*, 262, 166–177.

Kushner, T., & Knox, K. 1999. *Refugees in an Age of Genocide: Global, National and Local Perspectives During the Twentieth Century*. London: Frank Cass.

Landa, M. J. 1911. *The Alien Problem and Its Remedy*. London: PS King & Son.

Lauterpacht, H. 1946. The Grotian Tradition in International Law. *British Yearbook of International Law*, 23.

League of Nations 1930. *Ten Years of World Cooperation*. Geneva: Secretariat of the League of Nations.

League of Nations Archives (LNA). Geneva, Switzerland.

Legomsky, S. H. 2006. The USA and the Caribbean Interdiction Program. *International Journal of Refugee Law*, 18, 677–695.

Legro, J. W. 1997. Which Norms Matter? Revisiting the "Failure" of Internationalism. *International Organization*, 51, 31–63.

2000. The Transformation of Policy Ideas. *American Journal of Political Science*, 44, 419–432.

2005. *Rethinking the World: Great Power Strategies and International Order*. Ithaca, N.Y.: Cornell University Press.

Leibowitz, A. H. 1983. The Refugee Act of 1980: Problems and Congressional Concerns. *Annals of the American Academy of Political and Social Science*, 467, 163–171.

LeMaster, R., & Zall, B. 1983. Compassion Fatigue: The Expansion of Refugee Admissions to the United States. *Boston College International and Comparative Law Review*, 6, 447–74.

Leslie, R. F. 1956. *Polish Politics and the Revolution of November 1830*. London: Greenwood Press.

Levi, M. 1997. A Model, a Method, and a Map: Rational Choice in Comparative and Historical Analysis. *In*: Lichbach, M. I., & Zuckerman, A. S. (eds.), *Comparative Politics: Rationality, Culture, and Structure*. Cambridge: Cambridge University Press.

Levy, M. A., Young, O. R., & Zurn, M. 1995. The Study of International Regimes. *European Journal of International Relations*, 1, 267–330.

Lewis, C. 2005. UNHCR's Contribution to the Development of International Refugee Law: Its Foundations and Evolution. *International Journal of Refugee Law*, 17, 67–90.

Lewis, G. C., Sir. 1859. *On Foreign Jurisdiction and the Extradition of Criminals* [Online]. London: J.W. Parker and Son (reprinted by Thomson Gale). http://Galenet.Galegroup.Com/Servlet/MOML?Af=RN&Ae=F106524971&Srchtp=A&Ste=14 (Accessed July 8, 2007.)

Lewis, R., & Schibsby, M. 1939. Status of the Refugee under American Immigration Laws. *Annals of the American Academy of Political and Social Science*, 203, 74–82.

Lipson, C. 1991. Why Are Some International Agreements Informal? *International Organization*, 45, 495–538.

Lipstadt, D. E. 1982. Pious Sympathies and Sincere Regrets: The American News Media and the Holocaust from Krystalnacht to Bermuda, 1938–1943. *Modern Judaism*, 2, 53–72.

Lischer, S. K. 2005. *Dangerous Sanctuaries: Refugee Camps, Civil War, and the Dilemmas of Humanitarian Aid*. Ithaca, N.Y.: Cornell University Press.

Liu, R. 2002. Governing Refugees 1919–1945. *Borderlands* [Online], 1. www.Borderlands.Net.Au/Vol1no1_2002/Lui_Governing.Html.

Locke, J. 1993. *The Treatise on Government*. London: Everyman.

Loescher, G. 1993. *Beyond Charity: International Cooperation and the Global Refugee Crisis*. New York: Oxford University Press.

2001. *The UNHCR and World Politics: A Perilous Path*. New York: Oxford University Press.

2003. Refugees as Grounds for International Action. *In*: Newman, E., & Van Selm, J. (eds.), *Refugees and Forced Displacement: International Security, Human Vulnerability, and the State*. Tokyo: United Nations University Press.

Loescher, G., Betts, A., & Milner, J. 2008. *The United Nations High Commissioner for Refugees (UNHCR): The Politics and Practice of Refugee Protection into the Twenty-First Century*. Milton Park: Routledge.

Loescher, G., & Milner, J. 2005. *Protracted Refugee Situations: Domestic and International Security Implications*. Oxford: Oxford University Press.

Loescher, G., & Scanlan, J. A. 1986. *Calculated Kindness: Refugees and America's Half-Open Door, 1945 to the Present*. New York: Free Press.

London, L. 2000. *Whitehall and the Jews, 1933–1948*. Cambridge: Cambridge University Press.

Long, K. 2009. Early Repatriation Policy: Russian Refugee Return 1922–1924. *Journal of Refugee Studies*, 22, 133–154.

Lowes, S. 2012. The Legality of Extraterritorial Processing of Asylum Claims: The Judgment of the High Court of Australia in the "Malaysian Solution" Case. *Human Rights Law Review*, 12, 168–182.

Lyons, G., & Mastanduno, M. 1995. Introduction: International Intervention, State Sovereignty, and the Future of International Society. *In*: Lyons, G., & Mastanduno, M. (eds.), *Beyond Westphalia? State Sovereignty and International Intervention*. Baltimore: Johns Hopkins University Press.

MacCulloch, D. 2003. *The Reformation: A History*. New York: Penguin Books.

Maga, T. P. 1982. Closing the Door: The French Government and Refugee Policy, 1933–1939. *French Historical Studies*, 12, 424–442.

Malin, P. 1947. The Refugee: A Problem for International Organization. *International Organization*, 1, 442–459.

March, J. G., & Olsen, J. P. 1998. The Institutional Dynamics of International Political Orders. *International Organization*, 52, 943–969.

Mark, C.-K. 2007. The "Problem of People": British Colonials, Cold War Powers, and the Chinese Refugees in Hong Kong, 1949–62. *Modern Asian Studies*, 41, 1145–1181.

Markowitz, A. A. 1973. Humanitarianism Versus Restrictionism: The United States and the Hungarian Refugees. *International Migration Review*, 7, 46–59.

Marrus, M. R. 2002. *The Unwanted: European Refugees from the First World War through the Cold War*. Philadelphia: Temple University Press.

Marshall, G. 1947. Policy on Repatriation of Displaced Persons. *Department of State Bulletin*, 16, 1085.

Martin, D. A. 1990. Reforming Asylum Adjudication: On Navigating the Coast of Bohemia. *University of Pennsylvania Law Review*, 138, 1247–1381.

Mattingly, G. 1988. *Renaissance Diplomacy*. Mineola, N.Y.: Courier Dover Publications.

Mayall, J. 1990. *Nationalism and International Society*. Cambridge: Cambridge University Press.

2000. *World Politics: Progress and Its Limits*. Cambridge: Polity Press.

McAdam, D., McCarthy, J. D., & Zald, M. N. 1996. *Comparative Perspectives on Social Movements: Political Opportunities, Mobilizing Structures, and Cultural Framings*. Cambridge University Press.

McBride, M. J. 1999. *The Evolution of US Immigration and Refugee Policy: Public Opinion, Domestic Politics and UNHCR*, Centre for Documentation and Research. Geneva: United Nations High Commissioner for Refugees.

McClelland, J. S. 1996. *A History of Western Political Thought*. New York: Routledge.

McDonald, J. G. 1936. *The German Refugees and the League of Nations*. London: Friends of Europe.

1944. Refugees. *In*: Davis, H. E. (ed.), *Pioneers in World Order: An American Appraisal of the League of Nations*. New York: Columbia University Press.

McDowall, R. 1989. Co-Ordination of Refugee Policy in Europe. *In*: Loescher, G., & Monahan, L. (eds.), *Refugees and International Relations*. Oxford: Oxford University Press.

Mearsheimer, J.J. 1994. The False Promise of International Institutions. *International Security*, 19, 5–49.

Meissner, D. 1986. Reflections on the Refugee Act of 1980. *In*: Martin, D. A. (ed.), *The New Asylum Seekers: Refugee Law in the 1980s*. Dordrecht: Martinus Nijhoff.

Meron, T. 1995. Extraterritoriality of Human Rights Treaties. *American Journal of International Law*, 89, 78–82.

Meyer, J. 1980. The World Polity and the Authority of the Nation-State. *In*: Bergesen, A. (ed.), *Studies of the Modern World System*. New York: Academic Press.

Migration News. 2003. UK: Asylees, Safe Havens, Workers. 10. [Online] http://Migration.Ucdavis.Edu/Mn/More.Php?Id=57_0_4_0 (Accessed April 3, 2008.)

Milner, H.V., & Keohane, R. O. 1996. Internationalization and Domestic Politics: An Introduction. *In*: Milner, H.V., & Keohane, R. O. (eds.), *Internationalization and Domestic Politics*. Cambridge: Cambridge University Press.

Milner, J. 2004. *Golden Age? What Golden Age? A Critical History of African Asylum Policy*. Toronto: Center for Refugee Studies, York University.

2009. *Refugees, the State and the Politics of Asylum in Africa*. Houndmills, UK: Palgrave Macmillan.

Minear, L., Clark, J., Cohen, R., Gallagher, D., Guest, I., & Weiss, T. G. 1994. Humanitarian Action in the Former Yugoslavia: The UN's Role, 1991–1993. Providence, RI: Thomas J. Watson Jr. Institute, Brown University. [Online] http://Watsoninstitute.Org/Pub/OP18.Pdf. Occasional Paper 18.

Mintrom, M., & Norman, P. 2009. Policy Entrepreneurship and Policy Change. *Policy Studies Journal*, 37, 649–667.

Mooney, E. 2005. The Concept of Internal Displacement and the Case for Internally Displaced Persons as a Category of Concern. *Refugee Survey Quarterly*, 24, 9–26.

Moravcsik, A. 1999. "Is Something Rotten in the State of Denmark?" Constructivism and European Integration. *Journal of European Public Policy*, 6, 669–681.

Morgenthau, H.J. 1940. Positivism, Functionalism, and International Law. *American Journal of International Law*, 34, 260–284.

1978. *Politics among Nations: The Struggle for Power and Peace*. New York: Alfred A. Knopf.

Morris, J. C. 2003. The Spaces in Between: American and Australian Interdiction Policies and Their Implications for the Refugee Protection Regime. *Refuge: Canada's Journal on Refugees*, 21, 51–62.

Morris, M.D. 1985. *Immigration – the Beleaguered Bureaucracy*. Washington, D.C.: Brookings Institution.

Morris, N. 1990. Refugees: Facing Crisis in the 1990s – a Personal View from within UNHCR. *International Journal of Refugee Law*, 2, 38–57.

Müller, H. 1993. The Internalization of Principles, Norms, and Rules by Governments: The Case of Security Regimes. *In*: Rittberger, V. (ed.), *Regime Theory and International Relations*. Oxford: Clarendon Press.

2004. Arguing, Bargaining and All That: Communicative Action, Rationalist Theory and the Logic of Appropriateness in International Relations. *European Journal of International Relations*, 10, 395–435.

Nackerud, L., Springer, A., Larrison, C., & Issac, A. 1999. The End of the Cuban Contradiction in US Refugee Policy. *International Migration Review*, 33, 176–192.

Nadelmann, E. A. 1990. Global Prohibition Regimes: The Evolution of Norms in International Society. *International Organization*, 44, 479–525.

Nafziger, J. A. R. 1983. The General Admission of Aliens under International Law. *American Journal of International Law*, 77, 804–847.

Nettl, J. P. 1968. The State as a Conceptual Variable. *World Politics*, 20, 559–592.

Neufeld, M. 1993. Interpretation and the "Science" of International Relations. *Review of International Studies*, 19, 39–61.

Neuman, G. L. 1993. The Lost Century of American Immigration Law (1776–1875). *Columbia Law Review*, 93, 1833–1901.

2003. Qualitative Migration Controls in the Antebellum United States. *In:* Fahrmeir, A., Faron, O., & Weil, P. (eds.), *Migration Control in the North Atlantic World*. New York: Berghahn Books.

Neumayer, E. 2005. Unequal Access to Foreign Spaces: How States Use Visa Restrictions to Regulate Mobility in a Globalized World. *Global Migration Perspectives Working Paper No. 43*. Geneva: Global Commission on International Migration.

Nexon, D. H. 2009. *The Struggle for Power in Early Modern Europe: Religious Conflict, Dynastic Empires, and International Change*. Princeton, N.J.: Princeton University Press.

Ngai, M. M. 2003. *Impossible Subjects: Illegal Aliens and the Making of Modern America*. Princeton, N.J.: Princeton University Press.

Noiriel, G. 1991. *Réfugiés Et Sans-Papiers: La République Face Au Droit D'asile, XIXe-XXe Siècle*. Paris: Hachette Littératures.

Noll, G. 2000. *Negotiating Asylum: The EU Acquis, Extraterritorial Protection, and the Common Market of Deflection*. The Hague: Martinus Nijhoff.

Norwood, F. A. 1969. *Strangers and Exiles: A History of Religious Refugees*. New York: Abingdon Press.

Nyers, P. 1999. Emergency or Emerging Identities? Refugees and Transformations in World Order. *Millennium: Journal of International Studies*, 28, 1–26.

O'Brien, C. H. 1969. Ideas of Religious Toleration at the Time of Joseph II. A Study of the Enlightenment among Catholics in Austria. *Transactions of the American Philosophical Society*, 59, 1–80.

O'Brien, L. 1930. *Innocent XI and the Revocation of the Edict of Nantes*. Berkeley: University of California Press.

OCHA Internal Displacement Unit. 2003. *No Refuge: The Challenge of Internal Displacement*. Geneva: United Nations Publications.

Office of the United Nations High Commissioner for Refugees. 2006. *Convention and Protocol Relating to the Status of Refugees*. Geneva: UNHCR.

Ogata, S. 1993. Statement to the Forty-Ninth Session of the Commission on Human Rights. [Online] www.Unhcr.Org/Admin/ADMIN/3ae68fad1c. Html.

Oppenheim, L., & Roxburgh, R. 1920. *International Law, a Treatise*. London: Longmans.

Orchard, P. 2010a. The Perils of Humanitarianism: Refugee and IDP Protection in Situations of Regime-Induced Displacement. *Refugee Survey Quarterly*, 29, 38–60.

2010b. Protection of Internally Displaced Persons: Soft Law as a Norm-Generating Mechanism. *Review of International Studies*, 36, 281–303.

2010c. Regime-Induced Displacement and Decision-Making within the United Nations Security Council: The Cases of Northern Iraq, Kosovo, and Darfur. *Global Responsibility to Protect*, 2, 101–126.

2014. Implementing a Global Internally Displaced Persons Protection Regime. *In*: Betts, A., & Orchard, P. (eds.), *Implementation in World Politics: How Norms Change Practice*. Oxford: Oxford University Press.

Osiander, A. 1994. *The States System of Europe, 1640–1990: Peacemaking and the Conditions of International Stability*. Oxford: Oxford University Press.

Otterness, P. 2004. *Becoming German: The 1709 Palatine Migration to New York*. Ithaca, N.Y.: Cornell University Press.

Parker, G. 2001. *Europe in Crisis, 1598–1648*. Oxford: Blackwell.

Parry, C. 1969. *The Consolidated Treaty Series*. Dobbs Ferry, N.Y.: Oceana Publications.

Paul Weis Archive, Refugee Studies Centre. Queen Elizabeth House, University of Oxford, UK.

Payne, R. A. 2001. Persuasion, Frames and Norm Construction. *European Journal of International Relations*, 7, 37–61.

Peck, S. E. 1980. The Campaign for an American Response to the Nazi Holocaust, 1943–1945. *Journal of Contemporary History*, 15, 367–400.

Pellew, J. 1989. The Home Office and the Aliens Act, 1905. *Historical Journal*, 32, 369–385.

Penkower, M. N. 1988. *The Jews Were Expendable: Free World Diplomacy and the Holocaust*. Detroit, Mich.: Wayne State University Press.

Penrose, E. F. 1951. Negotiating on Refugees and Displaced Persons, 1946. *In*: Dennett, R., & Johnson, J. E. (eds.), *Negotiating with the Russians*. Boston: World Peace Foundation.

Percy, S. 2007. *Mercenaries: The History of a Norm in International Relations*. Oxford: Oxford University Press.

2008. *Mercenaries: The History of a Norm in International Relations*. Oxford: Oxford University Press.

Perruchoud, R. 1989. From the Intergovernmental Committee for European Migration to the International Organization for Migration. *International Journal of Refugee Law*, 1, 501–517.

Philip Noel-Baker Archive (NBKR). Churchill College, Cambridge University, Cambridge, UK.

Phillips, A. 2011. *War, Religion and Empire: The Transformation of International Orders*. Cambridge: Cambridge University Press.

Phillips, J., & Spinks, H. 2012. *Boat Arrivals in Australia since 1976*. Canberra: Parliament of Australia Department of Parliamentary Services.

Philpott, D. 1997. Ideas and the Evolution of Sovereignty. *In*: Hashmi, S. H. (ed.), *State Sovereignty: Change and Persistence in International Relations*. University Park, Penn.: Pennsylvania State University Press.

1999. Westphalia, Authority, and International Society. *Political Studies*, 47, 566–589.

2001. *Revolutions in Sovereignty: How Ideas Shaped Modern International Relations*. Princeton, N.J.: Princeton University Press.

Phuong, C. 2004. *The International Protection of Internally Displaced Persons*. Cambridge: Cambridge University Press.

Plaut, W. G. 1995. *Asylum: A Moral Dilemma*. Westport, Conn.: Praeger.

Plender, R. 1988. *International Migration Law*. Dordrecht: Martinus Nijhoff.

Porter, B. 1979. *The Refugee Question in Mid-Victorian Politics*. Cambridge: Cambridge University Press.

Powell, R. 1994. Anarchy in International Relations Theory: The Neorealist-Neoliberal Debate. *International Organization*, 48, 313–344.

Price, C. A. 1974. *The Great White Walls Are Built: Restrictive Immigration to North America and Australasia 1836–1888*. Canberra: Australian Institute of International Affairs.

Price, M. E. 2009. *Rethinking Asylum: History, Purpose, and Limits*. Cambridge: Cambridge University Press.

Price, R. M. 1997. *The Chemical Weapons Taboo*. Ithaca, N.Y.: Cornell University Press.

1998. Reversing the Gun Sights: Transnational Civil Society Targets Land Mines. *International Organization*, 52, 613–644.

2007. Nuclear Weapons Don't Kill People, Rogues Do. *International Politics*, 44, 232–249.

Price, R. M., & Reus-Smit, C. 1998. Dangerous Liaisons?: Critical International Theory and Constructivism. *European Journal of International Relations*, 4, 259–294.

Proudfoot, M. J. 1957. *European Refugees 1939–52: A Study in Forced Population Movement*. London: Faber and Faber Ltd.

Puchala, D. J., & Hopkins, R. F. 1982. International Regimes: Lessons from Inductive Analysis. *International Organization*, 36.

Pufendorf, S. 1749. *The Law of Nature and Nations*. London: J and J Bonwicke.

Putnam, R. D. 1988. Diplomacy and Domestic Politics: The Logic of Two-Level Games. *International Organization*, 42, 427–460.

Pyle, C. H. 2001. *Extradition, Politics, and Human Rights*. Philadelphia: Temple University Press.

Radzinowicz, L., & Hood, R. 1979. The Status of Political Prisoner in England: The Struggle for Recognition. *Virginia Law Review*, 65, 1421–1481.

Rae, H. 2002. *State Identities and the Homogenisation of Peoples*. Cambridge: Cambridge University Press.

Raitt, J. 1983. The Emperor and the Exiles: The Clash of Religion and Politics in the Late Sixteenth Century. *Church History*, 52, 145–156.

Raustiala, K. 2006. The Evolution of Territoriality: International Relations and American Law. *In*: Kahler, M., & Walter, B. F. (eds.), *Territory and Conflict in an Era of Globalization*. Cambridge: Cambridge University Press.

2009. *Does the Constitution Follow the Flag? The Evolution of Territoriality in American Law.* Oxford: Oxford University Press.

Raustiala, K., & Victor, D. G. 2004. The Regime Complex for Plant Genetic Resources. *International Organization*, 58, 277–309.

Read, J. M. 1962. The United Nations and Refugees – Changing Concepts. *International Conciliation*, 34.

Reaman, G. E. 1963. *The Trail of the Huguenots in Europe, the United States, South Africa, and Canada.* Toronto: Thomas Allen Ltd.

Rees, E. 1953. The Refugee and the United Nations. *International Conciliation*, 265–314.

1957. Century of the Homeless Man. *International Conciliation*, 193–254.

Reeves, J. S. 1925. The First Edition of Grotius' De Jure Belli Ac Pacis, 1625. *American Journal of International Law*, 19, 12–22.

Reich, E. 1905 [2004]. *Select Documents Illustrating Mediaeval and Modern History.* London: Kessinger Publishing.

Reimers, D. M. 1998. *Unwelcome Strangers: American Identity and the Turn against Immigration.* New York: Columbia University Press.

2002. Refugee Policies. *In*: Deconde, A., Burns, R. D., & Logevall, F. (eds.), *Encyclopedia of American Foreign Policy.* New York: Charles Scribner's Sons.

Reston, J. B. 1947. Negotiating with the Russians. *Harper's Magazine*, August, 97–106.

Reus-Smit, C. 1997. The Constitutional Structure of International Society and the Nature of Fundamental Institutions. *International Organization*, 51, 555–89.

1999. *The Moral Purpose of the State: Culture, Social Identity, and Institutional Rationality in International Relations.* Princeton, N.J.: Princeton University Press.

2004. Society, Power, and Ethics. *In*: Reus-Smit, C. (ed.), *The Politics of International Law.* Cambridge: Cambridge University Press.

2007. International Crises of Legitimacy. *International Politics*, 44, 157–174.

2011. Struggles for Individual Rights and the Expansion of the International System. *International Organization*, 65, 207–242.

Rigsby, K. J. 1997. *Asylia: Territorial Inviolability in the Hellenistic World.* Berkley: University of California Press.

Risse-Kappen, T. 1991. Public Opinion, Domestic Structure, and Foreign Policy in Liberal Democracies. *World Politics*, 43, 479–512.

1995. *Bringing Transnational Relations Back In: Non-State Actors, Domestic Structures, and International Institutions.* Cambridge: Cambridge University Press.

Risse, T. 1999. International Norms and Domestic Change: Arguing and Communicative Behavior in the Human Rights Area. *Politics and Society*, 27.

2000. "Let's Argue!" Communicative Action in International Relations. *International Organization*, 54, 1–39.

Risse, T., & Sikkink, K. 1999. The Socialization of International Human Rights Norms into Domestic Practice. *In*: Risse, T., Ropp, S. C., & Sikkink, K. (eds.),

The Power of Human Rights: International Norms and Domestic Change. Cambridge: Cambridge University Press.

Ristelhueber, R. 1951. The International Refugee Organization. *International Conciliation*, 470, 167–220.

Riveles, S. 1989. Diplomatic Asylum as a Human Right: The Case of the Durban Six. *Human Rights Quarterly*, 11, 139–159.

Robbins, R. 1956. The Refugee Status: Challenge and Response. *Law and Contemporary Problems*, 21, 311–333.

Roberts, A. 1998. More Refugees, Less Asylum: A Regime in Transformation. *Journal of Refugee Studies*, 11, 375–395.

Robinson, J. H. 1904. *Readings in European History*. Boston: Ginn.

Robinson, P. 2002. *The White Russian Army in Exile, 1920–1941*. Oxford: Clarendon Press.

Robinson, W. C. 1998. *Terms of Refuge: The Indochinese Exodus & the International Response*. New York: Zed Books.

Roelofsen, C. G. 1992. Grotius and the International Politics of the Seventeenth Century. *In*: Bull, H., Kingsbury, B., & Roberts, A. (eds.), *Hugo Grotius and International Relations*. Oxford: Oxford University Press.

Romain, G. 1999. The Anschluss: The British Response to the Refugee Crisis. *Holocaust Studies: A Journal of Culture and History*, 8, 87–102.

Roosevelt, F. D. 1941. *The Public Papers and Address of Franklin D. Roosevelt*. New York: Macmillan.

Rosenblum, M. R., & Salehyan, I. 2004. Norms and Interests in US Asylum Enforcement. *Journal of Peace Research*, 41, 677–697.

Roversi, A. 2003. The Evolution of the Refugee Regime and Institutional Responses: Legacies from the Nansen Period. *Refugee Survey Quarterly*, 22, 21.

Roxström, E., & Gibney, M. 2003. The Legal and Ethical Obligations of UNHCR. *In*: Steiner, N., Gibney, M., & Loescher, G. (eds.), *Problems of Protection: The UNHCR, Refugees, and Human Rights*. London: Routledge.

Rubinstein, J. L. 1936. The Refugee Problem. *International Affairs*, 15, 716–734.

Rucker, A. 1949. The Work of the International Refugee Organization. *International Affairs*, 25, 66–73.

Rudolph, C. 2006. *National Security and Immigration: Policy Development in the United States and Western Europe since 1945*. Palo Alto, Calif.: Stanford University Press.

Ruggie, J. G. 1982. International Regimes, Transactions, and Change: Embedded Liberalism in the Postwar Economic Order. *International Organization*, 36, 379–415.

——— 1992. Multilateralism: The Anatomy of an Institution. *International Organization*, 46, 561–598.

——— 1993a. Multilateralism: The Anatomy of an Institution. *In*: Ruggie, J. G. (ed.), *Multilateralism Matters: The Theory and Praxis of an Institutional Form*. New York: Columbia University Press.

——— 1993b. Territoriality and Beyond. *International Organization*, 47, 139–174.

——— 1998a. *Constructing the World Polity: Essays on International Institutionalization*. New York: Routledge.

1998b. What Makes the World Hang Together? Neo-Utilitarianism and the Social Constructivist Challenge. *International Organization*, 52, 855–885.

Rushton, S. 2008. The UN Secretary-General and Norm Entrepreneurship: Boutros Boutros-Ghali and Democracy Promotion. *Global Governance: A Review of Multilateralism and International Organizations*, 14, 95–110.

Rust, J. 2006. *John Searle and the Construction of Social Reality*. New York: Continuum International Publishing Group.

Rutinwa, B. 1999. *The End of Asylum?* The Changing Nature of Refugee Policies in Africa. Geneva: UNHCR.

Rwelamira, M. R. 1989. Two Decades of the 1969 OAU Convention Governing the Specific Aspects of the Refugee Problem in Africa. *International Journal of Refugee Law*, 1, 557–561.

Sadruddin, A. K. 1976. Lectures by Sadruddin Aga Khan on Legal Problems Relating to Refugees and Displaced Persons Given at the Hague Academy of International Law. [Online] http://www.unhcr.org/cgi-bin/texis/vtx/search?page=search&docid=3ae68fc04&query=Refugee%20Protection%20in%20International%20Law.

Salehyan, I., & Gleditsch, K. S. 2006. Refugees and the Spread of Civil War. *International Organization*, 60, 335–366.

Saloman, K. 1991. *Refugees in the Cold War: Toward a New International Refugee Regime in the Early Postwar Era*. Lund: Lund University Press.

Sandholtz, W. 2008a. Creating Authority by the Council: The International Criminal Tribunals. *In:* Cronin, B., & Hurd, I. (eds.), *The UN Security Council and the Politics of International Authority*. London: Routledge.

2008b. Dynamics of International Norm Change: Rules against Wartime Plunder. *European Journal of International Relations*, 14, 101–131.

Sassen, S. 1999. *Guests and Aliens*. New York: New Press.

Scharpf, F. W. 1997. *Games Real Actors Play. Actor-Centered Institutionalism in Policy Research*. Boulder, Colo.: Westview Press.

Schroeder, T. 1919. Political Crimes Defined. *Michigan Law Review*, 18, 30–44.

Schultz, H. 1970. The Principles of the Traditional Law of Extradition. *In:* Council of Europe (ed.), *Legal Aspects of Extradition among European States*. Strasbourg: Council of Europe.

Schuster, L. 2002. Asylum and the Lessons of History. *Race & Class*, 44, 40–56.

2003. *The Use and Abuse of Political Asylum in Britain and Germany*. London: Frank Cass.

2011. Dublin II and Eurodac: Examining the (Un) Intended (?) Consequences. *Gender, Place & Culture*, 18, 401–416.

Schuster, L., & Solomos, J. 1999. The Politics of Refugee and Asylum Policies in Britain: Historical Patterns and Contemporary Realities. *In:* Bloch, A., & Levy, C. (eds.), *Refugees, Citizenship and Social Policy in Europe*. London: Macmillan.

Scoville, W. C. 1952a. The Huguenots and Diffusion of Technology. I. *Journal of Political Economy*, 60, 294–311.

1952b. The Huguenots and the Diffusion of Technology. II. *Journal of Political Economy*, 60, 392–411.

Searle, J. R. 1995. *The Social Construction of Reality*. London: Free Press.

Seller, M. 1982. Historical Perspectives on American Immigration Policy: Case Studies and Current Implications. *Law and Contemporary Problems*, 45, 137–162.

Sewell, W. H. 1988. Le Citoyen/La Citoyenne: Activity, Passivity, and the Revolutionary Concept of Citizenship. In: Lucas, C. (ed.), *The Political Culture of the French Revolution*. Oxford: Pergamon Press.

Shacknove, A. 1993. From Asylum to Containment. *International Journal of Refugee Law*, 5, 516–533.

Shannon, V. P. 2000. Norms Are What States Make of Them: The Political Psychology of Norm Violation. *International Studies Quarterly*, 44, 293–316.

Sharpe, M. 2011. Engaging with Refugee Protection: The Organization of African Unity and African Union since 1963. *New Issues in Refugee Research* [Online], Geneva: UNHCR. www.Unhcr.Org/4edf8e959.Pdf.

Sherman, A. J. 1973. *Island Refuge: Britain and Refugees from the Third Reich 1933–1939*. Berkeley: University of California Press.

Sibley, N. W., & Elias, A. 1906. *The Aliens Act and the Right of Asylum*. London: William Clowes and Sons, Ltd.

Simmons, B. A. 2009. *Mobilizing for Human Rights: International Law in Domestic Politics*. Cambridge: Cambridge University Press.

Simmons, B. A., Dobbin, F., & Garrett, G. 2006. Introduction: The International Diffusion of Liberalism. *International Organization*, 60, 781–810.

Simon, R. J. 1974. *Public Opinion in America: 1936–1970*. Chicago: Markham.

Simpson, S. J. H. 1939. *The Refugee Problem: Report of a Survey*. London: Oxford University Press.

  1940. *Refugees: A Review of the Situation since September 1939*. London: Royal Institute of International Affairs.

Sinha, S. P. 1971. *Asylum and International Law*. The Hague: Martinus Nijhoff.

Sjöberg, T. 1991. *The Powers and the Persecuted: The Refugee Problem and the Intergovernmental Committee on Refugees (IGCR), 1938–1947*. Lund: Lund University Press.

Skanks, C. 2001. *Immigration and the Politics of American Sovereignty, 1890–1990*. Ann Arbor: University of Michigan Press.

Skran, C. M. 1988. Profiles of the First Two Commissioners. *Journal of Refugee Studies*, 1, 277–295.

  1995. *Refugees in Inter-War Europe: The Emergence of a Regime*. Oxford: Clarendon Press.

Smyser, W. R. 1987. *Refugees: Extended Exile*. New York: Praeger.

Soguk, N. 1999. *States and Strangers: Refugees and Displacements of Statecraft*. Minneapolis: University of Minnesota Press.

Soysal, Y. N. 1994. *Limits of Citizenship: Migrants and Postnational Membership in Europe*. Chicago: University of Chicago Press.

Spencer, I. R. G. 1997. *British Immigration Policy since 1939: The Making of Multi-Racial Britain*. London: Routledge.

Spitz, L. W. 1956. Particularism and Peace: Augsburg- 1555. *Church History*, 25, 110–126.

Spruyt, H. 1994. *The Sovereign State and Its Competitors: An Analysis of Systems Change*. Princeton, N.J.: Princeton University Press.

Stankiewicz, W. J. 1955. *The Edict of Nantes in the Light of Mediaeval Political Theory*. London: Butler and Tanner, Ltd.

State Department. 2004. *Refugee Admissions Program for Europe and Central Asia* [Online]. www.State.Gov/G/Prm/Rls/Fs/2004/28215.Htm (Accessed August 1, 2007.)

Stein, A. 1993. Coordination and Collaboration: Regimes in an Anarchic World. *In*: Baldwin, D. A. (ed.), *Neorealism and Neoliberalism: The Contemporary Debate*. New York: Columbia University Press.

Steinmo, S., & Thelen, K. 1992. Historical Institutionalism in Comparative Analysis. *In*: Steinmo, S., Thelen, K., & Longstreth, F. (eds.), *Structuring Politics: Historical Institutionalism in Comparative Analysis*. Cambridge: Cambridge University Press.

Sterling-Folker, J. 2000. Competing Paradigms or Birds of a Feather? Constructivism and Neoliberal Institutionalism Compared. *International Studies Quarterly*, 44, 97–119.

Stevens, D. 2004. *UK Asylum Law and Policy: Historical and Contemporary Perspectives*. London: Sweet & Maxwell.

Stewart, B. M. 1982. *United States Government Policy on Refugees from Nazism, 1933–1940*. New York: Garland.

Stoessinger, J. G. 1956. *The Refugee and the World Community*. Minneapolis: University of Minnesota Press.

Stoye, J. 2000. *Europe Unfolding 1648–1688*. Oxford: Blackwell.

Strayer, J. R. 1970. *On the Medieval Origins of the Modern State*. Princeton, N.J.: Princeton University Press.

Sundstrom, L. M. 2005. Foreign Assistance, International Norms, and NGO Development: Lessons from the Russian Campaign. *International Organization*, 59, 419–449.

Sutch, R., & Carter, S. B. 2006. *Historical Statistics of the United States: Millennial Edition Online*. [Online] Cambridge University Press. http://Hsus.Cambridge.Org/Hsusweb/Index.Do (Accessed October 4, 2006.)

Tannenwald, N. 2007. *The Nuclear Taboo: The United States and the Non-Use of Nuclear Weapons since 1945*. Cambridge: Cambridge University Press.

Taylor, P. J. 2003. The State as Container: Territoriality in the Modern World-System. *In*: Brenner, N. (ed.), *State/Space: A Reader*. Oxford: Blackwell.

Teitelbaum, M. S. 1984. Immigration, Refugees, and Foreign Policy. *International Organization*, 38, 429–450.

Teschke, B. 2003. *The Myth of 1648: Class, Geopolitics, and the Making of Modern International Relations*. London: Verso.

Thomas, D. C. 2001. *The Helsinki Effect: International Norms, Human Rights, and the Demise of Communism*. Princeton, N.J.: Princeton University Press.

Thomas, M. 2002. The British Government and the End of French Algeria, 1958–62. *Journal of Strategic Studies*, 25, 172–198.

Thompson, J. W. 1908. Some Economic Factors in the Revocation of the Edict of Nantes. *American Historical Review*, 14, 38–50.

Tichenor, D. J. 2002. *Dividing Lines: The Politics of Immigration Control in America*. Princeton, N.J.: Princeton University Press.

Tilly, C. 1992. *Coercion, Capital, and European States, AD 990–1992*. Cambridge, MA: Blackwell.

1996. *Citizenship, Identity and Social History*. Cambridge: Cambridge University Press.

Torpey, J. C. 2000. *The Invention of the Passport: Surveillance, Citizenship, and the State*. Cambridge: Cambridge University Press.

2005. Passports and the Development of Immigration Controls in the North Atlantic World During the Long Nineteenth Century. *In*: Weil, P. (ed.), *Migration Control in the North Atlantic World: The Evolution of State Practices in Europe and the United States from the French Revolution to the Inter-War Period*. Oxford: Berghahn Books.

Toulmin, S. 1990. *Cosmopolis: The Hidden Agenda of Modernity*. New York: Free Press.

Truman, H. S. 1955. *Memoirs*. New York: Doubleday.

Tsebelis, G. 2000. Veto Players and Institutional Analysis. *Governance: An International Journal of Policy and Administration*, 13, 441–474.

2002. *Veto Players: How Political Institutions Work*. Princeton, N.J.: Princeton University Press.

Tylor, C. 1892. *The Huguenots in the Seventeenth Century*. London: Simpkin, Marshall, Hamilton, Kent & Co., Ltd.

United Nations High Commissioner for Refugees Archives (UNHCR Archives). Geneva, Switzerland.

UNHCR. 1953. Report of the United Nations High Commissioner for Refugees and Addendum, 1952. [Online] UNHCR Refworld: www.Unhcr.Org/Cgi-Bin/ Texis/Vtx/Refworld/Rwmain?Docid=3ae68c664 (Accessed October 26, 2007.)

1954. Report of the United Nations High Commissioner for Refugees. [Online.] UNHCR Refworld: www.Unhcr.Org/Cgi-Bin/Texis/Vtx/Refworld/Rwmain? Docid=3ae68c968 (Accessed October 26, 2007.)

1957. *Memorandum Prepared by the United Nations High Commissioner for Refugees for Submission to the Committee on Social and Humanitarian Questions of the Inter-Parliamentary Union (Nice, 24 April 1957)* [Online]. www.Unhcr. Org/Admin/ADMIN/3ae68fd344.Html.

1961. *Forty Years of International Assistance to Refugees*. Geneva: UNHCR.

1966. Addendum to the Report of the United Nations High Commissioner for Refugees. Geneva: UNHCR. [Online] UNHCR Refworld:: www.Unhcr.Org/ Cgi-Bin/Texis/Vtx/Refworld/Rwmain?Docid=3ae68ca80 (Accessed April 2, 2008.)

1971. *A Mandate to Protect and Assist Refugees*. Geneva: Office of the United Nations High Commissioner for Refugees.

1986. Note on International Protection (Submitted by the High Commissioner). Geneva: UNHCR. [Online] UNHCR Refworld: www. Unhcr.Org/Cgi-Bin/Texis/Vtx/Refworld/Rwmain?Docid=3ae68c054 (Accessed November 7, 2007.)

1997. *The State of the World's Refugees: A Humanitarian Agenda*. Oxford: Oxford University Press.

2000. *The State of the World's Refugees: Fifty Years of Humanitarian Action*. Oxford: Oxford University Press.

2006a. *2005* UNHCR Statistical Report. Geneva: UNHCR.

2006b. *The State of the World's Refugees: Human Displacement in the New Millennium.* London: Oxford University Press.

2006c. *Statistical Yearbook: 2005.* Geneva: UNHCR.

2007a. *Note on International Protection. Report by the High Commissioner.* Geneva: UNHCR.

2007b. The Protection of Internally Displaced Persons and the Role of UNHCR. Geneva: UNHCR. [Online] www.Unhcr.Org/Refworld/Docid/45ddc5c04.Html (Accessed March 8, 2012.)

2009. UNHCR Deeply Concerned over Returns from Italy to Libya. Geneva: UNHCR. [Online] www.Unhcr.Org/4a02d4546.Html.

2012. *A Year of Crises: Global Trends 2011.* Geneva: UNHCR.

UNHCR Executive Committee. 1980. Conclusions No. 18 (XXXI) 1980: Voluntary Repatriation. Geneva: UNHCR. [Online] UNHCR Refworld: www.Unhcr.Org/Cgi-Bin/Texis/Vtx/Refworld/Rwmain?Docid=3ae68c6e8 (Accessed November 8, 2007.)

United Kingdom Public Record Office, Foreign Office Records (PRO FO). Kew Gardens, London.

United Nations. 1949. *A Study of Statelessness.* Lake Success, N.Y.: United Nations Publications.

United Nations General Assembly. 2005. Resolution 60/1: World Summit Outcome. New York: United Nations.

2012. *Approved Resources for Peacekeeping Operations* A/C.5/66/18, June 27.

United States Department of Homeland Security. 2010. *Yearbook of Immigration Statistics: 2009.* Washington D.C.: U.S. Department of Homeland Security, Office of Immigration Statistics.

United States Department of State Record Group 59, United States National Archives and Records Administration (NARA). Washington D.C.

United States Immigration and Naturalization Service. 1982. *1982 Statistical Yearbook of the Immigration and Naturalization Service.* Washington D.C.: United States Immigration and Naturalization Service.

van Selm-Thorburn, J. 1998. *Refugee Protection in Europe: Lessons of the Yugoslav Crisis.* Dordrecht: Martinus Nijhoff.

van Selm, J. 2003. Refugee Protection Policies and Security Issues. *In:* Newman, E., & Van Selm, J. (eds.), *Refugees and Forced Displacement: International Security, Human Vulnerability, and the State.* Tokyo: United Nations University Press.

Vattel, E. d. 1852. *The Law of Nations.* Philadelphia: T & J.W. Johnson.

Vayrynen, R. 2001. Funding Dilemmas in Refugee Assistance: Political Interests and Institutional Reforms in UNHCR. *International Migration Review,* 35, 143–167.

Vernant, J. 1953. *The Refugee in the Post-War World.* London: George Allen & Unwin Ltd.

Vialet, J. 1999. Refugee Admissions and Resettlement Policy. Washington, D.C.: Congressional Research Service, Library of Congress.

Victor, D. G., Raustiala, K., & Skolnikoff, E. B. 1998. *The Implementation and Effectiveness of International Environmental Commitments: Theory and Practice*, Cambridge: MIT Press.

Vincent, R. J. 1992. Grotius, Human Rights, and Intervention. *In*: Bull, H., Kingsbury, B., & Roberts, A. (eds.), *Hugo Grotius and International Relations*. Oxford: Oxford University Press.

Vincenzi, C. 1985. The Aliens Act 1905. *Journal of Ethnic and Migration Studies*, 12, 275–284.

Vink, M., & Meijerink, F. 2003. Asylum Applications and Recognition Rates in EU Member States 1982–2001: A Quantitative Analysis. *Journal of Refugee Studies*, 16, 297–315.

Walker, M. 1992. *The Salzburg Transaction: Expulsion and Redemption in Eighteenth-Century Germany*. Ithaca, N.Y.: Cornell University Press.

Walters, F. P. 1960. *A History of the League of Nations*. London: Oxford University Press.

Walters, W. 2002. Deportation, Expulsion, and the International Police of Aliens. *Citizenship Studies*, 6, 265–292.

Walzer, M. 1983. *Spheres of Justice: A Defense of Pluralism*. New York: Basic Books.

Ward, A. W. 1906. The Peace of Westphalia. *In*: Ward, A. W., Protero, G. W., & Leathes, S. (eds.), *The Cambridge Modern History*. New York: Macmillan.

Warren, G. L. 1951. UN Action on Status of Refugees and Stateless Persons. *Department of State Bulletin*, 25.

1953. The Escapee Program. *Journal of International Affairs*, VII.

Wasem, R. E. 2011. *U.S. Immigration Policy on Haitian Migrants*. Washington D.C.: Congressional Research Service.

Wasserstein, B. 1979. *Britain and the Jews of Europe, 1939–1945*. London: Institute of Jewish Affairs.

Watson, A. 1984. European International Society and Its Expansion. *In*: Bull, H., & Watson, A. (eds.), *The Expansion of International Society*. Oxford: Clarendon Press.

Weber, M. 1947. *The Theory of Social and Economic Organization*. New York: Free Press.

Weiner, M. 1996. Ethics, National Sovereignty and the Control of Immigration. *International Migration Review*, 30, 171–197.

Weis, P. 1954. The International Protection of Refugees. *American Journal of International Law*, 48, 193–221.

(ed.). 1995. *The Refugee Convention, 1951: The Travaux Preparatoires Analysed*. Cambridge: Cambridge University Press.

Weiss, C. 1854. *History of the French Protestant Refugees from the Revocation of the Edict of Nantes to the Present Time*. London: William Blackwood and Sons.

Weiss, T. G., & Korn, D. A. 2006. *Internal Displacement: Conceptualization and Its Consequences*. Oxford: Routledge.

Weiss, T. G., & Pasic, A. 1997. Reinventing UNHCR: Enterprising Humanitarians in the Former Yugoslavia, 1991–1995. *Global Governance*, 3, 41–57.

Weissbrodt, D., & Hortreiter, I. 1999. Principle of Non-Refoulement: Article 3 of the Convention against Torture and Other Cruel, Inhuman or Degrading Treatment or Punishment in Comparison with the Non-Refoulement Provisions of Other International Human Rights Treaties. *Buffalo Human Rights Law Review*, 5, 1–73.

Weldes, J. 1999. *Constructing National Interests: The United States and the Cuban Missile Crisis*. Minneapolis: University of Minnesota Press.

Welsh, J. M., & Banda, M. 2010. International Law and the Responsibility to Protect: Clarifying or Expanding States' Responsibilities? *Global Responsibility to Protect*, 2, 213–231.

Wendt, A. 1987. The Agent-Structure Problem in International Relations Theory. *International Organization*, 41, 335–370.

1992. Anarchy Is What States Make of It: The Social Construction of Power Politics. *International Organization*, 46, 391–425.

1999. *Social Theory of International Politics*. New York: Cambridge University Press.

2001. Driving with the Rearview Mirror: On the Rational Science of Institutional Design. *International Organization*, 55, 1019–1049.

Wendt, A., & Duvall, R. 1989. Institutions and International Order. *In*: Czempiel, E. O., & Rosenau, J. N. (eds.), *Global Changes and Theoretical Challenges: Approaches to World Politics for the 1990s*. Lexington, Mass.: Lexington Books.

Whelan, F. G. 1981. Citizenship and the Right to Leave. *American Political Science Review*, 75, 636–653.

Wight, C. 2006. *Agents, Structures and International Relations: Politics as Ontology*. Cambridge: Cambridge University Press.

Wijngaert, C. v. d. 1980. *The Political Offence Exception to Extradition: The Delicate Problem of Balancing the Rights of the Individual and the International Public Order*. Deventer, the Netherlands: Kluwer.

William III. 1699. William the Third, by the Grace of God King of England, Scotland, France and Ireland, &C. Charles Bill, and the Executrix of Thomas Newcomb deceas'd, Early English Books Online Ebook Collection. [Online] http://eebo.chadwyck.com/search/full_rec?SOURCE=pgimages.cfg&ACTION=ByID&ID=V151462.

Williams, J. 2002. Territorial Borders, Toleration and the English School. *Review of International Studies*, 28, 737–758.

Wolf, J. B. 1951. *The Emergence of the Great Powers, 1685–1715*. New York: Harper & Brothers.

Wolfers, A. 1962. *Discord and Collaboration: Essays on International Politics*. Baltimore: Johns Hopkins University Press.

Wood, G. S. 2009. *Empire of Liberty: A History of the Early Republic, 1789–1815*. Oxford: Oxford University Press.

Woodbridge, G. 1950. *UNRRA: The History of the United Nations Relief and Rehabilitation Administration*. New York: Columbia University Press.

Woods, N. 1996. *Explaining International Relations since 1945*. Oxford: Oxford University Press.

Wray, H. 2006. The Aliens Act 1905 and the Immigration Dilemma. *Journal of Law and Society*, 33, 302–323.

Wyman, D. S. 1985. *Paper Walls: America and the Refugee Crisis 1938–1941*. New York: Pantheon Books.

2002. *A Race against Death: Peter Bergson, America, and the Holocaust*. New York: New Press.

Younes, K. 2007. Iraq: U.S. Response to Displacement Remains Inadequate. Refugees International. [Online] www.Refugeesinternational.Org/Content/Article/Detail/9993.

Young, O. R. 1980. International Regimes: Problems of Concept Formation. *World Politics*, 32, 331–356.

1982. Regime Dynamics: The Rise and Fall of International Regimes. *International Organization*, 36, 277–297.

1986. International Regimes: Toward a New Theory of Institutions. *World Politics*, 39, 104–122.

1999. *Governance in World Affairs*. Ithaca, N.Y.: Cornell University Press.

Zacher, M. W. 1992. The Decaying Pillars of the Westphalian Temple: Implications for International Order and Governance. *In*: Rosenau, J. N., & Czempiel, E. -O. (eds.), *Governance without Government: Order and Change in World Politics*. Cambridge: Cambridge University Press.

2001. The Territorial Integrity Norm: International Boundaries and the Use of Force. *International Organization*, 55, 215–250.

Zolberg, A. R. 1983. The Formation of New States as a Refugee-Generating Process. *Annals of the American Academy of Political and Social Science*, 467, 24–39.

1995. From Invitation to Interdiction: U.S. Foreign Policy and Immigration since 1945. *In*: Teitelbaum, M. S., & Weiner, M. (eds.), *Threatened Peoples, Threatened Borders: World Migration and U.S. Policy*. New York: W.W. Norton & Co.

2006. *A Nation by Design: Immigration Policy in the Fashioning of the United States*. Cambridge, Mass.: Harvard University Press.

Suhrke, A., & Aguayo, S. 1989. *Escape from Violence: Conflict and the Refugee Crisis in the Developing World*. Oxford: Oxford University Press.

Zucker, B. A. 2001. Frances Perkins and the German-Jewish Refugees, 1933–1940. *American Jewish History*, 89, 35–59.

2010. American Refugee Policy in the 1930s. *In*: Caestecker, F., & Moore, B. (eds.), *Refugees from Nazi Germany and the Liberal European States*. New York: Berghahn Books.

Zucker, N. L., & Zucker, N. F. 1987. *The Guarded Gate: The Reality of American Refugee Policy*. San Diego: Harcourt Brace Jovanovich.

1989. The Uneasy Troika in US Refugee Policy: Foreign Policy, Pressure Groups, and Resettlement Costs. *Journal of Refugee Studies*, 2, 359–372.

Index

Lightning Source UK Ltd.
Milton Keynes UK
UKOW04f0744050716

277722UK00010B/446/P